AMNESTY IN BRAZIL

PITT LATIN AMERICAN SERIES

Catherine M. Conaghan, Editor

Amnesty in Brazil

Recompense after Repression, 1895–2010

Ann M. Schneider

University of Pittsburgh Press

Published by the University of Pittsburgh Press, Pittsburgh, Pa., 15260
Copyright © 2021, University of Pittsburgh Press
All rights reserved
Manufactured in the United States of America
Printed on acid-free paper
10 9 8 7 6 5 4 3 2 1

Cataloging-in-Publication data is available from the Library of Congress

ISBN 13: 978-0-8229-4693-9
ISBN 10: 0-8229-4693-9

Cover art: Photographs of political rallies in downtown Rio de Janeiro in 1979 (*top*), courtesy of the National Archive, and 1929 (*bottom*), courtesy of CPDOC/FGV.

Cover design: Melissa Dias-Mandoly

To Ricardo, Oliver, and Margot

CONTENTS

Acknowledgments   ix

List of Acronyms   xiii

Introduction: The Calculus of Restitution in Brazil   3

PART I—AMNESTY AS RECOURSE, 1890S–1910

Prologue: Two Admirals   19

1. Linking Restitution to Amnesty, "Even though Superfluous,"
   1890s   26

2. Amnesty as Penalty: An Inversion in the 1895 Law   44

3. The Shame of Amnesty: Black Sailors in Revolt, 1910   61

PART II—THE BUREAUCRATIZATION OF AMNESTY, 1930S–1940S

Prologue: The "Institution of Grace"   83

4. Revolutionaries and Bureaucrats: Amnesty in the Age of Vargas,
   1930s   91

5. A Democratizing Amnesty under Renewed Repression, 1945–
   1960s   110

PART III—AMNESTY AND TRANSITIONAL JUSTICE, 1979–2010

Prologue: What Got Written Down   133

6. Preempting an Inevitable Amnesty: Purges in Petrobras,
   1964–1985   141

7. Two Long Shadows: AI-5 and the Federal Police in São Paulo,
   1970s–2000s   167

8. Connected to Amnesty: From a Clandestine Life to the Inter-
   American Court of Human Rights, 1964–2010   189

Epilogue: The *Política* of Amnesty in Brazil   214

Notes   221

Bibliography   259

Index   277

ACKNOWLEDGMENTS

Researching and writing this book has been a labor of love that stretched over many years. For long spells since concluding its first draft in the form of a dissertation I had to set the project aside. The stories, however, would not let me go. As circumstances allowed, I returned to them to conduct further research and to puzzle over their broader significance and connections. Even when I was not actively working on the project, it was never far from my mind. But it is not mine alone. The actual completion of the book depended on the support, generosity, and inspiration of many. Not everyone who mattered in getting this to the finish line is mentioned by name below, but you know who you are, and I do too. Thank you!

The evolution of my dissertation into this book ran parallel to a now decade-long career as a forensic historian conducting research in support of human rights accountability work. This work has immersed me into the histories of countries throughout Latin America and given me opportunities to think comparatively about processes of reckoning with legacies of state-sponsored abuses. In addition to these more macro-level considerations, I have been privileged to meet and collaborate with a number of human rights scholars, defenders, and entrepreneurs whose work has led to innovations in human rights accountability throughout the region. I have also spent countless hours listening to the testimony of survivors, often over time and space, but sometimes face-to-face. I carry all of their stories with me too. They shape how I think about historical narratives, especially the stakes in centering individual experiences.

I would not have been able to complete the research for this book without generous financial support. A recent Fulbright Scholars Program grant allowed me to spend two consecutive summers doing additional archival work, including in collections that did not exist when I wrote my dissertation. I have not forgotten that I was able to accept the grant because of truly wonderful colleagues who made it easy for me to step away and very nice to return. During my doctoral program, a Fulbright-Hays Doctoral Dissertation Research Fellowship, together with a Social Science Research Council International Dissertation Research Fellowship, gave me the chance to live and study extensively in Brazil. Grants from the Tinker Foundation, the Mellon Fellowship in Latin American History, and the University of Chicago's Center for Latin American Studies and History Department funded additional short-term research trips.

My very first academic trip to Brazil in 2003 was in the form of a human rights internship supported by the University of Chicago's Center for Human Rights (now the Pozen Family Center for Human Rights). At that time, it was the only such center not housed in a law school and with a vision for and support of human rights work in the social sciences and humanities. In addition to the summer funding, the center provided students like me with year-round opportunities to make connections between scholarship and practice, including through the example of its then director, Susan Gzesh. I spent my internship assisting with cataloguing the archive of Grupo Tortura Nunca Mais, an advocacy organization in Rio de Janeiro. It was there that I began to see, or to see differently, some of the stakes in and complexities behind forms of reckoning with repression in Brazil. It was also there that I first learned a bit about the life story of Victória Grabois, which was one among those that would not let me go.

Before I was a graduate student, I was a high school Spanish teacher with an inclination to teach through topics in the news. In 1998, I watched unfold in real time the events surrounding the arrest in London, on a Spanish warrant, of Chilean dictator Augusto Pinochet. It was another story that grabbed hold of me, so much so that I decided to go to graduate school with an idea of working in human rights in Latin America. In the M.A. program at the University of Texas, Seth Garfield got me to think about the discipline of history and about Brazil. At the University of Chicago, Dain Borges taught me to be a historian of Brazil. For my dissertation, he urged me to think beyond the more recent past, and to interrogate and analyze the role and impact of amnesty over time. Also at the University of Chicago, Ana Lima tailored her Portuguese classes to the respective needs of her students, assigning just the right works of literature to complement and inform our research projects. Many of the literature works cited here I first read in her classes.

I likewise extend my gratitude to fellow graduate students whose examples, insights, and friendships, then and now, not only deepen my appreciation and love of the study of history but of those who pursue it. Among them, special thanks go to Patricia Acerbi, Pablo Ben, Julia Brookins, Nancy Buenger, Jessica Graham, Miranda Johnson, Sarah Osten, Jaime Pensado, Dora Sanchez-Hildalgo, Rosa Williams, and Julia Young.

In the intervening years, a number of scholars have provided advice and support for this project, as well as thoughtful comments and feedback on portions of the manuscript. I am especially grateful to Rebecca Atencio, David Fleischer, James Green, Mariana Joffily, Glenda Mezarobba, Carla Rodeghero, Nina Schneider, and Marcelo Torelly. The careful reading and incisive comments of the anonymous reviewers for the University of Pittsburgh Press improved my thinking and the manuscript.

The manuscript came together in the way that it did because of the expert advice and assistance of archivists and librarians, especially in Rio de Janeiro and Brasília, who helped me find my way to a wealth of material on the adjudication of amnesty. It also depended on the generosity of many *anistiados* themselves who shared their stories with me. Among them, I will make special mention of Victória Grabois and the late Mário Lima whose personal experiences with amnesty are told here. I also wish to thank the many other members of Grupo Tortura Nunca Mais and other former Reduc refinery workers who likewise were generous with their time and in the telling of their stories and who similarly informed this book.

My heartfelt gratitude goes to both my American and Brazilian families, who seemed to know when to ask about the book and when to refrain from doing so. I thank my parents for giving space to my early signs of wanderlust and support throughout the sojourns that followed. I thank my Brazilian family precisely for making me part of the family and always right at home.

Before closing, I want to remember Sarah Peckham, who had much to do with me taking the first steps on the path that has led me here. She would be so pleased.

The final acknowledgment rightly goes to Ricardo, Oliver, and Margot, who—in that order—came into my life and made it just as it should be. They have had to share my attention with this project for too long, may they now share in the satisfaction of its completion and the knowledge that, above all, I hope it makes them proud.

LIST OF ACRONYMS

ACA — Arquivo da Comissão de Anistia (Archive of the Amnesty Commission), Brasília

ADCT — Ato das Disposições Constitucionais Transitórias (Constitutional Transitional Provisions Act)

ADPF — Arguição de descumprimento de preceito fundamental (Claim of Non-Compliance with a Fundamental Precept)

AI-1 — Ato Institucional no. 1 (Institutional Act no. 1)

AI-2 — Ato Institucional no. 2 (Institutional Act no. 2)

AI-5 — Ato Institucional no. 5 (Institutional Act no. 5)

ALN — Ação Libertadora Nacional (National Liberation Action)

AN — Arquivo Nacional (National Archive), Rio de Janeiro and Brasília

ANL — Aliança Nacional Libertadora (National Liberation Alliance)

APERJ — Arquivo Público do Estado do Rio de Janeiro (Public Archive of Rio de Janeiro State), Rio de Janeiro

ARENA — Aliança Renovador Nacional (National Renewal Alliance)

CNV — Comissão Nacional da Verdade (National Truth Commission)

CONAPE — Originally Comissão Nacional dos Anistiados da Petrobras (National Commission of the Amnestied of Petrobras); subsequently Associação Nacional dos Anistiados da Petrobras (National Association of the Amnestied of Petrobras)

CPDOC/FGV — Centro de Pesquisa e Documentação de História Contemporânea do Brasil, Fundação Getúlio Vargas (Center for the Research and Documentation of Contemporary Brazilian History, Getúlio Vargas Foundation)

DASP — Departamento Administrativo do Serviço Público (Administrative Department of Public Service)

DESPS — Delegacia Especial de Segurança Política e Social (Special
    Police Station for Political and Social Security)

DHBB — *Dicionário Histórico-Biográfico Brasileiro* (Brazilian
    Historical-Biographical Dictionay

DOI-CODI — Destacamento de Operações de Informações, Centro
    de Operações de Defesa Interna (Detachment of Information
    Operations, Center of Operations of Internal Defense)

DOPS — Departamento de Ordem Política e Social (Department of
    Political and Social Order)

DPS — Divisão de Polícia Política e Social (Division of Political and
    Social Police)

DSI/MJ — Divisão de Segurança e Informações do Ministério da
    Justiça (Division of Security and Information of the Ministry of
    Justice)

MDB — Movimento Democrático Brasileiro (Brazilian Democratic
    Movement)

OBAN — Operação Bandeirantes (Operation Bandeirantes)

PCB — Partido Comunista Brasileiro (Brazilian Communist Party)

PCdoB — Partido Comunista do Brasil (Communist Party of Brazil)

Reduc — Refinaria Duque de Caxias (Refinery of Duque de Caxias)

UDN — União Democrática Nacional (National Democratic Union)

AMNESTY IN BRAZIL

The Calculus of Restitution in Brazil

In July 2003 at a weekly meeting in Rio de Janeiro of a human rights advocacy organization, a woman interjected a question into an evolving discussion taking place about amnesty and restitution in Brazil. The organization, Grupo Tortura Nunca Mais, had adopted in its name the call for "never again," and specifically for "torture never again," when it formed in 1985 during the political transition from a military dictatorship to democracy in Brazil. The woman who posed the question had been among urban university students who had joined groups mounting resistance to the dictatorship, which had taken a decidedly hard-line turn in late 1968. What happened to her over the months of her militancy, when she was not yet twenty years old, was both singularly devastating and yet commonplace for similarly situated middle-class students who had joined clandestine organizations.[1] Simply put, she was arrested, detained, and brutally tortured by state agents. Though some were tortured to death or disappeared while in custody, she was ultimately released. She then fled Brazil in exile, returning only after the passage of the 1979 amnesty. On that evening in July 2003, she asked the group: *Am I amnestied? Is my name on a list somewhere?*

Two years earlier, in August 2001, then president (and former political exile himself) Fernando Henrique Cardoso had created the Comissão de Anistia (Amnesty Commission) through a provisional measure. A law enacted in November 2002 formally instituted the commission under the auspices of the Ministry of Justice. The Amnesty Commission's purpose was to receive and rule on petitions for restitution and indemnity

made by individuals who had been targets of state repression.[2] The Brazilian government's move to pay reparations to victims of former regimes
followed similar steps taken elsewhere. Among the most striking, Switzerland announced in 1997 that it would sell gold reserves to fund payments to Holocaust survivors. The announcement followed allegations
that Swiss banks had profited from doing business with Nazis, and that
banking rules and associated bureaucracies had effectively dispossessed
descendants of Jewish victims. These allegations, while not new, prompted unrelenting negative press in the mid-1990s. Elazar Barkan, author
of *The Guilt of Nations*, remarked that the Swiss announcement—though
predicated by the exhaustion of an official explanation based on Switzerland's policy of neutrality during the war—shifted "world morality" and
drew attention to "amend[ing] historical injustice worldwide."[3] Indeed,
at the same time within Latin America, the Argentine government began to compensate victims and survivors of the 1976–1983 dirty war
there. Then, shortly after the establishment of the Brazilian Amnesty
Commission, a "soul-searching" Chilean government also budgeted for
indemnity payments as well as medical and psychological aid for surviving torture victims of the 1973–1989 dictatorship under General Augusto Pinochet.[4] Only the Brazilian program, however, referred to the
reparations as "amnesty."

The woman who posed the question that evening had just recently
made forays into political activism related to the reckoning with the dictatorship and had done so by frequenting the meetings of Grupo Tortura
Nunca Mais. The group met in their offices above a flower shop that is
across the street from the sprawling St. John the Baptist Cemetery in the
Botafogo neighborhood of Rio de Janeiro. Their weekly discussions occurred above the seemingly constant screech of bus brakes and car horns
on the busy General Polidoro Street that separates their second-story
windows from the cemetery. Among those buried in the expanse of
graves visible from their conference room are notorious former military
presidents whose tenures of terror are discussed in the pages that follow. They include Floriano Peixoto, the iron-fisted dictator of the earliest
days of the republic in the 1890s, and Emílio Garrastazu Médici, who
had overseen a period of particularly harsh repression during the Cold
War–era dictatorship.[5]

I was at the meeting that evening. One item on the agenda, in fact, was
introducing me, an American graduate student who had come to Brazil
on a fellowship to intern with a human rights organization. I would be
assisting Grupo Tortura Nunca Mais with indexing their archive, which
included many privately collected documents as well as published reports
and newspaper clippings about torture and forced disappearances com-

mitted during the 1964–1985 dictatorship. These materials joined the records of the group's advocacy since its founding following the return to civilian governance in 1985. The members had led efforts to denounce the abuses of the military regime. Though there would not be trials, the group had success early on in lobbying for, among other professional sanctions, the revocations of medical licenses for doctors who had monitored torture sessions and falsified autopsy reports and death certificates. They also advocated tirelessly for information about the disappeared.[6] Their archival materials had been carefully placed in plastic sleeves and collected in binders on shelves that lined their small conference room.

During my first months in Rio de Janeiro, and in subsequent research trips, I attended their weekly meetings and learned from them about a number of pressing human rights issues in Brazil. In a special way, however, something about that first meeting and the question posed about amnesty stayed with me. It is not a stretch to say that it planted the seed for this book. I was drawn to the complexities at play in the questions the woman asked. Trying to imagine her place, if any, in a new paradigm of reparations, she perhaps hoped for a procedural answer about required bureaucratic steps in petitioning to the Amnesty Commission. Yet there was something more philosophical about the question too. It had to do with what counted as amnesty and why it mattered.

QUEM CAUSA DANO REPARA
(THE ONE WHO HARMS MUST REPAIR)

The fact that the restitution extended to victims of past repression was dubbed "amnesty" stands out. In neighboring countries, far from representing a measure of justice, amnesty had long equated with impunity.[7] In Chile, for example, just as the Amnesty Commission in Brazil began receiving what would ultimately total tens of thousands of petitions for restitution from victims of state terror (and the Chilean government began paying for health services for torture survivors), lawyers and human rights activists worked to refine a legal theory that might strike down, or at least circumvent, a Pinochet-era amnesty law and thus enable investigations and prosecutions of past atrocities to proceed.[8] They argued successfully that a forced disappearance, in the absence of information about the whereabouts of the body, amounted to a kidnapping-in-progress and therefore could not be considered to have occurred during the 1973–1978 period covered by the amnesty.[9]

An ocean away, in South Africa, the years leading up to the establishment of the Amnesty Commission in Brazil had likewise been dominated by ideas about amnesty. There, rather than deny amnesty to perpetrators, the post-Apartheid Truth and Reconciliation Commission offered it in exchange for facts and information about the crimes they had committed. Though turning away from trials as the central avenue to address past atrocities, the South African commission nonetheless aimed to effectuate a form of reckoning. Their model of truth-for-amnesty had been designed to yield admissions of crimes from the perpetrators, acknowledgment of harm for the victims, and as a result, a foundation for a new society.[10] Supporters of the strategy argued, as Ruti Teitel explained, "that peace was a necessary precondition to democracy."[11] Under the direction of Archbishop Desmond Tutu, the commission envisioned the process as one that would create the spiritual conditions for forgiveness and ultimately reconciliation.[12] Unlike Chile, where amnesty acted as a shield for perpetrators, in South Africa it was to be the tip of the spear in a nation-building project.

At that time in Brazil, amnesty was somehow both and neither. The 1979 amnesty law had been a demand of a burgeoning civil society movement on behalf of those who had been targeted and persecuted by the military dictatorship. Enacted among other steps in the gradual return to civilian governance, the amnesty provided mechanisms for possible restitution to victims. Despite efforts to the contrary, the same 1979 law included language that has effectively secured impunity for state agents responsible for violations of human rights in Brazil.[13] Yet Brazil also has a much longer history involving amnesty. In categorizing restitution as "amnesty," the Amnesty Commission formalized and elevated a vocabulary that had been in use for a century or more. Indeed, in some ways, the commission itself was but the latest iteration of a familiar cycle in Brazilian history of making amends through amnesty.

The "amnesty" extended by the Amnesty Commission included formal acknowledgment of repression, monetary restitution, and eventually, an official apology on behalf of the state. Six years into the work of reviewing thousands upon thousands of petitions, the commission announced that the payment of reparations to victims of past political persecution signaled a return to "normalcy" in the judicial system. The commission articulated its contribution to the restoration of the rule of law in its responsiveness toward a fundamental principle of civil justice— namely, that the one who causes harm must repair.[14] In Portuguese, the deceptively simple precept is just four words: *quem causa dano repara*. Yet behind those four words lies a larger universe and longer history in Brazil about entitlement to restitution in the aftermath of repression. That history, just like the commission itself, is linked to the institution of amnesty. The reparations granted stood as a fulfillment of both the benefits guaranteed under the amnesty law as well as the larger spirit of amnesty more generally. Brazilians even utilize a substantive noun in Portuguese

FIGURE 1: TABLE - A CENTURY OF POLITICAL AMNESTIES IN BRAZIL

DATE	DECREE / LAW	
FIRST REPUBLIC (1889–1930)		
September 9, 1891	Decree no. 8	Conceded amnesty to those that took part in armed movements in the state of Pará.
August 5, 1892	Decree no. 72-B	Conceded amnesty to those implicated in revolts at the Forts of Lage and Santa Cruz.
September 16, 1892	Decree no. 83	Conceded amnesty to individuals who took part in revolutionary movements in the state of Mato Grosso and to those who directly or indirectly took part in the revolutionary movements in the state of Rio Grande do Sul.
September 12, 1893	Decree no. 174	Conceded amnesty to individuals implicated in the political events in 1893 in the state of Santa Catarina and in 1892 in the municipalities of Triunfo and others in the state of Pernambuco.
September 12, 1893	Decree no. 175	Conceded amnesty to persons implicated in the movements of March 2 in the state of Maranhão.
September 12, 1893	Decree no. 176	Conceded amnesty to the individuals who directly or indirectly took part in the movements that occurred in the Comarca of Catalão and the state of Goiás.
October 17, 1895	Decree no. 305	Conceded amnesty to the individuals implicated in the recent political events in the state of Alagoas and the city of Boa Vista in Goiás.
October 21, 1895	Decree no. 310	Conceded amnesty to all individuals who took part in revolutionary movements that occurred in the Republic up to August 23 of the current years (with restrictions).
May 5, 1896	Decree no. 406	Conceded amnesty to all who took part in the movement of September 4, 1896 in the state of Sergipe.
December 7, 1898	Law no. 533	Suppressed restrictions included in Decree no. 310 of October 21, 1895.
September 2, 1905	Decree no. 1,373	Conceded amnesty to all who took park in the movements in the capital on the night of November 14, 1904 and to related civil and military occurrences that preceded and followed it.
January 9, 1906	Decree no. 1,474	Exempted section of military personnel from restrictions included in Law no. 533 of December 7, 1898.
December 27, 1906	Decree no. 1,599	Conceded amnesty to all who directly or indirectly were involved in the most recent revolutionary movements in the states of Sergipe and Mato Grosso.
November 25, 1910	Decree no. 2,280	Conceded amnesty to navy insurgents.
December 13, 1912	Decree no. 2,687	Conceded amnesty to all implicated in the revolts of the navy battalion that occurred in Rio de Janeiro's port in December of 1910 as well as those in Manaus in October of 1910.
January 8, 1913	Decree no. 2,740	Conceded amnesty to all the civil and military personnel implicated in the revolts on the territories of Acre and Mato Grosso.

January 13, 1916	Decree no. 3,102	Conceded amnesty to all civilians and military personnel who were directly or indirectly involved in the revolutionary movements in the state of Ceará.
September 27, 1916	Decree no. 3,163	Conceded amnesty to all those involved in political or connected acts related to the matter of presidential succession that occurred in the state of Espírito Santo.
October 30, 1916	Decree no. 3,178	Extinguished all remaining restrictions placed on the amnesties of 1895 and 1898.
VARGAS ERA AND ELECTORAL DEMOCRACY (1930–1964)		
November 8, 1930	Decree no. 19,395	Conceded amnesty to all civilians and military personnel involved in the revolutionary movements of the country.
July 24, 1931	Decree no. 20,249	Conceded amnesty to all civilians and military personnel implicated in seditious movements that occurred in the capital of São Paulo on April 28, 1931.
July 30, 1931	Decree no. 20,265	Conceded amnesty to all civilian and military personnel implicated in seditious movements that occurred in the capital of Pernambuco on May 20, 1931.
October 23, 1931	Decree no. 20,558	Conceded amnesty to those responsible for electoral crimes committed up to October 24, 1930, as well as to civil and military personnel implicated in seditious activity in the country up to the same date.
May 28, 1934	Decree no. 24,297	Conceded amnesty to participants in the revolutionary movements of 1932.
July 16, 1934	Article 19, Transitional Provisions of the 1934 constitution	Conceded a "broad" amnesty to all who had committed political crimes before July 16, 1934.
April 18, 1945	Decree-law no. 7,474	Conceded amnesty to all who had committed political crimes from July 16, 1934 to the publication of the decree.
July 23, 1945	Decree-law no. 7,769	Conceded amnesty to military personnel who had been part of the Brazilian Expeditionary Force and had or were facing charges.
August 28, 1945	Decree-law no. 7,906	Extend the same amnesty granted under Decree-law no. 7,769 to personnel in the air force and navy.
September 10, 1945	Decree-law no. 7,943	Conceded amnesty to those accused of crimes of injury to public power and to those responsible for crimes related to political demonstrations.
March 11, 1946	Decree-law no. 9,050	Considered amnestied two generals who were administratively retired in 1930 and 1931.
September 18, 1946	Article 28, Constitutional Transitional Provisions Act (ADCT) of the 1946 constitution	Conceded amnesty to all citizens considered unsubmissive or deserters until September 18, 1946 as well as to laborers who suffered disciplinary actions as a result of strikes or labor disputes.
May 31, 1949	Law no. 721	Extended the benefits of Decree-law no. 9,050 to various other officers.

February 9, 1951	Law no. 1,346	Considered amnesty those who committed infractions against recently revoked electoral laws.
July 13, 1951	Decree-legislation no. 18	Conceded amnesty to those charged or tried for crimes related to labor strikes.
December 3, 1951	Decree-legislation no. 63	Conceded amnesty to those responsible for the crime of injury to public power or the agents who hold it.
July 6, 1955	Decree-legislation no. 70	Conceded amnesty to the participants in the conflict that occurred in "Tribuna Popular."
April 19, 1956	Decree-legislation no. 16	Conceded amnesty to journalists condemned under Decree-law no. 431 of May 18, 1938.
May 23, 1956	Decree-legislation no. 22	Conceded broad and unrestrictive amnesty to all civilian and military personnel who directly or indirectly involved themselves in revolutionary movements that occurred in the country from November 10, 1955 until March 1, 1956.
June 20, 1956	Decree-legislation no. 27	Conceded amnesty to the workers of state or private companies that had been charged with crimes related to strikes or other disputes over rights regulated in social legislation.
April 30, 1959	Decree-legislation no. 2	Conceded amnesty to former port workers in Rio de Janeiro who had lost their positions for political reasons.
December 5, 1959	Decree-legislation no. 17	Conceded amnesty to those involved in upheaval in municipalities of Paraná.
July 20, 1961	Decree-legislation no. 7	Conceded amnesty to workers or personnel of state or private companies for reasons related to strikes.
December 15, 1961	Decree-legislation no. 18	Conceded amnesty to those who directly or indirectly were involved in political crimes from July 26, 1934 until promulgation of the Additional Act.
September 11, 1963	Decree-legislative no. 15	Conceded amnesty to journalists and others charged with crimes of the press.
MILITARY DICTATORSHIP AND DEMOCRATIZATION (1964–2002)		
September 12, 1969	Decree-law no. 864	Altered article of Decree-legislation no. 18 of December 15, 1961 specifying that the amnesty does not give the beneficiaries any rights related to return to service, retirement, or back wages.
August 28, 1979	Law no. 6,683	Conceded amnesty to all who committed political or connected crimes from September 2, 1961 until August 15, 1979.
November 27, 1985	Constitutional Amendment no. 26	Conceded amnesty to civil servants and military members punished under exceptional acts, to authors of political crimes or crimes connected to them, to representatives of student and labor organizations, and to those who lost their jobs for political reasons.
October 5, 1988	ADCT of the 1988 constitution	Conceded amnesty to those who, during the period from September 18, 1946 to the promulgation of the Constitution, were punished for reasons exclusively political.
March 4, 1993	Law no. 8,632	Conceded amnesty to union leaders and representatives punished for political reasons.

December 4, 1995	Law no. 9,140	The Law of the Disappeared, oriented to the principles of reconciliation and national pacification expressed in the amnesty in Law no. 6,683 of August 28, 1979.
May 31, 2001	Provisional Measure no. 2,151	Provided the mechanisms and procedures to regulate and administer the amnesty granted in Art. 8 of the ADCT.
November 13, 2002	Law no. 10,559	Formalized Provisional Measure 2,151, establishing the regime of the "politically amnestied," including formal declaration as amnestied, and economic and other reparations.

Data for table, "A Century of Political Amnesties in Brazil," was derived from the compilation by the Brazilian Chamber of Deputies, *Anistia: Legislação Brasileira, 1822-1979*, and Mezarobba, *Um acerto de contas com o future: a anistia e suas conseqüências*, 251-265. Some of the amnesty laws were followed by additional decrees regulating their application. Those decrees, while not cited in this table, are addressed in the relevant sections of the chapters that follow.

to refer to those owed and paid such repair for repression: *os anistiados*, meaning "the amnestied."

This book is about the amnestied and these processes over more than a century in Brazil. It begins in the 1890s, in the earliest years of the republic, when Brazil was a new nation just emerging from colonial and then monarchical rule only to establish a military dictatorship and settle into a pattern of decidedly oligarchic rule. It then follows the role and impact of amnesty throughout and beyond the twentieth century, paying attention to when and why amnesty was linked to restitution. While not a continuous political process, debates about citizen rights transcended dramatic shifts throughout this history. Although admittedly the expectations about rights in the 1890s differed significantly from those in the 1980s, amnesty often factored into any equation of negotiation and settlement between opposition figures and the state. Over time, it evolved as a political convention that aimed variously to advance state legitimacy, secure civil peace, deliver justice, and otherwise guarantee citizenship rights.

Since the 1890s, at least forty amnesties have been granted for "political" crimes (see Table I.1).[15] A number of amnesties were granted for both regional and national revolts in the earliest years of the First Republic (1889–1930). The remedy, however, largely fell out of favor after being extended to Black sailors who had staged a mutiny in 1910. Amnesty returned to prominence as a political tool following a revolutionary movement that upset the oligarchy of the First Republic in 1930 and ushered in an era dominated by Getúlio Vargas. During the thirty-four years between the arrival of Vargas in power and the military coup of 1964, there were amnesties directed toward military personnel, civil servants, union representatives, and journalists, among others. During this same period, sectors of societies organized around and campaigned vigorously for amnesty, especially for one ultimately enacted in 1945. Similar activism led Brazil down a path that resulted in the 1979 amnesty law that signaled the military regime's willingness to again share power with civilians, including those among the opposition.

The beneficiaries of amnesty in Brazil from the 1890s to the present are a diverse group, including those who had been, or would be, presidents, senators, congressional representatives, high-ranking military officers, and esteemed intellectuals. They also include more common laborers, bureaucrats, enlisted military personnel, and students. Before being amnestied, many of those who would benefit from an amnesty decree had been—or had been seen as—revolutionaries or subversives. Some had devised, participated in, or were sympathetic to a range of activities, including armed revolt, against the government or against the military authority of their time. Others had been caught in a web of suspicion or a wave of repression. A number of anistiados had also been charged and convicted of political crimes in special courts or had suffered punitive measures by executive decrees. Others were subjected to torture and/ or fled Brazil in either self-imposed or forced exile, where they waited out the regime they opposed. Those who had been military personnel or government employees were often purged, losing at once their livelihood and any social status or economic security that their positions had provided. The decreeing of amnesty, however, freed those held in prisons, allowed for the safe return of exiles, and provided a means for readmission of former bureaucratic and military personnel.

In the chapters that follow the focus is on the processes behind any subsequent repair for the actions taken against these people. A few of the individuals are historical figures known in Brazilian history, but most are not. They include military officers in the 1890s; Black sailors in 1910; average bureaucrats and mid-level military personnel in the 1930s and 1940s; and oil refinery workers, police agents, and political militants in the 1960s and 1970s. The prevailing absence of their stories in the historiography leaves a hole in our understanding of amnesty. This book brings them in and provides a view to the mechanisms of, and stakes in, political amnesty over time in Brazil.

The twentieth-century French philosopher Paul Ricoeur described amnesty as that which is supposed to "interrupt" political violence by "bring[ing] to conclusion serious political disorders affecting civil peace—civil wars, revolutionary periods, violent changes of political regimes."[16] In the course of Brazilian history, grants of amnesty certainly did that. The state repeatedly, and perhaps habitually, managed the threat or consequences of upheaval, resistance, or rebellion via a well-timed amnesty. The political end of amnesty was linked closely with state capacity, which mattered deeply in precarious and delicate moments in the consolidation or transfer of power. The discourse surrounding amnesty in these moments typically celebrated its capacity to bring about peace by quieting the spirit of rebellion. Often evoking a metaphor of family, the enactment of amnesties promised to reunite Brazil and Brazilians. In this way, amnesties tapped into a more foundational notion of Brazilian culture as one rooted in harmony.[17]

Indeed, the granting of amnesties seemed to mark a symbolic return from an aberrant state of discord. Far from preventing bloodshed, however, such acts of conciliation came into play alongside violent disputes. As such, grants of amnesties were part of the persistent and parallel impulses in Brazilian political life toward both authoritarianism and accommodation. In a paradox shaped by patterns of paternalism, successive regimes in Brazil quickly and harshly disciplined opposition, only later to make a gesture toward ameliorating the punishment.[18] Rather than resolution, the gestures of conciliation often masked and obfuscated conflict.[19] The political philosopher Michel Debrun explained that the puzzling paradox of political conciliation, which ostensibly was a "fair and cordial compromise" between equals in Brazil, actually functioned as a "strategy of cooptation" and a "mechanism of discipline."[20] Viewed in this way, the various grants of amnesties drew from and deepened the broader conservative and long-standing political culture of conciliation in Brazil by neutralizing, averting, or co-opting challenges to authority.

Yet, as we will see, the institution of amnesty also served as a useful tool for those who ostensibly were, or would be, co-opted. Unlike a pardon or a commutation of sentence, amnesties had a certain leveling effect. An official pardon or sentence commutation, though alleviating criminal sanctions, did so through the reinforcement of a clear hierarchy: the benevolent ruler extending charity and mercy toward otherwise undeserving individuals. In contrast, amnesties were directed toward categories of crimes rather than toward specific individuals. Beyond alleviating punishment or the possibility of punishment, amnesties also removed the criminal characterization of designated acts or events. Derived from the Greek word *amnestia*, meaning forgetfulness (amnesia) or oblivion, amnesty was often described as the legal "forgetting" of an offense.[21] Beneficiaries made the case that any such forgetting required that the offense be treated as if it had never occurred. To do so implied a further obligation on the part of the state, namely, to address the consequences suffered by the amnestied individuals in relation to the forgotten offense. Over time, a consensus grew that anything short of recompense was an approximation rather than true amnesty.

Amnesty functioned, therefore, as both a singular event and a dynamic process. Although the enactment of amnesty laws in Brazil effectively resolved acute crises, they also created a forum of sorts through which further demands were made and additional negotiations took place. As a result, the status of being amnestied—with any corresponding rights or guarantees—was gained through a process that had scarcely begun with the decreeing of amnesty. The stakes involved in subsequent settlements ranged from the deeply moral to the everyday mundane, from issues of honor to those of memory, and from the granting of seniority to the concession of retirement pensions and reparations. For those who pursued it, the lived experience of amnesty unfolded largely away from public view in the months and years following the various decrees. These individuals most often considered amnesty as synonymous with restitution. That is, they described themselves as amnestied not at the moment of the decree but upon the approval of their return to their former posts or the bestowment of other compensatory concessions made possible by the decree. Such restitution stood as the material recognition of the rights-bearing status granted to them via the amnesty. More than other measures, therefore, amnesty not only "interrupted" violence but also served as the mechanism through which individual settlements were reached between a conciliatory state and its former enemies.[22]

This is why, perhaps, a companion term to *anistiado* emerged in Portuguese. The first president of the Amnesty Commission, José Alves Paulino, used the two terms together in the introduction to his compilation of the earliest plenary sessions held under his leadership. He referred to the "many, many politically persecuted people," as he dedicated the work to both the *anistiados* and the *anistiandos*.[23] The use of the gerund, *anistiando*, succinctly categorized those who were not yet formally amnestied but, rather, in the process of seeking such status; that is, those who were *amnesty-ing*. Both the amnestied and the amnesty-ing bring to the fore the ways in which political and revolutionary threat was perceived, managed, and punished throughout Brazilian history. Their efforts to become recognized recipients of amnesty likewise give us a glimpse at the prevailing and at times conflicting ideas about justice, especially in the determinations made about the limits of tolerable consequences for forms of political opposition and revolt.

The book is organized chronologically in three parts that reflect larger political shifts in Brazilian history. The periods include the First Republic (1889–1930), the Vargas era and the years of electoral democracy (1930–1964), and finally the period of dictatorship and redemocratization (1964–2010). Each of the three parts is subdivided into chapters that provide snapshots of the experience of amnesty for individuals in varying circumstances and at different moments. The narratives capture details of both the political repression inflicted and the subsequent path to some form of recompense. Taken together, the arguments in the chapters trace expectations over time regarding rights—including rights to recourse, opportunities, and exemptions—as well as notions about just restitution. Linked through the evolving institution of amnesty, the chapters show that access to the guarantees and the measurable results in individual lives were uneven and often surrounded by deep ambiguity.

The case studies trace the interpretations about the significance of amnesty over time in Brazil, but the book is not a history of the act or event of amnesty. Rather, it is a history of the amnestied and, more precisely, of the amnesty-ing. The dramatic moments of decreeing amnesty in Brazil were often noisy events that left behind front-page newspaper coverage, intense congressional debates, and voluminous other sources. Many of the individuals whose stories are told here, in contrast, have been protagonists of a quieter history. Their stories are found among the records of bureaucratic archives and disparate notations in newspapers, sometimes stretching over decades. Readers of these records, while perhaps establishing what happened to those who pursued amnesty, are less able, if not unable, to follow cases where efforts were abandoned or never made. Indeed, the collective application of amnesty paradoxically demanded individual efforts to legally secure its benefits, which resulted in uneven outcomes and necessitated some degree of resources and persistence on the part of the would-be amnestied person.

For those who pursued the guarantees of amnesty or challenged its limitations, the possibility for becoming amnestied was always subject to further review. Such review, in turn, often depended on new and evolving political situations. Similarly, the substance of what constituted amnesty also changed and evolved over time. In some moments and in some regards, amnesty meant the alleviation of punishment or signaled protection from the possibility of prosecution. At the same time, amnesty also represented various forms of restitution and reparations.[24] This book tells the history of these vagaries of amnesty. The cases that follow, not just from the more recent era but the earliest examples too, show lingering uncertainties as much as finality in seeking recompense through amnesty. Windows of opportunity for making successful claims opened, closed, and sometimes opened again over years following amnesty decrees. The historical problem of amnesty in Brazil lies precisely in this tension of amnesty as a settlement that is never quite settled.

When the woman posed her question at the 2003 meeting of Grupo Tortura Nunca Mais, the then newly created Amnesty Commission promised to bring a certain closure to an otherwise still contested past. Conceived of as a final chapter of sorts, the individual reparation payments were designed to act as the last words in a new national narrative. That narrative of remorse and acknowledgment on the part of the state, while important to many who had been targets of repression, also served a larger political function. The work of the commission would stand as the fruit of democratic process and the mark of state legitimacy. Its work, in turn, resulted in the amassing of an ever-growing collection of documents and rulings, which are themselves now an archive that in some ways frames the past contained within as one that ended with amnesty. Paulo Abrão and Marcelo Torelly, respectively a former head of the Amnesty Commission and a key advisor on it, interpreted the resulting association of amnesty with reparations and memory as the linchpin for the larger transitional justice process in Brazil. That association, they argued, makes possible an eventual evolution of amnesty as the final and definitive word signaling in Brazilian society the twin aspirations of truth about and justice for past state atrocities.[25]

The commission, however, outlasted its political visionaries and became a political target. In 2019, under the administration of right-wing reactionary Jair Bolsonaro, the commission was removed from the Ministry of Justice and relegated to a new ministry assigned to matters of "women, family, and human rights." In a sign that the past remained contested, new commissioners, unpersuaded by demands for forms of reckoning or transitional justice, announced that they would review prior rulings, possibly de-amnestying some former beneficiaries.[26]

A final assessment of amnesty in Brazil remains to be made. It is not, however, the simple sum of the deceptive and insidious politics of conciliation through which threats of and momentum for change in Brazil have long been muted. At the same time, neither is it a triumphal history that somehow culminates in a firm and final recognition of rights. What is sure is that amnesty marked and made both political and historical epochs. It also marked and made political and historical subjects who turned to amnesty both to express and to address issues involving rights. Those subjects are the protagonists of this book. Their histories, told in the chapters that follow, bring to the fore the deeper complexities at play in how, why, and to what extent amnesty served as a form of negotiation and settlement in Brazil. These histories show how the persistent idea of amnesty is one of conciliation, in which a contentious past is neatly placed in the past. Yet the details of the cases reveal that, far from creating closure, amnesty dragged on over time, reflecting ongoing and evolving debates about justice and just consequences.

Part I

Amnesty as Recourse, 1890s–1910

Prologue

Two Admirals

Admiral Eduardo Wandenkolk, 1892

In June 1892, from a remote outpost in the Amazon, Navy Admiral Eduardo Wandenkolk wrote a letter pleading that Brazilians "must know the inhumanity with which the political prisoners sent to Tabatinga are being treated." Wandenkolk and thirteen others had been banished to Tabatinga, near the border of Brazil with Colombia and Peru, by Floriano Peixoto, the "Iron Marshal." His letter reported that the local governor prohibited any aid or comfort to the exiles, "no matter what authority requests it or the individual's state of health." None of them could become ill, Wandenkolk concluded, "without it being a death sentence."[1]

Two months earlier, on April 6, 1892, Wandenkolk signed his name to the "Manifesto of the Thirteen Generals" denouncing Floriano's assumption of power as unconstitutional and calling for immediate elections for a new president. Until Floriano seized power, Wandenkolk had been the minister of the navy and a senator in the first Congress of the new Republic of Brazil.[2] The constitution to which Wandenkolk and the others appealed, in fact, had been put in place less than fifteen months earlier. In response to the manifesto against him, Floriano declared martial law in Rio de Janeiro (the capital city), suspended Congress, and ordered the immediate arrest and forced retirement from the military of eleven of the thirteen generals who had signed the manifesto, together with many other civilian and military figures. Within a week, dozens of detractors, including many of the signers of the manifesto, were either sent into exile to the far reaches of the Amazon region or detained in military forts.[3]

More than two decades before his banishment, Wandenkolk had been a decorated officer in the 1865–1870 Paraguayan War, a costly war that pitted Argentina, Brazil, and Uruguay against the expansionist project of the Paraguayan dictator Francisco Solano López. The war effort, complicated by unsavory imperial politics in Brazil, left an indelible mark on the Brazilian military as an institution. During the intervening years between the war and the events of 1892, Wandenkolk and his fellow war veterans were witness to and part of a transformation of the military, especially in its role in politics and governance. They rose in both rank and prestige over the next decade, feeling increasingly emboldened to involve themselves in imperial politics. In the 1880s, many of them, including Wandenkolk, joined a brewing conspiracy to oust the monarchy and establish a republic. Their coup was completed in 1889. A constitution signed in 1891 then consolidated the new form of government.

The recipient of Wandenkolk's 1892 letter sent from Tabatinga was Rui Barbosa. Barbosa had been one of the civilian conspirators against the monarchy in Brazil. He also was the primary author of the 1891 constitution, the first minister of finance in the republic, and a senator in the first Congress. In the years that followed, from 1893 to 1895, he would be a political exile himself. (In contrast to Wandenkolk, Barbosa spent his exile in Europe and Argentina, not in the Amazon.) Within days of the arrests and banishments in April 1892, Barbosa filed a petition for habeas corpus to the Supremo Tribunal Federal (Federal Supreme Court), a court established by the 1891 constitution to be the highest in the land. It named the thirteen generals and thirty others who had been either detained or banished by decree. The court, itself under threat from Floriano, denied the writ in late April and upheld the legality of Floriano's action as permissible under martial law.[4]

The somber, if not resigned, tone of his June letter aside, Wandenkolk did not perish in Tabatinga. By August 1892, martial law had been suspended, and Congress reconvened. The representatives quickly passed an amnesty for those "implicated in the events that resulted in the executive decree . . . declaring martial law."[5] Wandenkolk returned to Rio de Janeiro where, in June 1893, he assumed the presidency of the Navy Club and continued his opposition to Floriano. A month later, he commandeered the packet boat *Júpiter* in Buenos Aires, picked up weapons and ammunition, and set its course to the bay of the state of Rio Grande do Sul, where a local civil war had taken on decidedly national proportions.

Along the way Wandenkolk issued a proclamation calling for the navy to join the fray fighting against both Floriano and the state government of Rio Grande do Sul. His move was seen as an attempted coup, aiming "to depose the President . . . [and] subvert . . . the constitutional order of the Republic."[6] He and other rebels held the port for five days but ultimately were captured off the coast of Santa Catarina and imprisoned under military jurisdiction aboard the cruiser *República*. Wandenkolk was transferred to a prison in the Fort of Conceição, atop a hill in downtown Rio de Janeiro. From there, he had a bird's-eye view of a full-blown navy revolt against Floriano that would unfold just weeks later, in September 1893, in Guanabara Bay.[7] It had been less than eighteen months since he signed the Manifesto of the Thirteen Generals.

During the year that followed, politics took a turn in Brazil when an election brought a civilian to the presidency. Prudente de Morais, a planter from São Paulo, was inaugurated in November 1894. By the following July, Floriano had died and Congress was in the midst of negotiating the terms of an amnesty for those involved in the civil war in Rio Grande do Sul and the navy revolt in Rio de Janeiro. The amnesty became law in October 1895. Wandenkolk then retook his senate seat. Two years later, in October 1987, Prudente de Morais revoked Floriano's 1892 decree that had forcibly retired Wandenkolk and others. Wandenkolk returned to active duty as a navy officer, a position in which he remained until his death in 1902. Nearly two generations later, in 1945, the Brazilian navy honored Wandenkolk with the establishment of the Admiral Wandenkolk Center of Instruction for Officers of the Corps of Engineers. The motto of the center is "Here professionals of the sea are formed."[8]

Wandenkolk can rightly be thought of as belonging among the founding fathers of Brazil. Yet outside of the center for instruction that bears his name, his life is referenced only in history books and almost nowhere else. In comparison to another rebellious seaman who would soon follow, Wandenkolk's story has stayed static and firmly in the past. The story of that other seaman, João Cândido, continues to be a dynamic touchstone in the history of race in Brazil. Just seventeen years after Wandenkolk commandeered a ship in revolt, Cândido did the same. Following their respective revolts, both seamen were arrested and imprisoned. Both were also subsequently amnestied. The similarities between them end there, however. Their lives, and more precisely the contrasts between them, are bookends, of sorts, to a larger history about amnesty and rights in the early years of the period known as the First Republic in Brazil.

"ADMIRAL" JOÃO CÂNDIDO, 1910

On Christmas Day 1910, João Cândido and one other survivor were removed from a small prison cell on the Ilha das Cobras (Island of Snakes) near Rio de Janeiro. Fourteen other men imprisoned with them in the same cell had perished the night before. In a nearby cell another two survived the night, but eleven more had died. The bodies of the deceased were secretly buried. The imprisoned men, twenty-nine in total and all sailors in the Brazilian navy, had been arrested on Christmas Eve for allegedly violating terms of a 1910 amnesty. By some accounts, Cândido spent that torturous night in the very same cell in which the eighteenth-century revolutionary figure Tirandentes had been held prior to his execution. The two cells had become toxic during the hot night, having been disinfected with quicklime shortly before their arrival. The prisoners inhaled poisonous particles, which killed all but four of them by asphyxiation.[9]

Cândido was actually a helmsman, not an admiral. He was sent to a naval apprentice school at a young age and then enlisted in the navy by the time he was sixteen years old. He learned to read and write and was trained in complicated navigational skills. At some point, he also learned to embroider. His skill and work in the craft became the topic of academic discussion in the late 1990s, itself a testament to the continued resonance of this story of Black sailors in revolt nearly a century earlier.[10] Prior to the revolt he would lead, Cândido had been among sailors sent to England to receive specialized training and to be part of the crew that would bring home two new super dreadnaughts. The state-of-the-art ships promised to elevate Brazil's navy to be among the most technologically sophisticated.

In November 1910, however, the navy began preparations to sink those very ships when more than two thousand men (nearly half of all enlisted sailors) joined a revolt aboard the two new dreadnaughts and other ships. The sailors—many of whom, like Cândido, were one generation removed from slavery—demanded "liberty" and the abolishment of lashing as punishment aboard ships. Unlike Wandenkolk, who called for the ousting of the sitting head of state, Cândido demanded simply that sailors no longer be whipped. The fleet kept cannons aimed at Rio de Janeiro for four days. Cândido came to be called "Admiral" in the press and elsewhere, sardonically by many, after an anxious Brazil witnessed his successful maneuvering of the impressive ship within the Guanabara Bay in Rio de Janeiro during the revolt.[11]

The navy prepared a counterattack at the same time that Congress, through an emissary, negotiated a resolution that promised both to abolish lashing and to grant an amnesty to the rebel sailors. Barbosa, the same jurist to whom Wandenkolk had directed his 1892 letter, led the charge in Congress in support of an amnesty. Any relief the sailors may have felt in the negotiated resolution, however, was fleeting. Mistrust reigned on both sides. Weeks later, a second revolt erupted. Cândido, among others, remained loyal to the institution. Nonetheless, hundreds were arrested, including Cândido, and scores were summarily dismissed from the navy. In addition to the twenty-five who died in the two cramped cells on Christmas Eve, more than two hundred others spent that same evening aboard a merchant marine ship on their way to a forced exile in the Amazon region. Many did not survive the voyage. Those who arrived faced uncertain fates in dire conditions laying telegraph wires or working for rubber barons. Just two decades after the abolition of slavery, those in positions of power and influence were terrified by the fact that Black sailors had been capable of commandeering ships and aiming cannons at the city of Rio of Janeiro. They further abhorred that the Brazilian government had granted amnesty to the rebel sailors as part of the negotiated disarmament. Cândido spent months in prison before ultimately being acquitted of the charges against him.[12] He spent much of the rest of his life in poverty.

THE ARC OF AMNESTY, 1890S–1910

The institution of amnesty and, in particular, the person of Rui Barbosa stitch together the histories of Wandenkolk and Cândido, although these follow decidedly divergent trajectories. Barbosa received Wandenkolk's letter from Tabatinga. He also filed the habeas that was denied to Wandenkolk by the Federal Supreme Court in 1892. Years later and under different circumstances, Barbosa argued in Congress in favor of granting amnesty to Cândido and the rebel sailors aboard the new dreadnaughts. Once news broke of the fate of the mostly Black sailors banished to the Amazon, his was a leading voice condemning the government. Yet, a more ominous thread also runs between the trio of Wandenkolk, Barbosa, and Cândido. In 1890, Barbosa, together with Wandenkolk (then minister of the navy), drafted a new naval code permitting punishment of up to twenty-five lashes per day, and more if deemed necessary in the "prudent discretion of the commander."[13] Just before the revolt in 1910, a fellow seaman aboard the ship that Cândido would commandeer was subjected to a punishment of two hundred lashes.

During this brief twenty-year period from 1890 to 1910, which encapsulated the resistance mounted and the consequences endured first by Wandenkolk and then by Cândido, amnesty was planted and took root as an institution in Brazil. The particularities of each of their histories formed points on what would be an early arc of expansion and retraction in the reliance on and reliability of its guarantees. In the earliest months and year of the republic, when Wandenkolk and his counterparts challenged the authoritarian rule of Floriano, it would have been impossible to predict that amnesty, among other possible mechanisms, would emerge as a primary recourse to demand individual rights, however such rights were understood.

Yet it is precisely during this period that amnesty becomes this tool. Beginning in earnest with the 1895 amnesty granted under Floriano's successor, Prudente de Morais, many relied on the measure to make demands for certain protections and guarantees. In litigation and subsequent debates, amnestied individuals argued that the duty of the state did not end with the mere decreeing of an amnesty but, rather, also extended to restoring those who were amnestied to the positions and prestige they had once held. The arc of amnesty as a key resource for such demands ended, however, in reaction to what many viewed as dangerous overreach in the extension of such rights to Black sailors. Another two decades would pass before amnesty returned as the mechanism sought and granted to solve political strife. Only after a revolutionary movement brought Getúlio Vargas to power in 1930 does amnesty again factor prominently in the history of national conciliation and political consolidation.

To be sure, the appeal of amnesty—and more important, its linkage to restitution—was not a foregone conclusion but nonetheless occurred during the early years of the republic. This emergence of amnesty as an institution to secure rights and corresponding duties is traced in the following chapters, where the position of Wandenkolk and his colleagues is contrasted with that of Cândido's and his fellow sailors. The judicial and other maneuvers of one of Wandenkolk's elite compatriots, Army Marshal José de Almeida Barreto, are examined in chapter 1. Like Wandenkolk, Almeida Barreto was a senator and a signer of the Manifesto of Thirteen Generals against Floriano in 1892. Also like Wandenkolk, he was fired from his position (he had been a minister on what was then the highest military court) and banished to the Amazon region. Within a year of his exile, however, Almeida Barreto filed a civil suit for restitution. His attorney, Rui Barbosa, appealed to constitutional guarantees and made eloquent arguments about the imperative to balance power in the new republic. In this case, Barbosa included amnesty as an afterthought in articulating the obligation of the state for restitution to its citizens.

In hindsight, these arguments in 1893 were nonetheless a dress rehearsal for a lawsuit Barbosa filed two years later, on behalf of a group of nearly four dozen military men who had been dismissed as deserters for having taken part in the rebellions against Floriano. Their story is told in chapter 2. These military men sued the state over the terms of the 1895 amnesty that provided for their eventual return to military service but only after an interim period of two years. Barbosa argued that the two-year suspension amounted to a penalty and was thus the very inversion of amnesty. His arguments were ultimately unsuccessful in the courts but persisted as a foundational narrative in the decades that would follow. Indeed, in large-scale mobilizations for amnesty that occurred during the latter-half of the twentieth century, allusions abound to the debates and demands that surrounded the 1895 amnesty. A common trope about amnesty in Brazil, in fact, credits those debates with delineating the mechanism of amnesty as intrinsically linked to restitution.

Finally, the history of Cândido and some of his fellow sailors is told in chapter 3. On a spectrum with the 1895 matter, the case of the mutinous Black sailors and their fate shows the force of the legacy of slavery and some of the limits of amnesty at that time to pacify and conciliate. The debates in Congress and in subsequent judicial proceedings about the Black sailors contrast starkly with those that had occurred over a decade earlier with regard to the four dozen military men who had filed a lawsuit over the 1895 amnesty. For those amnestied by the 1895 decree, adherence to notions of entitlements resonated, even if they did not wholly prevail. Less than a generation later, appeals to matters of basic dignity for the Black sailors had far less purchase. The saga of the sailors, however, remained a salient topic in history for generations to come.

Although amnesty fell out of fashion temporarily following its extension to the Black sailors, it nonetheless became firmly instituted in Brazilian politics during this period. As protagonists of this history, Wandenkolk and his colleagues, Cândido and his fellow seaman, and Barbosa, their shared advocate, all left their mark on the struggle to define rights and citizenship in Brazil. Their failures as much as their successes—whether arguing in a court of law or in the court of public opinion—lend insight to the ways in which rights were construed and negotiated in the young republic of Brazil. Their histories, moreover, bring to the fore the inception of amnesty as a purveyor of citizen rights in Brazil. That notion endures today.

CHAPTER 1

LINKING RESTITUTION TO AMNESTY, "EVEN THOUGH SUPERFLUOUS," 1890s

On May 8, 1893, José de Almeida Barreto filed a civil action before a federal judge in Rio de Janeiro for the restitution of his salary and other financial benefits that had been withheld since he was forcibly retired by a presidential decree issued thirteen months earlier. The April 7, 1892, decree that ousted Almeida Barreto and several other high-ranking military officers was the response of Floriano Peixoto, the first vice president of the new republic of Brazil, to a manifesto published the day before. Known as the Manifesto of the Thirteen Generals, the missive decried Floriano's assumption of the presidency after his predecessor stepped down and demanded that new elections be held. Almeida Barreto, an army field marshal, had signed it. Navy Admiral Eduardo Wandenkolk had signed it as well.

At the time Almeida Barreto added his name to the manifesto, he was a senator and held an active appointment as a minister on the Conselho Supremo Militar (Supreme Military Council). The following year, a decree replaced the council with a special military court and solidified the position of the Federal Supreme Court as the pinnacle of the judiciary in Brazil. Just a few years earlier, Almeida Barreto had been among the military leaders who lent critical support to the Republican-led conspiracy against the Brazilian Crown. He also served as an elected constituent to a national assembly that followed. The assembly wrote the 1891 constitution and elected two military men to govern the new republic of Brazil, Deodoro da Fonseca as president and Floriano as vice president. Within months and amid a deepening crisis, Deodoro stepped down and Floriano stepped in. Bolstered by a vote of confidence by Congress in January 1892, Floriano responded to his political critics as if their actions had been a matter of military indiscipline.

Just days after Floriano forcibly retired officers such as Almeida Barreto and Wandenkolk from the military, he also had them, and dozens of others, arrested and either banished to the far reaches of the Amazon or detained in military forts. Wandenkolk was sent to Tabatinga, where he wrote to Rui Barbosa imploring that the world must know the conditions under which they lived. Almeida Barreto was exiled to Cucuhy. A fellow exile, José Joaquim Seabra, described their corner of the Amazon in much the same way Wandenkolk explained the deplorable conditions in Tabatinga. Months later, Seabra, a Recife law school professor and member of the lower house of Congress, known as the Chamber of Deputies, explained that those in Cucuhy had sought shelter in one of two straw shacks that had been used as storage for rubber tappers in a remote village. They lived by hunting and fishing, navigating around swamps that "opened up here and there like glazed eyes." Those swamps, Seabra said, demanded that a terrible tribute be paid and got it by "ambushing" the exiles with malaria.[1]

In justifying their banishments, Floriano cited to the constitutional duty of the executive to "secure order and maintain national institutions" against the "crime of sedition."[2] In a message published in the *Diário Oficial* soon after, Floriano explained that his detractors had shown an "unseemly spirit of indiscipline, disorderly conduct, and the seed of anarchy."[3] Assailed by Floriano, they had a champion in Barbosa, who acted quickly on their behalf. He filed a lengthy petition for habeas corpus to the Federal Supreme Court on April 18, 1892, naming Almeida Barreto, Wandenkolk, Seabra, and more than forty other men, including both civilians and additional military members.

In spite of his passionate argument, Barbosa did not persuade the court. Rather than habeas corpus, the exiles found relief via an amnesty, which Congress passed in August of that year. Within the year that followed, Barbosa would represent Almeida Barreto in his civil suit for restitution.[4] In both the habeas petition and the case for restitution, Barbosa made arguments about constitutional guarantees and the balance of power in the newly established republic. In hindsight, these arguments then served as stepping stones for his further advocacy in the face of new affronts that would soon follow. Indeed, he echoed—and sometimes refined—the ideas he put forth in the habeas matter and Almeida Barreto's case for restitution in his collection of writings related to a broad amnesty granted in 1895. In those writings, known as *Anistia Inversa* (Inverted amnesty), Barbosa outlined nothing short of an imperative for restitution through amnesty. Subsequent generations, in fact, have viewed Barbosa's arguments as a treatise about amnesty and rights in Brazil. Before those arguments were made, however, Almeida Barreto's case concluded with a grant of restitution for the rights that had been taken from him by Floriano's 1892 decree. The final ruling occurred shortly after Floriano's death and just a few weeks before the granting of the 1895 amnesty that would be at the heart of the *Anistia Inversa* matter. The 1895 amnesty, granted by Floriano's civilian successor, extended to individuals involved in a civil war in the state of Rio Grande do Sul and a navy revolt in Rio de Janeiro in 1893, two related crises that were predicated on and exaggerated by the events of 1892.

Republican Beginnings through a Military Coup

On November 6, 1889, on what would be one of the final days of the monarchy, a positivist and Republican conspirator against the Brazilian Crown, Benjamin Constant, received what was for him some very good news: Marshal Almeida Barreto would join the military effort to topple Emperor Dom Pedro II.[5] At the eleventh hour, Almeida Barreto decided to put aside his differences with a fellow marshal, Deodoro, and join the conspiracy. Deodoro, an unlikely revolutionary, personally admired the emperor and politically was sympathetic to the monarchy. Nonetheless, he had been convinced by Republican conspirators and influenced by his junior officers to lead a military coup.[6] Elsewhere in the military hierarchy, Almeida Barreto was placed in command of a brigade of more than a thousand men. Rather than defend the monarchy, he stood with Deodoro and the rebel forces. Wandenkolk, who also supported the ousting of the monarchy, opened the navy arsenal to the army-led campaign. Firepower, however, proved unnecessary. On November 15, the weary emperor, long weakened by disease, quickly accepted the military ultimatum to step down. In many ways, his deposing was a coda to the process of abolition that had reached fruition just the year before. Indeed, as Lilia Moritz Schwarcz explains, slavery was the great paradox of the Brazilian empire, "both its foundation and the only thing that could destroy it."[7] Dom Pedro II retreated with his family to Portugal. His exile ended a sixty-six-year period of monarchy in Brazil, which had been preceded by three centuries of Portuguese colonial rule.

The actual end of the Brazilian monarchy was nonetheless a rather bland event. There was no real revolution, no mobilization for broad citizenship rights, and in some far-flung places little to no news about the political changes that had transpired. In the most general terms, the monarchy fell to a quiet military coup that had been led by Deodoro but engineered by civilian Republican conspirators. Among them were

Barbosa and Aristides Lobo, who had famously noted that "surprised" masses in Rio de Janeiro mistook the proclamation of the republic for a military parade.[8] Barbosa, for his part, spent the fateful day of November 15, 1889, in Rio de Janeiro in the house and company of Constant.[9]

Constant, named after the French revolutionary figure, left his mark in the Brazilian military academy where, as a devotee of positivism, he influenced a generation of officers that ultimately moved against the monarchy. These most likely included the junior officers who had convinced Deodoro to lead the coup. For Constant and many late nineteenth-century thinkers in Brazil, positivism outlined a promising path to overcome what they understood as their collectively inherited deformities. Indeed, since the 1850s (and with rigor since the 1870s), a number of intellectuals, politicians, and military brass looked especially to Comtean positivism and its motto of "order and progress" as the route to modernization in Brazil.[10]

Auguste Comte's thesis argued that human society moved through three historic phases: the theological, the metaphysical, and the positive. Knowledge of the world and human destiny derived, respectively, from explanations about gods and spirits, from other abstractions, and from observable relationships or experience or, rather, from *positive* data. Progress through these phases depended, in many ways, on order. This thesis fortified the movement for the institution of a republic.[11] The coalition of conspirators against the monarchy, in fact, linked order and progress so fundamentally to the idea of a republic in Brazil that the positivist *ordem e progresso* motto was inscribed on the Brazilian flag in the days following the proclamation. Given, however, that Brazil seemed further from progress than other nations, the positivist founding fathers could scarcely afford the orthodoxy of observing Comte's three stages unfold naturally. Indeed, it was generally accepted that more order would be necessary. This call for order elevated the military to a new level of political importance and responsibility. The prevailing sentiment was in favor of a military dictatorship, which was duly installed.[12] Thus, Deodoro assumed leadership of the provisional government following the ousting of Dom Pedro II and installed what would become the first of two successive military dictatorships that inaugurated the First Republic in Brazil.

For subsequent generations, the lack of widespread upheaval in the upsetting of the monarchy became a fitting metaphor for the particularities of Brazilian social and political life. The idea of the bloodless revolution especially appealed to Brazilian mentalities throughout the twentieth century. It reinforced a notion, perhaps most famously articulated in the work of Gilberto Freyre, that Portuguese colonialism was of a gentler form than that of other European powers and thus that Brazil inherited a legacy of and tendency toward the abhorrence of violence.[13] Viewed through this lens, other revolutionary episodes added to the myth-making. Subsequent amnesties of rebels and opponents, then, under-scored the Brazilian proclivity toward conciliation. The irony, however, was that in the absence of any real revolution, violence nonetheless pro-liferated. In the case of the 1890s, in fact, the precarious early years of the First Republic belied the strikingly peaceful transfer of power from the monarchy. Bitter conflict, tense uncertainty, and outright civil war plagued the new republican regime. Indeed, the events of those years in some ways institutionalized violence as a form of political process.[14]

Clashes, in fact, erupted during a constituent assembly in 1890–1891, which had been convened to draft the constitution of the new republic and to elect its first president. Written primarily by Barbosa, the con-stitution instituted a liberal federative republic modeled on that of the United States. Notably, it abolished the "moderating" power, which Bra-zil's first constitution had enshrined in 1824, following the severing of ties to Portugal, to make the Brazilian emperor the ultimate arbitrator of state affairs during the nineteenth century. The 1891 constitution also retooled the parameters of habeas corpus and the concession of amnes-ty. Soon, both mechanisms would be invoked in the face of Floriano's repression.

Under the 1891 constitution, habeas corpus was to be granted "when-ever an individual suffers, or is in imminent danger of suffering, violence or coercion by illegality or abuse of power."[15] Barbosa would subsequent-ly argue that its recourse extended beyond the protection of physical lib-erty to include as well freedom of thought. Asserting that "the individ-ual is not free because he can change his position on the surface of the earth, like an animal," Barbosa argued that violence against freedom of thought and expression was a "more degrading, more painful" and "more insolent abuse of power."[16] Without setting out a formal hierarchy, he nonetheless elevated freedom of thought and expression as "supreme" liberties that should also be protected by habeas corpus. He noted that high courts in free countries broadened—rather than restricted—such individual guarantees.[17] It would not be so, however, in Brazil.

As for amnesty, the 1891 constitution gave Congress, comprised of the Chamber of Deputies and the Senate, the sole prerogative to enact it, subject to executive approval.[18] Under the 1824 constitution in place during the monarchy, the authority to grant amnesty fell within the pur-vey of both the legislature in its role to "make, interpret, suspend and revoke laws" and the emperor, as the "Moderating Power." Any amnesty extended through the emperor's moderating power was to be reserved for extraordinary circumstances and in cases of emergency in which such a decree was "advisable for the sake of humanity and the good of the State." Unsurprisingly, since amnesties tended to be part of a response to extraordinary circumstances, more than twice the number of decrees were issued by the emperor than by the legislature between the years 1824 and 1850.[19] Yet before the 1824 constitution granted either power such authority, an amnesty had helped to shape the contours of a then new form of government. Within twenty-four hours of the famous 1822 "Shout of Ipiranga" that claimed Brazilian independence from Portugal, an amnesty was granted. Similar to amnesties that would follow, this one, for "all past political opinions," included a caveat: anyone who opposed the cause of independence had to leave the country within four months.[20]

Yet before either habeas corpus or amnesty would be invoked by some of the constituents of the 1890–1891 assembly themselves, they would first elect Deodoro as president and Floriano as vice president. Deodoro nominated Admiral Wandenkolk to be the minister of the navy. (Wandenkolk had received the secondmost votes, behind Floriano, for vice president). Deodoro also named Barbosa as minister of the treasury.[21] Almeida Barreto was placed on the Supreme Military Council. Wandenkolk, Almeida Barreto, and Barbosa were then elected as senators in the first Congress of the new republic. It is important to note, however, that the electorate was a narrow swath of Brazilians. It included only those who occupied the patron side of the patron-client divide and categorically excluded women.[22] Nonetheless, the election for the presidency sanctioned Deodoro's provisional government, giving him a clear mandate to continue as president.

It was Floriano, however, who received the applause and congratulations on behalf of the powerful Military Club for having been elected vice president. Extending well beyond the military, Floriano's followers, known as Florianistas, included the most radical wing of the Republican parties, who called themselves Jacobins. Not all Florianistas were Jacobins, but all Jacobins were decidedly Florianistas. They were primarily urban, drawing members from among small shopkeepers, bureaucrats, and members of the liberal professions. They unequivocally supported governance via military dictatorship and were adamant to protect the new institutions from monarchist infiltration. Like their French namesakes under Robespierre a century earlier, the Brazilian Jacobins fought suspected saboteurs and potential treason everywhere.[23]

Deodoro and his minority of supporters, in contrast, had adhered to the movement to fell the monarchy more on terms of military honor

than on terms of republican principles.[24] Indeed, Deodoro took a conciliatory approach to the monarchists, commuting death sentences to life
imprisonments and annulling after one year the banishment orders of a
number of elite political figures who were sympathetic to the monarchy
and hostile to republican rule.[25] He was not, however, without gratitude
for the Republicans. In fact, in May 1890, Deodoro sought to bestow the
military title of brigadier general on his civilian ministers in recognition
of their work in organizing the republic. Barbosa, for one, refused, explaining that such honors were incongruent in "a person so essentially
civilian . . . whose life, in every way, has been a radical negation of the
arts of war."[26]

If Deodoro's support had already waned in the military by the time
of his formal election by the assembly, his influence in Congress quickly
plummeted following the election. A growing financial crisis only added
to his problems. Aimed to stimulate industrialization in the wake of abolition, an economic plan devised by Barbosa resulted in rising inflation
and a recession.[27] In response to related political problems, Deodoro attempted to assume the historic "moderating power" by closing Congress
on November 3, 1891, just months after the new constitution had abolished it. The authoritarian move gave fodder to accusations that he had
become a dictator. Under the burgeoning opposition, and in increasingly
poor health, Deodoro resigned later that month. By early December,
Floriano had replaced Deodoro at the head of the fragile republic, the
exiled emperor, Dom Pedro II, had died, and during the year that followed, in August 1892, Deodoro also passed away.

Upon the resignation of Deodoro in late 1891, Floriano declared a
state of siege. Congress, led by representatives of the state of São Paulo, then gave him broader authority in a motion passed on January 21,
1892. To "consolidate" the republic, the motion granted the "use of all
means, even the most energetic that the circumstances may demand, to
maintain order, to severely punish any who disturb or attempt to disturb public peace and tranquility, [and] to reestablish the true federative
regime that was defiled by the act of November 3," when Deodoro attempted to close Congress.[28] In his tenure from 1891 to 1894, Floriano
jealously guarded his rule against numerous attacks and under repeated
accusations of illegitimacy. To do so, the Iron Marshal resorted to almost
continuous declarations of martial law and allowed Jacobin agitation to
flourish. A number of his sharpest critics including Barbosa fled Brazil
under death threats. The Manifesto of the Thirteen Generals, published
on April 6, 1892, was the first in what would be a series of challenges to
Floriano's rule. Arguing that the constitution required the convening of
new elections if the president had not yet served at least half of the orig-

Figure 1.1. Almeida Barreto, J. J. Seabra, and other exiles in Cucuhy, 1892. Courtesy of CPDOC/FGV.

inal term, the signatories called for just such elections. Four of the thirteen had served in the constituent assembly and had signed their names to the constitution. In a defining act, Floriano responded by purging the officers and others of similar standing through forced retirements. Many then found themselves banished or detained in military forts.[29]

THE 1892 HABEAS CORPUS, A BRAZILIAN *MARBURY V. MADISON*

Almeida Barreto, in a missive that would be read in the Senate a month later, described how, on April 10, 1892, he was surprised at home by a brigadier general and several officers who came to arrest him on the orders of Floriano. He invoked, to no avail, his rights to immunity as a senator. He learned on April 13 that he had been banished to Cucuhy, on the border with Venezuela, for the crime of conspiracy and sedition. En route aboard a packet boat, he and others attempted, while docked in the state of Pará, to obtain a writ of habeas corpus from a local court. It was denied, however, because another had been filed on their behalf before the Federal Supreme Court. They were not allowed to wait for a ruling from the higher court and were forced to continue the journey to Cucuhy (see figure 1.1). Almeida Barreto explained that, at that moment, he found himself "absolutely deprived of the exercise of legal defense and suffering the most extraordinary constraints . . . in the memory of republican countries ruled by a liberal constitution."[30]

Barbosa filed the habeas corpus petition before the Federal Supreme Court on behalf of "the citizens illegally arrested and held in durance or threatened therein" by the decrees of April 10 and 12, 1892, that declared martial law in the capital.[31] The first two of more than forty individuals named were Wandenkolk and Almeida Barreto, identified as senators and with their respective military titles. The list included a total of eleven members of Congress, seven of whom, like Wandenkolk and Almeida Barreto, were commissioned military officers. One of them, First Lieutenant João da Silva Retumba, would also be among several dozen military men who, represented by Barbosa, would later file a lawsuit contesting restriction placed on the 1895 amnesty (see chapter 2).[32] Another, Lieutenant Colonel Gregorio Thaumaturgo de Azevedo, like Almeida Barreto, would file a civil suit for restitution. Seabra, the law professor who had been exiled with Almeida Barreto to Cucuhy, was also named in the habeas petition. In addition to representing the state of Pernambuco in the Chamber of Deputies, Seabra had tenure and a chair in the Recife law school until Floriano stripped him of that position.

The Federal Supreme Court considered the petition on April 23, 1892. Barbosa described the matter before the eleven ministers as one of "greatest civic importance, fraught with the most far-reaching moral consequences."[33] Floriano for his part had let the ministers know of additional, and decidedly more personal, consequences: "If today they grant the habeas corpus," he wondered aloud, "who will be around tomorrow to grant them habeas corpus when they need it?" Whether influenced by the overt threat or not, the measure was denied. Only one minister, Joaquim de Toledo Pisa e Almeida, dissented from the majority opinion.[34]

In his argument to the ministers, Barbosa evoked a metaphor of slavery. If they denied the habeas, he said, it would mean nothing less than a reembrace of the corrupt institution. Such a reference was most certainly jarring. Abolition had come incrementally and quite late in Brazil. It began with the Free Womb Law of 1871, which guaranteed free status to any child born to an enslaved woman, continued with the Sexagenarian Law of 1885, which granted freedom to any enslaved person over sixty-five years old, and arrived at a total abolishment of slavery only in 1888. This prolonged process of abolition ran parallel and was integral to the gradual decline of support for the monarchy, especially among the military.[35] Barbosa lamented that the efforts of the "revolution of November 15" that ousted the monarchy would all be for naught if Floriano's actions stood. They would have, in Barbosa's estimation, "accomplished nothing more than to transfer to ourselves the bondage from which . . . we had freed our slaves."[36] This equivalence, both in moral and political terms, aimed to heighten the stakes in the decision.

Barbosa continued, sidestepping if only momentarily any mention of race, to define the fundamental difference between a free person and an enslaved person by explaining that the former is subject to law while the latter is subject to a "tyrant's will." If the habeas were not granted, he argued, it would be to accept the submission of civil society to military dominance, which he then compared to the submission of enslaved Black people to the control of white men. Barbosa told the court that the petition represented its first opportunity "to perform with all solemnity its important duty in the most delicate and most serious of its relations with the moral life of the country"—that is, to place itself "between the unarmed rights of individuals and the violent blows of authority." If, Barbosa warned, "aggrieved citizens find no corrective in your justice, whose model should be that of the United States . . . then the country is virtually converted into a military camp," where liberty depends on a ruler's whim and the constitution is but a façade masking "the omnipotence of the harshest military despotism."[37]

This forceful reaction to Floriano's authoritarian moves is illustrative of what the historian José Murilo de Carvalho has described as "citizenship in the negative." Among other examples, Carvalho points to the movement for abolition as among ruptures in the conditional acceptance of a status quo in Brazil. These ruptures tended to involve a segment of society that pushed back against the breach of an implicit pact, aiming to show that the government "could not put its foot on the neck of the people."[38] Like other such moments of civil society engagement, the exiled political foes of Floriano did not make demands for a fundamentally equal society per se but, rather, for a more particularized protection from state interference in their lives.

Barbosa, in fact, argued separately for what he described as three classes of individuals impacted by the events and with a right to habeas corpus. In these discussions, the arguments are far more technical. The first class, comprised of eleven individuals, had all been arrested before the declaration of martial law. This group included Seabra who, as Barbosa noted, should have enjoyed the protection of constitutional immunity. The second class, comprised of Wandenkolk and one other, were arrested after the official declaration that put an end to martial law. The encroachment on the rights of both of these classes seemed more straightforward given the temporal confines of the authorities granted under martial law.[39]

The last class included those who were arrested during the period of martial law. This was arguably a more difficult case to make. To do so, Barbosa maintained they had a right to habeas corpus because their suspensions had violated the constitution. He also cited William Blackstone, an eighteenth-century English jurist who, in his *Commentaries on the Law of England*, made an impassioned plea for those "delivered . . . to the privacy of prison walls, where [their] sufferings are unknown or forgotten." Blackstone contrasted the response to imprisonment, which he described as "an invention of arbitrary force less likely to move one's feelings or excite his indignation," to the "cry of tyranny" one could expect if the state deprived someone of life or property. As such, Blackstone concluded that imprisonment was "far more dangerous." Barbosa then told the court, such was the situation in Brazil, emphasizing the bitterness incurred under the rule of republican government.[40]

The risk, as Barbosa continued, lay not just in what had happened to those named in the petition but in what might happen to additional victims of tyranny who were sure to follow. Barbosa reminded the ministers on the court that they met for only four months during every year. The events of the previous six months, he argued, allowed them "to imagine the possibility" of one or more "suspensions of guarantees," during which many other people would be imprisoned and banished. Calling again on the tenets of republicanism, Barbosa told the court that banishments were simply incompatible with "the spirit and principles of this form of government," and he lamented that individuals "segregated at the nod of one man, should pine in prisons at penal stations, or be poisoned by the malaria of marshes, without help from the courts of justice." The court must not, Barbosa argued, allow them to remain "excluded all alone, perhaps as criminals, perhaps as innocent martyrs, from the general communion of the law, from the common protection of the courts." The single remedy to the calamity, Barbosa told the court, was that of habeas corpus, "in its august simplicity, with its unforbiddable faculty of penetrating wherever the violence of authority is felt."[41]

Barbosa made a special plea on behalf of the eleven members of Congress who were among those banished and who were named in the petition. They had been "unconstitutionally torn from the seats in which the People and the States had placed them," he explained. Considering that congressional sessions were subject to the whim of the executive, such violence to the elected members represented for Barbosa the decimation of the constitution. If the court would grant the habeas corpus "to which they and their companions in misfortune are entitled," it would not just restore them to their rights but would be no less than "the revival of dejected and discouraged Brazilian society."[42]

Barbosa further argued that the words of an American Supreme Court justice, Joseph Story, should be read as gospel in every meeting of the court. Story, who served on the US Supreme Court from 1811 to 1845, was the authoritative figure on constitutionalism in the nineteenth century. He famously wrote the 1841 opinion in the Amistad case, deciding in favor of fifty-three Africans who killed the captain and took over the schooner that was heading toward the Caribbean where they would be sold into slavery. Captured off the coast of Long Island, their plight galvanized abolitionists in the United States. The US Supreme Court found in their favor, stating that they had been illegally held.

The particular Story passage that Barbosa wanted read at every session of the Brazilian Federal Supreme Court was part of his 1833 *Commentaries on the Constitution* and intended to compel its members to act: "fortunately . . . the functions of the judiciary, in deciding on constitutional questions, is not one which it is at liberty to decline. While it is bound not to take jurisdiction if it should not, it is equally true, that it must take jurisdiction if it should." Unlike the legislature, Story explained, the court could not "avoid a measure, because it approaches the confines of the constitution." Rather, "it must decide it," because "it has no more right to decline the exercise of a jurisdiction, which is given, than to usurp that, which is not given." Either to decline or to usurp in such matters, Story explained, "would be treason to the constitution."[43]

The model in the United States was the 1803 US Supreme Court case *Marbury v. Madison*, a landmark case in US jurisprudence that firmly established the judiciary as an equal partner in power and asserted its authority as arbiter in constitutional matters.[44] The case had to do with a judicial commission in Washington, DC, granted to William Marbury in the final hours of the administration of John Adams. James Madison, the secretary of state for the succeeding administration of Thomas Jefferson, denied Marbury's commission and those of others that had been similarly granted by Adams. In response, Marbury and his co-petitioners filed for a writ of mandamus that would compel delivery of the commissions. Chief Justice John Marshall ruled against Marbury and the co-petitioners, based on the argument that the issuance of the requested writ was beyond the scope of the court's power. He found that a section of the 1789 Judiciary Act may have provided such authority, but the relevant section was inconsistent with the US Constitution and thus not valid. It was the first time that the US Supreme Court had declared a law unconstitutional.

Paradoxically, this decision that limited the power of the Court in the matter before it also established the larger prerogative of the judiciary to determine if laws were constitutional. In short, it enshrined the principle of judicial review.[45] Nearly ninety years after the *Marbury v. Madison* case in the United States, Barbosa argued that the Brazilian court faced a similar question of power and authority and that it must exercise its duty to settle what amounted to the assumption by the new administration of a "moderating power" in force during the monarchy. The members of the Brazilian court, however, were not persuaded. They found it was permissible under the 1891 constitution for the president, while the Congress is in recess, to declare martial law and suspend constitutional guarantees for the sake of national security. They specified that it did not matter whether the danger was posed by "external threat or internal commotion." The court further found that during a state of siege the president is authorized to impose, as a security mechanism, detention and banishment to other sites of national territory.[46] The appeal to habeas corpus, therefore, failed as a remedy for these men. Just a few months later, however, Congress enacted an amnesty. The amnesty, granted on August 5, 1892, allowed them to return from banishment and resume their former lives, but did not restore everything to them. Thus, in April 1983, exactly one year after the habeas corpus matter, Almeida Barreto filed a civil suit demanding restitution.

Illustrious Victims

As both an army field marshal and a minister on the Supreme Military Council, Almeida Barreto held not one but two lifelong appointments on the day he was forcibly retired by Floriano. His lawsuit for restitution argued that Floriano's action against him amounted to a violation of article 74 of the 1891 constitution, which guaranteed the inviolability of commissioned and lifelong appointments. Barbosa, as his attorney, maintained that such rights, enshrined in the constitution, could not be altered without deliberation and an act of Congress. The extraordinary power afforded the government under the declaration of martial law, moreover, did not include authority to impact the tenure of such positions. As in the habeas corpus matter, Barbosa contended that the judiciary had the right and duty to examine the constitutionality of legislative and administrative acts and to deny them if they infringed on any individual constitutional right.[47] In Barbosa's estimation, Almeida Barreto had been "charged, tried and sentenced, . . . without judicial intervention—as if the head of state was the supreme justice of the country."[48] (Barbosa would return to this idea in the *Anistia Inversa* case just a few years later.) The basis of a republican constitution, Barbosa stated further, depended on "the impenetrability of the wall of guarantees that encircles an individual like a sash fortified . . . by guardian courts, and in the reparative intervention of federal justice in all cases of violence against constitutional right."[49]

Perhaps stinging from the court's refusal to assert its authority in the habeas matter, Barbosa maintained that the judiciary's check on legislative power was balanced by the legislature's prerogative in matters exclusively political. This said, he maintained that politics could not be defined in any way to include an act that infringed on individual constitutional rights. Since Floriano's forced retirements violated an article of the 1891 constitution, they could in no way be considered political matters and therefore fell within the purview of the judiciary. Barbosa referenced again the 1803 US Supreme Court case *Marbury v. Madison*, arguing that Floriano's actions were unconstitutional, indeed "a veritable exploitation," because Almeida Barreto had been retired "without his consultation and against his will." As Barbosa pointed out, military retirement was only permissible on three grounds: age, physical incapacity, or habitual bad behavior. While conceding that the third, in theory, might apply, he reminded the court that, by law, the government had to hear the opinion of an inquest and consult with the Supreme Military Council, of which Almeida Barreto was a member.[50]

The sum of Almeida Barreto's payments as a member of a Supreme Military Council included his military pay and other financial benefits. His forced retirement resulted in a reduction of his compensation by nearly one-third over what he previously received.[51] Almeida Barreto's claim to the total value was based solely on the type of post he held within the military. As Barbosa quipped, "there are jobs, and then there are jobs."[52] He did so to distinguish between positions in which the employee is subject to dismissal by his or her administrator and those that are *vitalícios*—that is, those positions that belong to the holder for life or until he or she renounces the position. In response, the defense argued that Floriano's actions had been legitimized by the mandate Congress had granted him in January 1892 to take all action necessary to consolidate the republic.[53]

Presidential elections were held in March 1894, while Almeida Barreto's case was pending. Prudente de Morais won, which placed the government in the hands of the planter class of São Paulo upon his inauguration in November 1894. Floriano died in July 1895. Just months later, in October 1895, Prudente de Morais signed a sweeping amnesty to rebels involved in both the 1893 civil war in Rio Grande do Sul and the navy revolt in Rio de Janeiro. Debates about the 1895 amnesty made news as Almeida Barreto's case wound through the courts. Those debates helped to frame acts of restitution as a fulfillment of amnesty. Yet in the Almeida Barreto case, Barbosa mentioned amnesty only tangentially to his central arguments about constitutionality.

In fact, Barbosa addressed the matter of amnesty in spite of the fact, as he noted, that it was "superfluous" to the question at hand. Specifically, Barbosa argued that, even if legally decreed, the forced retirements in April 1892 were revoked by the amnesty of August 1892.[54] Rather than serving as the fundamental basis for a claim to some sort of restorative justice, Barbosa's discussions of amnesty in this case were additive. They reinforced other claims articulated on the basis of constitutional guarantees of individual rights. Nonetheless, the enactment of the 1895 amnesty decree during the litigation of the Almeida Barreto case provided an opportunity for Barbosa to begin to theorize about the nature of amnesty and how he thought it ought to function in Brazil.

What Barbosa sketched out in the Almeida Barreto case included a brief argument concerning the nature of amnesty, which was a kernel of the longer explanation he would defend a few years later in the *Anistia Inversa* case. Referring both to the Brazilian penal code and to European legal scholars, he argued that amnesty was a law "not of pardon, but of forgetting." A pardon implied a wrong that was being deliberately overlooked, creating a certain debt between the pardoner and the pardoned. Forgetting, by contrast, created no such debt of gratitude or taint of unworthiness. It simply "extinguished all effects of punishment and placed the matters in perpetual silence," as if the accused had never committed the crime. In that forgetting, the "citizen is completely reintegrated to his rights, regaining them in all their fullness." Perhaps most strikingly, Barbosa further underscored that beneficiaries of amnesty could not refuse the recourse because it operated in the public interest.[55] The interest, it would seem, had to do with the balance of power and the prerogative of the legislature to "take away any penal consequences" via amnesty. An amnesty, he explained, extinguishes "the vestiges and specific characteristics" of those consequences.[56]

The court sided with Almeida Barreto and, on appeal in September 1895, the Federal Supreme Court upheld the decision. In so doing, it nullified the executive act that forcibly retired Almeida Barreto. The court also found that Almeida Barreto had a right to a position on the highest military court, based on an 1893 decree that regulated the transfer of ministers from the Supreme Military Council to the court that had replaced it in a restructuring of the judiciary. The Federal Supreme Court further ordered that Almeida Barreto be paid his salary and all benefits that were denied him as a result of his illegal dismissal.[57]

More than a half century later, another Bahian jurist condemned Floriano's actions as vengeful and lauded Barbosa's swift and thoughtful response. Rubem Nogueira—whose education in Salvador, Bahia, had taken place in a school named after Barbosa—viewed Floriano's actions of April 1892 as the beginning of a nefarious practice in Brazilian politics. Floriano had "injur[ed] . . . legitimate rights of a group of men, through the immoderate use of the extraordinary recourse of a martial law." His "revenge," by retiring the military officers and summarily stripping the academics of their chairs, "would be, in the last analysis, the unfortunate seed that would germinate" in Brazilian politics. From that earliest moment forward, presidents "would take actions against figures of the elite, opinion leaders, men of thought, through arbitrary removal from lifelong appointments." Nogueira argued that Floriano's actions "vulgarized in Brazil one of the most unfortunate mentalities of its governments, namely, the contempt, greater or lesser, for men, their basic liberties, and the exercise of their right to criticize the conduct of their government." More succinctly, Nogueira stated that "intolerance prevails in Brazilian life."[58]

Nogueira's analysis, first published in 1949, was framed through the lens of hindsight. In the fifty-seven years between Floriano's actions against his detractors and Nogueira's publication, Brazil had undergone major political transformations that, like those of Floriano's time, included purges of opponents from military and civilian posts. More would follow in the decades after Nogueira penned his critique, and he would have a front row seat. Beginning as a state-level representative in the late 1940s, he was elected to several terms in the Chamber of Deputies, including a final stint from 1967 to 1971, during the hard-line turn of the military dictatorship when political opponents were met not just with purges but often with torture and sometimes disappearance too. A second edition of his 1949 book on Rui Barbosa was published in 1967 and followed two other books he wrote, in 1954 and 1956, also on Barbosa and his work.[59]

If Floriano's example replicated itself, it was not, therefore, for lack of recognition of the implications. Nogueira opined that "Rui [Barbosa] felt that, at its core, the presidential act firing or retiring political adversaries for momentary conveniences was more than an attack on traditional judicial norms" and, rather, "a fatal example that could corrupt . . . compromising the future." On balance, Nogueira affirmed that "Barbosa was right." He had knocked on the doors of federal justice to argue for a ruling on the unconstitutionality of decrees issued by Floriano in April 1892 and, as a result, to obtain the "reparation of the damages that they caused their numerous and illustrious victims."[60]

Not all who opposed Floriano, however, had been forcibly retired, nor were they all commissioned officers and "illustrious victims" like Almeida Barreto and Wandenkolk. Many, especially dozens involved in the navy revolt against Floriano in 1893, were lower-level officers and seamen who had been declared deserters. These military men, like Wandenkolk and Almeida Barreto before them, would seek representation by Barbosa. They did so to challenge the terms in the 1895 amnesty decree that provided for their eventual return to the military but allowed it only after a two-year interim and subject to the perceived needs of the commanders. In response—and following on the heels of the Almeida Barreto case for restitution—Barbosa developed his *Anistia Inversa* arguments. He would anchor these juridical arguments, presented in defense of the military men's immediate and automatic return to service, in an understanding of amnesty as amnesia and erasure.

REINTEGRATION AS A "COROLLARY" TO AMNESTY

Before focusing on the nature of amnesty in the *Anistia Inversa* matter, Barbosa concluded his argument about amnesty in the Almeida Barreto case by referencing a precedent. He cited that, even in the "bad times" of the monarchy, a law school professor who had been tried and convicted, and who had completed his sentence for his involvement in an 1848 uprising in the state of Pernambuco, was returned to his formerly held chair in the law school immediately and automatically when an amnesty was granted. Under the "noble representatives of republican justice," therefore, it followed that even legally decreed retirements and dismissals connected with or resulting from the period of the state of siege would necessarily be revoked by the amnesty.[61]

In two executive actions issued a month after the passage of the 1895 amnesty, Prudente de Morais took steps in that direction. Referencing the Federal Supreme Court decision in the Almeida case in both matters, Prudente de Morais revoked Floriano's April 1892 decree that forcibly retired military officers and fired civilians in public service. One act revoked the part of Floriano's decree specifically related to Lieutenant Capitan Duarte Huet de Barcallar Pinto Guedes and other unnamed military officers "involved in crimes of conspiracy and sedition." The officers, the act explained, had been retired without their consent and without justification. Citing the decision in the Almeida Barreto case, the act affirmed that the decree retiring the officers had violated article 74 of the 1891 constitution, which guaranteed in full the rights of those holding military posts, and therefore was unconstitutional. It did not matter, the act further explained, that the retirement had occurred during a period of martial law, as martial law only permits the executive to make arrests and banishments. Finally, the act states that the officers' crimes had been amnestied by the 1892 legislative decree. Prudente de Morais affirmatively stated that amnesty "wipes away the prosecution, the sentence, and the crime itself."[62]

Prudente de Morais's other act addressed the situation of Seabra and another civilian, Arthur Fernandes Campos da Paz. Floriano had removed the two men from their respective chairs in the law school of Recife and the medical school in Rio de Janeiro. Prudente de Morais's act affirmed that their positions, like Almeida Barreto's, were lifelong appointments. As in the other executive act, he explained that martial law allowed for their arrests and banishment, but Floriano had no authority to remove them from their posts. Similarly, the August 1892 amnesty involved, "as a corollary," their reintegration to the posts from which they had been deprived.[63] In so doing, Prudente de Morais linked restitution to amnesty in an essential way.

CHAPTER 2

AMNESTY AS PENALTY

An Inversion in the 1895 Law

In early 1895, upon hearing the news of the favorable ruling by the lower court in the Almeida Barreto case and while he himself lived in exile in London, Rui Barbosa showed little faith that the decision would be a harbinger of a more liberal regime. In a letter to a friend he complained that they may have persuaded the court, but to his mind the guarantee of individual freedoms in Brazil was hardly a fait accompli. In any other country, Barbosa said, the decision "would be considered a charter of republican liberties." Brazil, however, lacked liberal institutions to ensure such protections. "Among us," he concluded, "I do not know what value it will have." If Barbosa lamented the decision's potential value as foundational jurisprudence, others worried about the costs in other terms. London newspapers reported that the sum of the indemnity granted through the subsequent reintegration of former military officers in Brazil would reach forty thousand pounds sterling. This news, the press explained, had been received "very unfavorably" by Floriano's friends and supporters.[1]

Nonetheless, there was cause for some optimism in and about Brazil. For many, that optimism was embodied in the new civilian president, Prudente de Morais, whose election brought an end to Floriano's dictatorship. Within Prudente de Morais's first year in office, peace accords were brokered in the bloody civil war in Rio Grande do Sul and the amnesty was passed for those who had participated both in the civil war and in the 1893 navy revolt in Rio de Janeiro. In September 1895, soon after the peace accords were signed and while Congress was hashing out the details of the amnesty, workers from the war arsenal gathered at the national palace to celebrate Prudente de Morais, the peace accords, and the amnesty. A poem distributed at the event and subsequently published in the *Jornal do Comercio* linked Prudente to peace, and peace to amnesty: "over cadavers of the brave / . . . an immortal being cried / . . . 'who's crying?,' a voice asked / 'It's me,' responded the Fatherland / . . . 'don't cry anymore,' said the voice / 'I am the angel of peace! / . . . your children will fight no more / . . . your immortal name / radiates an aura of peace / the clarions echo in the air / Prudente! Peace! Amnesty!'"[2] The convulsion of violence that had followed the installation of the republic in 1889 seemed to be behind them.

Barbosa, for his part, returned from exile and joined the debates in Congress over the amnesty. Initially proposed in May 1895, the amnesty would extend only to civilians and exclude any military personnel who took part in either the civil war or the navy revolt. Subsequent iterations expanded the scope to include military members. In the version that became law in October 1895, a caveat limited the eventual return of amnestied military members to active duty and their former posts. Many took issue with the restriction, and forty-seven, all former military members subject to the caveat in the amnesty, sought out Barbosa to represent them in an effort to have the restriction declared unconstitutional. Barbosa took the case, returning to and expanding on some of the arguments he had put forth in the Almeida Barreto matter and in his opposition to Floriano's tyranny more broadly. He published his arguments about the amnesty, and its restriction, under the title *Anistia inversa: caso de teratologia jurídica* (Inverted amnesty: a case of juridical teratology).[3] A sign of the broader interest in the case and in Barbosa's arguments, the publication went through two editions in 1896 alone, and the hearing to rule on the appeal before the Federal Supreme Court in early 1987 was watched by "citizens of all social classes."[4]

Barbosa curiously used the scientific/medical terms *inversa* and *teratologia*, which denote a sort of essential or congenital deformity, to describe the imposition of what he deemed a penalty in the 1895 amnesty. This inverted or malformed amnesty prohibited the officers from immediately and automatically returning to active duty, leaving any such reincorporation to the exclusive prerogative of the executive branch of government and, notably, only after a two-year interim. Barbosa characterized his clients as "convicted" by the amnesty, having been subject to a penalty (a minimum two-year suspension) without the benefit of due process and a fair trial.[5] The 1895 amnesty, he argued, was an abomination against what true amnesty was meant to be and do.

The *Anistia inversa* case (ultimately lost before the Federal Supreme Court) elevated amnesty as an important recourse for and safeguard to citizenship rights in Brazil. It also marked the beginning of the institutionalization of amnesty in the Brazilian political process, especially in moments involving broader transitions or liberalizations. In subsequent debates throughout the twentieth century, some treated Barbosa's arguments as settled thought about amnesty. Politicians and activists appealed to his arguments, often quoting large sections, to emphasize that Brazil had a certain tradition of amnesty. As in the 1890s, amnesty continued to be a key part of settling civil and political strife. It served as a tool of government both to secure peace and to pivot toward a new political regime. Yet amnesty was not exclusively in the purview of those with the levers of governing. Beginning with the plaintiffs in the *Anistia inversa* case, those who had opposed and been targeted by a repressive regime in subsequent decades demanded not just amnesty but also restitution as an essential and integral part of any amnesty.

DIAGNOSING A BRAZILIAN PROBLEM

The broader context of politics during these earliest years of the First Republic were marked by elite privilege, power struggles between military and civilian elites, and deference to European culture and ideas, including theories about eugenics. There are markers of all of these in Barbosa's arguments on behalf of the military personnel impacted by the amnesty, but he framed the case in terms typically reserved for physical abnormalities. That he did so underscores the reach and salience of eugenics in Brazilian thought at that time. It was widely agreed in those days that miscegenation had uniquely weakened the Brazilian "race." By extension, there was also agreement about inherent physiological inferiority in its people, which served to explain an array of ills afflicting the larger society. Brazil was a young nation, but it was often described with metaphors of physical decline. As historian Dain Borges notes, the dominant concept of the nation at that time was that of "a sick man."[6]

Two works about events in the 1890s, one fiction and the other nonfiction, demonstrate the pervasiveness, and thus the power, of the notion that something was not quite right in the formation of Brazil as a nation. The work of fiction by Afonso Henriques de Lima Barreto, *Triste Fim de Polycarpo Quaresma* (published in English as *The Sad End of Policarpo Quaresma*), satirizes the 1893 navy revolt. The work of nonfiction by Euclides da Cunha, *Os Sertões* (published in English as *Rebellion in the Backlands*), describes and reflects on the rise and decimation of a millenarian movement in Canudos, in the northeastern state of Bahia, in the mid-1890s.[7] Barbosa's arguments in the *Anistia inversa* case tap into the same insecurities concerning the new nation that are expressed in these works and then offer the court a seemingly rare opportunity to correct the nation's course.

Lima Barreto published his bitter satire about the 1893 navy revolt against Floriano, *The Sad End of Policarpo Quaresma*, nearly a generation after the events. Born in 1881, exactly seven years to the day before the abolition of slavery, he felt deeply and wrote poignantly about prejudice. Two generations removed from slavery (his maternal grandmother had been enslaved), he was famous for saying: "It is difficult not to be born white, race for white people is a *conceito* [concept], for Black people it is *preconceito* [preconception]." Growing up in Rio de Janeiro, Lima Barreto would have witnessed firsthand the revolt and its aftermath in those earliest years of the republic.[8] The hapless antihero in his novel, Policarpo Quaresma, is a Brazilian twist on Don Quixote. While Miguel de Cervantes's Don Quixote leaves the reader to ponder who the real fool is, Lima Barreto's Policarpo Quaresma leaves little room for doubt. Indeed, the novel's title, *The Sad End of Policarpo Quaresma*, foreshadows that it is not a hero's tale. Policarpo, like Quixote, is obsessed with books, yet his reading leads not to deeper knowledge and insight but, rather, to a naïve and overly patriotic fervor. That fervor drives him to exalt that which is native in Brazil in the face of a generalized devotion and deference among Brazilians for all things European.

Policarpo's quest takes the form of a series of harebrained schemes for radical reforms in Brazil, for which he pays successively higher personal costs. Among these schemes is a campaign to have the official language changed from Portuguese to Tupi, the language spoken by the indigenous inhabitants of Brazil. His efforts are met with biting ridicule in the Brazilian press. Retreating to the countryside, he attempts to elevate Brazilian agriculture and, in doing so, becomes embroiled in political battles that result in his economic ruin. He turns, then, to the military, which is suddenly facing a navy revolt against the rule of Floriano. Certain of the worthiness of the battles and of the man he had come to defend, Policarpo sends a letter to Floriano to report a distressing scene he had witnessed of Floriano's troops executing rebel prisoners. Expecting that Floriano would instantly recognize the loyalty and nobility shown in his calling attention to what he assumed was a lamentable aberration, Policarpo instead finds himself accused of treason and facing a firing squad himself, the very sad end referred to in the title.[9]

There are echoes not just of Cervantes's Don Quixote in the character of Policarpo, albeit with a twist, but also of Gustave Flaubert's Bouvard and Pechuchet. Flaubert's unfinished novel was published posthumously in 1881, the same year that Lima Barreto was born. In this satire of France and the French Revolution, the characters Bouvard and Pechuchet take up farming, convinced that, "with common sense and a little study," they could not fail. Nonetheless, they do fail, and do so over and over again. Flaubert uses the characters, described as "epic heroes of failure," to satirize any assertion of authority, whether the product of formal study or rooted in accepted wisdom.[10] In spite of these similarities with more classic literary characters, Lima Barreto's Policarpo is nonetheless distinctly Brazilian. Through Policarpo, Lima Barreto renders the new republic born under Floriano as cruel and arbitrary. Yet, his critique arguably goes one step further: Policarpo's end is sad, but not tragic. At every turn, he could have avoided his ultimate fate had he not willfully ignored the evidence of his own dispensability and the realities of Brazil at that time. On a fundamental level, Policarpo simply failed to recognize that something was off, and perhaps intrinsically so, in Brazil.

In this regard, Lima Barreto's tale, published first in installments in a newspaper, stood as a fictionalized account of destruction by the Brazilian republic. A decade before his story circulated, the Brazilian journalist Euclides da Cunha had published *Rebellion in the Backlands*, providing a contemporaneous description and reflection on the consolidation of that republic through the decimation of a movement in the northeast of Brazil. The movement had taken root in the small village of Canudos in the impoverished interior of the state of Bahia. It was led by Antônio Vicente Mendes Maciel, known as Antônio *Conselheiro*, an adopted surname that means "Counselor," who had been a wandering religious figure in the *sertão*. With his charisma and the resonance of his criticism of corrupt priests, Conselheiro gained a large following, which ultimately settled in Canudos. He also gained powerful enemies both in politics and among local priests, who resented his criticism and growing influence. A dispute with a judge in a neighboring village spiraled outward and reached national proportions. The judge had stopped the delivery of wood ordered by the Canudos community for the construction of a new church. When they went to claim the wood, the judge requested state forces to stop the "invasion." A battle ensued between the state forces and the Canudos movement. After heavy losses, the state forces retreated. As news of the defeat spread, the settlement in Canudos came to be viewed as a distinct political threat, fueled in part by increasing suspicion disseminated in the press that the settlement was conspiring with monarchists intent on restoring the old form of government. Conselheiro had written about the divine authority of kings, and indeed credited divine inspiration for the abolition of slavery in Brazil, but the aims of the settlement in Canudos were more immediate and decidedly local.[11]

Da Cunha's account of the rise of the millenarian movement and the slaughter of its members by the Brazilian military in successive campaigns in 1896 and 1897 drew parallels to revolutionary France. He reportedly considered entitling the work *Our Vendée*, to evoke the civil war between royalists and republicans during the French Revolution in the west-central coastal region of Vendée.[12] Ultimately, his emphasis on geographical determinism to understand the Brazilian episode was reflected in the official title, *Os Sertões*, referring to the arid *sertão* (*sertões* in the plural) region of the northeast of Brazil. Da Cunha's depiction in his first two chapters of "the land" and "the man" mixed contempt with a sort of nostalgic admiration for the place and the people he saw as obstacles to progress. That place and those people, it followed, were part of the unique challenges that Brazil faced as a new nation.

What is known, and knowable, about the struggle and final slaughter of the Canudos settlement fascinated, and perhaps haunted, not just Da Cunha but subsequent generations of intellectuals, politicians, and literary figures. A lifetime after Da Cunha published his work, the Peruvian Nobel Prize–winning author Mario Vargas Llosa made him a bespectacled character in his historical-fiction account of Canudos, entitled *The War of the End of the World*. Vargas Llosa explained in an interview that after reading *Rebellion in the Backlands*, he was drawn not just to the story of Canudos but also to the person of Da Cunha, who had helped to shape the narrative about the conspiracy animating the movement, "then discovered that he had been wrong." The idea about the conspiracy, Vargas Llosa explained, was "this ghost" that hardened into a false reality, with tragic consequences.[13] Then and now, the events in Canudos represent the imposition at all costs of the new republic as much in the major central-south cities of Rio de Janeiro and São Paulo as in the far reaches of the northern hinterlands. The defeat of the Canudos settlement stood as the final routing of the challenges to the new order and, more symbolically, of what had been holding Brazil back. It was followed by the "Belle Époque" transformations of Rio de Janeiro that began in the late 1890s, and the corresponding entrenchment of oligarchic politics that dominated until 1930.

The rise of the movement in Canudos in the northeast and the subsequent military campaigns that decimated the community ran parallel to the legal arguments taking place in Rio de Janeiro over the *Anistia inversa* matter. Rui Barbosa's legal advocacy on behalf of Almeida Barreto and then of the forty-seven military men from 1892 to 1897 pointed to similar anxieties explored by Lima Barreto and Da Cunha about perceived inherent weaknesses among Brazilians or within the institutions and government of Brazil. Indeed, Barbosa's characterization of the amnesty as deformed mapped onto conclusions about other political and social problems of late nineteenth-century Brazil. In no other arena did this notion play out more succinctly than in that of race. For many at that time, the doctrine of racial degeneration explained the position of Brazil among the world's nations. For these thinkers, the nation unfortunately was embodied in inferior beings.[14] The prevailing impression was that Brazil stood further away from progress for fundamentally physiological reasons. Barbosa most assuredly tapped into this elite sense of unease about "normal" and "delayed" development in critiquing the penalizing amnesty as an absurdity of justice inflicted upon his clients.

Of the forty-seven who sought Barbosa to represent them, just four were from the army, ranging in rank from major to colonel. The rest were navy personnel who had taken part in the 1893 navy revolt. They were mostly lower in rank than their fellow plaintiffs from the army and included seventeen first lieutenants, twelve midshipmen, four second lieutenants, three lieutenant captains, three lieutenant commanders, and one captain of land and sea. The remaining three were of unspecified rank. Of the forty-seven, a few had also been among those, together with Wandenkolk and Almeida Barreto, who had been detained or banished by Floriano and for whom Barbosa sought a writ of habeas corpus in 1892. These included Major Sebastião Bandeira and Colonel Antonio Carlos da Silva Piragibe from the army, and navy First Lieutenant João da Silva Retumba.

Retumba, younger than both Almeida Barreto and Wandenkolk, had been just eight years old when the Paraguayan War broke out, but he grew up in the context of the evolution of the military in Brazil. With Almeida Barreto and Wandenkolk, among others, he joined in the movement to unseat the monarchy and was likewise elected, as a representative from the state of Paraíba, to serve on the constituent assembly that wrote the 1891 constitution. The next year, just as with Wandenkolk and Almeida Barreto, he was also forcibly retired from the navy on the orders of Floriano. In the subsequent decree that exiled Almeida Barreto and Wandenkolk to the Amazon, Floriano ordered Retumba held in Fort Lage in the Guanabara Bay of Rio de Janeiro. A little more than a year later, while Wandenkolk was watching the September 1893 navy revolt from prison on a hill in Rio de Janeiro, Retumba took an active part.

The revolt itself was inextricably linked to a civil war that was raging in the southern state of Rio Grande do Sul, also known as the "Federalist Revolution." This war began in February 1893 between forces that defended federalism and forces that favored a strong central government and presidentialism like that instituted by Floriano. The federalist forces attempted to prevent Júlio de Castilhos from assuming power as governor. Floriano sent troops to support Castilhos and the Castilhistas. Waged with political assassinations, merciless executions, and the slaughter of noncombatants, the civil war left a bloody mark on Brazilian history. Indeed, the signature method of execution was the *degola*, the same slit from ear to ear used to slaughter goats. The violence forced tens of thousands to flee the national territory into Uruguay and elsewhere. Floriano's escalation of the conflict in Rio Grande do Sul infuriated his many enemies, especially in the navy. By September, sedition compounded civil war. Led by Admirals Custódio José de Melo and Luís Filipe de Saldanha da Gama, the navy staged a revolt. The rebels then took on Floriano on two fronts, in Rio de Janeiro, the capital, and in the ongoing conflict in Rio Grande do Sul. The leaders demanded Floriano's resignation in great part for having sided with the Castilhista forces.[15]

The conflict also spread north from Rio Grande do Sul to the state of Santa Catarina, which declared its capital, Desterro, as the capital of a provisional national government in 1893. Floriano defeated these rebels in April 1894 and then had the city renamed Florianopolis in homage to himself and as punishment for their rebellion. In the course of some of the revolts against him, Floriano issued amnesties, including one in September 1893 for all implicated, whether directly or indirectly, in the "revolutionary movements" in Santa Catarina and the "political events" in the city of Triumpho and elsewhere in Pernambuco. Two additional amnesties decreed on the same day were extended to those who had been "directly or indirectly involved in political movements" in Maranhão and Goiás.[16]

In response to the multipronged threats to Floriano, the Jacobin faction among his supporters, which had formed in the wake of the breakdown of the heterogeneous revolutionary alliance and the sharp division between Deodoro and Floriano, formed "Patriotic Battalions" to defend him. It was one such battalion, in Lima Barreto's account, that Policarpo had witnessed executing prisoners and that would soon execute him on orders of Floriano. In many ways, the Jacobins found their raison d'être in fighting for Floriano. A cult of personality developed around him. Their fervor did not diminish with Floriano's exit from power following the 1894 election, nor even with his death in July 1895. The Jacobin movement began to disintegrate only after its members were implicated in an assassination attempt against Prudente de Morais as he was reviewing troops that had just returned from the final battles at Canudos in 1897. The movement ended, following a subsequent attempted coup, amid a revolt that emerged in resistance to obligatory vaccinations in Rio de Janeiro in 1904.

Of the forty-seven former military members and new clients of Barbosa, at least thirty-five, perhaps more, had been officially designated as deserters in the course of the conflicts in 1893.[17] Upon assuming office,

Prudente de Morais addressed the matter of deserters, decreeing a pardon on January 1, 1895, for the enlisted personnel in the navy and the national guard who had deserted to participate either in the civil war in Rio Grande do Sul or in the navy revolt in Rio de Janeiro, if they returned to duty by March 1. In the United States, the *Washington Post* noted that "the leaders of the revolution or those conspicuously engaged in its incitement are not included in this decree, and the government as yet has not made its policy definitely known with regard to this class of political offenders." With a more colonial gaze, the article added that "the chances are that they will be dealt with severely, in accordance with the usual South American practice." The writer then advised that the government of Brazil "consider carefully the happy and ameliorative results, which attended the magnanimous and altogether different policy pursued by the United States at the close of the late civil war." That policy of pardon "and the absence of all measures of retaliation or penalty" toward those who fought against the federal government of the United States "greatly aided in the ultimate restoration" of relations. Unless the Brazilian officers "are bent on self-destruction," the writer argued, Prudente de Morais could "well afford to do" what the United States had done.[18] Within ten months, likely owing little to the criticism from abroad, the Brazilian Congress enacted an amnesty law that extended to the rebel military officers, albeit with a caveat.

THE 1895 AMNESTY

The road to amnesty that resulted in the 1895 decree began with a single article bill proposed on May 7, 1895, by José da Costa Azevedo, a senator from the state of Amazonas. The proposed law would provide amnesty to "all Brazilians who directly or indirectly took part in the revolt of September 6 promoted by a part of the national fleet." Purportedly extended to "all Brazilians," it actually applied only to civilians, and only to those who participated in the navy revolt. A single paragraph attached to the article stated that the amnesty excluded military personnel. That exclusion bothered some in Congress. In debates that followed, one senator puzzled over the distinction between military personnel and civilians since "before the law all who took part in the revolt are criminals." Another, Quintino Bocaiúva, the former president of the Republican Party, argued for including as well those who had taken part in the civil war in Rio Grande do Sul in addition to those involved in the navy revolt. While acknowledging the dilemma of extending amnesty to those still in arms, he heralded its potential for pacification. If the amnesty were broad, he said, "it would end up injuring the prestige of the Government." On the other hand, if it were partial, it would be "discouraging" for the rebels. But either way, broad or restricted, "amnesty would be a measure of high politics, of efficient action and an opportunity to reach great social benefit." Manuel Ferraz de Campos Sales, then a senator from São Paulo who would later succeed Prudente de Morais as president of Brazil, agreed. For those concerned with extending amnesty while the war raged on, he assured that "no one wants to disarm the Republic before the rebels." Rather, he explained, "what we want is to give it one more weapon, a weapon of pure moral value, to arrive at peace. . . . It is not the rebels with weapons in their hands who would be amnestied, but rather those who disarm, who have abandoned being a rebel."[19]

Campos Sales then authored a substitution to the first proposal for amnesty. His bill extended the amnesty beyond the "September 6, 1893 revolt" by the navy to also include "the revolution initiated in February 1893 in the south." It required that all recipients turn over their weapons and present themselves to competent authorities within ninety days. The new bill included military personnel, but excluded the military leaders of the revolutionary movements. It also specified that amnestied military personnel had no right to reintegration to their former positions. The requisite legislative committee backed Campo Sales's version, but with the further qualification that the leaders to be excluded were the "heads" who had devised, incited, or directed the revolts. A final amendment proposed broadening the scope of the amnesty to include the officers, but granting the executive the prerogative to approve when it was proper for any personnel to return to active duty. In the interim, all navy and army officers would be placed in a special reserve status.[20] The bill failed to pass the Senate by a single vote.[21]

In the Chamber of Deputies, a similar proposal would amnesty anyone who had "directly or indirectly" been involved in revolutionary movements, including those "in the south" and "in Rio de Janeiro" up to the date of the peace accords signed on August 23, 1895, that brought the civil war to an end. Additional proposals likewise addressed the matter of military leadership and the prospect of reintegration. One bill proposed that amnestied officials were to remain, at the government's discretion, in the reserves. Another clarified that the amnesty did not institute a right for military officers to return to service, noting that the government had the prerogative to determine the time it thought necessary before anyone returned to active duty. The Chamber of Deputies ultimately approved the bill with an amendment excluding amnestied officials for two years in September 1895. The bill returned to the Senate, where it was approved, then was signed into law by Prudente de Morais in October 1895. It extended amnesty to all persons who, directly or indirectly, were involved in revolutionary movements through August 23,

Figure 2.1. Rui Barbosa, undated portrait. Courtesy of CPDOC/FGV.

1895. Return to active duty for army and navy officers would be possible only after a two-year interim and only if "deemed appropriate."[22] Just four months later, Barbosa filed a case against the federal government on behalf of forty-seven officers who were among those prevented from returning to active duty because of the amnesty.

INVERTED AMNESTY

In his advocacy for the military personnel, Barbosa built on his recent success in the Almeida Barreto case. Barbosa's argument in the *Anistia inversa* case had to do with both individual remunerative entitlements and larger questions about the separation of powers. Both issues stemmed from the two clauses stipulating the mandatory, and arguably indefinite, suspension from active duty. The initial filing submitted by Barbosa maintained that the suspension was unconstitutional in two ways: it denied officers' rights and corresponding benefits inherent in their positions, and it ascribed to the legislature punitive power reserved for the judiciary. Yet, it was not just the fact that the officers had been denied rights inherent in their position; their treatment differed in concrete ways from that of other officers and of civilian personnel as a whole. In solid economic terms, the forty-seven officers who filed suit were granted only their salary and time counted toward retirement but were denied other benefits. Other officers who had been exonerated in the courts prior to the amnesty, as well as amnestied civilian federal employees in general, faced no such restrictions.

Barbosa argued that the central problem with the 1895 amnesty was not that it included a restriction but that what was being described as a restriction was actually an "inversion" of the sui generis of amnesty. In most basic terms, the amnesty imposed, instead of alleviated, a punishment. Barbosa argued that it created for his clients "an exceptional juridical situation of diminishment of their rights, based on having participated in revolutionary movements." This affront to their rights consisted of the "ad hoc penalty" imposed by Congress "for a crime already committed and provided for in previous laws." That is, Congress, in one act, (1) legislated a penalty, (2) issued a sentence, and (3) applied that penalty. In effect, the amnesty defied the principle of retroactivity and ascribed to the executive branch of government indefinite control to deprive the officers of the rights associated with their position. The punishment imposed on them by the amnesty was done without formal accusation and without defense, due process, or judgment. Such a situation, Barbosa argued, "constituted an intolerable aggression," especially against the presumption of innocence until proven guilty.[23]

As in the Almeida Barreto case, the constitutional question at stake in the *Anistia inversa* matter involved the guarantees inherent in lifelong posts and positions. In addition to article 74 of the 1891 constitution, which enshrined the guarantee in full for holders of commissioned and other lifelong appointments, Barbosa also cited article 85, which guaranteed that even "when not in commission, [the holders] will receive all benefits in addition to their salary." Article 85 clearly linked benefits to a specific position, regardless of duty status, and this called into question, in Barbosa's view, the justification of the extraordinary classification of the "in reserve" amnestied officers.[24]

In the first instance, the court agreed. In a decision on July 27, 1896, Judge Aureliano Campos determined that the officers were free from the

restrictions placed by the amnesty and ruled that the government had
to pay them their salaries and all benefits.[25] The decision explained that
restrictions on amnesty are valid only if and when they do not violate
the "fundamental pact of the Republic." The government appealed the
decision. Six months later, on January 20, 1897, the Federal Supreme
Court reversed the decision with a narrow majority of three votes to two.
In the majority decision, the court found that amnesty is essentially a political mechanism conceded for the shared social interest in "forgetting"
certain events or crimes. Amnesty, the court explained, can be general,
restricted, absolute, or conditional. The decision noted that only the legislature can establish the guarantees and conditions deemed necessary,
weighing the interests of the state, the preservation of public order, and
the demands of justice. In short, the court found that Congress intended
to restrict the 1895 law and doing so was an exercise of its legitimate
authority. It would therefore be judicial overreach to alter the law.[26]

A dissenting opinion argued that the political nature of amnesty
could never legitimate the denial of rights of the amnestied. Minister
José Higino, who had written the majority decision in the Almeida Barreto case, emphasized the competency of the court to deny the application of an unconstitutional law, as well as to consider part of a law
unconstitutional, while finding other parts constitutional. He agreed
with Barbosa's arguments, finding that the restrictions in the law were
unconstitutional because they amounted to a sentence imposed by the
amnesty law. The law, as such, could not exercise any authority to impose
punishment because it was beyond the scope of congressional power.
Amnesty, he affirmed, is forgetting and therefore abolished not just the
crime but also its consequences.[27]

The majority decision was a controversial one both in terms of substance (as described above) and on procedural grounds. Procedurally, the
decision fell short of a true majority. Federal Supreme Court decisions
typically required six voting ministers among eleven total ministers. Six
ministers, however, recused themselves in this case, leaving only five to
rule on the matter. Attempts to annul the decision on those grounds,
however, also failed. On August 8, 1897, the court refused to consider
the objection and advised that those seeking review of the procedure
would have to file a special petition, known as an *ação rescisoria*. Barbosa subsequently received numerous requests to utilize the recourse but
opted against that strategy. In Almeida Barreto's case, arguments about
the amnesty were largely additive, but here they had been at the core
and they had failed. Rather than filing further petitions to the court,
Barbosa instead opted to continue litigating questions related to amnesty
in Congress.

While the decision in the first instance was pending before the Federal Supreme Court, the Chamber of Deputies debated a related question about the reintegration of former civil servants. In an earlier judicial decision, a court had granted restitution to former employees of the Ministry of Justice and the Ministry of Interior for the time in which they were denied their posts by executive power. The committee in the Chamber of Deputies that studied the questions raised by the ruling found that the executive could not, by a simple resolution, reintegrate former purged employees for two main reasons. First, they argued that the constitution granted the president the authority to nominate and to remove but did not include any power to reintegrate. The argument centered on the nature of reintegration, which "always has the character of reparation, of a distribution of justice" and "can only occur if the removal was illegal or unjust." Any power to reintegrate, therefore, would assume a tolerance for, or support of, unjust or illegal action. Second, reintegration directly impacted the National Treasury, especially in cases in which the individual had been replaced. Such reinstatement would require an additional power to create a place for two officials and funding for such when the legislative had approved only one.[28]

THE AFTERMATH AND ANOTHER PATH

In February 1897, during the month following the Federal Supreme Court's decision, Retumba requested that the Ministry of the Navy remove his name from the special reserve class created by the 1895 amnesty. Those assigned to the class were to remain there for at least two years. He argued that he could not be so assigned because on the day the amnesty became law, he was not a member of the navy. Rather, he had been forcibly retired by Floriano by decree more than three years earlier, on April 12, 1892. Since only those formerly in the navy could be assigned to special reserve class, he argued that the restrictions in the amnesty could not apply in his case.[29] Nine months later, in November 1897, Prudente de Morais partially resolved the matter for Retumba and others. By decree, a total of sixty-seven individuals, including both Retumba and Wandenkolk, as well as thirty-one of the forty-seven plaintiffs in the *Anistia inversa* case, were returned to active duty from the reserve status. The decree noted that all had already completed the two years away that were stipulated by the 1895 amnesty.[30] An additional forty-five men from the army were similarly returned by another decree on the same day, including the four officers who had been party to the *Anistia inversa* case.[31]

The following year, Barbosa introduced a bill in Congress to strike all "restrictions placed on the amnesty via legislative or executive deliberations."[32] Prior to a lengthy justification by Barbosa, the congressional debates both rehashed old arguments and presented new considerations. Some worried about the possible dangers of formerly rebellious officers rejoining the military. Others focused on the simple unfairness of suspension for officers in the military but no corresponding suspension for civilian federal employees who had taken part in the rebellions.

One senator, seemingly responding to longer-standing arguments about the nature of amnesty, criticized what he called "the doctrine of the unconstitutionality of restricted amnesty." In response, Barbosa denied that such a doctrine had been proposed or developed and justified his bill on the simple principle of equal treatment. The suspension was unfair, he argued, because it only affected those officers whose cases for reinstatement were either in progress or had not yet been heard when the amnesty was decreed. His argument contained, however, further comments about the nature of amnesty, stating that "here we are not dealing with a restriction, but with a verifiable inversion of amnesty." The inversion in this instance was not that the amnesty instituted and imposed a punishment but, rather, that those who had been in court prior to the issuing of the amnesty did not face the same consequences. Many had been absolved and therefore faced no restrictions on their careers. Those who had not "were subject to a punishment that they would not have been had they gone to court." They were, Barbosa argued anew, "citizens who were convicted without having been tried."[33] The bill passed on December 7, 1898, striking the two-year restriction placed on the 1895 amnesty (but more than three years after it had been enacted) and effectively undoing the Federal Supreme Court's ruling.

The matter of *Anistia inversa*, in many ways, laid the foundation for amnesty as a convention for settling rights claims amid political flux. The fall of the monarchy left a power vacuum of sorts, one that military and civilian elites of varying ideological and personal alliances attempted to fill. In the midst of the power conflicts, political and ideological debates arose regarding the seemingly simultaneous imperatives both to uphold liberal rights and to maintain order. The arguments made in the 1896–1897 *Anistia inversa* case took on those questions concerning political power and privilege. In striking the clauses from the amnesty that placed the rebel officers' return to active duty under various conditions, the Congress reconsidered the price to be exacted and paid for political rebellion and sedition. In part, the Congress had simply found a balance among myriad mitigating factors and political allegiances. Not least among them was the growing consensus of the patently unconstitutional and dictatorial nature of Floriano's rule.

Barbosa's systematic argument about "legal amnesia" linked the act of amnesty to the action of restitution. In turn, this argument helped to establish a category of rights-bearing political actors—namely, the amnestied. Yet, these early cases of amnesty and restitution involved a rather narrow guarantee of acquired rights associated with more elite stations and status. More specifically, the cases involved military personnel and their rights during what were, for all practical purposes, authoritarian military regimes. The contemporary debates about the case were, in fact, as much about individual constitutional guarantees as about power in the new republic. Moreover, the intended legal legacy had more to do with judicial review and the supremacy of constitutional guarantees than about amnesty per se.

The championing of *Anistia inversa* as a legal treatise throughout the twentieth century, however, focused on the act, the action, and the actors involved in amnesty and restitution. Subsequent generations treated the work as gospel in future demands about amnesty and its corresponding rights. Large sections of Barbosa's arguments, in fact, would be recited verbatim in tense debates during the precarious political liberalization in 1945, and again in 1979 in the transition from military dictatorship to civilian rule. The most frequently repeated trope from the case was Barbosa's appeal to broad-ranging examples of the resolution of civil strife throughout world history via amnesty. In a litany beginning with an example from ancient Greece, Barbosa linked amnesty to democracy in a seemingly essential way, extolling its pacifying power. He spoke admirably about the application of amnesty throughout French and American history, including the amnesty granted following the American Civil War.[34] *Anistia inversa* came to serve as a shorthand way to refer to some sort of perceived tradition for the protection of variously claimed constitutional, citizenship, political, or human rights via amnesty in Brazil.

The actual demands of the forty-seven military plaintiffs in the *Anistia inversa* case were, by some measures, rather modest and circumscribed. They made no claim for indemnity, reparations, or even reintegration to their formerly held commissions. Rather, they claimed rights to salary and benefit based on guarantees in force at the time of the sanctions that deprived them of portions of their income. Furthermore, Barbosa made no claims in his arguments for broad or universal application and, in fact, conceded that amnesty could be restricted. The central issues at stake in the case—as to what "inverted" amnesty—had nothing explicitly to do with universal rights in the face of authoritarian excess. The rights at stake were those that had been acquired—that is, those that were inherent to a position or status in society. Just the same, invoking the text in the decades that followed helped to justify claims for more universal application and broader rights to restitution and reparations after episodes of state repression.

THE HALF-LIFE OF THE *ANISTIA INVERSA* CASE

Both the intended consequences of the *Anistia inversa* case as well as its popular legacy tell us something about the history of restitution and the ways in which it was linked to amnesty over time in Brazil. In many ways, the *Anistia inversa* case institutionalized amnesty as part of political process in Brazil. What is certain is that the logic of Barbosa's arguments in the 1890s continued to make sense for those claiming rights via amnesty in other moments of political crises or upheaval in the decades that followed. It was not just the intellectual arguments that persisted. In response to an amnesty granted in a constitution enacted in 1934, a group among the descendants of the original forty-seven plaintiffs, including descendants of Custódio José de Melo, filed a lawsuit against the National Treasury in connection with the original case. Arguing that the 1934 amnesty, which was extended "to all who had committed political crimes" up to the date of its enactment, necessarily included their ancestors whose political crimes had been less than amnestied by the 1895 law.

The lawsuit requested payment of salary and benefits for the time prior to the reintegration of the original plaintiffs decades earlier.[35] A lower court rejected their argument in 1943, agreeing with the position of the attorney general that amnesty and reparation were not two sides of the same coin. Rather than an act of reparation as a font to generate indemnity, the attorney general said that amnesty "is itself already a favor" because "it is an act of the forgetting of a crime." The Federal Supreme Court unanimously upheld the decision in August 1947. The high court found that the plaintiffs' ancestors had enjoyed the full benefit of amnesty once the original restrictions in the 1895 law were eliminated by Congress. In response to their efforts, the court ruled that "no matter how much one tortures the text, there is no way to twist that which is straight."[36] Yet before these efforts to expand on and legitimate the arguments about amnesty made by Barbosa in the mid-1890s, there would be a further contraction and an endpoint, of sorts, in the reliance during the First Republic to utilize amnesty as a pacifying and unifying tool. The amnesty in 1910 of rebel sailors (most of whom were Black and descendants of enslaved people), while they still had cannons trained on the city of Rio de Janeiro, was seen by many as an abomination.

CHAPTER 3

THE SHAME OF AMNESTY

Black Sailors in Revolt, 1910

A *New York Times* headline on November 28, 1910, announced that "Sailors had been tortured" in Brazil. The article ran the day after the government had retaken control of warships commandeered by mutineers. João Cândido, a Black sailor, had led the revolt. Cândido and his fellow sailors, mostly forced conscripts and, like him, sons of formerly enslaved people, kept cannons aimed at Rio de Janeiro for four days. The revolt of these sailors occurred seventeen years after the navy had revolted against Floriano in the earliest years of the young republic. Except for the fact that both were navy uprisings, the two revolts had little in common. The first included high-ranking officers who sought nothing short of the ousting of the head of state, the second was a revolt of Black enlisted men demanding better treatment from their officers. Unlike their more elite counterparts who rebelled against Floriano in 1893, the rebel sailors in 1910 made no calls for broad political change, nor did they cite any individual constitutional protections. Their demands were more politically circumspect but also more poignant. Although the *New York Times* article in November 1910 made no mention that the sailors were primarily Black, it explained that the "principal grievance . . . was the employment by the officers of a leather whip called a 'chibata'" and that the "stories of the punishment inflicted upon the men . . . show it to have been veritable torture."[1]

Days later, a related article provided further context in an account from a former Brazilian sailor. This particular sailor had taken part in the plotting of the revolt aboard the new state-of-the art dreadnaught, the *Minas Geraes*, but deserted the navy just before it unfolded. He said that the "conditions in the Brazilian Navy were very bad . . . for the slightest thing a man would get the rope's end."[2] One such unfortunate man was Marcelino Rodrigues de Menezes, a sailor from Bahia, who was flogged with between 200 and 250 lashes on the evening of November 21, 1910, aboard the *Minas Geraes*.[3] The revolt was not a spontaneous reaction to this specific flogging, but the spectacle of violence ushered it in for those who had long plotted to rebel. The very next evening, nearly half of the enlisted sailors (2,379 out of 5,009) revolted against their officers.[4] The ships involved included the new dreadnaughts, the *Minas Geraes* and its sister vessel, the *São Paulo*. The crews of an older dreadnought, the *Deodoro*, and a cruiser, the *Bahia*, also joined the fray on the side of the rebels. The *República* cruiser did not participate in the affront, but the crewmen abandoned their posts to lend manpower aboard the *São Paulo*.[5]

The revolt began with shouts of "Down with the lash" and "Long live liberty."[6] On the *Minas Geraes*, João Cândido emerged as the leader only after an initial spasm of violence. The ship's commander, João Batista das Neves, and three other officers were killed by the rebels, one of whom desecrated the corpse of Neves by urinating on it. The officers had gone down fighting so some rebels were also killed during the melee. On the *Bahia*, another officer and at least one rebel died. Officers of the *São Paulo* abandoned the ship, except for one who ultimately committed suicide.[7] The uprising came to be called the *Revolta da Chibata* (Revolt of the Lash), a title the journalist Edmar Morel used to describe the events in his book of the same name that was first published in 1959. Showing the enduring interest of this episode in Brazilian history, his book went through at least five additional editions, in 1963, 1979, 1986, 2009, and 2016. The title framed the events of the revolt around the sailors' demand that corporal punishment be abolished in the navy.[8] Their other demands included the removal of "incompetent and undignified" officers who were not fit to serve, an increase in their salaries, better food, and an amnesty so they would not be punished for rebelling.

After three days under the barrels of cannons on the most potent vessels in the Brazilian navy, an anxious Congress passed—and the president signed—an amnesty. It extended to "the insurgents in possession of the ships of the National Navy," with the condition that "they submit themselves to authorities under the terms established by the Government." Those terms included disarmament, but mistrust reigned on both sides. Within three days of the amnesty, another decree followed that authorized the removal of enlisted men from the navy "whose continuance in the service would be detrimental to discipline."[9] The decree

Figure 3.1. João Cândido (right) and fellow sailor, 1910. Courtesy Museu da Imagem e do Som, Rio de Janeiro.

circumvented a disciplinary council in place to handle such matters. Arrests and purges soon followed. Between December 2 and 6, nearly 130 sailors were arrested; by December 8, sailors were being dismissed from service, especially those among the crews of the *Minas Geraes* and the *Bahia*. A day later, a second revolt broke out that was followed with the harshest repression, including summary executions, lethal conditions in detention, and exile to the farthest reaches of the Amazon.[10]

During the first revolt, while a congressional emissary negotiated with the rebels, the military made plans for a counterattack. Problems with logistics and capacity, however, thwarted a military assault on the rebels. The simultaneous, if secret, pursuit of both conciliation and counterattack brings to the fore some of the tensions in Brazil at that time. On one hand the resort to amnesty as a mechanism to secure peace ran parallel to the impulse to quash any threat, especially when it had come from poor Black sailors. The *New York Times* had described the treatment of Brazilian sailors as "torture," but the Brazilian press did not. Indeed, many politicians, military elites, and journalists largely looked at the revolt, as well as the subsequent amnesty granted to the rebel sailors, through the lens of honor. The framing of these events as such marked in some ways a certain continuity. The more elite rebels of the 1890s had understood and argued for restitution of the rights afforded them by their relative position in Brazilian society. The sailors of 1910, however, had no such clout and relied instead on notions concerning basic human dignity.

These norms based on honor therefore ran parallel to principles of dignity. In contrast to the experiences of more elite military personnel in the 1890s who asserted both constitutional protections and rights against the tyranny of Floriano, the sailors involved in the Revolt of the Lash instead appealed to universal standards of humane treatment. The drama of the latter goes some distance in explaining the long-standing fascination with the events that transpired over a few days in Rio de Janeiro in late 1910. Yet in each of the navy uprisings, amnesty was a mechanism both sought and extended. Placing these events side-by-side exposes the reach and limits of amnesty as a political resource and institution during the years of the First Republic in Brazil.

In the 1950s the Brazilian sociologist Gilberto Freyre aptly described the Revolt of the Lash as "a small-scale version of the drama of Brazil at the turn of the century." For Freyre, this drama played out in a contradictory quest for modernization at the expense of human development. An impersonal state, in a race to make up for the industrial laziness of the empire, had focused on technological advancements. As Freyre explained, that unflinching commitment to the latest technology came at a cost. The republic had no time to properly educate, train, and reform the recruits. The new technological acquisitions also required additional crew, which only aggravated the problem. To solve the shortage, the military "scour[ed] the ports for instant technicians, machinists, and firemen, incorporating native thugs and foreigners with anarchist ideas into a Navy accustomed to the old styles of discipline, including that of the lash." The result, he explained, was the breakdown of traditional discipline, "hastened by the moral, religious, and educational neglect suffered by the regular crews." The regular crews were comprised mostly of formerly enslaved people or their descendants, whom Freyre described as "accustomed to the patriarchal conditions and disciplines of the slave quarters."[11] As such, violence served as an organizing tool for the navy.

The sailors, however, ultimately answered that violence with the threat of even greater destruction.

It was not just the lack of investment in Brazilians themselves but also the barbarity with which the lowly were treated that underscored the contradiction in the government's pursuit of technological advancement. The news of the exceedingly brutal response to the second revolt seemed to confirm a growing perception that the use of corporal punishment marked the Brazilian navy as singularly uncivilized. Such an accusation cut to the heart of the Brazilian government's initiatives at the time, and especially in Rio de Janeiro, the capital of the republic, where all efforts had been aimed at pulling Brazil into modernity and placing it firmly among "civilized" nations. These efforts were made in a context where patronage, as in the nineteenth century, still wielded enormous influence in the public and private lives of Brazilians. Ties of patronage wove a web in which each person had a place, even if that place was outside of the web. These patron-less individuals were referred to as the *desprotegidos*, or "unprotected ones." Ultimately, claims to honor in this social structure depended on one's vertical relationship to others.[12]

By the turn of the twentieth century, the system of patronage had mapped itself somewhat onto European theories about eugenics. For Brazilian elites, eugenics both explained physical inferiority and drew a map for the improvement of the Brazilian "race." Crucial social and political distinctions had ostensibly been lost with the abolition of slavery in 1888 and the declaration of a republic in 1889, which were crystalized in a notion that all were citizens and none were slaves. Yet theories about degeneration reinforced more traditional social markers. Since, in the logic of the time, enslaved people, free Blacks, and multiracial individuals bore the most obvious marks of a perceived genetic weakness, they "naturally" remained socially inferior. Patronage ties, however, also underscored a shared national destiny. If miscegenation over time had weakened the Brazilian "race," the nation itself was also weak and sickly.[13]

The "body" in the First Republic, therefore, was at once a physical body of an individual and the embodiment of the nation. In assessing the physical health of Brazilians, intellectuals and other elites concluded that the masses were prone to disease and bore the marks of degeneration. Such physical maladies compounded, limiting the health and capacity of the nation. Rui Barbosa had tapped into a prevailing anxiety about the strength of the republic when he framed the 1895 amnesty as "inverted," connoting a sort of congenital deformity. Notably, this understanding of the nation as the sum total of its parts coexisted with a much narrower definition of the Brazilian nation—that is, a nation consisting exclusively of a small circle of elites. The Brazilian anthropologist Roberto DaMatta described these dual conceptions of the Brazilian nation as one based on "solidarity and cordiality" and the other as composed of "exclusive categories organized in a scale of respect and deference."[14]

Lima Barreto's 1916 *The Sad End of Policarpo Quaresma* brings this duality to the fore. Policarpo, a consummate Brazilian patriot, sees the destined greatness of Brazil especially in the heritage of the indigenous and the rural poor. He is disheartened by their seeming lack of patriotism and what he views as limited intellectual capacity, but Policarpo's convictions about them do not waiver. During the 1893 naval revolt against Floriano, Policarpo's sentiments are echoed by a lieutenant who scolds his admiral for complaining about some soldiers. He reminds the admiral that "the patria is just beneath the masses." In spite of a few like-minded comrades, Policarpo is confronted by the much more limited version of the nation and its inherent goodness when he rushes to defend Floriano, only to be executed as a traitor himself (see chapter 2). As a prisoner awaiting his execution, Policarpo realizes that the "patria that he had wished for was a myth; it was a fantasy he created in the silence of his study."[15]

By the turn of the century, legislation targeted the masses as the primary obstacle to national strength. Much of this legislation aimed at purifying and healing physical bodies and spaces. Among the reforms, the federal government subsidized white immigration, to improve the Brazilian "race," and focused on issues of hygiene and disease control as "civilizing" mechanisms. The implementation of such reforms, however, often clashed with social and cultural norms because the reforms blurred the lines between private and public realms. Nonetheless, debates over national health critiqued more than the condition of the masses. As Dain Borges points out, by the 1910s questions about degeneration and national health "often implied criticism of the 'moral corruption' of republican politics."[16] In this way, the well-being of the nation depended not only on its exterior physical robustness but also on its interior moral integrity.

The Revolt of the Lash was not the only contradictory situation that led to violence in the early years of the twentieth century. On the heels of the decimation of the millenarian movement in the backlands of Canudos, politicians redoubled their modernizing efforts. Technology, among possible engines of reform, seemed a viable remedy to Brazil's lack of development. Under the administration of Francisco de Paula Rodrigues Alves (elected in 1902), Brazil invested in everything from street lamps and trolley cars to the very super dreadnoughts that became the site of the 1910 sailors' revolt.[17] In the city of Rio de Janeiro, reformers targeted issues of disease and hygiene as part of a larger modernizing project during what came to be known as the "Belle Époque" (1898–1914).[18] Yet in sharp contrast with this lofty nomenclature, epidemics swept quickly and frequently throughout the city. Sanitation lagged further as the population increased—and indeed doubled just between the years 1900 and 1920.[19]

In response to the threat of disease, Alves's minister of public health, Oswaldo Cruz, announced in 1904 that vaccination against smallpox would be obligatory. In spite of its potential benefits, riots broke out.[20] The cross-class resistance to Cruz's required vaccination gained momentum along two trajectories: medical fear of vaccination and ideological opposition to the obligatory aspect of the inoculation program. The ideological resistance centered on state encroachment in the home. This opposition, as Jeffrey Needell points out, "was founded on constitutional grounds, [namely] the sanctity of the individual's rights against the coercive powers of the state."[21] Employing DaMatta's assessment that the home and, by extension, the body were the domain of private power, the vaccine revolt can be understood as the response to a perceived affront to one's honor. Viewed in this way, the obligatory vaccine dishonored men because it forced them to acquiesce to state power within their own homes. Uninvited officials would, in the words of one labor leader, "penetrate his home . . . and brutalize his daughters' and wife's bodies [with injections]."[22] Such boundary-crossing violated an unwritten pact between citizens and the state. As José Murilo de Carvalho explained, citizens forswore active participation in public affairs in exchange for government noninterference in their daily domestic life. Since the government had violated its side of the pact, "the population felt within their rights when they reacted violently."[23] Limits on state encroachment in the home would, in the logic of the time, ensure the enjoyment of citizen rights by protecting personal honor.

The revolt against the vaccine included ideological opposition to obligatory inoculation, but some rebels opposed much more than the vaccination. As Needell further argues, the revolt must be understood in two contexts: that of the poor fighting against state interference in their private lives and that of the military, or rather sectors of the military, plotting against Alves's administration.[24] Alves, the third in a succession of presidents from São Paulo, inherited and continued the exclusionary politics of the oligarchy that had been brokered with Floriano late in his term. Facing a war in Rio Grande do Sul and the navy revolt of 1893, Floriano sought the assistance of moderate Republicans from São Paulo. In so doing, he alienated his more radical support base. The radical elements, of course, did not simply disappear. Indeed, about three hundred

Jacobins in the military attempted to wrest power from Alves during the upheaval of the vaccine revolt. Interestingly, General Hermes Rodrigues da Fonseca, the man who would be president during the Revolt of the Lash (and a nephew of Deodoro da Fonesca), foiled their plan.

When Hermes da Fonseca prevented the coup attempt against Alves in 1904, he earned the trust of civilian elites. His subsequent campaign for the presidency in 1910, however, pitted *militaristas* against *civilistas*. Hermes's opponent, who cast himself and his administration as firmly and fully civilian, was Rui Barbosa. After a rigorous campaign (the most campaigning ever in the short history of the republic), Hermes defeated Barbosa with the support of the Republican Party machine. One week after his inauguration, Hermes faced the crisis of the Revolt of the Lash. On the fateful evening in November 1910, while attending the opera, Hermes got word about the events aboard the dreadnaughts. In their first, well-scripted message sent to the president, the "sailors, citizens, and Republicans" explained that they could "no longer endure the slavery of the Brazilian navy nor the lack of protection." They called for the removal of "incompetent and undignified officers," the reform of the "immoral and shameful code" that ruled over them, outlawing the use of the lash and similar punishments, an increase in salaries, and training. They gave Hermes twelve hours to reply or risk the annihilation of the "Fatherland."[25] Other more spontaneous communiqués consistently reiterated the sailors' demand that corporal punishment be abolished in the navy and added the condition of a general amnesty. José Carlos de Carvalho, who had previously proposed a wage increase and was mentioned in their original manifesto, served as Congress's negotiator with the sailors and was himself a navy officer. He reported that the sailors also demanded better food.[26]

In the view of many of the time, the republic faced an impasse. "Degenerate" Black sailors had mutinied against their white officers; Brazil's prize technology had turned against its capital city; the familiar, and inflammatory, political issue regarding the limits of state power over one's body had been reignited; and the divide between *militaristas* and *civilistas* had deepened. The reactions to the Revolt of the Lash, though varied, are a window to how events challenged and shaped the government's modernizing mission. Both the revolt and the government's responses to it had to seek justification through appeals to political norms. The justifications for the revolt, the amnesty, and the repression were all framed in a shared political language. This common language, however, drew from diverse logics about citizenship, rights, and the state. On one hand, the government's amnesty resembled a favor granted by a patron to his client, an act of charity that can be given and taken away. On the other hand, it stood, albeit very briefly, as an affirmation of a universal right not to be in any way enslaved.

THE MILITARY AS SOLUTION AND PROBLEM

The quest for modernity and technology as a solution to national weakness played out in the military. Beginning in 1904, the government committed itself, at great expense, to modernize the navy. The two new dreadnoughts involved in the revolt, the *São Paulo* and the *Minas Geraes*, were among a recently acquired fleet. Their purchase gave Brazil standing among the best equipped navies in the world.[27] The maiden voyages of these ships in the early months of 1910 briefly enhanced the prestige of the navy in national and international circles. President-elect Hermes da Fonseca accompanied the *São Paulo* home. During the journey, he reportedly grew quite fond of the crew. The *Minas Geraes* also performed a ceremonial role. To honor the memory of the much-esteemed Brazilian ambassador to the United States, Joaquim Nabuco, the *Minas Geraes* went first to the United States to make a convoy with the American ship transporting his remains to Brazil.[28]

The crews of these ships had received the best training to date in the Brazilian navy. They spent nearly two years in England learning how to operate and maintain the new ships, all the while plotting their revolt. Inspired by the Russian sailors' 1905 mutiny on the *Potemkin*, and in the midst of tremendous union movements in England and the anti-monarchy revolution of 1910 in Portugal, these Brazilian sailors returned home determined to challenge repressive authority as their international brethren had done. Indeed, when the leadership of the revolt lost footing in their negotiations with the government, some sailors invoked the spirit of the Russian sailors who had not wavered and had earned the backing of the populace.[29]

Instead of guaranteeing defense for Brazil and increasing its honor, the investment in the new dreadnoughts and their crews threatened the nation with the most sophisticated naval power available at that time. The navy officers drafted plans to attack the mutinous ships, but their relative weakness against the rebel ships' capacity soon convinced the government that diplomacy offered the most likely route for resolution. The irony that it was the best ships that turned against the government did not escape notice. One political cartoon depicted a Brazilian navy ship growling at a caricature of the republic only later to show deference to a foreign dignitary.[30] Rui Barbosa echoed a similar sentiment when he reminded his fellow senators that Brazil's navy power had traditionally posed a much greater threat to Brazil itself than to any potentially hostile foreign power.[31]

The prevailing metaphor of the nation as a body created political space for a revolt on those same terms, but it also co-opted the revolt from the rebels. In step with some abolitionist thought (wherein the evil of slavery rested in the corrupting influence of the enslaved on the slaveholder), the locus of the attention in the revolt shifted from the injury on the physical body of the victim to the moral wound on the nation. Indeed, opposition to slavery called attention not just to the obvious and regrettable welts and scars on the body of the enslaved but also, and perhaps more so, on the insidious marks left on the honor and soul of the master.[32] Similarly, the problem of the sailors' revolt in political discourse rarely addressed the bodies of the sailors themselves and instead concerned itself primarily with the honor of the officers and, by extension, the nation.

In the military, this concern for honor existed alongside a sincere promotion of social leveling. By the beginning of the twentieth century, the military had negotiated a new institutional role within the government, making itself a protagonist in the modernizing project of the First Republic. The military's zeal for being the generator of citizenship, however, was tempered by its rigid hierarchy and its vulnerability to elite privilege. Perhaps more than in any other institution, the dilemma over honor, cruelty, and the legitimate use of violence played out in the military.

The military both provided particular solutions and posed troubling problems for the political elite of the time. Faced with worrisome social problems, vagrancy, and crime, government officials on both national and local levels looked to the military as the answer for their troubles. Beginning in the period of the empire, the military served as a depository for criminals and suspected criminals, mostly poor and multiracial (in the army) or Black (in the navy). In fact, "recruitment" into the military was itself a form of punishment. Overburdened courts reserved themselves almost exclusively for homicide cases and a few other high crimes. Marginalized adolescent boys, enslaved men, *capoeiras* (practitioners of the Afro-Brazilian martial art), and other *desprotegidos* (unprotected ones, signifying their lack of a "patron") were rounded up and forced into military service both as a punitive and as a preventive measure for crime. As a perfect marriage of punishment and reform, military service was intended to imprison the criminal, thereby making the streets safer, while training him in skills that served the larger society. Beyond "recruiting" men and boys as punishment, much of the work of the military, though contradictory, involved policing streets and guarding prisons.[33]

Impressment as a solution for the weak justice system and ambitious city planners, however, posed sticky problems in times of more traditional military crisis. Even though forced recruitment of social misfits seemed to make up for a lack of volunteers, the resulting stigma associated with military service worked against attracting more "honorable" men to volunteer. The crisis of the Paraguayan War (1865–1870) clearly brought to the fore the detrimental aspects of impressment for the prestige of and numbers in military service. Emperor Dom Pedro II and the military devised numerous strategies to inspire volunteers to serve, but to little avail. Men of means simply captured or bought less fortunate free or enslaved men to serve in their place.[34] Peacetime recruitment fared no better. Between 1840 and 1888, apprentice schools, the halfway houses to military impressments, sent 8,586 minors and 6,271 other forced recruits to the navy. During this period the same agencies trained and sent a paltry 460 volunteers.[35] For 1910, the year of the sailors' revolt, the navy reported 924 "recruits" from the apprentice schools compared with 49 volunteers.[36]

By the turn of the twentieth century, the military began to see and speak of itself as the key generator of patriotism and modernity for the republic. Officers claimed that the soldiers were "nothing more than the people-in-arms" and that the army was the "school of citizenship."[37] Brazilians from all regions and backgrounds, the military argued, could be trained in useful skills as well as fortified physically in the barracks. Those that passed through the barracks, in fact, would emerge as robust and ideal citizens. This conflation of citizen and soldier proved contradictory. As DaMatta points out, the Brazilian citizen, (a rather narrow category) had the guarantee of social equality, while the soldier remained in his place in the military hierarchy.[38]

BRAZILIAN SAILORS

In many ways Cândido, the leader of the Revolt of the Lash, is emblematic of any Brazilian sailor of the time. Born in 1880 to an enslaved woman, he was guaranteed his freedom upon maturity through the 1871 Law of the Free Womb. He was sent to a naval apprentice school at the age of thirteen and then enlisted into the navy at the age of sixteen. Sailors lived to some degree on the whims of their officers and often suffered abuse, but the military nonetheless provided opportunities not otherwise available to them. Cândido, for example, learned to read and was trained in complicated navigational skills. He was also among the crew sent to England to receive training on and to accompany home the two new super dreadnoughts.

At the time that the Revolt of the Lash erupted, the harsh conditions for Brazilian sailors was no secret. Corporal punishment in the navy fit well into its institutional role in the larger penal system in Brazil.[39] Given the isolation of a ship at sea, navy commanders enjoyed a relatively high degree of autonomy. The War Ministry included a court system, but few cases from the navy ever reached its courtroom. Rather than delay hearings, judgment, and punishment, the officers simply dealt with disciplinary situations on deck. In addition to lashings, other penalties included fines, wage garnishment, isolation, reduced rations (bread and water), and hard labor. Considering that many had been impressed into service and had suspect backgrounds, the gravest crimes of the sailors in the eyes of their officers were those that threatened order. Fighting among sailors on board, drunkenness, and lack of due respect to an officer were seen as the most menacing behaviors.[40]

Fifteen years before the Revolt of the Lash, Adolfo Caminha, a late-nineteenth-century Brazilian writer, published a controversial novel, *Bom Crioulo*, that broached the topics of race, violence, and sexuality in the Brazilian navy and commented on the physical and moral fitness of both the lowly and the powerful. The title character, Bom Crioulo, had escaped from an enslaved past but then was forced into naval service. Control over his labor and sustenance had in some ways simply changed masters, but Bom Crioulo nonetheless experiences a sense of liberty for the first time while at sea. The expanse of that liberty seemed to be reflected in his own physical health, first in its fullness and then in its unmistakable decline. Indeed, as he begins his naval career, Bom Crioulo seems physically perfect, "with a formidable set of muscles, giving an impression of almost superhuman strength."[41] With that freedom, he allows himself to fall in love and have a relationship with a young, white cabin boy. His perfect physique then begins to slowly show the wear of an internal moral collapse.

The first hint of his decline comes in a scene of lashing. Bom Crioulo's strong body had previously withstood brutal punishment, but a single drop of blood betrays him after 150 lashes, surprising even the guard who whipped him.[42] Other signs of degeneration followed. He grows thin and struggles with a "deep drowsiness." His relationship with the cabin boy seems to have eroded his physical prowess.[43] By the end of the novel, Bom Crioulo cannot hide his frailty. Subsequent lashings leave him "bathed in blood."[44] Rushed to the hospital to recover, he only weakens further. His body simply would not heal from the lashing. All this occurs while the cabin boy grew physically stronger in a secret love affair with their former landlady. As a turn-of-the-century Brazilian Othello, Bom Crioulo then kills his former lover in a jealous rage, a crime of passion that suggests to the reader that Bom Crioulo has a sick, uncivilized soul.

The novel demonstrates the pervasive idea at that time that the physical body stands as proof of interior qualities, but it also questions such assumptions. In his study of race, Borges examines a tendency in Brazil to be mindful that appearances can be deceiving. Any confidence in the thinking of the time that inferior human qualities could be detected on the physical bodies was tempered by an accepted warning against being duped by making such assumptions.[45] Caminha's treatment of race, violence, and sexuality arguably plays with this contradiction and provides a point for consideration of Peter Berger's insights about honor and dignity.

Berger argues that the claims to rights based on "honor" or on "dignity" arise from opposing frameworks. The relationship of the "true self" to the physical body and sexuality in conceptions of both honor and dignity are illustrative of this opposition. In the conception of honor, the "true self" is revealed in the full "regalia" of his roles (a knight in armor riding out to do battle, for example), while the "naked man in bed with a woman represents a lesser reality of the self." In the framework of dignity, on the other hand, one's institutional roles are a mere "disguise." Berger argues that it is "precisely the naked man, and even more specifically the naked man expressing his sexuality, who represents himself more truthfully."[46] Caminha's tragic character is not presented as honorable, but he does inspire sympathy. Conversely, the "regalia" of the navy is exposed as a façade hiding a corrupt and cruel institution.[47]

Coming to terms with the revolt on the prized ships, the minister of the navy, Joaquim Marques Baptista de Leão, only partly faulted the rebel sailors. He saw them as having weak moral backgrounds and succumbing to brainwashing by "ill-formed" political ideas while in Europe. Their officers, therefore, were also to blame because they had failed to impose "proper" political ideology.[48] The revolt itself made the question of corporal punishment in the navy, a matter that had been under debate for some time, an issue of utmost urgency. Two contradictory codes, civilian and military, regulated the use of the lash as punishment in the navy; both were largely ineffective. On the civilian side, Rui Barbosa and others maintained that corporal punishment had been clearly abolished on at least three occasions throughout Brazil's history. In a speech in the Senate just a few days after the amnesty had been granted to the rebel sailors, Barbosa reminded his fellow senators that the third act of the republic in 1889 had abolished corporal punishment in the navy. This act, he continued, simply reinforced the guarantees against torture and other cruel punishments that had been granted in the 1824 constitution during the empire, which was again held in force in the 1891 constitution of the republic. Barbosa concluded his speech with an indictment of the officers. The open violation of laws forbidding corporal punishment by superiors, Barbosa said, had planted "a permanent seed of sedition" in their sailors.[49]

Military code allowed officers to use corporal punishment within certain legal limits, even though this was prohibited in the various constitutions. For example, the code permitted up to twenty-five lashes per day. If a sailor was sentenced to more, the lashing was to be administered over several days.[50] The use of corporal punishment, however, was a tricky recourse for navy commanders. Lashing a sailor in the presence of his fellow crewmen demonstrated the officer's authority on the ship and had an impact on the sailors witnessing it. Yet it also posed certain risks for the commander. If the offender withstood the punishment bravely, he enjoyed a hero's status among his peers. If the offender suffered tremendously, the commander faced another set of problems, ranging from the loss of the sailor's labor during his recovery to criminal charges for excessive punishment.

One anonymous apologist for the lash, a particularly racist navy officer, maintained that corporal punishment offered the only recourse to control the offensive conditions and habits of the enlisted men. The first impression of these sailors, he said, was one of "decay and physical weakness . . . they dressed poorly, and did not know how to eat or sleep." He blamed the "depravity" shown by the sailors on the color of their skin and lamented that the "other races gave themselves over" to their influence since the Black sailors were "always in the majority." At sea, he explained, twelve or fifteen virtually defenseless officers, "abandoned" by the navy, were left to command four or five hundred of these sailors. The lash, therefore, was the only guarantee of discipline. The crews themselves, in this officer's estimation, viewed the lash as their protection against depraved fellow crewmen.[51]

Another officer, facing charges for excessive punishment in 1893 in the War Ministry's court, successfully defended the use of the lash on different terms. He argued that, to be effective, the general rules of punishment must be tailored to the specific offender.[52] The day limit of twenty-five lashes might sufficiently punish some weaker sailors, but for others it would hardly be a punishment at all. (He had ordered five hundred lashings on a single day, twenty times the "legal" limit.) His defense rested on the logic that, even though the number of lashes might seem excessive, the effects of the punishment were, in fact, not. He had allowed the man to wear two shirts, which afforded some protection. He claimed further that this sailor required no extraordinary medical attention after the whipping and in fact returned to work within days of the punishment.[53]

This apparent tolerance for corporal punishment in the navy and the military court cannot be attributed to insensitivity toward violence. Nor can it be assumed that all commanders who employed the lash did so out of impulsive cruelty. In fact, much discussion among military officers and would-be reformers at the turn of the century considered lashing essential, though regrettably so. Peter Beattie points out, in fact, that the military was deeply concerned with its institutional role as manager of "legitimate" violence as a sort of social guardian, protecting the honest by punishing the wrongdoers.[54] Framed in this way, the recourse to violence seemed to some as more of a duty than a choice.

Joaquim Maria Machado de Assis, who died two years before the Revolt of the Lash, had masterfully exposed the moral quandary of violence as a social organizing tool. In his short story "The Rod of Justice," a young man is disturbed by the cruelty of his godfather's girlfriend toward an enslaved girl. He vows to intervene should the woman resort to violence. Yet, when she demands that he hand her "the rod" to whip the girl, the young man complies. He had sought the woman's intercession in an effort to convince his father to allow him to leave the seminary. His debt for her intercession leaves him feeling trapped by his own circumstances, which prevent him from helping the young girl to escape hers. Not surprisingly, his choice "pricked [him] with an uneasy sense of guilt." In the end, the young man feels himself to be as much a victim of the "system" as the girl, although the girl would surely disagree.[55]

FOR SHAME

Once military leaders and government officials learned that part of the navy had mutinied, they began immediate plans to end the uprising and return order and discipline to the ranks. Their plans developed along opposing trajectories. They would negotiate with the rebels while secretly preparing a counterattack. The task of negotiation fell primarily to Congress whose representative in discussions with the rebel sailors was the above-mentioned Carvalho, a member of the Chamber of Deputies as well as a navy officer. The newly appointed navy minister, Leão, coordinated the military's plans for the counterattack. Carvalho and Leão had contradicting aims, yet both emphasized the limited options available to them and the importance of maintaining honor. For Carvalho, ideas about the reciprocal duties tied to honor limited the range of options for the government's response. He argued that the discipline observed by the rebel sailors throughout the revolt obliged the government to respond accordingly. For Leão, however, the mutiny itself proved an utter lack of discipline; the sailors and their revolt, therefore, had to be put down forcefully. Leão explained that the government's options were limited not by Carvalho's more abstract notions of duty but, rather, by more practical constraints of time, technology, and the military's relative strategic disadvantage vis-à-vis the rebels.

Carvalho's account described the scene aboard the ship as one of strict order. He reported that the sailors had received him with "all the honors inherent in my position," that the ship's safe was under heavy guard, and that there was no alcohol on board. Carvalho noted that the sailors were willing to submit to legitimate authority, as evidenced when Cândido obeyed his order to anchor the ship, a maneuver that Cândido had "executed . . . with precision."[56] Thus, not only were the ships under strict control, but the rebel sailors were also able seamen. Carvalho's emphasis on the sailors' deference to him underscored the duty the government then owed them. The sailors, in Carvalho's view, knew their place in the social hierarchy; therefore, a violent response was not only unnecessary, but also indefensible. In Congress, Barbosa explained that he had read Carvalho's statements with admiration and announced to his fellow representatives, "Gentlemen, this is an honest revolt!"[57]

Carvalho's reports showed sympathy toward the sailors and their plight, but Leão described the revolt as a "massacre of officers." Any duty owed, therefore, was to the officers. In eulogizing one of them, who "alone and defenseless against more than one hundred armed men had put up a fearsome fight," Leão called for his "legacy of heroic resistance" to receive "homage among the most outstanding of our history."[58] Even before the congressional negotiations began on the morning of November 23, 1910, the navy had already devised the first of two counteroffensive attacks. It involved the division of destroyers, which had remained under military command. The plan was to arm them with torpedoes. A series of embarrassing errors and miscalculations, however, prohibited the navy from transferring warheads. At a point of near desperation, navy officers even weighed the possibility of laying mines in the port to put down the rebellion. Good judgment prevailed once they realized the damage that would be caused to commerce by mining an international port.[59]

Congress ultimately curtailed the navy's chance to respond militarily by granting an amnesty. In short order, a patchwork of arguments was stitched together by the obvious political expediency of the measure to resolve the crisis. Barbosa had led the charge, and the proposal to amnesty the rebels passed unanimously in an often divided Senate. Only a few opposed it in the Chamber of Deputies.[60] The representatives seemed reassured by Carvalho's faith that the sailors would comply with the negotiated terms of surrender. With the immediate peril behind them, however, critics forcefully condemned the grant of amnesty. The most refined critiques regretted that the granting of amnesty to the sailors while still in arms might set a dreadful precedent.[61] Most were concerned, however, with the more immediate insult to military honor, and they fumed at Congress.[62] One contemporaneous political cartoon described the amnesty as "the lashing of our soul."[63] Another depicted Cândido, the Black "Admiral," surrounded by white officers saluting him. Under the caption, "the discipline of the future," Cândido threatened the officers saying that he "did not think he could put up with them without using the lash."[64] A generation later, a 1949 editorial in the *Correio da Manhã*, that appeared on the anniversary of the 1910 revolt, repeated the old indictments by criticizing Congress for allowing the "noble, political instrument of amnesty to benefit criminals without any political program."[65]

Some international critics seemed to agree with those offended by the amnesty. On the front page of *Correio da Manhã* on December 22, 1910, a London foreign correspondent complained that the grant of amnesty cost Brazil much prestige in Europe. Acknowledging that the European press could not fully understand the dilemma facing the Brazilian Congress, he thought it had acted hastily. "It seems," he said, "like a reckless course for a congress and a government to amnesty rebels that assassinated their officers and who still threatened the capital of the country with their cannons." He concluded by reporting that, "if the impression in Europe of the uprising was bad, that of the amnesty was a disaster."[66] Headlines in the press in the United States were similarly negative. Just after the amnesty was granted, the *New York Times* ran an article entitled, "Brazil Gives Way; Rebel Fleet Gone, Congress, After Fisticuffs, Votes Amnesty to Mutineers—Then, Can't Find Ships."[67] A *Washington Post* editorial a month later assured that "Disgraceful Affair in Brazil's Navy Has No Parallel in American Services."[68]

Amnesty was not, however, without its defenders. Most emphasized the social peace and public order secured by extending amnesty.[69] It was because of the amnesty, in fact, that the sailors turned the cannons away from the city of Rio de Janeiro and returned the ships to the command of the officers. For those same officers, however, the amnesty was utterly untenable. How could they reassume command when the mutiny had gone unpunished? Soon, new codes were enacted to circumvent the amnesty and Hermes signed a decree that provided the navy with the power to summarily dismiss any sailor deemed a threat to discipline.[70]

When tensions over these practices mounted, a second revolt erupted among a marine infantry battalion on the Ilha das Cobras and aboard the *Rio Grande do Sul* late in evening of December 9, 1910. The officers regained controlled of their ship, but the naval base on the Ilha das Cobras remained in the hands of the insurgents. Before dawn, the government's forces opened fire on the island, retaking control by mid-afternoon. Estimates of killed and wounded servicemen vary widely; sources confirmed at least twenty-three killed and from eighteen to more than one hundred wounded. Reports of the chaos pointed a finger at the amnesty and pressured Congress to suspend individual rights through a state of siege until order was reestablished, which it did.[71] The amnesty that had been extended to the rebel sailors to resolve the acute crisis had ended up sparking further conflict.

Rebels, as well as nonrebels, were rounded up and detained, including Cândido, who had remained loyal to his commanders during the second uprising. Nearly thirty of those arrested were held in lethal conditions on the Ilha das Cobras on Christmas Eve, from which only Cândido and three others survived.[72] Rather than securing governmental control, the state of siege in many ways seemed a relinquishment of it. Indeed, the prison fatalities horrified the reading public. One journalist compared the "sinister scene" to the drama of the *Divine Comedy* and argued that only a vigorous response to the events could salvage Brazil's tainted image, but only partially.[73] On the same day that the bodies were pulled from the prison cells, over two hundred people, a mixture of sailors and other suspicious individuals who had been captured during the state of siege, were sent into exile aboard a steamer, the *Satélite*. A number of them were summarily executed en route, including one who reportedly "jumped" overboard.[74] News of these events was suppressed for several weeks but eventually came out and deepened the crisis in Brazil. Thus, both the revolt and the harsh repression that followed brought scandal to Brazil.[75]

THE END OF AMNESTY

Unlike Floriano's many foes attempting to unseat him in the 1890s, the rebel sailors in 1910 did not attempt or even desire a revolution in the strictest sense. Rather, they fought for forms of protection and inclusion in Brazilian society. Their initial demands declared them "citizens and Republicans." It was a striking claim given the slavery-like system of the Brazilian navy at the time. Much was at stake for them in the revolt. Overworked and abused, they risked further repression, if not death, at the hands of their officers should the revolt fail. As it happened, they faced the same risks even though the grant of amnesty initially signified their success. The amnesty offered the most reasonable course of action in order to resolve the initial crisis of the rebellion, but within a few short weeks it came to seem imprudent. Similarly, the use of corporal punishment in the military had initially offended republican sensibilities as they debated the amnesty, but these same republicans soon sanctioned the repression unleashed during the state of siege.

In the conceptualization of the time, the sailors' demand to outlaw lashing as punishment in the navy implied not only a limit of the reach of the state over their physical bodies but a more spiritual boundary as well. The government would not touch an esteemed man because to do so would be to dishonor him. Dishonoring an esteemed man, in turn, brought dishonor to the nation. The sailors' demand to end corporal punishment, therefore, was seen by some as a claim for honor, whether deserved or underserved. Yet their claim also reveals a logic at work that ran counter to honor. By contrasting the realities in the navy with the promises of the republic, the sailors' demanded a minimum social-leveling right of bodily integrity based more on notions of basic dignity.

Much was also at stake for the military in putting down the revolt. The question of corporal punishment challenged military authorities to reconcile the political project for modernization with an unflinching defense of the status quo. The same cannons that threatened them had come at tremendous expense and commitment. In fact, the very ships on which the sailors mutinied had promised to enhance the international standing of Brazil but, instead, had brought shame and embarrassment. The revolt over the use of the lash, furthermore, exposed the contradictions within the government's civilizing program. Hygiene and health initiatives to strengthen the citizenry certainly seemed incongruent with whipping. Similarly, the changing role of the military in society and the growing faith in reform did not align with the abysmal conditions of sailors in the Brazilian navy.

The outcomes for the Black sailors in 1910 stand in stark contrast to those of the higher-ranking officers during the 1890s. The issues surrounding amnesty for the officers revolved around entitlements based on constitutional guarantees. For many of the sailors, however, amnesty was a matter of life and death. The officers faced a sanction via the 1895 amnesty, but many had the resources and influence to contest and ultimately reverse the punitive measures through an act of Congress. The sailors had no resources for any recourse and no long-standing allies. As a result, the amnesty did not hold. Taken together, the two cases highlight the parameters of citizenship during the First Republic in Brazil and underscore the ways in which ideas about amnesty, restitution, and legitimate political opposition were both challenged and changed. The more elite officers in the 1890s were successful in gaining, over time, full standing as beneficiaries of amnesty; the Black sailors in 1910 were not.

The extension of amnesty to Black sailors seemed, in some ways, to sully it as a recourse and to harden the opposition to granting it in moments of crisis. More than a decade earlier, Barbosa's arguments about amnesty had elevated the measure as a guarantor of rights. The impressive reach and impact of Barbosa's arguments is perhaps evidenced in the very fact that the sailors themselves had explicitly demanded it together with the abolition of whipping as a punishment. Yet, the amnesty did not hold for these sailors, and for two decades afterward amnesty largely disappeared as a political tool. Through successive administrations in the 1920s, in fact, the suggestion of amnesty was an absolute nonstarter in dealing with the dramatic and ongoing protests for reforms that were led by junior military officers known as the *tenentes*, or lieutenants. The tenentes' movement helped fuel the subsequent revolution that brought Getúlio Vargas to power in 1930. After fruitless efforts for amnesty during the 1920s, a grant of amnesty was part of the revolutionary program. Under Vargas, the use of amnesty became both broader and more bureaucratized.

The events of the Revolt of the Lash marked, therefore, an end to amnesty, at least temporarily. At the same time, those events were the beginning of an enduring fascination with these sailors in Brazilian history and historiography, though not within the navy itself. In 2008, then President Luiz Inácio Lula da Silva ("Lula") saw fit to address the lingering injustice, and he did so in posthumously conceding amnesty to Cândido and his companions by signing a law that essentially restored the 1910 amnesty.[76] Efforts to amnesty the sailors anew had begun in 2002, shortly after the creation of the national Amnesty Commission, which drew broad attention to historic injustices. For any sailors still living, the proposed law would provide a pension, reflecting promotions in the navy as if they had remained in active service. For those deceased, the pension would go to surviving family. For many, the compensation was not merely symbolic. In 2005, just before a planned demonstration in Brasília for the families of the sailors, Cândido's then eighty-one-year-old daughter explained one painful result of the family's persistent poverty. Unable to afford a permanent grave, her father's remains had been exhumed and cremated.[77] A few months after Lula signed the amnesty into law in 2008, he attended the presentation of a statue honoring Cândido in Praça Quince, a public square in downtown Rio de Janeiro. In response to a press query about the event, a navy representative commented that the revolt was a "sad episode in their history" and added that they "do not recognize heroism in that movement."[78]

PART II

THE BUREAUCRATIZATION OF AMNESTY, 1930S–1940S

PROLOGUE

THE "INSTITUTION OF GRACE"

In 1933 Geminiano da França, a judge on the Federal Supreme Court, published a three-part series on the "Juridical Institution of Grace" in the principle legal journal in Brazil, *Revista Forense*. His arguments in the section entitled "Amnesty" began with a discussion about pacifying impulses that occurred throughout the world following the devastation of the First World War. He mentioned successive programs seeking to improve economic and social relations that, if left unchecked, might be a germ of future wars. Although there was little to show for those efforts, Da França urged his readers not to grow discouraged. Then he turned to the topic of benevolence and its power to diffuse rather than inflame conflict. The "most expressive manifestation" of such benevolence, he argued, was amnesty, which comforts the vanquished and acts as a check on the victor.[1]

His reflections in 1933 were made in the wake of the revolution that brought Getúlio Vargas to power, but he focused primarily on the 1895 amnesty and the arguments made by Rui Barbosa. Indeed, as Barbosa had done in his litany in the *Anistia Inversa* case, Da França buttressed his argument with examples from ancient time to the recent past to show the effectiveness of amnesty as a political tool. Turning his attention to the question of a "partial amnesty," he noted that the restrictions in the 1895 amnesty were met with vigorous protests, which then solidified in the *Anistia Inversa* case brought by former military members over the caveat that their possible reintegration be predicated on a two-year suspension. He explained how the 1897 Federal Supreme Court ruling found that the restrictions placed on the amnesty "did not offend *rights* but, rather, only injured *interests*," and that the prerogative of the legislature to concede amnesty in the way "best suited to public interest."[2] Based on that same prerogative, Da França added that the Federal Supreme Court's ruling against the military personnel's claim for immediate restitution could not, and did not, prevent Congress "from later recognizing its mistake and abolishing all the restrictions, which had been adopted as providence of the moment." The legislature, he explained, restored the amnestied to the fullness of their rights.[3]

Nearly a decade later, in early 1942, Jorge Amado, a then-emerging literary and political figure in Brazil, made a similar argument about benevolence and amnesty, albeit in a different form. From exile in Argentina, Amado wrote and published *Vida de Luis Carlos Prestes: o cavaleiro da esperança* (The life of Luís Carlos Prestes, the cavalier of hope). He described the work as a "political book, written for the amnesty campaign, for the freedom of Prestes."[4] His exalted biography of Prestes is a hero's tale about the former military officer who had led a "Long March" of protest through the interior of Brazil in the 1920s. The march ended in his own exile, first to Bolivia and then elsewhere in South America. Unlike many other rebel officers, Prestes did not back the revolution that brought Vargas to power in 1930. Instead, he began what would be a slow conversion to communism and indeed moved to Moscow in 1931, where he remained until 1934. The following year, and in opposition to Vargas, Prestes prepared to lead a communist-backed revolutionary movement that would begin with coordinated revolts in military barracks. The resulting Intentona Comunista—or communist "attempt," as it is known—failed.[5] In response, Vargas began along a track that would ultimately lead to the institution of a fascist-styled dictatorship, the Estado Novo. Prestes was arrested soon after the revolts were put down and remained in prison until the passage of an amnesty in 1945. Amado's book was written and published during Prestes's imprisonment as part of a burgeoning campaign for amnesty that seized upon his plight.

Only nine years separate the publication of Da França's legal arguments and of Amado's political treatise, but their respective historical moments seem much more distant. Da França wrote with an eye to the past, urging hopefulness in a post–First World War context. Amado's context, in contrast, was the active and staggering global threat posed by Adolf Hitler in the Second World War and the repression of Vargas's Estado Novo at home. Looking back on the work in 1979, just months before another amnesty would mark the beginning of the end of the Cold War–era military dictatorship in Brazil, Amado would nonetheless insist that the book was born from, and for, an obstinate faith in the future.[6]

DA FRANÇA AND THE LESSONS OF THE PAST

Da França's analysis of amnesty, and of grace as a political institution more generally, fits within a broader shift in mentalities from the generation of the 1890s to that of the 1930s. This shift is more famously apparent in Gilberto Freyre's seminal *The Masters and the Slaves*, which was first published the same year as Da França's reflections on amnesty. Freyre rebutted the preceding generation's trope of racial degeneration with arguments about a perceived harmony made possible by Brazil's particularized colonial legacy. Indeed, he credits what he describes as the benevolence and adaptability of the Portuguese patriarch with yielding a milder and more informal form of colonialism in Brazil.[7] Da França made no comparable sweeping comments on the merits of Brazilian society but nonetheless seemed to reject some of the prior generation's premises.

In the 1890s Rui Barbosa had tapped into prevailing anxieties about Brazil, and about Brazilians, by applying the more scientific language of "inversion" to criticize the 1895 amnesty. Forty years later, Da França looked at that same amnesty in a different way. He did not see deformity so much as expediency. Barbosa framed his advocacy on behalf of the military officers in terms that revealed larger insecurities about race in Brazil, whereas Da França worried over the specter of political agitation. For Barbosa, the situation of the 1895 amnesty required corrective justice for offenses to individual rights. For Da França, amnesty served primarily as a political tool in urgent situations involving threats to public order—that is, amnesty provided first and foremost for public peace. Notably, any subsequent restitution to individuals made possible by amnesty, Da França argued, had to take into account the rights subsequently acquired by others.

Born in 1870, Da França was a contemporary of Barbosa. He witnessed firsthand the upheaval of the 1890s. In 1893, he was serving as the chief of police in Niteroi, the sister city across the bay from Rio de Janeiro, when the navy revolt against Floriano broke out. From 1919 to 1922, Da França then served as chief of police in Rio de Janeiro. From that post, he campaigned vigorously against the increased influence of communist and anarchist thought in the transforming city.[8] He took action against what he described as the "degrading spectacle" of "malnourished and diseased vagrants, prostitutes, and anarchists" in downtown Rio de Janeiro.[9] From there, Da França rose in the judiciary, ultimately being appointed in 1922 to the Federal Supreme Court. His appointment occurred the same year that the Partido Comunista Brasileiro (the Brazilian Communist Party, PCB) was formed, and reform-minded junior officers staged the first of a series of rebellions that would evolve into columns of Prestes's Long March.

Just a few months after the revolution of 1930, however, Da França lost his judgeship. In a sign of his close ties to the previous regime, he was retired by a decree issued by Vargas.[10] The decree itself cited the "imperative demands of public order," as well as a previous decree that reduced the number of ministers on the court. Four other judges were likewise retired because of "illness, advanced age or other conditions of relevant nature" that made them "incompatible" with the requirements of the position.[11] Da França died in December 1935, just after the eruption and quick suppression of the barracks revolts that aimed to ignite a broader revolutionary movement.

A number of events during the preceding decades set the stage for the upheaval that occurred in 1930. Economically, coffee had replaced sugar as the main crop. Political power shifted with that economic change, moving from the sugar barons of the northeast to the coffee barons of the central-south. The turn from a system of slavery to one of wage labor resulted in an influx of immigrants and, with them, ideas. Immigrant workers from southern Italy, in particular, introduced more radical ideologies to an otherwise conservative political landscape. At the same time, the cities expanded, along with the public bureaucracies within them, as well as the commercial white-collar middle class. In the first decade of the twentieth century, self-styled visionaries worked to transform Rio de Janeiro from a depressing and disease-ridden international port to a more modern capital city, modeled on Paris. The transformations included the addition of trolley cars, streetlights, and promenades, as well as the expulsion of the poor and destitute from the center of the city to the high rocky mounds that surround it.[12]

In his 1933 analysis of amnesty, Da França both extolled its unique virtues and warned of its potential grievous misuse. He described amnesty as a pact of honor that must be "religiously upheld," by which he meant the government must not act in any way with regard to crimes that had already been amnestied. Doing so, he said, constituted a crime and, as with Lady Macbeth, would leave a stain on the hands of the state that an "ocean's worth of water could not wash away." His parting words were a warning that a despotic government might utilize amnesty as a trap to more surely exact its vengeance. He reached back to the sixteenth century and across the ocean to Europe to describe as an example the massacre of Huguenots in Paris on St. Bartholomew's Day.[13] He neglected to mention other possible examples of such traps from more recent history in Brazil, especially the amnesty extended to Black sailors who had revolted a generation earlier in Rio de Janeiro.

At the core, Da França laid out how amnesty operated as a "legal fiction," in which an action that yesterday was a crime and tomorrow would continue to be a crime, today is not. He mused that amnesty "is not exactly a law because laws look to the future and amnesty looks to the past." In precise terms, he viewed amnesty as a political tool that "aimed for immediate results . . . attending first and foremost to the imperative of public order." He emphasized that the power of amnesty, however, does not include the power to renounce subjective individual rights legitimately acquired by third parties. The general rule of law, he explained, is that each person can claim reparation of prejudices suffered.[14]

This preoccupation with balancing rights marked a departure from the sort of settlement ultimately reached in the 1895 *Anistia Inversa* matter and even from that of the 1910 mutinous sailors. The shift reflected a more general move toward rational bureaucratic process. Rather than deference to the constitutional protections afforded the more elite citizens, as in the *Anistia Inversa* matter, or even the utter lack of any such protection as in the case of the lowlier sailors, a new concern about justice emerged. Da França's reflections underscored the pressing call for the state—and perhaps confidence in the state—to mediate conflicting claims.

AMADO AND WHAT THE FUTURE MIGHT HOLD

Born in 1912, Amado did not live through the military dictatorships that quickly replaced the monarchy in the 1890s. But like Barbosa, he was from the state of Bahia, studied law, and at points in his life was exiled from Brazil. Trained as a journalist, Amado was also among a small circle of Brazilian writers at that time who had studied outside of Brazil. One of his earliest works—*Jubiabá*, published in 1935 when Amado was just twenty-three years old—was praised by Albert Camus. It tells the story of Antonio Balduino, a young, poor, Black man from Bahia. Its purpose, summarized succinctly by Celso Lemos de Oliveira, is "to show the development of a hero with an enlightened political consciousness through a character who starts out with the odds against him."[15] Indeed, the work delights in seeming contradictions. It begins, for example, with Balduino, a successful boxer, defeating the central European champion, who happened to be a blond German. Toward the end of the novel, the beautiful and privileged Lindinalva, who has fallen on dire misfortune and turned to prostitution, entrusts her son to Balduino as she is dying.

Jubiabá is one of six novels that the young Amado published during the six years between 1931 and 1937. During this period he also attended law school and involved himself with the Aliança Nacional Libertadora (National Liberation Alliance, ANL), a political group founded early in 1935 and composed mostly of members of the underground PCB. The ANL called for revolutionary action and was among the forces behind the November 1935 barracks revolts. In the aftermath, Amado was accused of subversion and jailed. After two months in prison in 1936, Amado began to travel outside Brazil, including to Mexico where he met with the famed muralists Diego Rivera and David Siqueiros, among other communist intellectuals. In an article published in 1936 in Argentina, Amado argued that a novel was, or should be, a "political being" and a "weapon for fighting."[16] A year later, in 1937, he was arrested in Manaus and then was taken to Rio de Janeiro where he was held until 1938. He would not publish another work of fiction until 1943.[17]

Amado wrote the *Life of Luís Carlos Prestes* while he was in exile in Argentina. He had left Brazil in 1941 to escape the repression of Vargas's dictatorial Estado Novo. In the preface to the first edition published in Brazil in 1945, he described the work's prior life in terms that fit in with his politics. The clandestine copies that circulated in Brazil, he said, "never became anyone's individual property" but, rather, passed from "hand to hand." He described the book as a weapon "in the struggle for amnesty, for democracy, and against the Estado Novo, but principally against fascism." The clandestine copies circulated under various titles that further elevated the person of Prestes. The titles included *Life of Saint Luis, Life of King Luis,* and *Mischief of Little Luis.*[18] It was first published in a Spanish edition in Argentina, but the book was soon outlawed there too. Juan Perón, the ambitious army colonel who rose to power in Argentina, reportedly ordered the Argentine police to confiscate and burn any and all copies of the work. Its repression, both in Brazil and abroad, added to the intrigue surrounding both the book and the person of Luis Carlos Prestes.[19]

An amnesty decreed in 1945 resulted in Prestes's release from prison. That year, both he and Amado were elected as senators from the newly legal PCB, and they served in a national constituent assembly that drafted a new constitution in 1946. The party's legality and their mandates, however, were short-lived. By 1947, with the advent of the Cold War, the PCB again became illegal and was pushed underground. For Amado, another period of exile followed. In the 1950s, disillusioned with the staggering crimes of Joseph Stalin, he largely abandoned politics and dedicated himself to literature.[20]

THE BUREAUCRATIZATION OF AMNESTY

In his 1933 articles, Da França looked to amnesty as a viable political tool and reflected on its potency as a harbinger of peace. In his 1942 biography of Prestes, Amado argued for amnesty as a sign of justice and vindication in a longer political struggle. After a period during which presidents of Brazil eschewed amnesty, the time in which Da França and Amado were writing about it marked a certain return and institutionalization of amnesty in Brazil. This brief period and the transformations brought to and wrought by amnesty in political life in Brazil are examined in the two chapters that follow.

If amnesty had been seen as a recourse utilized by the earliest political opponents of Floriano in the 1890s, it began to take on the contours of a full-fledged political institution during the Vargas era. Indeed, a cycle of repression, followed by amnesty, followed by renewed repression would mark the lives of many during this period. What emerged and took shape was somewhat of a contradiction. Discussions of amnesty circled around themes of pacification and unity. Letters directed to Vargas pleaded with him as a patron and father-figure to unite Brazil through amnesty. The lessons learned and re-learned from the world wars added urgency to the work of securing peace. Social movements also came together around the issue of amnesty and argued passionately and personally for it. Yet like the shift from the poetry of a political campaign to the prose of governing, amnesty also seemed to undergo a transformation of sorts after it became law. A far cry from the public drama surrounding the granting of amnesty, its application proceeded on a case-by-case basis and fell largely to ad-hoc commissions. In step with a broader move toward a more compartmentalized and rational bureaucracy, these commissions were instituted to handle, fairly and dispassionately, all claims to benefits enumerated in the amnesty. Beginning with the amnesty of 1945, such commissions were instituted in the laws themselves. These commissions did not replace court cases entirely, but no subsequent case came close to rivaling, in either scope or significance, the *Anistia Inversa* case that was argued by Barbosa before the Federal Supreme Court in the 1890s.

Arguably, the implementation of amnesty through bureaucratic entities ensured a level of efficiency and fairness in its application. With the bureaucratic solution, however, came bureaucratic problems. A favorable ruling from the commission, for example, did not translate into guaranteed reintegration into one's former post, which often required a series of additional administrative steps and determinations. Additionally, the seemingly impersonal application of the law through a commission was subject to decidedly personal interventions, especially as the optimism and openness of the immediate end of the Second World War gave way to the Cold War and renewed political repression.

A return to a practice of granting amnesty took place following the 1930 revolution in Brazil and extended to the 1964 dictatorship. With the return of amnesty came the inception and progressive entrenchment of a bureaucracy to mediate claims to the rights enumerated in various amnesty laws. This work is examined in the chapters that follow. Negotiations regarding the placement of amnestied military personnel in the early 1930s and the first-of-its-kind Comissão Revisora (Review Commission), instituted to handle claims from civilians who had been purged from the federal workforce, are discussed in chapter 4. The period of the Estado Novo and the emblematic and celebrated amnesty of 1945, including the ad hoc commissions tasked with adjudicating restitution granted by the amnesty, are discussed in chapter 5. For some former military personnel and civil servants who initially appealed to these commissions in the 1930s and 1940s, their efforts to return to their previous jobs spanned decades.

The work and results of these various bureaucratic commissions give us both a view of the complex history that was shaped by Vargas and his legacy and a look beyond Vargas to trace the evolution of ideas about rights and justice in Brazil. What was deemed threatening to the Brazilian nation evolved from the internalized racial anxieties of the first generation of the republic through the new fears and pressures brought by the external realities of the Great Depression, the Second World War, and the coming Cold War. Notably, the framing of conflict and conciliation during this period frequently relied on metaphors about a Brazilian "family" and depended on the sway held by patterns of paternalism.

CHAPTER 4

REVOLUTIONARIES AND BUREAUCRATS

Amnesty in the Age of Vargas, 1930s

In November 1924 Herculino Cascardo, a young first lieutenant in the Brazilian navy, commandeered a dreadnaught, the *São Paulo*, in Guanabara Bay. His insurrection occurred in the same bay and on the same ship that João Cândido had led the famous Revolt of the Lash in 1910. The twenty-four-year-old Cascardo intended to join a month-old rebellion against the federal government that was under way in the state of Rio Grande do Sul, which had been the site of a civil war in 1893. All of the more senior officers of the *São Paulo* stood down, so Cascardo, together with six second lieutenants, took charge of a crew of more than six hundred men. They set sail from Guanabara Bay in Rio de Janeiro for the southern state.[1] The rebellion in Rio Grande do Sul was being led by an army captain, Luis Carlos Prestes, who had hoped to seize control of a military base from which to launch a broader revolution.[2]

The events of November 1924 marked a continuation and an expansion of a revolutionary movement already afoot. The movement began, as many do, in bitter defeat. Just over two years earlier, on July 5, 1922, military rebels took over Fort Copacabana overlooking Guanabara Bay in Rio de Janeiro aiming to defend the military against what they viewed as egregious civilian political affronts. With the fort surrounded and under fire, including from the *São Paulo*, hundreds surrendered. Eighteen, however, held out against the government's forces; sixteen of them perished in a confrontation on Copacabana Beach. Both Cascardo and Prestes were in the vicinity of the revolt. Prestes had hoped to join the rebels but was too ill with typhus to be of any use. Cascardo,

Figure 4.1. Luis Carlos Prestes in exile in Bolivia, February 1928. Courtesy of CPDOC/FGV.

assigned to the *São Paulo*, was onboard as the dreadnaught fired on the fort.[3]

Two years later both men were in active revolt. By October 1924 Prestes was at the head of the rebellion underway in his home state of Rio Grande do Sul; a month later Cascardo commandeered the *São Paulo* in an effort to provide Prestes with critical aid. The events in Rio Grande do Sul in October had inherited and built on a rebellion in São Paulo that had begun and ended in July 1924 (described as a second July 5 in reference to the events in Rio de Janeiro two years earlier). The young rebel officers briefly took control of São Paulo city. They held it until the end of the month, when they retreated and set out on a "column" traversing the backcountry. These military rebels—part of the broader *tenente* movement—lacked a clear vision for political reform but railed against corruption and entrenched oligarchic politics.[4] The roots of *tenetismo*, the movement associated with these junior officers, are traced to Antônio de Siqueira Campos and Eduardo Gomes, the two survivors of the famed (if failed) July 5, 1922, revolt at the Copacabana Fort in Rio de Janeiro.

The column from São Paulo was three months into their march when Cascardo set the *São Paulo* on a course from Rio de Janeiro south to Rio Grande do Sul. Cascardo, however, never arrived to provide his intended support. Climatic conditions prevented him from docking in Rio Grande do Sul. He was forced to continue on to Uruguay, where he had to turn the ship over to the Uruguayan authorities, who promptly returned it to Brazil. Cascardo would spend the next six years in exile, returning clandestinely to Rio Grande do Sul in time to participate in the 1930 revolution that upended the established political elites and ushered in the era of Getúlio Vargas.

Prestes's effort in Rio Grande do Sul also failed. In the absence of a firm geographic base from which to expand the rebellion, he instead led a column of rebel soldiers, similar to the one from São Paulo, on what would become a three-year, twenty-four-thousand-kilometer march through southern and western states in Brazil. The "Prestes Column" quickly became the stuff of legend and earned Prestes the nickname the "Cavalier of Hope," immortalized in the biography written by Jorge Amado. Even within the military, which sent a campaign to subdue him and his followers, Prestes enjoyed the status of a folk hero. To some degree, the military appropriated the exploits of his column of rebels as if they had been part of the formal military and not fighting against it.[5]

The legend might have been romantic, but the conditions were not. The column, numbering some fifteen hundred men, fought skirmishes with the military campaign sent to quash it. The military forces were commanded by none other than Cândido Rondon, who had famously accompanied Teddy Roosevelt on his ill-fated expedition into the Amazon in 1914. Fatigue and illness also took hold within the column. By December 1925, Prestes and four hundred others had malaria.[6] With dwindled numbers and weakened capacity to battle, the exhausted and isolated column retreated into exile in Bolivia in 1927. That same year, Cascardo, still in exile in Uruguay, was convicted in absentia in Brazil and sentenced to eleven years and eight months imprisonment for his involvement in the revolt onboard the *São Paulo* three years earlier.[7]

Cascardo, however, would not serve a day of that the sentence. Soon after returning clandestinely to Rio Grande do Sul in 1930, he made his way to Rio de Janeiro where, on October 3, he was part of the revolution that one month later placed power in the hands of Vargas. Once installed as the provisional president of Brazil, Vargas acted quickly to decree an amnesty to "all civilian and military members who, directly or indirectly, involved themselves in revolutionary movements."[8] The November 8 decree marked a return of sorts to the reliance on amnesty in Brazilian politics. In the preceding years, the unwillingness to extend amnesty had hardened. Indeed, neither the surviving members of the standoff at Fort Copacabana nor the members of the rebel columns in the 1920s had benefited from an amnesty during what would be the last years of the First Republic. At the same time, a burgeoning opposition movement increasingly demanded it. Thus, within days of taking power, Vargas reversed this course, bestowing amnesty on those whose resistance ultimately had brought him to power.

A RETURN TO AMNESTY

Within the first years of his rule Vargas would rely on amnesty not only for those who had helped bring him to power but also for those who had opposed, or had been perceived as opposing, his assumption of power. These included the military leaders who staged what they called the "Constitutionalist Revolution of 1932" in São Paulo, as well as of former civil servants who had been purged from their positions as Vargas consolidated his power. Amnesty for these sectors came in a 1934 law and as part of the 1934 constitution. The constitution also provided for the first-of-its-kind federal commission to accept and rule on petitions from purged civil servants to be returned to their former positions. Thus, beyond a return to amnesty as a political tool, the early years of the Vargas era also marked the beginning of a broader bureaucratic response to issues arising from the implementation of amnesty laws.

The shift toward more bureaucratic management of amnesty can be seen in the evolution of how Vargas addressed issues arising from three groups: (1) members of the military movement whose resistance in the 1920s brought him to power, (2) members of the military movement who rebelled against Vargas once he was in power, and (3) cadres of civil servants who lost their posts under Vargas. When the implementation of the 1930 amnesty resulted in grievances among the military members who had helped bring him to power, Vargas responded with further decrees and arbitration. In attempting to settle with the segments of the military who revolted against him in 1932, Vargas worked in reverse, first attempting decrees to reintegrate and reclassify them before conceding amnesty. For the ousted civilian servants, he appointed a Comissão Revisora, or Review Commission, that required applicants to submit petitions for reinstatement and await a ruling from the commission.

What emerged during this period, both in the negotiations related to military personnel and in the bureaucratic review of civilian petitioners, was the need to balance competing claims to rights. The central questions had shifted from those surrounding the amnesties involving high-ranking officers in the 1890s and mutinous sailors in 1910. Rather than elite constitutional entitlements for the former and the utter lack of any such rights or protection for the latter, the problem in the 1930s involved settling demands for restitution from former employees in light of the obligations owed to those who had replaced them. Lawsuits continued to be filed and individual or small group resolutions were arranged ad hoc, but the federal government also took steps to manage the implementation of amnesty—including formalizing bureaucratic structures to categorize and account for amnestied personnel. If, in the earliest years of the First Republic, Rui Barbosa had defined the debates about amnesty within the realm of individual constitutional rights, during the Vargas era the focus shifted to managing and regulating the application of amnesty within a dedicated bureaucracy.

Cascardo and Prestes were only two among an impressive, largely army-led military movement against the political elites of the 1920s. By that time, Brazil had settled into an oligarchy ruled by the agricultural elites of the powerhouse states of São Paulo and Minas Gerais. After an uninterrupted twelve-year run by Paulista planting elites, beginning with Prudente de Morais, the power-sharing arrangement—dubbed *café com leite*, or coffee with milk—alternately delivered the presidency to elites in São Paulo (the coffee state) and Minas Gerais (the dairy state), with the tacit support of the political elites in Rio de Janeiro and Rio Grande do Sul.[9] The rural oligarchy managed their populations via debts of labor and gratitude. The poorer classes linked to them provided the manual labor for the coffee export economy as well as the numbers to ensure desired electoral outcomes. The oligarchs were linked as well, via family or other ties, to an emerging and upwardly mobile class of urban merchants who oversaw the exportation of coffee and the importation of elite material goods. The government bureaucracy, for its part, served further patronage ends, providing nonmanual labor jobs and social status to another emerging sector that would otherwise have been left out of the spoils.[10]

After nearly a decade of armed opposition to the oligarchic politics, the tenentes collaborated with a political coalition that had formed in 1928. The Aliança Liberal (Liberal Alliance) consisted mostly of politicians from the states of Rio Grande do Sul and Minas Gerais who had been increasingly edged out of power by the São Paulo elites. Indeed, the disruption of the power structures in 1930 owed much to the Liberal Alliance. Their platform included a secret ballot, administrative reform, freedom of the press, and notably, an amnesty for the rebels of the 1920s. Elites before and after the 1920s spoke of amnesty as a gesture of political acumen, but no amnesty was granted during any of the tenente revolts of the 1920s. In the heat of the conflicts, President Artur Ber-

Figure 4.2. Liberal Alliance political rally in Rio de Janeiro, 1929. Courtesy of CPDOC/FGV.

nandes (1922–1926) wanted to keep military power in close check and flatly refused to consider an amnesty. Bernardes's successor, Washington Luís (1926–1930), viewed amnesty as a show of state weakness. In fact, two congressional amnesty projects were struck down by the majority who supported him.[11]

In 1930 the Liberal Alliance nominated Vargas as their candidate for the presidency. He narrowly lost to the appointed candidate, Júlio Prestes, who had been supported by the outgoing fellow Paulista, Washington Luís. Amid accusations of fraud, the Liberal Alliance began to plot against Washington Luís and the larger São Paulo political machine. They looked to the tenentes for military backing—and largely got it. The collaboration of the tenentes with the Liberal Alliance landed Vargas in the presidency and themselves in positions of power for the first time. Vargas repaid their support first with a general amnesty and then with key appointments to administrative positions, including as the *interventors* who replaced the former state governors. Cascardo joined those who assumed a formal position in the Vargas regime. Prestes, however, continued as a resistance figure and would become a formidable enemy of Vargas by late 1935. Before the conflict intensified between Vargas and Prestes, both the unseated old elites and the various sectors of the heterogeneous coalition that brought Vargas to power made competing claims. During the years from 1930 to 1935, Vargas negotiated terms of powers with these varied sectors of consequence, including the tenentes who had supported him and the redoubtable revolutionaries in São Paulo who opposed him. Ultimately, Vargas assuaged or dominated critics and opponents enough to maintain both his authority and his effective power until 1945.

AMNESTY AND AGGRIEVED SUPPORTERS, 1930

Within five days of taking office in November 1930, Vargas decreed a sweeping amnesty. He had arrived in Rio de Janeiro to assume the presidency accompanied by a contingent of soldiers from his native Rio Grande do Sul. They symbolically marked the event by riding in on horseback and hitching their animals to an obelisk on the central avenue in downtown Rio de Janeiro.[12] The amnesty that soon followed extended "to all the civilians and military personnel who, directly or indirectly, involved themselves in the revolutionary movements that occurred in the country."[13] Decades later, it was touted as "one of the most broad-sweeping amnesties of the Republican era."[14] It placed, among others events, Cascardo's insurrection and the resulting criminal conviction "in perpetual silence." It also ostensibly protected Prestes from the possibility of prosecution for his leadership of the revolt in Rio Grande do Sul and the rebel column that followed.

A notable achievement for those who had been clamoring for amnesty for the rebels of the 1920s, the decree itself included just two articles. The first, in three brief sections, set forth the scope of potential restitution—namely, it denied the beneficiaries any right to their salaries "relative to the time in which they were prisoners, on trial, serving a sentence, or for any other reasons that they were absent from service." It stipulated that such time would nonetheless count "for all other legal effects," which were taken to include advancement by seniority and the calculation of military pensions. Finally, it mandated that all cases and related sentences would be held in "perpetual silence, as if they had never existed."[15] The second and final article simply revoked any regulation that might counter it. This initial decree, however, required a number of additional ones to manage and resolve issues raised by its implementation.

The implementation of the amnesty, and the issues arising from it, took different tracks in the navy and the army. For navy personnel, Vargas brokered a new settlement that largely customized the amnesty for them. He did so through a series of decrees issued from November 1930 through February 1931. The first, issued just a week after granting the amnesty, addressed a technicality specific to the navy. The decree stipulated that "the period of time in which [naval officers] were removed from service be counted as time aboard a war ship." Doing so rendered these officers, in an administrative sense, as having fulfilled the service time on the open sea that was required for promotion.[16]

In another decree, issued on December 24, 1930, Vargas qualified the clause prohibiting the payment for time in which a beneficiary of the amnesty had been "imprisoned, on trial, completing a sentence, or for any other reason absent from service." It stipulated that the restriction on payment applied only to such time out of service that occurred prior to January 1, 1930. This small adjustment applied not just to navy officers but to all beneficiaries of the amnesty, with one specific exception. It would not apply to former students of the Military School who had been nominated or commissioned as first lieutenants. For any possible payments, these tenentes were restricted to the time since the issuance of the amnesty decree on November 8, 1930. In addition to Vargas and other senior leaders, this December 24 decree also bore the signature of Conrado Heck in his capacity as a vice admiral and the minister of the navy under Vargas. Thirty-five years earlier, Heck had been a young midshipman among the more senior officers who sued over the restriction in the *Anistia Inversa* case.[17] By December 1930, and among those wielding power in the new government, he signed his name to a decree that, while providing for some indemnity, nonetheless qualified and differentiated the application of amnesty to a new generation of military personnel.

Less than a month later, on January 22, 1931, Vargas amended the amendment regarding payments. In yet another decree, he clarified that it applied to amnestied officers only and not to enlisted personnel, excepting again the former students who had been nominated or commissioned as first lieutenants.[18] By this time, Cascardo had assumed the post of special assistant to Heck.[19] He responded to the further adjustment in a missive sent to Vargas a week later. In it, he explained that the revised stipulations for payments created a serious ethical dilemma in the navy. Cascardo reminded Vargas that the motivation for altering the original decree had been to "remedy the injustice" that the amnesty would unwittingly inflict on military officers who had "persevered on the side of the revolution" that brought him to power, in contrast to those who had abandoned the revolution and returned to service earlier.

The January 1931 decree created a clear distinction between the rank and file, including noncommissioned officers, who would not receive any salaries, and the commissioned officers who would. In a wry aside, Cascardo opined that such a situation might have worked in the army but would not do so in the navy. Navy officers, he told Vargas, could not accept the payment "without grave injury to their conscience." Many officers, in fact, had already promised their subordinates that they would be paid. Based on that guarantee, enlisted men had made various purchases "fixed their houses, bought plots of land . . . etc." Cascardo concluded his letter with an ultimatum. If everyone could not be paid, he explained, the officers would forfeit their salaries from 1930 and quit their positions in the cabinet and ministries.[20] Two days later, Vargas issued a decree to put the matter to rest. In it, he suspended the application of the previous decree for the navy and provided an indemnity payment of the equivalent of eight months of salary to the beneficiaries of the amnesty, provided they present themselves by February 15, 1931. That time frame to avail themselves of the benefit was then extended to March 12, 1931.[21] For the navy, therefore, the seemingly straightforward amnesty became, in its implementation, both circuitous and contentious. Nonetheless, through additional concessions, a resolution was brokered.

In the case of the army, the process devolved into prolonged conflict, especially over seniority among the amnestied officers. It pitted the tenentes and other junior officers who had participated in the revolts of the 1920s against those who had not. Cascardo may have been referencing brewing tensions on this matter in his comment surmising that the army might accept an unjust solution with regard to the amnesty, but the navy would not. In what came to be called the "case of the amnestied lieutenants," a mediation initiated by Vargas and the war minister resulted in a lengthy decree issued on June 3, 1932, more than a year and a half after the amnesty. In it, Vargas stipulated the disposition of competing claims for the purpose of "regulating the relation of rights" among two categories of officers.[22] The two categories were those that had participated in the revolts of 1922 and/or 1924 (and who were subsequently amnestied under the 1930 decree) and those who had entered the military school and been commissioned after those events. The "Amnestied Revolutionary Officers," as they referred to themselves, "considering themselves more senior than their comrades," who had entered the academy after the defining events of July 5, 1922, at Copacabana Fort. At the mediation that preceded the decree, representatives for the two groups reportedly pledged solidarity, but both sides affirmed their prerogative to take issues over seniority to the courts for resolution.[23]

The solution defined in the decree included the creation of a parallel track within the army for the amnestied officers. A similar parallel track had been established in the navy following the revolt of 1893 to reintegrate the amnestied navy officers.[24] The 1932 decree specified, in fact, that while amnestied individuals were owed its benefit, the granting of said benefits must not "injure the rights" of others.[25] Therefore, rather than return to the normal track for promotion and advancement, the amnestied would be placed in a separate track. Moving forward, in the case of vacancies, the same promotion would be given on both tracks.

Other issues would be left to the courts for resolution.[26] The decree further stipulated that the most advanced students, who had already been commissioned as first lieutenants at the time of their ousting, would be stationed for a period in a unit within the First Military Region before being assigned elsewhere. The younger students were to be re-registered in the Military School or another institution, to complete their course work. For any who had moved on from the military and were in a civil service job, they could include the time from their ousting from the military until their appointment in the civil service as part of their tenure in government employment.[27]

More than a decade later, Luis Gallotti, then the attorney general of Brazil, explained that some of the amnestied officers had misunderstood the reach of the amnesty. In assuming they had seniority over those who entered the military academy after them, they acted "as though there had never been a movement of 1922" and maintained "that they should be considered officers from the date in which they would have concluded their courses, if they had not been dismissed." But, he explained pragmatically, "who could say which ones would have passed the exams, would have gone to class, had good conduct, and the like?" Gallotti then argued that amnesty could only reestablish the rights that the amnestied individual already held. It did not, and could not, create "new" rights—that is, amnesty could only account for what had been, and not, as some would argue, for what might have been. In doing so, Gallotti emphasized what had come into clearer focus for many over the preceding years, that the rights of the amnestied were to some extent held in check by the possible detriment of rights acquired by third parties.[28]

AMNESTY AND DISPOSSESSED ELITES, 1934

The political power brokers of São Paulo arguably lost the most in the upheaval of the revolution that brought Vargas to power in 1930. The revolution, in fact, had been aimed directly at them. Washington Luís, the president, was a Paulista; Júlio Prestes, the president-elect, was as well. At that time, the political power of the São Paulo elites on a national scale was matched only by their economic power. The state had prospered at an unprecedented pace under the combined conditions of the international demand and price for coffee and the 1891 constitution, which allowed the planters the autonomy to exploit their economy by directly negotiating international investment and loans. Given their economic prowess, the state stood a world apart from its poor northeastern counterparts, which remained, in the eyes of many, the obstacle to modernization that Euclides da Cunha had described in *Rebellion in the Backlands* a generation before.

With the loss of political and economic power, which was most certainly exacerbated by the world economic crisis and the plummeting price of coffee, Paulistas of all stripes began to see Vargas and his revolution as a dictatorship. A "United Front" formed from among the old oligarchs and reformers who had initially supported the revolution. With military men and civilian volunteers, the front staged an armed rebellion under a banner of liberal constitutionalism that lasted from July 9 to October 2, 1932. Similar to the civil war in Rio Grande do Sul and the campaign against the settlement in Canudos in the 1890s, the revolt in 1932 highlights the misfit of the myth of peaceful political process in Brazil. In less than three months of fighting, over one thousand were left dead. The conflict was brought to a negotiated end when anticipated support from other states never materialized, owed perhaps to the rebels' embrace of regionalist separatism.[29] The rebels, outmanned and outarmed by loyal federal troops, began to discuss terms of surrender. Their terms included an amnesty.

A long-standing, but soon to be erstwhile, ally of Vargas from Rio Grande do Sul, José Antônio Flores da Cunha, endorsed a "sketch of a formula for the pacification of the country" that had been provided to him by a mission led by the archbishop of Porto Alegre, the capital city of Rio Grande do Sul. (Four years earlier, in 1928, Flores da Cunha had proposed, without success, an amnesty for the rebels of the 1920s, earning himself the informal title of the "Champion of Amnesty.") The plan for São Paulo began with a "full and absolute amnesty," provided that all who took up arms turn over their weapons to federal authorities. As proposed, the amnesty would "extinguish" the crimes committed in revolting against the government and would return the rebels to the status and positions they formerly held.[30] The actual settlement, however, did not include an immediate amnesty. In fact, when the fighting ceased, Vargas cut a swath through the military officer corps. The shakeup included the forced retirement of 372 army officers, well over half at the rank of lieutenant, as well as 48 higher-ranking officers, including 7 generals.[31] By the end of 1933, the shakeup in the military was so complete that 36 of the 40 generals on active duty had been promoted to that rank by Vargas's new government.[32] Vargas nonetheless partially assuaged the São Paulo rebels by convening a constituent assembly to write a new constitution. He also placed a Paulista as the interventor of the state.

In January 1934, Vargas issued a decree that provided for the reinstatement of military personnel who had been ousted.[33] Eighty-seven second lieutenants, in fact, returned to their post the next day. Specifically, the decree reinstated all "captains and subalterns who had been administratively retired or transferred to reserve status because of their direct or indirect involvement in the events that took place in the country beginning in June of 1932." This decree also canceled the acts that had canceled the commissions of second lieutenants and sergeants for the same reasons. Those officers would be reinstated and allowed to continue with the same commission that they had held, provided that there was enough service to warrant such reappointments. Perhaps owing to a lesson learned from the case of the "amnestied lieutenants" from 1930, the officers who returned would provisionally be placed in "Block A," so as not to prejudice the officers in the "Ordinary Block." Those who returned could be placed in the "Ordinary Block" when and if another officer from that block was promoted, or if additional posts were created. The officers had no right to back pay or indemnity and had thirty days to apply for the reinstatement.[34]

This and other similar decrees in early 1934 were followed by a more general amnesty granted in late May. Vargas resolved to grant amnesty, the decree explained, because it was, at that moment, a "national aspiration," and because other civilian and military personnel that had been involved in seditious movements since the revolution of 1930 had already been amnestied. The participants in the "revolutionary movements of 1932," therefore, should likewise be afforded amnesty.[35] It seemed a sweeping measure of restitution, but not everyone was pleased by the amnesty. Euclides Figueiredo, one of the key leaders of the 1932 rebellion, criticized the decree for failing to meet the expectations of the rebels. It could never achieve its purported "confraternal ends," he argued. Given its shortcomings, he said he could not in good conscience return to active service in the army. The path for former military personnel nevertheless seemed more straightforward than the situation in which the amnesty had left civil servants. He noted that these individuals, "who were less guilty than he," faced numerous obstacles in returning to their formerly held positions.[36] Indeed, the decree stipulated that the reinstatement of ousted civil servants depended on the availability of vacancies and required a case-by-case review by special commissions. This would be the first of many assertions made by Figueiredo in support of immediate and automatic reinstatement of amnestied personnel from the 1930s through the 1940s (see chapter 5).

As in the fallout of the 1930 amnesty, the simple decree faced complicated pragmatic issues. In the military, the problem arose of how and where to place amnestied personnel returning to duty. Legally, the conundrum continued to revolve around protecting the new rights of the amnestied without infringing on the existing rights of those who had taken the places opened by the earlier dismissals or, alternatively, of those who had stayed faithful to the federal government during the tumult. As for the government employees, there is no evidence that any special commissions were instituted to make determinations about reinstatement. Roughly six weeks later, however, the Disposições Transitórias (transitional provisions) of the new 1934 constitution provided for just such a commission. The transitional provisions aimed to stipulate procedures for situations likely to arrive from the implementation of the new constitution.

Among such possible situations, the framers of the new constitution anticipated increasing demands for reintegration and restitution from military personnel and civil servants who had lost their posts since Vargas ascended to power. One provision allowed the president, "in due course" to establish a commission, or various commissions, to address these demands. Any such commissions were to be presided over by a federal judge who, "taking into account the grievances of the petitioners, [would] write opinions about the appropriateness of approving their return as soon as possible to the posts or public functions they exercised and from which they had been removed by the Provisional Government." The inclusion of the phrase "as soon as possible" later opened up the government to sharp criticism for a lag in, if not disregard of, placing those approved for reinstatement into posts. The same provision further stipulated that those who were returned to their previously held posts were not entitled to the payment of back wages or any indemnity. The very next provision, extended a general amnesty "for anyone who had committed political crimes up to the present date."[37] The descendants of Admiral Custódio José de Melo and other military officers who rebelled against Floriano and were amnestied in 1895 would appeal to this provision in making a claim for the payment of wages withheld nearly forty years earlier.

BUREAUCRACY FOR THE BUREAUCRATS (IN A STATE OF WAR)

In the months following the issuance of the 1934 constitution, Vargas appointed one centralized commission for the review of petitions for reinstatement from former civil servants. The Review Commission held ninety-three sessions from September 1935 through November 1937.[38] In lofty rhetoric that at once recognized the recent repression and served as an apology for it, the president of the commission explained that the mechanisms adopted by the provisional government, though legitimate for the defense of the state, did not "coincide exactly with the ideal of justice" but instead were "many times supplanted by momentary imperatives of political or social necessity." In response, the commission devoted itself "unequivocally [to] the realization of what was just . . . with the objective of putting an end to the excessive impulses that are always inevitable in the course of revolutions."[39] He stated further that the work of the commission would silence "any discussion not congruent with equity."[40] This equity took the form of reconciliation between the state and its workers who, he explained, "deserved the benefit of the doubt [and] to be allowed, again, to exercise activities whose salary meant the security of their homes." Indeed, the commission emphasized the "intolerable weight" of the economic stress and the excessive cost of living at that "moment in the world." Much like the discourse surrounding amnesty, the president of the commission added that this "noble gesture" was in step with the "rhythm of the Brazilian heart, in which the fraternity of its people allows for the separation of ideas, but not disunity by unconquerable hate or unforgettable resentments."[41]

The commission, however, did not function in a vacuum. While its members met to determine reintegration of purged federal employees from the earliest days of Vargas's regime, a new threat emerged, and renewed repression took hold. In November 1935, in fact, just two months after the first meeting of the Review Commission, the communist-backed barracks revolt broke out. It occurred just months after Luis Carlos Prestes returned from his years living in Moscow. Once in Brazil, but in hiding in Rio de Janeiro, Prestes had helped coordinate the recently launched ANL, which operated as a front organization for the then illegal PCB. It garnered an impressive urban middle-class following ranging in estimates from seventy thousand to one hundred thousand members. The ANL advocated for the nationalization of industries, land reform, broad civil and social rights, and the cancellation of foreign debt.[42]

Cascardo, who a decade earlier had attempted to aid Prestes in the revolt in Rio Grande do Sul, served as the ANL's titular head. By mid-1935, just months after its founding, the organization began calling for more outright revolutionary action, which drew the ire of Vargas and resulted in the arrest and summary trial of several of its leaders. Plans for revolutionary action continued nonetheless and had the attention of the Communist International (Comintern), which approved armed revolution for Brazil at its Seventh Congress in July 1935. Prestes, "fundamentally still more tenente than Communist," had always thought the route to revolution in Brazil ran through the military rank and file more than a labor- or agrarian-led movement. The revolts that broke out in November 1935 in Natal, Recife, and Rio de Janeiro, however, cannot be fully credited to the ANL, the PCB, Prestes, or the Comintern. They were, in the estimation of Leslie Bethell, "a series of minor, poorly coordinated military insurrections influenced as much by tenetista as by Communist ideology and sympathies," and they failed.[43]

The military disparagingly dubbed the insurrections an *intentona* (meaning an "attempt") and more specifically as the Intentona Comunista. So defined, the uprising came to represent the specter of a communist-inspired and -led revolt from within the military itself. It fed a myth that, as Maud Chirio explained, "established a simplistic, unnuanced national narrative of constant threat."[44] More immediately, it served to legitimize Vargas's longer-standing repressive posture. Indeed, Vargas met the threat with disproportionate violence, unleashing a wave of increasing merciless political policing and violence. An initial declaration of a national emergency expanded to a congressionally approved state of siege and, by March 1936, the declaration of a state of war that remained in force until June 1937.[45] Between the November 1935 revolt and the declaration of a state of siege the following March, over three thousand were arrested, nine hundred of whom were civilians. The majority of those arrested, indeed over 85 percent, were released by the early months of 1936; those released would have included Jorge Amado. By May 1937, while the Review Commission was still ruling on petitions for readmission, however, the number of arrests as well as prisoners still in custody more than doubled.[46] A special Comissão de Repressão do Comunismo (Commission for the Repression of Communism) was responsible for the detention of many from the left more broadly, not just members of the ANL or PCB, some of whom were also tortured.[47]

In addition to approving and extending a state of siege and then a state of war, Congress strengthened national security laws that were already in place and passed constitutional amendments that gave Vargas a series of discretionary powers, including the power to dismiss public servants and to cancel the commissions of military officers.[48] A new wave of purges in the military and civil service quickly followed. Before the end of 1935, 23 officers involved in the uprising in Rio de Janeiro lost their commissions by decree. During 1936, over 100 officers and 1,136 enlisted personnel were discharged from the military.[49] In September 1936, Congress also instituted the Tribunal de Segurança Nacional (National Security Tribunal), following a request from Vargas for a special court to prosecute the individuals involved in the revolt (see chapter 5). Initially an arm of military justice, the court ruled on cases of both civilians and military personnel who were accused of "attempting to subvert the political and social institutions of the nation."[50]

By November 1937, during the same month that the Review Commission concluded its meeting, Vargas signed a new constitution, replacing the largely reaffirming 1934 constitution with a blueprint for his Estado Novo, or "New State," modeled on European fascism.[51] In the previous months, news of a plot for an imminent communist coup, the "Cohen Plan," had been leaked to the press. Vargas capitalized on the fear and confusion that followed by postponing scheduled elections that would have ended his presidency, censoring the press, further bolstering political policing, and intimidating and persecuting enemies at every turn. Under the charter of the Estado Novo, Vargas expanded his authority in national security matters and further entrenched existing repressive measures. One article, in particular, granted the authority to dismiss personnel based on "the prerogative of the regime or in the interest of public service."[52] Brazilians would later learn that the Cohen Plan had actually been a fabrication, precisely to create the conditions necessary to justify imposing the Estado Novo.[53]

During its twenty-six months of activity—which overlapped with the ramping up of repression after the 1935 revolts and concluded the same month that the Estado Novo was instituted—the Review Commission ruled on a total of 800 cases. The commission found in favor of the petitioner in 512 individual rulings, or nearly two-thirds of the cases, while denying petitioners in 288 rulings. Just over one-fourth of the cases came from former employees in the Ministry of Treasury, while approximately one-fifth came from both the Ministry of Justice and the Ministry of War. The three departments combined amounted to two-thirds of the total petitions. The rest came from applications from the Ministries of Transportation, Agriculture, Navy, Education, Labor, and Exterior.[54] The daily newspaper, *Jornal do Brasil*, reported on the meetings, which were held at the National Archive in Rio de Janeiro. The reports included the cases assigned to each minister for the upcoming session, the rulings reached by the commission, and in some select cases, announcements of reappointments for those who received favorable rulings.[55]

At one of the earliest meetings, the commissioners ruled on the case of Amaro Magalhães da Silva who had been fired on orders of the Vargas-appointed interventor of Rio Grande do Sul in 1931. The interventor had the authority to fire him because he was a state rather than a federal employee. Those circumstances were not unique among applications, at least among the nearly one-third whose petitions were denied. The commission argued that because he was not a federal employee his case fell outside its purview and that the federal government bore no responsibility for the acts of a state official.[56] One commissioner, Eugenio de Lucena, while agreeing with the conclusions reached in the case, voted separately. He found that if Vargas did not set up another commission to handle claims from state and municipal employees it would be incumbent on the Review Commission to do so.[57] A letter to *Jornal do Brasil* likewise advocated for state commissions, stating that "the states and cities were under the direction of the federal government" since Vargas assumed power, and they continued to be so after the enactment of the 1934 constitution. As such, the author argued, each state should have a commission duly nominated by the federal government "to rule in its name."[58] Within weeks, just such state commissions were established, first in São Paulo, which had more than six hundred cases to consider, followed within a month by a commission in Rio de Janeiro.[59]

At the midpoint of its work, the commission approved the request of a federal collector who had held his post for less than a month in 1931. Benigno do Couto had been named to the post in Rio Casea by decree on August 24, 1930, but did not take office until February 16, 1931. On March 10, 1931, he was fired by decree. In its session on July 14, 1936, the commission unanimously approved his petition for reintegration. Some months later, and "in view of the ruling of the *Comissão Revisora*," he was reappointed as a federal collector, this time in Bom Desparecho.[60] It was a somewhat exceptional occurrence, however, for him to actually be placed in a position. A second lieutenant in the navy, Aristoteles de Souza Imenses, had likewise received a unanimous favorable ruling for either reintegration to his former post or assignment to a new appointment, but neither happened. In response, he filed a security measure with the Federal Supreme Court. A letter published in August 1936 summarized the status of cases that, like Aristoteles's case, had received approval but nothing further, explaining that "no matter how many times government officials say they will honor the decisions of the commission, so far only four or five former public servants have been reintegrated or newly approved."[61]

A former congressional representative who had taken part in the drafting of the 1934 constitution expressed similar frustration. In his letter published in *Jornal do Brasil*, he explained that the inclusion of the phrase "as soon as possible," in reference to the return of former workers in the very article of the transitional provision that created the commission, was not open to interpretation. The qualification, he maintained, only alleviated the state from the obligation to create new positions, which would add expenditures, but in no way granted arbitrary power to delay reappointments.[62] Yet complaints about the failure to place individuals back into public service continued. By October 1936, an announcement ran in newspapers asking everyone who had received a favorable ruling to attend an urgent meeting to consider legislation that had been proposed in the Chamber of Deputies.[63] The proposed legislation would grant reintegration to all those who had favorable rulings from the Review Commission.[64] It did not advance. Former federal employees who had been readmitted to their posts, however, were able to count the time they were separated from their position as time in service.[65]

By December 1936, letters published in newspapers were charging the government with cronyism and corruption. One complained, with some hyperbole, that while those that formerly occupied posts were confronting all manners of difficulties, their replacements enjoyed remunerations that would easily support ten large families.[66] Another complained that "the government continues to delay reparation," and that "those who formerly held appointments had been put in the street to open space for allies."[67] Soon after, in early 1937, a somewhat familiar solution emerged. Vargas published a message directing the legislature to create a special category for those who had a favorable ruling from the commission for having been fired "arbitrarily in the revolutionary confusion of 1930." These individuals would belong in the special category until a vacancy opened to which they could be appointed.[68]

By March 1937, the newspaper announced under a heading of "Promised Reparations," that though many had already had favorable rulings from the commission, only some had actually returned. The great majority remained "deprived of their right . . . to the occupation of their posts."[69] In June, as the decree of the state of war expired, a certain consensus settled that it was impossible for the civil service to reincorporate all those who had been granted reintegration by the commission.[70] In response, a new law required preferential treatment to those previously approved for readmission for any and all jobs in newly created judicial zones in the Federal District. The preference, however, could not infringe on the "acquired rights of third parties."[71] An appointment made a few weeks later seemed to go to just such a third party; the person nominated to the new post was not among those who had petitioned to the Review Commission.[72]

BALANCING ACTS

In his reflections in 1933, Geminiano da França had made a case for the necessity to protect third-party rights in fulfilling the guarantees of amnesty. After a period in which no amnesties had been granted, the return of the measure in 1930 was accompanied by concern that its application could not infringe on the subjective individual rights legitimately acquired by others. The general rule, Da França explained, is that each can claim reparation of prejudices suffered.[73] In some ways, the notion of negotiating among rights that emerged in this period not only called on the government to be the arbiter but also revealed a certain confidence in the state to do so. Special blocks established within the military to accommodate amnestied officers and the Review Commission established to determine the status of former civil servants both stand as early examples of the state taking on that role. It did so through the creation of new tasks for existing bureaucracies and, increasingly, entirely new bureaucracies.

Yet, parallel to this designing of an ostensibly rational and bureaucratic state ran the mentalities of a decidedly more paternalistic order. This was evident in, among other ways, Vargas's gesture to reach a settlement with navy personnel. At the same time, it was evident in the perception of the generation of officers of the 1920s with regard to what they viewed as acceptable consequences for their prior rebellion. Giving up seniority, they made clear, was not among these consequences. It was also evident in the ways in which the Review Commission framed its work. As a gesture of "humanity and solidarity," the state described itself as benevolently taking former workers back into the fold, even if in word only. Finally, the context of increasing repression that ran parallel to the reintegration of formerly purged personnel underscored the violent tensions present just beneath the surface and the degree to which any such guarantees could quickly become attenuated.

The model of an ad hoc bureaucracy nonetheless took root and would be repeated in instances of amnesty that followed. An amnesty granted in 1945, which signaled both an end of the repression of the Estado Novo and an emerging faith in the power of amnesty to be a democratizing force, included the creation of just such commissions. In doing so, the law linked individual petitions for restitution inextricably to amnesty, and amnesty to a subsequent bureaucratic process. As under Vargas in the 1930s, the commissions associated with the amnesty of 1945 functioned in a context of increasing repression and were shaped by both old and new political battles. What stands out is both the length of time it took to arrive at a resolution in many cases and the instability of any and all resolutions reached.

CHAPTER 5

A DEMOCRATIZING AMNESTY UNDER RENEWED REPRESSION, 1945–1960S

In 1947, a former low-ranking corrections guard, Braz Antônio da Silva, received quick approval from the Comissão Especial para o Retorno dos Funcionários Anistiados (Special Commission for the Return of Amnestied Functionaries), for readmission to his post. Da Silva, like many others, had been arrested in 1936 by a special police force responsible for ensuring "political and social security." He was subsequently fired from his post. The power to purge him and others from the civil service had been granted in an amendment to the 1934 constitution. Enacted in December 1935, less than a month after the barracks uprising known as the Intentona Comunista, the amendment provided for the dismissal of personnel for the "exercise of activities subversive to political and social institutions." Da Silva's arrest and dismissal occurred while the Review Commission was still adjudicating hundreds of claims for the readmission of civil servants who had been ousted just a few years earlier during the consolidation of the revolution that brought Getúlio Vargas to power in 1930. Da Silva first began making appeals to various authorities to return to his post following his release from prison in 1937. Ten years later, the commission unanimously approved his request, finding that his dismissal had been politically motivated.[1] His story, however, did not end there.

The Special Commission for the Return of Amnestied Functionaries that reviewed Da Silva's petition was instituted by a general amnesty granted in April 1945. The amnesty had been one among several liberalizing measures taken during the final months of 1944 and the early months of 1945, which included lifting press censorship, providing for mass political parties, and even legalizing the PCB. These and other measures effectively dismantled Vargas's 1937–1945 Estado Novo dictatorship and marked the beginning of a period of electoral democracy in Brazil.[2] The discussions about amnesty in the press captured the optimism about and imperative for peace and democracy that were taking hold in Brazil and globally in the final months of the Second World War. Indeed, in 1944, when Brazilian soldiers joined the Allied forces fighting in Italy, Vargas's Estado Novo regime grew increasingly untenable in Brazil.[3] Public campaigns for amnesty in Brazil, in fact, framed the granting of amnesty as a moral and historical victory against fascism at home precisely at the moment that it was being defeated abroad. This emergence of a trope linking amnesty to a broader process of democratization expanded on more established narratives of amnesty as a harbinger of peace. The campaign for amnesty largely focused on the plight of political prisoners. Most of them had been arrested in the wake of the barracks uprising of November 1935, but some had resisted Vargas's regime from other ideological frameworks. Their immediate release with the granting of the amnesty stood as a marker of a broader political transition underway that was shifting Brazil from more authoritarian to more liberal politics. Indeed, some of these prisoners would soon be elected to form part of a constituent assembly drafting a new constitution. Their plight served as an effective lens through which the "drama" of Brazil's recent past and near future could be condensed and narrated.[4]

During these few months, though largely away from any spotlight, a quieter aspect of the political transition was also set in motion. In addition to the release of political prisoners, the amnesty provided for the establishment of commissions like the one that had reviewed Da Silva's petition to return to his post. The former civil servants who filed the required paperwork to these commissions had been part of an expanding bureaucracy and the increasing bureaucratization of the state. Given the opportunity for advancement, job stability, and pensions, many had occupied enviable positions.[5] The loss of employment and career opportunities, therefore, proved a particularly insidious form of repression. In addition to the consequences of prison time served, petitioners complained of loss of status and chronic unemployment or underemployment.

The history of the numerous individual petitions to such commissions gives a behind-the-scenes glimpse into Brazil's midcentury transition from dictatorship to democracy. Within entire branches of the military service as well as in small departments of governmental ministries, it was ad hoc committees, administrators, and judges who interpreted and applied the amnesty. Their interpretations and applications in many ways shaped, if not determined, the careers of individuals ranging from high-ly visible political figures to mid-level bureaucrats and junior officers to more humble and anonymous laborers and soldiers. Their history shows the complexity—and at times, frailty—of being or becoming amnestied.

For many, the 1945 decree unfolded into a saga that would span the length of the nearly twenty-year period of electoral democracy (1945–1964) and beyond into the years of the military regime (1964–1985). Da Silva, for example, in spite of having been unanimously approved by the commission, faced decades of bureaucratic and legal battles before he was finally reinstated in the public service. His readmission granted by the special commission in 1947 had been blocked by executive power as part of renewed repression of communists and suspected sympathizers in the coming of the Cold War. Others likewise faced lengthy battles in their attempts to be readmitted to their former posts. Considered sep-arately, these outcomes show the reach of the state—in both authori-tarian and liberalizing forms—in the lives of individuals. Considered collectively, these outcomes bring to the fore the parameters of measures of restitution and aspects of the mechanics of what we now refer to as transitional justice.

Two Men against Vargas

Two men in particular played key roles in the events related to the 1945 amnesty. Both had, at best, long-standing and antagonist relationships with Vargas, albeit from different ideological perspectives. In many ways Luis Carlos Prestes, captured and imprisoned following the failed 1935 uprising, became the face of the subsequent amnesty campaign, signi-fying the plight of the political prisoners. He was, as well, a singular and formidable obstacle to its granting. Euclides Figueiredo, who had resisted the consolidation of the Vargas regime as a leader in the 1932 revolt in São Paulo, would again take up arms against Vargas in 1938, lending military know-how to disgruntled adherents of *integralismo* (in-tegralism), a nationalistic and fascist-inspired movement whose militan-cy grew parallel to that of the communists. Following the 1945 amnesty, both Prestes and Figueiredo were elected to Congress and served in a constituent assembly that drafted a new constitution in 1946. In that process, Figueiredo became a key voice for former government employ-ees and military personnel, attempting at every turn to make readmis-sion to their posts both automatic and swift. Both men also sought to obtain the benefits of amnesty in the years that followed.

In 1930, first Prestes, then Figueiredo, were approached by the Lib-eral Alliance, the political coalition of those who had been edged out of power during the period of the First Republic, to lead revolutionary forces in the bid to install Vargas in the presidency after his narrow electoral defeat. Both refused.[6] Prestes was pressured by many fellow tenentes to join them in adhering to the Liberal Alliance, but he disapproved of Vargas. He issued a manifesto from exile in Argentina, calling for "agrarian and anti-imperialist revolution," in response to a vague and only timidly revolutionary manifesto published by Vargas after his loss in the 1930 election.[7] Figueiredo, for his part, refused to lead the Liberal Alliance's revolutionary forces based on his expressed loyalty to constitutional order. When those forces arrived in Rio de Janeiro on October 3, 1930, they detained and imprisoned Figueiredo, albeit only briefly. Figueiredo would later describe the victory of the revolutionary forces in 1930 as "a true disaster, a catastrophe."[8]

Some of the former members of the Liberal Alliance would have perhaps agreed. Once in power, the heterogeneous alliance did not hold. Disputes between the more liberal constitutionalists advocating elections and the more authoritarian-minded tenentes resulted in a tense power struggle.[9] When Vargas postponed elections it seemed that the tenentes had gained the advantage. Figueiredo soon joined a group of conspirators opposed to the direction Vargas was heading and assisted them in their planning of an armed revolt. The conspirators called their rebellion the "Constitutionalist Revolution," which was actually a brief civil war in which the revolutionary forces, led by Figueiredo and others, were far outnumbered and outarmed by the forces loyal to Vargas.[10] After subduing the revolt, Vargas initially granted small concessions to the rebels and ultimately amnestied them in 1934 (see chapter 4). These were somewhat characteristic gestures of statesmanship that would later earn him a reputation as a great conciliator, yet one beholden to none. Vargas's conciliating overtures, in fact, were frequently mistaken for allegiance, first among tenentes that helped bring him to power in 1930 and later among the new and ideologically driven *integralistas*.

Figueiredo and his fellow conspirators in São Paulo in 1932 ultimately received an olive branch from Vargas. Prestes and his comrades got only his heavy hand. Since the beginning of his presidency, Vargas and his administration pursued a hard line against communist activity, specifically, and socialist agitation in general, cracking down on leftist newspapers and distributing prolific anticommunist propaganda aimed especially at the working class. His chief of police, Filinto Müller, and the newly appointed war minister, Góis Monteiro, impressed upon Vargas the imminent threat that communists and their sympathizers posed for his administration. Müller recommended purges of suspects in the military and civil service, stricter immigration laws, and "work colonies for captured Communists."[11]

With the institution of the Estado Novo, it seemed that Vargas had adopted the political tenets of the emerging political ideology of integralism. The rightist integralista movement was tied to fascism in Italy; it bitterly opposed communists and socialists and often started bloody skirmishes in the streets. Under the leadership of Plinio Salgado, these Brazilian "Green Shirts" justified extremist measures in the face of economic and political problems, especially those exacerbated by the Great Depression.[12] In spite of any apparent or real ideological sympathies, Vargas nonetheless kept the integralistas themselves at bay. Frustrated by their failure to gain power, some integralistas began to conspire against Vargas. The leadership of this group approached Figueiredo and invited him to spearhead the military planning. Figueiredo participated in a number of meetings with the integralistas, and he ultimately assumed the role of strategist for the armed revolt. The police, however, discovered his scheming, and he was jailed. A planned attack on the government palace in Rio de Janeiro took place, nonetheless, in May 1938.[13] Vargas, his daughter, and loyal guards traded gunfire with the rebels. In the end, not only was the revolt put down but it also gave Vargas a certain license to crack down on the extremists from the right as he had those of the left. The archenemies communists and integralistas soon found themselves imprisoned together.

The repression unleashed in the wake of the 1935 barracks revolt would not be reined in until late in 1944, during the waning months of the Second World War. Police abuse and brutality were common, though unevenly applied. Prestes himself eluded the hunt for him until March 1936, when information obtained under torture led the police to his hiding spot. He was arrested together with his wife, Olga Benário, who was seven-months pregnant with their child. Prestes had met Olga, a young German Jewish Communist Party member and security specialist, on his return voyage from Moscow to Brazil in 1934. She had been sent to pose as his wife in the hopes of deflecting suspicion. In the midst of their three months of travel to Brazil, the professional cover arrangement between them had evolved into something much more personal.[14]

Others caught in the hunt for communists suffered barbaric tortures, though perhaps none more so than the German national Arthur Ewert, who used the alias Harry Berger in Brazil. He had been sent to Brazil, together with his wife, Elise, by the Comintern. Ewert's court appointed attorney before the National Security Tribunal, Sobral Pinto, appealed to norms regarding the humane treatment of animals in a largely fruitless effort to improve conditions for him.[15] For her part, Elise was deported to Nazi Germany where she died of pneumonia in prison. Prestes's wife, Olga, was likewise deported. She gave birth in a women's prison, before being transferred to a Nazi concentration camp. Her daughter, Anita, was released to the care of her paternal grandmother, Leocádia Prestes, and returned to Brazil. Olga was killed in a gas chamber in 1942.[16]

Although it was initially founded to prosecute those arrested in connection with the 1935 barracks revolt, the mandate of the National Security Tribunal expanded with the institution and entrenchment of the Estado Novo. By 1938, the court was granted broader authority to prosecute enemies of the regime in general, which by then included those involved in the integralistas revolt. From its founding in 1936 until the end of 1944, it handled almost six thousand cases, which named a total of just over nineteen thousand defendants. The court convicted and sentenced a total of 16 percent of those defendants, while acquitting 40 percent. The remaining 44 percent had their cases dismissed, were excluded from among those named in the case, or were transferred to another court.[17] Nearly half of those convicted were tried and sentenced between the court's inception in September 1936 and the end of 1937, the period in which it overwhelmingly, if not exclusively, tried those accused of involvement in the 1935 barracks revolt. The court sentenced Prestes to sixteen years and eight months in prison and Ewert to thirteen years and four months.[18] Later on, for his part in the 1938 integralista uprising, the court sentenced Figueiredo to four years' imprisonment.[19] Nearly six hundred people, including Prestes and Ewert, were still in prison when the 1945 amnesty was decreed.

THE 1945 AMNESTY

Calls for amnesty began soon after arrests were made of individuals involved in the barracks revolt. Following the 1938 integralista revolt, additional voices joined the cry. Statements issued by the underground PCB in September 1939 referenced the new world war in Europe in calling for the release of political prisoners in Brazil. The statements referenced Prestes, "the cavalier of hope," among the hundreds of political prisoners then detained and concluded with a demand for amnesty as the only viable path to internal peace in Brazil.[20] That same year, in a letter to Oswaldo Aranha, then minister of foreign relations, one father of a young integralista prisoner urged Vargas to reconcile with his former enemies, much as the Spanish dictator, Francisco Franco—at least in the estimation of this father—was doing in the wake of the Spanish Civil War. He explained that his son and other young people had simply been "caught up in the folly of youth."[21]

Another letter directed to Aranha described amnesty as nothing less than the "first and indispensable step for internal peace."[22] An army doctor also published an open letter to Vargas in defense of amnesty. Likewise appealing to Vargas's "generous hand extended to the vanquished," he argued more pragmatically that a grant of amnesty posed no risk for Vargas's regime. Although there remained "Comunistas and Integralistas" in Brazil, he maintained that the majority of Brazilians were "Republican Democrats" and ready to assist in the defense of Brazil, which would surely defeat both movements. He ended his letter saying that Vargas's greatest strength lay not in bayonets or cannons but in his heart: "you do not know how to hate nor are you vindictive; and winning, you extend a generous hand to the vanquished."[23]

Relatives of political prisoners also appealed directly to Vargas, framing their demand for amnesty in terms of what would bring about greater peace and the reconciliation of the Brazilian "family." One 1941 letter from São Paulo, signed by nearly eight hundred people, explained that such a gesture coming from Vargas, "as exemplary spouse, and above all, as a nurturing father," would put him "in the enviable position as the peacemaker of the Brazilian home, as the man who with just one act would make all hate and recriminations disappear."[24] A similar appeal with more than twelve hundred signatures called on Vargas to grant an amnesty for the sake of the innocent victims of economic hardship left in the wake of the prior political conflict. The letter reminded Vargas that "many honest Brazilians continue separated from their homes, whose children, wives, and even younger siblings endure the difficult test of the absence of their providers." The letter concluded in frank economic terms, citing the continual price increase for staple foods and for rent. Borrowing from biblical language, they pleaded that, "if in such circumstances the life of the poor is a vale of tears, even more dire is the life of the families whose heads are prevented from providing for them because they find themselves imprisoned."[25]

Such emotional appeals aside, both a growing amnesty movement and the lingering resistance of the Vargas regime to grant amnesty hinged in many ways on the figure of Luis Carlos Prestes. Pro-amnesty groups used the image and the name of Prestes to portray the unjust plight of the political prisoners and the necessity of amnesty for the larger project of democratization. The movement gained ground in 1942 when the exiled Bahian writer Jorge Amado published his biography of Prestes. Years later in a new preface to the book, written during a subsequent campaign for amnesty in 1979, Amado explained that he wrote it "with the fundamental objective to further the cause of amnesty for the political prisoners and exiles." It was, notably, an aim he felt had been achieved.[26]

As early as 1942, Vargas's advisors worried about the "problem of the political prisoner," but they were opposed to granting an amnesty.[27] Vargas's war minister and eventual successor, Eurico Gaspar Dutra, initial-ly favored a pardon, which would signal the benevolence of the regime while denying any moral vindication for the prisoners. Army generals, incensed about the 1935 revolt, however, opposed any easing of pres-sure, especially via an amnesty, and made that position clearly known to Dutra.[28] By early 1944, with Prestes's support for Brazil joining the Allied forces, Dutra reportedly began to be persuaded about the poten-tial that amnesty might have "in the formation of an internal atmosphere of mutual understanding and even of cooperation of all for the spiritual unity of the country." Dutra even discussed the possibility of freeing po-litical prisoners via an amnesty with a police agent who had interviewed Prestes several times in jail. Attempting to assuage critics from the mili-tary, he advised a decree modeled on the 1895 amnesty, which had come to be a point of pride within army history.[29]

By the time the broader amnesty movement began to organize rallies in 1944 and 1945, communists and their sympathizers posed a greater li-ability for Vargas in prison than they did outside. Indeed, as general dis-dain for fascism grew in Brazil, so did sympathy for political prisoners. The public campaigns on behalf of the prisoners continued to emphasize the unifying and democratizing potential of amnesty. The Bahian sec-tion of the Ordem dos Advogados do Brasil (Brazilian Bar Association), for example, urged the minister of justice in 1944 to support an amnesty since, given its "amplitude and objectivity," it inspires confidence, which would in turn foster national unity. Only then, the association explained, could Brazil participate, "indivisible and strong, in the liquidation of the fascist enemy and the democratic reedification of the free world of tomorrow."[30]

By March 1945, with hope for peace increasing in Europe, argu-ments for amnesty in Brazil extolled it as a peacemaker. The *Correio da Manhã* newspaper highlighted the broad scope of support for amnesty by publishing a list of six hundred individuals and associations, "with-out distinction of class, political leanings, or religious beliefs," who had organized pro-amnesty committees. Amado was among those named.[31] Other intellectuals also called for amnesty, including the poet Carlos Drummond de Andrade. In his "Poem of March 1945," the very word *anistia* reverberates like a life force throughout Rio de Janeiro. It was "aboard trains and trolley cars, in stores and at lunch counters." It cried out "from rocks, insects, and even umbrellas," and from the poor suburbs to the wealthier neighborhoods of Ipanema and Leblon. "Everything that squeaks," the poem declared, was "calling for amnesty."[32]

Beyond peace, the amnesty was also touted as a necessary base for de-mocracy. The organizing committee of the National Pro-Amnesty Week, which was to take place on April 8–15, 1945, published an editorial seeking to put the past political crimes in a larger historical perspective. The committee explained in the editorial that "those who find themselves prisoners or in exile are not criminals in the current sense of the term" but, rather, had "simply disagreed in a more or less radical or violent way with the ruling regime." Such divergences, and even armed revolt, the committee stated, "is a basic right of human consciousness, when not, as it many times is, a debt of patriotism or humanity." The committee then urged that the political crimes be viewed not for the acts themselves but, rather, for the motives behind them. The committee concluded by making a case for a step-by-step process of democratization, which necessarily began with amnesty, since only through amnesty would the liberty and political rights of citizens excluded from the "national community" be restored. Elections could then follow because, when the country was reunified, they would elections be a true "expression of the feelings of a nation."[33] The posters advertising the week of campaigning declared that "only fascists and the fifth column are against amnesty" while "all true patriots demand a broad, unrestricted and immediate amnesty."[34]

In the final moment, Vargas did not exclude Prestes or any other remaining political prisoners from the amnesty. The decree itself included all "political crimes" and "connected common crimes" committed from 1934 until the publication of the decree on April 18, 1945.[35] In general terms, both political and connected common crimes were understood to be those prosecuted under the National Security Tribunal. Of the roughly 3,000 individuals convicted by the National Security Tribunal from 1936 to 1945, exactly 563 remained in prison when Vargas decreed the amnesty. The rest either had already served their full or commuted sentences or had been absolved or pardoned. Of those still in prison, almost 20 percent were incarcerated on the notorious island prison of Ilha Grande. Among them, the longest sentence being served totaled eighty-four years while the lightest was two years.[36]

The remaining political prisoners were the most obvious and immediate group of *anistiados*, but the scope of the decree was broader. The brief text, in fact, reflected a disposition toward restitution but did not go as far as offering reparations or any indemnity. Its first article established the parameters of temporal and legal inclusion—namely, "political crimes dating from July 16, 1934," which was the date that the 1934 constitution entered into effect, including the amnesty granted therein. Two subsections of the 1945 amnesty dealt with the handling of "common crimes" under the decree, clarifying, respectively, those that were not able to be amnestied and those that were. Criminal acts not covered included "common crimes not connected to political crimes" as well as crimes committed in wartime against state security. Criminal acts considered "connected to political crimes," and thus able to be amnestied, were those "committed with political end," which "may have been prosecuted in the National Security Tribunal." (This notion of crimes "connected to political crimes" is also included in the 1979 amnesty; see chapter 8). The next two articles of the decree specified that the return of qualifying military personnel to their former posts or a similar position would depend on a case-by-case review by commissions nominated by the president. Although the decree made career restitution possible, its restorative quality was checked in its final article, which stated that "under no circumstances" would a beneficiary of the amnesty have "rights to back pay or the equivalent, nor to any sort of indemnity."[37]

The release of the political prisoners, the first and most visible outcome of the amnesty decree, accompanied, and in many ways seemed to set in motion, the other aforementioned liberalizing measures, including the legalization of the PCB and the convening of a constituent assembly to write a new constitution that would replace the authoritarian 1937 charter of the Estado Novo. Elections were also set for December 1945. In this first election of Brazil's "democratic experiment," the ballot presented a choice between two military men, General Dutra, who had been a critical figure in Vargas's regime, and Brigadier Eduardo Gomes, who had survived the 1922 revolt at Fort Copacabana and had been the effective leader of the opposition to Vargas since the middle of 1944.[38]

Although military men were set to control the political transition from above, the former archenemies Prestes and Vargas captured burgeoning political mobilization, especially among the urban working class. If the inclusion of Prestes in the amnesty was unexpected, even more so was Prestes's about-face with regard to Vargas.[39] Rejecting the choice between the "fascist" supporters of Dutra and the "reactionaries" associated with Gomes, Prestes supported what he called a "genuine democracy" through a constituent assembly, which implied that Vargas would continue in the presidency in the interim and until a new constitution could be put in place. Indeed, Prestes got behind the more populist pressures for "a Constitution with Vargas," explaining that it was the only way "to crush Nazism."[40] Both Prestes's PCB and Vargas's *queremistas* (as in *queremos Vargas* or "we want Vargas") exploited the political opening by coordinating unprecedented popular protests focusing on economic conditions, especially low wages and the rising cost of living.[41] Speculation and fear increased that Vargas would meddle to postpone or otherwise impact the elections. In the end, Vargas neither asserted himself as a candidate nor interfered in the pending elections. Military mistrust of his intentions, however, resulted in the delivery of a military ultimatum in October 1945 that he step down or be forcibly removed. He acquiesced.[42] In December, Dutra won the election. A constituent assembly, without Vargas, got to work early in 1946 on a new constitution.

"THE BEST DEMOCRATIC TEST OF THE REPRESENTATIVES"

Prestes had been the face for amnesty in both the public campaigns and the debates behind closed doors. Figueiredo, on the other hand, emerged as a critical voice for amnesty at the Constituent Assembly of 1946. He saw the assembly as an opportunity to correct the 1945 amnesty decree to match what he described as the spirit of the measure and to meet the expectations of the Brazilian citizens. In the early weeks of the assembly in March 1946, in fact, Figueiredo presented a motion for a vote that would urge the executive to suppress the second and third articles of the 1945 amnesty, which specified that the return of qualifying military personnel and civil servants, respectively, depended on the review of presidentially nominated commissions. Some fellow representatives proposed a more deferential motion, asking the executive for "details with regard to the providences that had been taken to put the amnesty decree into effect."[43]

In support of his motion, Figueiredo reminded the representatives that many had voted for the broad amnesty of 1934 and argued that the circumstances were strikingly similar. Details about the debate that followed are memorialized in a newspaper clipping that was collected and included in a police dossier on the campaign for amnesty. Figueiredo reportedly told his colleagues that military men and civilians faced difficult situations and that "their families [were] going without even today because of having been removed from their positions." Noting that some had yet to be returned to their posts, Figueiredo insisted that, "what they had was half-amnesty." If, however, the articles were suppressed, as he proposed, those who benefited from the amnesty would be immediately reintegrated into their former positions, instead of having to petition to and be approved by a special commission. It was "contrary to the very spirit of the [amnesty] law," Figueiredo argued, to require each and every military and civilian beneficiary to pass through "sieves," wherein the cases are judged one by one, and "with such slowness."[44]

His argument garnered support from unlikely quarters. Shortly before the vote a PCB representative to the assembly, Mauricio Grabois, declared Figueiredo's motion as "the best democratic 'test' of the Representatives." Echoing Rui Barbosa's arguments in the 1890s, he emphasized that the 1945 decree freed political prisoners but was not truly amnesty. Amnesty, Grabois said, "means forgetting," but they could see "that the government did not forget." Flores da Cunha, who had championed amnesty for the tenentes in the 1920s and helped to broker an amnesty for the rebels of São Paulo in the 1930s, also supported the motion and likewise turned to arguments made by Barbosa in the 1895 *Anistia Inversa* case. Amnesty, he said, "cannot be restricted. Either you concede it, or you deny it."[45]

Others, however, vehemently opposed the motion. The possibility of former rebels returning to the ranks of the military, in fact, incensed a good number of constituents. One representative, particularly disgusted with the lofty talk of national unity and conciliation, reminded the assembly about the purported crimes that had been committed during the 1935 revolt, in which, he claimed, "military men were killed while sleeping in the barracks." With an argument framed in terms of military honor and dishonor, this representative emphatically declared, "in the Army, in the Navy, and in the Air Force there are no places for enemies of the Fatherland."[46] In the end, this view held sway. Figueiredo's motion did not pass.

Efforts to alter the amnesty continued as the assembly drafted the new constitution, but with similar results. A proposed article for the constitution that would strike the same clauses from the amnesty decree garnered only 81 votes in favor against 159 votes opposed. A separate proposed article, which affirmatively provided reinstatement of all civil servants excluded from their posts for political reasons since 1930, was likewise defeated, although more narrowly, with 106 votes in favor against 115 opposed. The assembly passed, however, an article providing an amnesty for military deserters. It also passed one for those involved in labor strikes, even in the face of an unfavorable decision by the chair of the legislative committee that had reviewed the proposal.[47] Criticism emerged during the debates that was directed at the PCB representatives for having applauded the amnesty in 1945 only to push to change it at the assembly. Prestes explained that, at the moment the "dictatorial decree" was signed, it meant the freeing of political prisoners, which "truly represented a step ahead" for democracy and national unity. But in the present moment, "in a constitutional text . . . after having achieved other phases in the march for democracy," he argued, "of course much more should be demanded."[48]

SPECIAL COMMISSIONS AND THE ADJUDICATION OF AMNESTY

In the months immediately following the 1945 amnesty, a number of former civil service and military personnel petitioned to return to their posts in accordance with the articles in the amnesty decree. Special commissions formed as needed. The Ministry of Finance established one such committee, following the suggestion of the Departamento Administrativo do Serviço Público (Administrative Department of Public Service, DASP) for a three-member panel, to include a representative from the DASP as well as from the Ministério da Justiça e Negócios Interiores (Ministry of Justice and Internal Affairs, MJNI).[49] The military formed their own committees, publishing a decree in early 1946 to streamline the application and hearing process. According to the decree, discharged military personnel had 120 days to file; their petitions had to include the date of the official act that resulted in their discharge and their current address, as well as a list of the professional activities they had undertaken during their absence. They also had to pass a physical exam. Since amnesty "restores but does not create," if approved, the petitioner would return to the same post and level previously held.[50]

Caseload varied from commission to commission. The air force in Rio de Janeiro dealt with at least fifty requests from personnel involved in the 1935 revolt alone.[51] The "Commission for the Military Police in Rio de Janeiro" heard a total of thirty-four cases, involving both individuals accused of communist activities and participants in the 1938 integralista uprising.[52] Cumulative details from all the commissions, unfortunately, are unknown. Unlike the Review Commission instituted by Vargas in 1935, there is no evidence that a final report or comprehensive data was either requested or collected. Moreover, unlike the duly documented number and names of political prisoners freed by the amnesty, the scope of persons eligible for and who secured the right to return to their former jobs in 1945 seemed to have been neither projected nor calculated.

The commissions operated roughly from 1946 to 1948. This brief window of time had opened with a series of democratizing events but closed with a step back toward more authoritarian politics. By 1948, there was intensifying political policing, purges in the military and civil service, and renewed criminalization of the PCB. The cases heard in the various amnesty commissions mirrored this corresponding contraction toward more authoritarian politics. The imperative for pacification and national reconciliation that was so prominent in the public campaigns for amnesty and the higher-level political pronouncements gave way to a mixture of competing demands within the various commissions. The demands ranged from the height of national security concerns to the much lowlier depths of old squabbles, political and otherwise.

The "Special Commission for the Return of Amnestied Officers" of the army, navy, and air force reviewed a number of requests but none as high-profile, or arguably as vehemently, as that of Luis Carlos Prestes. The former army captain's application was rejected by the committee on three separate grounds: moral, professional, and patriotic. Morally, the commission emphasized that Prestes was the person principally responsible for the barracks revolt and that the military "in act and speech" was against communist ideology as a "danger to public order, family habits, individual liberty, and the democratic spirit of the Brazilian people." Professionally, the committee simply noted that it had been a long time since Prestes had exercised any military function and that, due both to his age and to the expansion in number and complexity of duties of officers, his return was "inconvenient." Patriotically, the commission explained that Prestes, as a current senator and secretary of the PCB, had vowed publicly that he would not take up arms against Russia if Brazil became involved in a war. A soldier "who expresses himself in this manner," they said, "does so under the penalty of being found a traitor." Moreover, they argued that an officer espousing such an ideology would pose a risk of acts of espionage or sabotage to the military. In sum, the commission found that Prestes's request "deals with a person without patriotic spirit and who is undesirable within the ranks of those committed to the defense of the homeland."[53] Other officers were similarly refused.[54]

Prestes did not take the news lying down. He filed a complaint against the *A Noite* newspaper for publishing the conclusions of the commission, noting that on its front page the paper had printed that Prestes was "undesirable in the Army," and further on that he was a "person without morals."[55] Figueiredo, in contrast, had an easier time of it. Administratively retired by decree in 1938 during the integralista uprising, he returned to service in April 1946 and was promoted to brigadier general. In October 1951 he requested the benefits extended in a 1950 law bestowed upon individuals who had served in a war zone during the Second World War. Testing the limits of the reach of amnesty, he argued that he was available and disposed to serve at that time but could not because he had been ousted. The petition on that point was denied in 1953.[56]

Elsewhere in the bureaucracy, the outcomes of cases like that of José Duarte, a machinist for the Northwest Railroad, show how continued political militancy came at a price. Duarte lost his job in 1942 after being convicted by the National Security Tribunal.[57] He was one of the nearly six hundred released from prison with the amnesty decree in 1945, midway through serving a sentence of six years and six months.[58] Following the amnesty, he was hired for a second federal job at the same time as he petitioned for restitution to his former post. In July 1945, after less than two months on the new job, and before the amnesty commission heard his case, Duarte was fired again. His dismissal, based on "excessive absences constituting abandonment," was, ostensibly, entirely disciplinary. After reviewing his case and employment history, the special commission quickly denied his petition to return to his first job, noting that his employment record included a long list of absences "for extremist activities" as well as nine administrative suspensions and various punishments for minor offenses. The commission also noted that his file contained a PCB document that he had signed and reportedly circulated. Because of his continued militancy, the commission ruled that "the return of said employee would be improper for the administration."[59]

In May 1946, a secret memo to the head of the DASP from Dutra's secretary explained a policy that was to be applied to personnel involved in the "exercise of communist activities." Any such activity by civil servants who did not have tenure (*estabilidade*) would result in his or her immediate dismissal. Those who did have tenure would be subject to the "competent administrative process." A note included in the file situated this new policy in relation to international standards, pointing out that the US Congress maintained a permanent committee (the Dies Committee) to investigate any and all "anti-American" activities of public servants. The note further commented that on a daily basis in the United States "various civil servants are fired due to their extremist or anti-American ideas."[60] It is worth noting that in Brazil, this policy was instituted, albeit secretly, during the brief period when the Communist Party was legal, indeed a full year before the party would again be declared illegal. The director of the DASP, however, warned of trouble in perusing it. He returned three cases of tenured individuals from the War Ministry that had been sent to him as the "competent administrative authority" and advised that any such inquests should obey the dictates of the existing statutes "in order to protect against possible criticism" of the government.[61] The new policy, at least for nontenured employees, was put into place nonetheless and was accompanied by renewed investigation and surveillance of employees suspected of communist activities.[62]

Braz da Silva, the corrections guard, fell victim to this very policy. Since he lost his job based on an explicitly political amendment to the 1934 constitution—namely, for "the exercise of activities subversive to political and social institutions," his case neatly fit the parameters of the amnesty and received a unanimously favorable ruling before the special commission. His readmission was blocked, however, by President Dutra himself, who sat as the final arbiter for a number of cases.[63] The undeniably political motives for his forced retirement in 1936, while at first securing him the benefits of the amnesty earlier in the work of the special commission, made him all the more susceptible to the renewed repression that quickly followed. In contrast, the case of Manoel Miguel de Mello, a member of the military police, never made it to Dutra's desk, having been denied by the special commission in October 1948.

Although the policy to dismiss public employees who participated in "communist activities" was quietly put in place in 1946, by the time the commission heard De Mello's case in 1948, the PCB was again illegal and the repression of its member quite in the open. The frequent purges of current employees in the military and civil service spelled doom for former employees like De Mello who were attempting to secure readmission.[64]

In the military, the problem posed by the return of soldiers who had been involved in the revolt of 1935 beleaguered the commissions. The military had touted the individual bureaucratic hearings as the way "to appreciate and respond appropriately to the dozens, hundreds of different and complex cases." Once the repression of communist activity was in full force, however, all the petitions were collectively denied and the cases closed.[65] Surely knowing the liability, the above mentioned De Mello vehemently denied any affiliation with the PCB in his petition to the special commission. Whether such affiliation was real or falsely suspected, he characterized his 1935 dismissal as the result of a personal vendetta against him by integralistas on the police force. The accusation of "communist activity," moreover, could be easily explained. At that time, he said, the unofficial slogan on the force was "who was not an *Integralista* was a *Comunista*."[66]

Thus, not only did the grander national security concerns of the moment weigh on the outcomes of commission hearings, but so too did the muddled reality of old political and personal squabbles. The expectation that amnesty might act as a purveyor for national reconciliation on a large scale got lost in translation at the department level. De Mello's case, among others, brings this to the fore. According to his petition, he and another officer were arrested in a sting while having coffee. He was summarily dismissed from the force when it was discovered that his companion had communist propaganda in his pocket. Later, he learned that the other officer had been allowed to continue on the force, confirming in his mind that he had been the victim of a deliberate trap. The commission, however, found no evidence of such. The commander of the military police, moreover, submitted documents recording "habitual bad conduct," which left De Mello "morally unfit for military life and the police profession." As in other cases, the commission denied De Mello's petition since the official reason for his dismissal was disciplinary, not political. The commission acknowledged that he may have suffered harassment but found that his other disciplinary infractions also would have merited his dismissal. A far cry from the rhetoric of national reconciliation, in more editorial comments justifying the ruling, the commission seemed to recognize both the potential abuse of power by the commander and the potential for opportunistic behavior from a former troublesome employee. De Mello continued to solicit readmission, though to no avail, at least until 1959.[67]

Accusations of targeted political harassment went in both directions. Tomas Ribeiro de Carvalho, for example, did not deny his affiliation with integralistas, explaining that the Acão Integralista Brasileira (Brazilian Integralist Action), was a "party legally constituted and registered in the Supreme Electoral Tribunal." In his defense, he explained that, from when he entered the special police force in late 1932 until his dismissal in late 1937, there was never a complaint against him. In fact, he described himself as an exemplary employee who worked overtime as treasury and accounting chief without ever receiving or asking for corresponding benefits. His dismissal, which he noted had occurred without any investigation of a suspected irregularity, had to be understood as simply the "discretionary act of a dictatorial government." His commander, however, disagreed. He described Ribeiro de Carvalho as "undisciplined," an "avowed integralista by his own admission," and a "political fanatic," who had been suspended several times prior to his dismissal for discussing political matters in the precinct. The commander added that his opposition to the return of Ribeiro de Carvalho to the force extended well beyond the norms of disciplinary policy to the moral landscape of the recent past. He blamed *integralismo* in Brazil for sharing in the ideology of Nazi fascism, which had inflicted untold suffering upon millions.[68]

The political currency of such anti-fascist rhetoric, and the corresponding extension of that rhetoric to integralism in Brazil, had resonance during the final months of the public campaigns for amnesty in 1944 and 1945. It seems, however, to have lost its luster and purchase power in the commission hearings in the years that followed. As in other cases, dealing with the overtly political, and even moral, backdrop to Ribeiro de Carvalho's case was easily sidestepped with a bureaucratic technicality: he had submitted his petition after the deadline. In his review of the matter, Dutra agreed that Ribeiro da Carvalho was ineligible to petition for readmission. Upon Dutra's order, his application was simply archived.

A good number of petitioners shared the same initial fate as Ribeiro da Carvalho, though others entered a bureaucrat maze in which their cases were transferred (or at least marked for transfer) to other ad hoc commissions. The special commissions had particular trouble settling claims of petitioners who had been tried by the National Security Tribunal for political crimes but had technically lost their job based on article 177 of the 1937 constitution of the Estado Novo. Being dismissed under article 177, "by the prerogative of the regime or in the interest of public service," connoted no overt political motive and therefore was technically beyond the scope of the amnesty. Their convictions by the National Security Tribunal, however, lent credence to their claims of politically motivated persecution. These petitioners thus found themselves in a nebulous category in which they simultaneously fit and did not fit the scope of the amnesty decree. It was precisely this muddled situation that Figueiredo attempted to simplify during the Constituent Assembly in the early months of 1946. By late 1947, a bill was introduced in the Chamber of Deputies to create a commission to rule on the readmission of those fired under article 177. The amnesty commissions then tabled their review of all relevant cases, noting that they would later pass them on to an article 177 commission, should it come into being.[69]

The law passed, as did other legislation, regulations, and rulings concerning the return of amnestied former civil servants and military personnel in the 1950s and 1960s.[70] Sectors of civil society continued to campaign for the expansion of the 1945 decree. Among them, members of the PCB, as before, relied on the image of the Prestes, who spent the 1950s living clandestinely, attempting to reorganize the underground PCB, and avoiding an outstanding warrant for his arrest. In 1961 Congress decreed just such an amnesty, applicable to all those who participated directly or indirectly in political crimes from the date of the promulgation of the 1934 constitution up to the date of the publication of the 1961 decree.[71] Based on the new legislation, the results of other cases, and especially the 1961 amnesty, some individuals who previously had been denied or blocked from readmission persisted in their pursuit.

Among them, Ribeiro de Carvalho, the aforementioned integralista whose petition was simply archived by Dutra because he had missed the deadline, not only persisted but also solicited the help of Plinio Salgado, a former leader of the integralistas and a member of the Chamber of Deputies. Salgado wrote to the minister of justice in 1959 on behalf of his "old friend and follower." Showing disgust at the "huge injustice" inflicted on Ribeiro de Carvalho, Salgado reminded the minister that then President Juscelino Kubitschek, while governor of Minas Gerais, had reinstated all former integralistas who had been fired from the state police force during the Estado Novo. With rhetorical flourish, he lamented that so many cases similar to that of Ribeiro de Carvalho's had passed "from Herod to Pilate" in the "Holy Bureaucracy" and that some "miracle" was in order to bring back to life, and to the "sunlight of their legitimate rights," this and other Lazaruses "trapped in the tombs of injustice." The reply from the minister read simply: "I regret the impossibility to attend to your request, once the interested party allowed the deadline to expire for his application to return to the post from which he was fired on Nov. 11, 1937." Ribeiro de Carvalho was, nonetheless, readmitted by decree on January 20, 1964, just weeks before a military coup ended Brazil's "democratic experiment." His file contains no notation explaining the justification for his readmission, which occurred more than twenty-six years after he was fired.[72]

For Ribeiro de Carvalho and others, the stakes in being amnestied likely would have changed over time. More than two decades after being fired, readmittance would have mattered more in terms of securing a military or civil service pension, as these former employees reached retirement age. Braz da Silva, the corrections guard who—in spite of having been unanimously approved by the commission in 1947—faced more than twenty years of bureaucratic and legal battles. He was reinstated in 1963 by an administrative decision and "as an act of reparation" for the injustices he suffered. His administrative reinstatement was followed by a judicial ruling that found Dutra's action in blocking his readmission both arbitrary and in violation of the law. Braz da Silva was awarded and paid retirement benefits, this now under the military regime, based on years of service since 1936.[73] Not all the individual histories, however, ended so well, or even, just ended. In 1969 the military regime—by then under the third of five successive military presidents—revoked the 1961 amnesty and suspended the reinstatement of all military personnel who had benefited from it.[74]

CONTRARY-TO-FACT LANGUAGE IN LEGAL TERMS

In his contemporaneous reflections on the 1946 constitution, the jurist Francisco Cavalcante Pontes de Miranda weighed in about amnesty. After repeating a litany of amnesties originally presented by Rui Barbosa in the 1895 case of *Anistia Inversa* and citing, among others, the sagacious use of amnesty in Athens, at the conclusion of the American Civil War, and at key moments of strife in Brazil, he explained that the word "amnesty" derived from the Greek word *amnestia* and denoted forgetting. As such, amnesty was a "peace that forgets and the forgetting that pacifies." The Roman concept of *lex oblivion* provided a procedural model for this legal amnesia—that is, amnesty required that political crimes be treated as if they had never taken place.[75]

Fellow constitutional scholars agreed. Carlos Maximiliano commented that the conciliatory aims of amnesty set it apart from other measures, especially pardon and mercy. The distinctions, in fact, were crucial. Pardon and mercy, like amnesty, alleviated criminal sanctions, but they acted merely as gestures of a ruler's charity or benevolence toward otherwise undeserving individuals. Amnesty, in contrast, was "not conceded out of sentimentalism, simple goodwill, sympathy for the losers or personal mercy." Rather, historical circumstances "called for forgetting infractions and for impunity for certain crimes" as a way "to quiet spirits and pacify a region." As such, amnesty was "a highly political measure adopted for motives that did not humble the citizen who benefited." Granted collectively, amnesty "forgot" a punishable act.[76]

This contrary-to-fact language proved easier to manage in the philosophical realm than in the procedural one. Philosophically, amnesty served a collective aim of national reconciliation by "forgetting" the moments and events of strife and division. Procedurally, amnesty dealt with individuals whose lives were marked by and changed in those moments and events. Politicians, advocates, and amnestied individuals argued with some success that "forgetting" required measures of restitution, both material and moral. There were limits, however. In Brazil, as elsewhere, the state measured its response to its authoritarian past with priorities of the moment. The collective goal of national reconciliation through amnesty did not fully translate in the individual cases of the amnestied.

In many ways, this history underscores the pragmatic limitations of measures of restitution and reparation and the stubborn unevenness of their guarantees. Not only did the political context change, but arguably, so did the priorities of those seeking amnesty—the *anistiandos* (amnestying)—themselves. It is not difficult to imagine how some must have grown suspicious of the process, or weary of bureaucracy, and cut their losses or simply forged different paths. What had been a collective measure to amnesty all who had committed political crimes devolved into a process of individual initiative within a compartmentalized system where resources, perseverance, and political will mattered. Ultimately, the process ground to a halt before the more complicated cases could be resolved.

Expectations about amnesty, and specifically what the "forgetting" should look like, did not go away, however. Indeed, many continued to push for restitution and the recognition they saw at the heart of what it meant to be amnestied. Pontes de Miranda, among others, nonetheless argued that amnesty could only "return to a point in time but could "not proceed from that point on a road that could have been taken but was not." Amnesty, he said, "reestablishes, rather than establishes; it restores, but does not create."[77] Such understandings of the limits on any restorative imperatives of amnesty persisted, and indeed won the day, in the sometimes decades-long adjudications related to the 1945 amnesty. Yet the idea of amnesty as something more than what it had been also persisted. In 1979, fifteen years into the military dictatorship that would rule Brazil, Euclides Figueiredo's son, General João Figueiredo, then the fifth and final president of the regime, signed an amnesty into law. The amnesty set in motion a gradual political opening and the subsequent return to democracy after what would be twenty-one years of dictatorship. It also was the beginning of a slow expansion of rights framed as amnesty, and of amnesty as an institutionalized mechanism of transitional justice in Brazil.

PART III

AMNESTY AND TRANSITIONAL JUSTICE, 1979–2010

PROLOGUE

WHAT GOT WRITTEN DOWN

Just before the title page, and again in a final note, Bernardo Kucinski tells the readers of his historical novel, *K*, that "everything in this book is invented, but almost everything happened."[1] It is an allusion to the phrase with which Primo Levi concluded the preface to his 1947 *Survival at Auschwitz*: "it seems unnecessary to me to add that none of the facts are invented."[2] In doing so, Kucinski separates his work from the genre of atrocity testimony, exemplified in Levi's searing account of his survival in the Nazi death camp. While authority rests with Levi's recollection of events as a survivor, Kucinski's book is based on what he imagined must have happened to his sister when she was disappeared in 1974 by the São Paulo secret police. An accomplished journalist, Kucinski opted for literature to tell his sister's story. As Rebecca Atencio explains, his reliance on fiction both reflects particularities about the Brazilian postdictatorship reckoning and highlights the related capacity of literature to raise "critical awareness about different kinds of injustices."[3]

The dictatorship that followed the 1964 coup in Brazil lasted twenty-one years and is among the longest of the Cold War–era dictatorships in Latin America. Since the transition to civilian governance in 1985, Brazil has been recalcitrant in addressing the human rights abuses that were committed during the dictatorship, a fact that helps explain the relative place of fiction in Brazil's postdictatorship processes. In neighboring Argentina and Chile, for example, truth commissions accompanied the political transitions of the 1980s in efforts to delineate the new governments from the past regimes and to condemn, in the terms possible at that moment, the previous period of state terror.[4] In Argentina, where the military had been weakened by defeat in the Malvinas/Falklands War, trials also briefly proceeded against members of the junta. The efforts, however, became a cautionary tale about the unintended consequences of pursuing criminal trials parallel to a larger political transition.[5]

As a result, the countries in the region settled on a paradigm of truth-telling in lieu of prosecutions. Framed as a necessary trade-off, societies would know what happened to the victims of state violence, but the perpetrators, to the extent they were identified or identifiable, would not face any criminal sanctions. The consensus view held that reporting on incidents and patterns of egregious violations of human rights acknowledged the victims without the risk that trials posed for upsetting the political transitions themselves. With the exception of Argentina, the transitions had been the result of negotiated settlements rather than military defeats, and the new governments proceeded cautiously so as to minimize risk from the military to their consolidation.[6] At the time, Samuel Huntington famously synthesized advice for "democratizers" addressing past atrocities, noting that "the least unsatisfactory course may well be: do not prosecute, do no punish, do not forgive, and above all, do not forget."[7]

It was a turn, as Ruti Teitel explained, from the more "single-minded focus on individual accountability" of the post–Second World War model to a "more communitarian conception," where transitional justice became a "private matter . . . for victims to reconcile and recover from past harm." The choice between "punishment and amnesty" in the post–Cold War transitions in South America, she noted, "was complicated by the recognition of dilemmas inherent in periods of political flux."[8] The truth-telling that did occur, while not a panacea, nonetheless did critical work of substantiating facts. Such facts mattered acutely, especially in the face of institutionalized patterns of denial, dissembling, and obfuscation about instances of torture and forced disappearances, particularly shocking features of many of the Cold War–era dictatorships and dirty wars in Latin America.[9]

Although it was contemporaneous, the political transition in Brazil did not adopt the paradigm of truth-telling that was undertaken elsewhere in Latin America. In fact, it took more than a generation for an official truth commission to be mandated in Brazil. Finally instituted in 2012, the commission completed its report in 2014, fifty years after the coup and nearly thirty years after the transition.[10] In the moment of transition from dictatorship to electoral democracy, rather than address its legacy of state violence in the then novel way, Brazil went down a more familiar, and particularly Brazilian, path. It turned to amnesty. The amnesty law enacted in 1979 marked the beginning of the end of the dictatorship, signaling a willingness on the part of the regime to re-share power.[11] It also marked, in the eyes of many, a certain vindication for the victims of violence and persecution at the hands of the state and provided, as in previous amnesty laws, for the possibility of some forms of restitution.

This is not to say that amnesty did not factor into political transitions elsewhere. Quite the contrary was true. Amnesty laws accompanied, and often predicated, liberalizing steps and broader peace agreements throughout the region.[12] Amnesty laws stand, in fact, as the most commonly utilized mechanism of transitional justice in Latin America.[13] In Argentina, laws enacted after the transition brought the trials to an end and prevented further investigation, functioning as de facto amnesties. In Chile, a self-amnesty was securely in place before Augusto Pinochet conceded to the results of the referendum that would end his rule.[14] The subsequent truth commission in Chile deliberately did not "name names" of perpetrators in deference to dictates of due process. Further north, in El Salvador, an amnesty law was enacted just days after the truth commission there issued a report that, unlike the Chilean report, identified those it had determined bore responsibility for instances of egregious human rights violations.[15] In these and other countries in the region, amnesty came to equate with impunity and became a stubborn obstacle for accountability efforts as they evolved in the decades after the democratic transitions.[16]

Only in Brazil did the path to acknowledge victims run through amnesty. At the same time, the amnesty law also served to guarantee impunity for perpetrators of human rights violations in Brazil, as it did elsewhere in Latin America. And it remains an entrenched impediment to accountability in Brazil today. In 2010, while trials of some known perpetrators moved forward in other Central and South American countries, Brazil's Federal Supreme Court affirmed an interpretation of the 1979 amnesty as "bilateral" and thus covering crimes, including torture and forced disappearance, committed by state agents.[17] This affirmation from the highest court arguably limited the impact of the Brazilian Truth Commission, instituted two years later, to effectuate a deeper reckoning with the legacy of state violence.

The Brazilian Truth Commission was able to confirm, albeit belatedly, some details of the torture, death, and disappearance of Kucinski's sister. None of the individuals identified as responsible, however, have been held to account. Kucinski's sister, Ana Rosa, was thirty-two years

old and a postgraduate lecturer at the prestigious Institute of Chemistry at the University of São Paulo on the day in April 1974 that the
secret police detained her. They detained her husband, Wilson Silva, the
same day. At the time of their disappearance, both Ana and Wilson were
militants in the Ação Libertadora Nacional (National Liberation Action, ALN). The ALN had been founded and led by Carlos Marighella,
who had defected from the PCB in frustration with the party's position
against armed resistance to the dictatorship. Marighella then emerged as
a leading theoretician of urban guerrilla tactics. Together with another
guerrilla group, the ALN most famously kidnapped the US ambassador
to Brazil, Charles Elbrick, in September 1969. They successfully negotiated the release of Elbrick in exchange for fifteen political prisoners. A
wave of repression soon followed.[18] The dreaded chief of the São Paulo Departamento de Ordem Política e Social (Department of Political
and Social Order, DOPS), Sergio Paranhos Fleury, killed Marighella
in a shootout in São Paulo two months later. In October 1970, Fleury tortured to death Marighella's successor, Joaquim Câmara Ferreira.
Following these events, the ALN redirected its effort. A final wave of
arrests and forced disappearances in 1974, including of Ana and her husband, largely decimated the ALN.[19]

Testimony to the Truth Commission from a former sergeant of the
feared Destacamento de Operações de Informações, Centro de Operações de Defesa Interna (Detachment of Information Operations, Center of Operations of Internal Defense, DOI-CODI) in São Paulo confirmed that the couple had been transferred from the DOI-CODI in São
Paulo to the clandestine torture center known as the "Casa da Morte"
(House of Death) in Petrópolis, an hour's drive from Rio de Janeiro. He
also confirmed that DOI-CODI agents attempted to extort money from
her family. A former DOPS agent admitted to the Truth Commission
that he took the couple's bodies in the trunk of his chevette from the
House of Death to the Usina Camhayba factory. The factory had large
brick ovens where their bodies, and those of nearly a dozen other victims
of the House of Death, were apparently incinerated. He also reported
that Ana Rosa's body bore signs of having been brutally tortured.[20]

The details that emerged about what happened to Ana in testimony
to the Truth Commission occurred after Kucinski wrote and published
K. In the larger void of information as he wrote, Kucinski tells the fic-
tional story of a father's desperate search for his disappeared daughter.
He does so in a series of vignettes, born of "fragments" from his memory,
and conveyed "just as they came, after being buried for years, without
confirming them through research."[21] Indeed, it would have been difficult for Kucinski to confirm much through research at that time. For one

chapter, Kucinski relies on brief minutes of a university council meeting that had been dutifully recorded and were available to him. While the more recent testimony to the Truth Commission detailed the violent end of the lives of Ana and her husband, the council meeting minutes simply recorded perfunctory notes for each item on the agenda. Kucinski reads between the lines to tell the story of a more symbolic assault on Ana, not by the state's repressive apparatus per se, but by her colleagues and the university bureaucracy.

The first item on the agenda for the council meeting was a vote on whether to rescind Ana's contract for "dereliction of duty." The recommendation to fire Ana had been made, in part, by a retired professor seeking reappointment. A vote on his reappointment, Kucinski notes, was the second item on the agenda. An indignant philosophy professor, in Kucinski's imaginings, sees through this opportunistic move. He thinks to himself, "everyone knows she was taken by the secret police," even if the authorities deny it. Yet, instead of acting on that knowledge, the council relied on more verifiable data. The institution, "renowned for its scientific rigour," looked to the indisputable evidence that she had been absent from work since April 23, 1974, and therefore found that she had failed to complete the requirements of her job.[22] The secret vote returned two spoiled ballots, one abstention, and thirteen votes to rescind Ana's contract. It stood, in Kucinski's telling, as another insidious way in which Ana had been terminated, drawing a subtle parallel between the utter disregard shown to Ana by the secret police in the grotesque acts of torture and forced disappearance to the banal administrative actions of her colleagues who had her fired.

The fact that Kucinski had access to the council meeting minutes that resulted in Ana's being fired but had nothing that could shed light on her death reveals something about repression and its tendrils in Brazil. It also reflects the landscape and evolution of transitional justice as it played out in Brazil. Those processes proceeded apart from the framework and pace in the region and have resulted in Brazil being viewed as lagging behind. There have nonetheless been some breakthroughs. Following the transition to civilian governance in 1985, for example, the compilation *Brasil nunca mais* (Brazil never again) appeared in bookstores and newsstands. Based on records of the military courts made available on a limited basis to adjudicate matters related to the 1979 amnesty, the report compiled data on torture and other crimes that were gleaned primarily from testimony in court proceedings. The report included the names, if known, of state agents complicit in torture.[23] The same year, a constitutional amendment affirmed the 1979 amnesty and expanded its reach to additional persons who had been targeted by the regime but whose circumstances did not fit within the narrower confines of the law. That amendment then led to an article in the 1988 constitution that broadened the scope and reach of possible indemnity for victims of state repression.

In December 1995, the Brazilian state officially recognized individuals who had been killed and disappeared during the dictatorship, issued an apology, and began a reparations program. Law 9,140, known as the Lei dos Desaparecidos (Law of the Disappeared), included an annex in which it named 136 people formally recognized as having been disappeared by the military regime. Ana and her husband are among those named.[24] It also established the Comissão Especial sobre Mortos e Desaparecidos Políticos (Special Commission on Political Deaths and Disappearances) that ultimately reviewed 475 cases and authorized reparation payments to the families of more than 300 victims.[25] The law itself was framed as an extension of the 1979 amnesty. The second article, in fact, declared the new law's application as grounded in the "principle of reconciliation and national peace-building" expressed in the earlier amnesty.[26] In turn, the establishment five years later of the national Amnesty Commission, which would review tens of thousands of petitions for restitution, is viewed as an extension of the reparations program administered under the Law of the Disappeared.

This progression—from the original amnesty in 1979, to expansions on it under laws passed in the 1980s, 1990s, and 2000s—marks a further institutionalization of amnesty but also the continued striving for a deeper realization of amnesty itself. In her previous scholarly work, Glenda Mezarobba, who would serve as a lead researcher for the Brazilian Truth Commission, contrasted what was striking and widespread mobilization for amnesty in the late 1970s with the agonizingly slow and labored arrival of the fulfillment of the restitution it was to effectuate in the Amnesty Commission. She argued that the amnesty law of 1979 served as "pragmatic conciliation" as the military navigated its exit from power. Only in 1995, with the passage of the Law of the Disappeared, did amnesty expand to include acknowledgment. And only following additional years of concerted efforts on the part of those who had been persecuted, did amnesty come to represent financial reparations in the establishment of the Amnesty Commission.[27] Mezarobba also notes that the Brazilian state, in contrast to some of its neighbors, has only conceded in administrative matters, setting up the Special Commission on Political Deaths and Disappearances and then the Amnesty Commission. It has utterly failed, she argues, to fulfill its duties to ensure justice and truth about what had happened.[28]

This was true in Ana's case. No one has been held to account, but there were some actions taken at the Institute of Chemistry where she worked. Following the 2011 publication of Kucinski's book, a memorial was inaugurated to recognize the "grave injustices committed by the University of São Paulo against [her] memory." Also, in a symbolic but meaningful gesture in 2014, the Institute of Chemistry issued a formal apology and voted unanimously to nullify the decision made forty years earlier to dismiss her from her position.[29]

The chapters that follow are case studies in a much larger universe of diverse experiences related to the recent history of amnesty in Brazil. In some ways, the individual stories are quite distinct from that of Ana Kucinski and from each other. They converge, nonetheless, in analysis of the outcomes of their respective petitions for restitution based on the 1979 amnesty, from its enactment under the dictatorship to its perceived fulfillment in the Amnesty Commission. The trajectory of their claims from the period of the dictatorship to the very recent past shows the ways in which the Brazilian state formulated and responded to dictates regarding the defense of human rights and citizenship. Far from comprehensive, the cases examined represent a spectrum of abuses meted out by the state and the strategies adopted and adapted to seek restitution by those who had been targeted.

In chapter 6 we look at the 1964 coup and the immediate steps taken to discipline some sectors of the work force through the events at one oil refinery on the outskirts of Rio de Janeiro and in the lives of roughly forty employees who worked there. As part of the majority state-held Petrobras company, the refinery was among the first to be taken over by the military regime after the coup, and the labor leaders there were among those immediately targeted. These petroleum workers, or *petroleiros*, however, were not targeted with the exceptional powers the regime granted itself. Rather, they lost their jobs—and quite deliberately so—under ordinary labor legislation. This fact complicated their path to eventual amnesty and restitution, which was ultimately gained through a politically brokered agreement. We follow the history of these petroleiros from their being fired in 1964 to their readmission in 1985 and beyond and examine the ultimate resolution of their cases by the Amnesty Commission in the mid-2000s.

In chapter 7 we look at another group of forty some employees but in a different city nearly a decade later. This case focuses on police agents in São Paulo who lost their jobs in the 1970s under the infamous Fifth Institutional Act (AI-5) and tells the parallel stories of the impact of AI-5 both through the torture and disappearances committed by state agents in São Paulo and the simultaneous purges from within the ranks of the repressive apparatus itself. It follows the cases of the fired agents, from the public accusations of corruption and extortion that predicated the purges through their efforts for reappointment, first under the 1979 amnesty and then through the subsequent laws that expanded the possibilities for indemnity over the decades that followed. The focus is on their cases before the national Amnesty Commission and the evolving calculus in Brazil of recognizing and offering restitution for repression.

After chapters dominated by events in the lives of men, in chapter 8 we look at the life under and after repression of one woman, Victória Grabois. Her story is told with attention to the paradoxical impact of a clause in the 1979 amnesty—namely, that of granting amnesty for crimes "connected" to political crimes. The interpretation of the clause defined her life in two distinct realms. First, she committed just such a "connected crime" when she lived and worked clandestinely during the dictatorship with identification documents in someone else's name. The clause, therefore, was her path to resuming her identity without facing charges for fraud. That same clause, however, perversely also shielded those responsible for the disappearance of her father, brother, and husband who were part of the Guerrilha do Araguaia (Guerrilla Movement of Araguaia) in the early 1970s. When efforts for justice, and even for information, were stymied in Brazil, she took part in a case before the Inter-American Court of Human Rights. Her story underscores an absurdity at the heart of the postdictatorship reckoning in Brazil.

These case studies are certainly not exhaustive but nonetheless are a window into some of the processes of repression under the dictatorship as well as those of subsequent restitution. The stakes in amnesty during this period were framed, as never before, in the language of human rights, especially in light of the prevalence of torture and the practice of forced disappearance by the military regime. What emerges is the ways in which Brazil stayed the course with amnesty in what amounted to an incremental approach in a decades-long pursuit to refine, perfect, and institutionalize a vision of amnesty as it was meant to be—and not as it had been.

CHAPTER 6

PREEMPTING AN
INEVITABLE AMNESTY

Purges in Petrobras, 1964–1985

In the immediate days following the 1964 coup, one police team from DOPS worked on intelligence gathering at an oil refinery in a poorer lowland area, known as the Baixada Fluminense, on the outskirts of Rio de Janeiro. The refinery, located in the municipality of Duque de Caxias, was known by its acronym Reduc (Refinery of Duque de Caxias). It had opened just a few years earlier as part of the expansion of the state-run oil company, Petrobras. Military leaders who had plotted against and then overthrown the government of João Goulart had serious concerns about the levels of possible resistance from labor leaders at the plant. Those labor leaders, in fact, at first had plans to resist but then abandoned them and went into hiding when the military occupied the refinery.[1] In the weeks following the coup, the DOPS team working at Reduc and elsewhere in Petrobras aimed to make the company "immune to extremist ideological infiltration" through a system of *ficharia*, or the production of confidential individual files. Throughout the months of April and May 1964, agents sent nearly daily updates regarding the climate at Reduc and the level of cooperation with the regime, as well as details about specific individuals identified as the most radical.[2] In those earliest days, there were records on about forty employees, all of whom were fired in the coming weeks and months. Those forty or so were, in turn, among more than thirteen hundred employees who were purged from the company nationwide in the first wave of crackdowns.

In numerous other cities and within other ministries and industries, scores of Brazilians found themselves targets of the regime and faced repression through actions taken to remove them from their jobs and positions. Many elected officials lost their mandates, labor leaders such as those at Reduc were pursued by the intelligence services, military personnel opposed to the coup were disciplined and often discharged, and civil servants throughout the bureaucracy were fired. Often the regime took such actions under arbitrary authority it granted itself in one or more of "institutional" or "complementary" acts, the first of which was enacted just days after the coup on April 9, 1964. Other times, as was the case for Ana Kucinski, bureaucracies dismissed employees under ordinary regulations.

The same bureaucratic logic that was applied in 1974 to justify rescinding Ana's contract at the University of São Paulo had in fact been used a decade earlier to purge employees from Reduc and elsewhere in Petrobras. Those at Reduc, a site of urgent national security concern for the military in 1964, were immediately targeted by the regime yet technically did not lose their jobs under the repressive apparatus. Rather, they were fired through the enforcement of ordinary regulations. Moments in the histories of three of them—Wilson, Francisco, and Newton, all of whom had been hired with the inauguration of Reduc during the second semester of 1961 and then fired in 1964 following the coup—provide a glimpse at some of the ways the regime's repression played out and the paths taken to forms of restitution. Of the three, Newton had the longest tenure with Petrobras at just three years and one month. He was an administrative assistant, Wilson was an auxiliary analyst, and Francisco was a machine operator. Fifteen years later, Wilson, Francisco, and Newton, together with the majority of the others previously under surveillance at Reduc, petitioned to return to their posts before a commission formed under the 1979 amnesty. The amnesty, as outlined in its first article, extended to any and all individuals who "had committed political crimes or crimes connected to them; had committed electoral crimes; had their political rights suspended; or had been punished by Institutional and Complementary Acts implemented during military regime."[3] Since, like Ana, the refinery workers were fired under internal employment regulations, often for absences from work after they went into hiding or were refused admission to the plant, the commission overwhelming refused to consider their petitions.

In October 1985, however, following the political transition to civilian governance and after more than twenty years away from their jobs, 528 former petroleum workers—or *petroleiros*, as they are known—including Wilson, Francisco, and Newton, were readmitted to their jobs at Petrobras.[4] Their "reintegration" followed an expansion of the amnesty through a constitutional amendment and was facilitated by a deal brokered with the new civilian government to address the particular situation of the petroleiros. Most did not stay but, rather, retired soon after returning with pensions adjusted to reflect years of service up to their retirement date. Years later, they also petitioned to the Amnesty Commission that was created in 2001. In fact, the petroleiros were among some of the earliest petitioners. For many of them, amnesty meant vindication and a recognition of the political motivation behind their dismissals. The pursuit of amnesty, in turn, was a central part of a larger struggle for labor rights, one for which they had organized and advocated over decades.

THE PETROLEUM INDUSTRY AND NATIONAL SECURITY FROM VARGAS TO THE 1964 COUP

Petrobras opened in 1954, the result of the most intense public policy debate since the dismantling of Getúlio Vargas's authoritarian Estado Novo and the democratization of 1945. The campaign surrounding the founding of Petrobras, titled "O petróleo é nosso!" (The petroleum is ours!), was emblematic of the larger nationalist turn in economic policies in Brazil and elsewhere following the global economic crisis of 1930. To be sure, the depression had hit Brazil hard. Its export-led economy suffered; coffee revenues alone dropped over 50 percent within four years after the crash. Economic recovery, it seemed, depended on insulating Brazil, as much as possible, from external shock. A plan for industrialization was the result. The petroleum industry, besides being a key motor for industrialization in its own right, held the added interest and responsibility of national security.[5]

The campaign for nationalizing the petroleum industry belonged, in many ways, to Vargas. In 1950, five years after accepting the military ultimatum to leave office or be deposed, Vargas returned to national politics and was elected president. Within a year he sent the Petrobras bill to Congress. The bill proposed a mixed public-private corporation (what would be called a "mixed-economy" company), with majority ownership in government hands and a state monopoly on drilling and new refineries. Existing refineries and distribution would remain under private ownership. Strongest in Rio de Janeiro, "The petroleum is ours!" campaign pitted the nationalists against those they called *entreguistas*, who would "hand over" the oil industry to American "imperialists." A fierce debate about establishing a mixed-economy oil company continued for two years and fueled intense nationalistic and explicitly anti-foreign sentiments that surpassed those expressed by Vargas. Although the campaign had grown more radical, Vargas reasserted his claim on it by signing the 1953 law creating Petrobras on the anniversary of the date on which he first assumed power in 1930.[6] Petrobras was, in the end, Vargas's attempt to balance nationalism and orthodoxy in economic policy.

If the campaign belonged to Vargas, the nascent company belonged to his legacy.[7] Petrobras opened in May 1954, in the midst of an increasingly untenable situation for Vargas. His ever more nationalistic statements coupled with the appointment of João Goulart to the Labor Ministry ultimately drew the battle lines between Vargas and his enemies. Goulart, a fellow native of Rio Grande do Sul, was a Vargas protégé and a young up-and-coming leader in the Partido Trabalhista Brasileiro (Brazilian Workers' Party), the major party of the left in Brazil and the prime base of support for Vargas. Populist support for Vargas increased in the early 1950s, but opposition festered within a newly empowered group of anti-communist military officers. Thomas Skidmore notes that these officers were particularly incensed when Goulart added to the populist fervor by proposing a significant increase in the minimum wage in February 1954. The focus on increasing workers' wages did not sit well with these officers, whose real salaries had taken a hit with surging inflation. They compared Goulart to Juan Perón, who had engineered a brief boom in the Argentine economy that was quickly followed by a seemingly bottomless economic crisis.[8]

To assuage critics from the middle class and stave off conspiracies brewing among members of the officer corps, Vargas fired Goulart before the end of the month. By May 1954, he nonetheless implemented a 100 percent increase in the minimum wage, larger even than what Goulart had proposed. In response, opposition to Vargas grew stronger than ever. It had been, in part, fueled by Carlos Larcerda, an influential Vargas critic who used his newspaper, *Tribuna de Imprensa*, to relentlessly criticize the president.[9] Lacerda was a leading voice in the União Democrática Nacional (National Democratic Union, UDN), which had been founded in 1945 as the opposition to Vargas and had become during the intervening years the main conservative party. Bryan McCann notes that in a play to middle-class fears, Lacerda reported in his columns that the minimum wage hike would mean that "office boys would earn almost as much as law school graduates."[10] In August 1954, one of Vargas's bodyguards tried to kill Lacerda. The failed assassination attempt nonetheless resulted in the murder of an air force officer who had been with Lacerda. Investigations by the air force quickly traced the murder to Vargas's staff, increasing an already unbearable political crisis for Vargas.[11] Military officers then delivered, as they had in 1945, an ultimatum: either he stepped down or he would be deposed. If they expected he would retreat, as he had in the impasse nearly a decade earlier, they miscalculated. Rather than step down, he committed suicide.

Figure 6.1. Reduc Refinery, 1961. The text reads, "We proudly deliver our first gasoline. Mission Accomplished. Other achievements will follow." Courtesy of CPDOC/FGV.

The outpouring of veneration for Vargas, seen by many as a victim and a martyr, set his opponents back on their heels. His suicide note condemned the coalition of international and national forces that allied to block "workers' guarantees" and the creation of Petrobras. He blamed "a subterranean campaign" for his defeat and ended by saying to all Brazilians that "I gave you my life. Now I offer my death."[12]

The more nationalistic forces took Vargas's final statement as a bequeathing of his legacy to them. Petrobras, for its part, became one of the key sectors of labor militancy and, as such, a continued target of anti-Vargas forces. Within Petrobras, the more radical nationalists organized to lobby for the total nationalization of the petroleum industry, including the refineries and distribution companies that had remained in private hands. During the construction of the Reduc refinery outside Rio de Janeiro in 1958, one such group established Movimento 2004 (Movement 2004) in a nod to Law no. 2004, which had established Petrobras.[13] The movement identified the more orthodox administrators as the main enemies of Petrobras, "destroying the company from within . . . by making incentives for corruption and embezzlement, suffocating the protests and criticisms of its patriotic workers with threats of dismissal, persecution and terror."[14] Movement 2004 joined the new trade unions in expanding pressure and strikes related to personnel decisions.

The unions gained significant ground when Goulart assumed the presidency after the unexpected resignation of Jânio Quadros in 1961. Quadros had been elected as the UDN candidate in 1960; his campaign symbol of a broom to sweep away corruption and lethargy resonated broadly.[15] His adherence to the UDN, however, was attenuated. Not long after assuming office in January 1961, Quadros seemed to veer away from economic austerity as the path to combat inflation. He also presented Che Guevara with the order of the Cruzeiro do Sul, the highest honor that can be bestowed on a foreigner. The gesture to honor the Argentine comrade of Fidel Castro infuriated Lacerda and UDN leaders. Rather than engage in a back-and-forth with his critics, Quadros stunned the nation by simply resigning in August 1961, a mere eight months after taking office. Quadros perhaps assumed that Congress would bring him back rather than allow Goulart, the vice president, to assume the mantle of the presidency. (Goulart had become vice president by running against the UDN candidate under election laws that allowed for split-ticket voting.) Congress, however, did not bring Quadros back.[16]

At the time of Quadros's resignation, Goulart was completing a goodwill tour of China. The possibility of his assumption of the presidency prompted key military leaders to move to block him. They warned that as Vargas's labor minister, Goulart had conspired to place "agents of international Communism" among union leadership. A countermovement organized by the Brazilian Workers' Party and emboldened by the muscle of Goulart's brother-in-law Leonel Brizola—who was then the governor of Rio Grande do Sul and who had an ally in the commander of the Third Army based in his state—forced the opposition to compromise. The compromise retained Goulart as the executive but reduced his power by shifting Brazil to a parliamentary system. In January 1963, a plebiscite returned Brazil to a presidential system, restoring full presidential power to Goulart.[17] Fifteen months later, in the events from March 31 to April 1, 1964, the military ousted him in a coup.

Between the establishment of the first union in 1958 and the military takeover in 1964, the ranks of Petrobras had nearly doubled, from 17,704 to 34,184 employees. Over 25,000 of them worked in and around Rio de Janeiro.[18] Among salary and personnel demands, the unions began to advocate for the takeover of the remaining private refineries. Tensions between the unions and the military escalated during the brief tenure of General Osvino Ferreira Alves as president of Petrobras. Named to the post by Goulart in January 1964, Alves, known as the "People's General," consistently allied with labor in internal disputes. The military grew increasingly concerned with the possibility of sabotage at a Petrobras plant and the general national security repercussions of the petroleum unions' strikes, a suspicion compounded by the trips of a few union leaders to Cuba and the Soviet Union in the preceding months. A rally staged by Goulart at the central station in Rio de Janeiro on March 13, 1964, marked a saturation point for the military. Among other measures, Goulart decreed the final steps toward nationalizing the remaining private refineries. Francisco and others from Reduc were there, among a crowd estimated to be between 150,000 to 250,000, many of whom were waving red flags.[19] Less than three weeks later, the military ousted Goulart, closed Congress, and took over Petrobras, including the Reduc refinery.

OPERATION "CLEAN UP," 1964

The military conspirators that ousted Goulart took immediate steps to redirect the political and economic course of Brazil. Reduc, a problematic and worrisome site for the military, was occupied immediately as part of the unfolding coup. Alves was detained in his office on March 31 and spent the next three months in prison. Initially, General Humberto de Alencar Castelo Branco, the first of what would be five military presidents over a twenty-one-year dictatorship, announced that he would simply finish Goulart's term, but then delayed the presidential elections scheduled for 1965.[20] Part of his strategy was to rule via institutional acts. The First Institutional Act (AI-1) was decreed on April 9, 1964, and empowered the regime to revoke the political mandates of elected officials and to suspend the political rights of any citizen for a period of ten years. Such actions—known as *cassação*, or cassation (removal or banning)—were explained as being in "the interest of peace and national honor."[21] They were also exempt from constitutional limits and judicial review. In addition to the attack on political rights, AI-1 also removed constitutional and legal guarantees related to job security and tenure in the military and public service, making the holders of such guarantees subject to being summarily fired or retired.

The very first list of *cassados*, or those subject to such cassation, included 122 military officers and 102 civilians. Goulart was among them, as were 41 representatives in the Chamber of Deputies; Luis Carlos Prestes, the leader of the PCB; Alves, the recently deposed president of Petrobras; and 29 labor leaders. Days later, another list included an additional 24 military officers and 67 more civilians. By the end of 1964, approximately 3,500 Brazilians had been punished under AI-1, including 980 members of the military.[22]

Even before the regime issued AI-1, purges were already underway within Petrobras. The first list of employees to be fired was issued on April 6, 1964. Over the coming months, military security personnel and

Petrobras leadership identified, tracked, and ultimately purged scores of employees. From the earliest days, the situation at Reduc seemed to frustrate the military security personnel. The DOPS, in fact, complained that the superintendent, Adalberto Mendes da Silva, proved ever "more and more useless" to DOPS and helpful to the "reds."[23] Into the month of May, the security agents reported that the "communists held control" of Reduc and pleaded for a new coordinator in Duque de Caxias, adding that knowledge of the petroleum industry should be a secondary qualification to a strong hand to "rid the area of communists."[24]

The DOPS kept close tabs on at least forty-six employees of Reduc, including Wilson, Francisco, and Newton. Among them, agents noted several "professional agitators"; many officers of the Sindipetro union; three members of "Movimento Comunista 2004"; three more, who had reportedly been to either Cuba or the Soviet Union, including Newton; and another three supposed hired assassins, or at least individuals "willing to take out fellow petroleiros for the cause." By May 1964, nine of these forty-six were in DOPS or other custody; the whereabouts of six were unknown; two had been prohibited from working, sent home, and told to wait until further notice; three were working; and the rest, ostensibly, remained under surveillance.[25]

The reluctant replacement for Mendes at Reduc, Roberto Coimbra, quickly asked to be relieved of his duties. In a lengthy letter making the request, he explained that he was first asked to take the post on April 22 but declined. The following day in a meeting with, among others, the new president of Petrobras, Marshal Ademar de Queiroz, Coimbra was "practically ordered to take it." He said that he made it clear, upon assuming the post on May 12, that his administration would not tolerate the insertion of politics in any internal matters at the plant. Less than three weeks later, he submitted his resignation in indignation. Over several pages, he explained what happened, beginning with the assertation that operations at Reduc had returned to normal during his brief tenure. He learned, however, that he was the target of a rumor planted among his employees by staff from the director's office at Petrobras. The rumor was that he would soon be replaced because of involvement in "political activities." The activities in question, he explained, involved the defense of a former colleague, "whose actions and service, and [whose] quality of character merited as much," after learning that the employee's name appeared on the second list of people who would be fired from Petrobras. Coimbra maintained that their work together preceding the military takeover had always been apolitical, and that his defense of this "good . . . enthusiastic, disciplined, honest and hard-working employee" was too. He lamented the economic hardship the individual would surely face since it would be "nearly impossible to find a job paying even 50 percent of the wages he made in Petrobras." He concluded, stating sharply, "we could not allow exemplary and innocent colleagues to be fired without doing anything in their defense. This is the minimum a MAN can do."[26]

The general climate of surveillance meant that intelligence work and investigatory cooperation could be demanded of any Petrobras employee. Indeed AI-1—in addition to providing for the dismissing, relieving of duty, or retiring of federal and other government employees—also provided for the creation of "General Commissions of Investigations" wherever required. On one day in mid-April, eighty-one Petrobras employees were ordered to appear before just such a commission.[27] Some employees, however, did not need to be compelled to support the cleansing operation underway. One disgruntled former employee, who was certain his anti-communist sentiments resulted in his dismissal a few months prior, enthusiastically offered his assistance in a letter to Queiroz. Upon his dismissal from Petrobras, the author of the letter "declared that he would one day return, perhaps with a machine gun, to retake the company from the communists." Since "the country was now in the hands of the true democrats," he explained that he was cooperating with DOPS and their affiliates within Petrobras "in the fight against the communists still at large." He also promised that upon Queiroz's inaugural arrival to the Petrobras presidency, he would be among security personnel "with a 32 tucked in his waist and ready to enter into action if necessary."[28]

WHAT WAS WRITTEN DOWN

Upon arrival at the helm of Petrobras, Queiroz acted quickly to effectuate dismissals.[29] Yet unlike the purges under AI-1, petroleiros overwhelmingly lost their jobs under ordinary worker regulations, many simply because they failed to appear at their posts. For example, one former high-ranking Petrobras executive reported via his wife and attorney that his political asylum in the Paraguayan Embassy prevented him from appearing at work. He therefore requested, citing labor laws, an extension of the requirement to appear or else lose his job. In response, a lawyer advising Petrobras granted that political asylum constituted a positive international right, but given the constitutionality of the ruling regime and its institutional acts, he could not see how "the exercise of the right of asylum might be invoked" to justify any such extension. Petrobras proceeded with the time line of the notification of his pending termination. He learned that he had been fired while he was still in the Paraguayan Embassy.[30]

The ordinary nature of their dismissal made petroleiros a somewhat exceptional case among those who lost their jobs under the military regime. As a sector of interest to national security, Petrobras and its employees fell well within the mandate of political policing, and many of the company's labor leaders were among key suspects in the military crackdown. The petroleiros, however, were also regular employees of a mixed-economy corporation subject to and protected by the consolidated labor legislation in force since the Vargas era.[31] This entanglement of overlapping legislation resulted in deeply politicized investigations of employees followed by totally depoliticized sanctions. A common situation involved individuals who were in jail, in hiding, or in exile being dismissed from their posts at Petrobras for absences constituting abandonment of their jobs.

In the immediate wake of the purges, leaders from the Associação dos Engenheiros da Petrobras (Association of Petrobras Engineers) in Rio de Janeiro met with the directors of Petrobras and pressed them on behalf of detained and dismissed employees and their families. They formally asked for details about the location of those in prison in order to inform and calm their families, a guarantee for the best possible treatment of those individuals, and a commitment to provide moral and material assistance to their families. Queiroz responded by stating he hoped that a climate of work and peace would soon be reestablished at Petrobras and he counted on the "strong voices" of these engineers to make known that there was neither persecution nor vendettas happening within Petrobras.[32]

Queiroz formulated a policy to handle dismissals, first with a memo in May 1964 and then with a formal resolution in September. In the May memo, Queiroz delineated three levels of subversion and the requisite authority that could so classify troublesome employees. In order of severity, the first included employees whose ideological commitments and subversive activities were in opposition to the company. The second included employees who were implicated in corruption or other administrative irregularities. The final category included employees who willfully or otherwise participated in activities "contrary to the interests of Petrobras." Only the Conselho de Segurança Nacional (National Security Council) could classify those falling into the first category, the latter two could be determined via recommendations of either the National Security Council or by Petrobras directors. In the September resolution, Queiroz established "definitive norms for the application of penalties to employees incriminated by their participation in ideological-subversive activities." Those norms involved the application of sanctions from existing labor regulations to any and all "employees incriminated in the investigations and commissions that brought to light participation in ideological-subversion and other grave irregularities contrary to or dis-

Figure 6.2. Ernesto Geisel (center foreground), Ademar de Queiroz (center behind), and others in a visit to Reduc, February 1971. Courtesy of CP-DOC/FGV.

tant from the objectives of the Company."[33] The resolution justified these measures on the basis that Petrobras was an industrial company whose functioning was in the interest of national security.

The forty-six petroleiros from Reduc who were initially targeted by the DOPS lost their jobs under this policy. Among them, Wilson, Newton, and Francisco were all fired between August and October of 1964. In their reporting, the DOPS described Wilson as "highly familiar with Marxism, a doctrinaire," as well as "polite and cultured." They noted that he was "always present at strikes" and in fact had incited strikes and intensely promoted Marxism with the aim of recruiting "for the cause."[34] He was fired at the end of August. By the time Wilson was fired, Newton had become a suspect in a DOPS investigation of the infiltration of unions to make them "focuses of subversion." The inquest concluded that Newton was in violation of national security law and recommended preventative detention. In October he was fired from Petrobras. For his part, Francisco, in addition to his participation on the March 13 Goulart rally, reportedly had close ties to Max da Costa Santos, a representative in the Chamber of Deputies who had been purged from Congress in the first wave of actions taken by the military against oppositional legislators. The DOPS also noted that Francisco was once absent for thirty days without notice during which time he went to the northeast to "promote agitation." He was fired from his post as a machine operator at the end of September.[35]

Asked decades later about the ordinary dismissal of petroleiros in the months following the military takeover, Ernesto Geisel, who during the 1970s was both the president of Petrobras and then the fourth of five military presidents, remembered that Queiroz had been a particularly "conspicuous conspirator." According to Geisel, Queiroz surprised his colleagues when he refused to utilize the regime's institutional acts to fire workers from Petrobras. Instead, he looked for justifiable bases in ordinary labor regulations, which he thought may be even better suited to address the problem of radicalized labor in the petroleum industry. Suspecting that "in a few years, an amnesty will come allowing those punished by the Institutional Act to come back," he surmised "through the [labor laws] it would be more difficult."[36] Indeed it was.

THE 1979 AMNESTY

The men targeted and fired in 1964 at Reduc—and they were all men—had lost their jobs when they were still young. Their average age at that time was thirty-four, which made them nearly fifty when the regime sent a proposed amnesty to Congress in 1979. The proposal—sent by General João Figueiredo, the son of Euclides Figueiredo and the fifth and final president of the military regime—was the regime's response to an impressive civilian movement that had emerged and united disparate opposition.[37] The amnesty campaign itself became the emblematic movement for broader democratization and in many ways signaled the reentry of civil society into political life.

The earliest social organization focused exclusively on amnesty was the Movimento Feminino pela Anistia (Women's Movement for Amnesty). It formed in 1974 and was spearheaded by Terezinha Godoy Zerbine, an attorney and the wife of a general who had been purged under AI-1. By 1977 the group was publishing a newsletter, which they named *Maria Quitéria*, in homage to the early nineteenth-century woman who, passing as a man, joined the Brazilian army to fight in the 1822 War of Independence.[38] Exiles also organized; a group in Portugal set up the Comitê Pró-Anistia Geral do Brasil (Pro-General Amnesty Committee of Brazil), and similar groups formed in Sweden, France, and Italy.[39] The Comitê Brasileiro pela Anistia (Brazilian Committee for Amnesty) then formed in 1978 to provide coordination for the various groups, which coalesced around a demand for a "broad, general, and unrestricted" amnesty. At the committee's nationwide conferences in São Paulo in 1978 and in Salvador in 1979, a number of professional organizations pledged their support for amnesty on behalf of their colleagues who had lost their positions or had their careers derailed for ideological reasons during the military regime. Among them were the national associations of architects, bankers, and lawyers, to name but a few. Key civil society organizations, including the Ordem dos Advogados do Brasil (Brazilian Bar Association), the Associação Brasileira de Imprensa (Brazilian Press Association), the Catholic Church, and the Sociedade Brasileira para o Progresso da Ciência (Brazilian Society for Scientific Progress) formally adopted amnesty as a central tenet of their missions by 1978. An international conference for "Amnesty in Brazil" had just written a resolution when the regime announced its amnesty proposal in 1979.[40]

What came to be seen as a doctrine of Brazilian amnesty was developed in a number of books published in 1978 and 1979.[41] Members of Congress recited some passages from these books verbatim during the debates over the proposed amnesty. Roberto Ribeiro Martins, a journalist and former political prisoner, elaborated on five centuries of political conciliation in Brazil, dating back to the conquest, to make a case for a tradition of and imperative for amnesty in *Liberdade para os brasileiros* (Liberty for Brazilians). Speaking for the Brazilian Bar Association, José Ignacio Ferreira, an attorney and politician purged under AI-1, referenced fifty-six previous political amnesties in Brazil in a book entitled *Anistia, caminho e solução* (Amnesty, path and solution). In *O poder da graça* (The power of grace), Railda Saraiva de Moraes emphasized the collective nature of amnesty as distinct from other forms of executive pardon and, thus, its potential for national reconciliation.[42] Together with the broader social mobilization, these works added to public pressure for amnesty that in many ways forced the regime to acquiesce, which it did, but on its own terms.

The proposed amnesty sparked a number of debates and an intense period of campaigning and protests before being signed into law in late August 1979. The most salient debate centered on the exclusion from the amnesty of certain "common" crimes and, therefore, of a subsection of the opposition. A related debate focused on the implicit inclusion of other crimes described as "connected" to political crimes, which many feared would be interpreted to include torture and the state agents who had been complicit in such gross human rights abuses.[43] Both the protested exclusion and the controversial inclusion of crimes under the scope of the amnesty were stipulated in its first article. The next several articles set out the terms for the possible reinstatement of civil servants and military personnel who had been fired, retired, or otherwise separated from their posts and included setting up special commissions to review petitions for such reintegration. The first article, however, dominated the attention of the broader public and thus the congressional committee responsible for reviewing the proposed law and any possible amendments to it.

As proposed in article 1, the amnesty extended to all who, during the period from September 2, 1961, to December 31, 1978, "committed political crimes or crimes connected to them" and to those who had their political rights suspended or were punished on the "basis of the Institutional and Complementary Acts."[44] The two subsections of article 1 contained, respectively, the possible inclusion of state agents who had been complicit in human rights violations and the overt exclusion of a small sector of the opposition who had been convicted of specific crimes. The first subsection defined the reference to "connected" crimes included in the amnesty as being of any nature "related to political crimes" or committed because of "political motivation." The second subsection specified that anyone convicted for crimes of terrorism, robbery, kidnapping, or assault were excluded from the amnesty.[45]

In response, many who had been advocating for amnesty argued that both situations were antithetical to true amnesty. The issue of the exclusion of certain crimes, however, overshadowed the possible inclusion of others, especially after fourteen prisoners in Rio de Janeiro who would be among those excluded from the amnesty began a highly publicized hunger strike in protest, which grew to include other prisoners in other states.[46] Some politicians then lobbied on their behalf, making the most of both the international disfavor for the excesses of the military regimes throughout the Southern Cone and the political capital of appeals to principles of human rights and democracy. These efforts went some distance in subverting the narrative of the regime, which emphasized the amnesty as a grand gesture of conciliation that would welcome home thousands of exiles, to one that shone a spotlight on the several dozens of individuals who had been left out. In the Senate, the president of the committee responsible to review the proposed amnesty law, Teotônio Vilela, followed the lead of the social movements and adopted the mantra of a "broad, general and unrestricted" amnesty. He traveled to visit the prisoners over the congressional break, which resulted in an accusation by the minister of justice that he was "desperate for publicity."[47] Press coverage of his visits nonetheless helped soften public perceptions about the prisoners. The regime had framed them as "terrorists," but some narratives of their hunger strike and visits by members of Congress described them as political prisoners who had participated in armed struggle against an oppressive regime.[48]

The regime supported its exclusion based on the nature of the crimes themselves and consistently emphasized the scope of those covered by the amnesty, especially the "five thousand exiles" who would be able to return home. Early discussions mentioned that the amnesty would include 166 Brazilians who were still under AI-1's ten-year suspension of their political rights, as well as 960 who had already completed their suspension. Within the armed forces, the amnesty would cover 1,261 who had been purged under the institutional acts. Individuals who had been convicted of crimes, however, fell into two categories: 1,729 who had committed "political crimes" would receive the benefit of amnesty; 195 who were convicted of so-called blood crimes would not.[49] In a gesture of goodwill, the government all but guaranteed a pardon by Christmas for those excluded.[50]

In a formal tally just weeks after it was enacted, the amnesty reportedly excluded a total of 450 individuals. Their names were catalogued in a forty-two-page government report and noted the charge for which they had been convicted, the sentence imposed, and the court. Among them was Ines Etienne Romeu, the lone survivor of the House of Death in Petrópolis, where Ana Kucinski had been tortured to death. There was also a list of 1,259 individuals whose crimes were included in the amnesty. This list noted each person's case number and the court before which they had appeared.[51] Among those named as amnestied were Dilma Rousseff, who would later be elected to two terms as president of Brazil, and José Genoíno, who was among the founders and would serve as president of the Partido dos Trabalhadores (Workers' Party) during the party's rise and tenure in power. During the dictatorship, both belonged to clandestine organizations involved in armed resistance and both were captured, tortured, and convicted of crimes.[52]

It is not clear if any similar lists were generated after the enactment of the amnesty law to account for those who had been fired, retired, or otherwise separated from their posts—at least not until 2000, when the Chamber of Deputies compiled just such a list.[53] Indeed, the public focus on the urgent issues surrounding the hunger strike, and the accompanying opportunity to condemn the regime on human rights grounds, obscured other exclusions of the amnesty and other sectors that had been the target of persecution and repression, among them the petroleiros. During the two months from the proposal of the amnesty to its enactment on August 28, 1979, few amendments to the bill addressed the issue of and the process for restitution to bureaucratic and military careers. As proposed, the amnesty law would grant civil servants and military personnel a period of 120 days to petition to return to their former posts. If granted, petitioners would return to the same position or job held on the date of his/her dismissal. Their return, however, would be conditioned on the existence of vacancies and/or the "interest of the administration." Those who did not petition or whose petitions were denied would be considered retired. The time in which they were separated from their positions would count toward their pensions.[54]

The proposed amendments to these articles sought to include broader sectors of society and to strike the requirement of case-by-case review, aiming to make readmission both uniform and automatic. Support came from various sources. An association founded in early July in Rio Grande do Sul, under the telling acronym AMPLA, which means "broad" and therefore called further attention to the slogan for a "broad, general, and unrestricted amnesty," advocated for "ex-officio" reintegration that would be independent of availability of positions.[55] Seeing the uphill battle facing the amendments, Representative Marcelo Linhares submitted an entirely separate bill proposing "reintegration, pure and simple." His bill echoed one of the proposed amendments to the amnesty but took amnesty, "whether coming from the initiative of the Executive or otherwise," out of the equation. The language addressed what he described as the "technical-juridical error" in which employees of mixed-economy companies like Petrobras had been fired under normal labor regulations rather than through one of the institutional acts. The petroleiros supported Linhares's bill, pointing out that it reached the same ends as the amendments to the proposed amnesty but without restrictions and ambiguities.[56] Linhares's proposal would never become law. But in intense sessions of voting in late August 1979, and with few modifications to the original proposal, the Brazilian Congress passed—and Figueiredo signed—the amnesty law.[57]

THE AMNESTY COMMISSIONS, 1980

It did not take long for the special commission established in Petrobras under the 1979 amnesty to deny the majority of the petitions filed by former employees. Perhaps aware of the likely outcome, only 337 applied to return to the posts from which they had been purged. Of those, the commission approved just 7 (2 percent) for return to Petrobras, all of whom had been the subject of direct requests by current administrators. The committee refused to consider 289 (86 percent), including the petitions of Francisco and Wilson, because they had not lost their jobs as a result of the enforcement of any of the regime's institutional or complementary acts and therefore fell outside the scope of the amnesty. The commission granted retirement to the remaining 41 (12 percent), one of whom was Newton. The petitions of the 41 granted retirement technically fit the scope of the amnesty, but the committee cited "lack of administrative interest" in having them return to work.[58] Soon after, both Wilson and Francisco were nonetheless similarly retired. For Francisco, it happened through an intervention by the Ministry of Labor in 1981 that "amnestied" him and other former union directors and representatives. Because the action had been taken under the amnesty law, their retirements were designated as "exceptional."[59]

Commissions in other agencies and departments similarly ruled on petitions from former employees to return to their posts. In the Ministry of Transportation, of 300 petitions reviewed, 30 individuals were approved to return to work while 230 were placed in retirement status. The remaining 40, the commission found, "had nothing to do with the amnesty."[60] In the Ministry of Justice (see chapter 7), of 146 petitions reviewed only nine returned to their previously held jobs, while thirteen were denied. The rest were granted retirement, including three cases in which the resulting pensions went to the widows of the former employees.[61] In the Ministry of Agriculture, as of the end of March 1980, seventeen former employees had been "amnestied" and another twenty-one were still under consideration. Notably, the seventeen had not requested that they return to their posts. As such, they were formally retired, with the time since their dismissal included in their pensions. Four of the seventeen were already deceased so the benefits went to their dependents.[62] Also by March 1980, the navy released information about the first list of amnestied former personnel, which included twenty-one officers, fifty enlisted personnel, and twenty-five civilians. None of them, however, returned to service because they had all "surpassed the age limit."[63]

Perhaps the most striking aspect about the various commissions was not so much the outcomes but the across-the-board low rate of applicants. If, in just the initial months of the regime, more than 1,300 petroleiros lost their job, and those numbers reached nearly 5,000 by the end of the regime, it is difficult to ignore the fact that only 337 total former employees filed paperwork with the commission. Though arguably many knew it would be a losing battle, the numbers of applicants to other commissions handling petitions for amnesty were similarly quite low. In addition to the 146 to the Ministry of Justice and 300 to Transportation, the data reported on applications among former military members cited just 300 from the army, 400 from the air force, and 500 from the navy. This was true in spite of the fact that a full 44 percent of those immediately purged by the military regime had been military members.

The ranks of the purged from the military swelled to total nearly 7,500 during the dictatorship.[64]

For many former military personnel, the amnesty process instituted under the 1979 law began poorly and devolved into an exercise in humiliation. They resented the requirement that they affirmatively had to petition for reinstatement. If granted, the military placed them in the rank they held at the time of their expulsion. Such reinstatements, while viewed as demeaning, were also few. Most eligible for amnesty were informed that there were no vacancies available to them. Those officially retired under the amnesty law were granted time counted since their expulsion. They found this concession frustrating, however, because the pension was modest and associated with the lower rank they had held. In comparison with what was accorded their peers who had not been purged, it was a pittance.[65]

A subset among former military personnel—namely, members of the Associação de Marinheiros and Fuzileiros Navais do Brasil (Association of Brazilian Sailors and Marines)—found themselves in a situation quite similar to that of the petroleiros.[66] Like the petroleiros, these lower-ranking members had not been purged under one of the institutional acts but, rather, on grounds of misconduct. In the weeks and months leading up to the coup, they had been watched with increasing suspicion and had been subjected to harsher discipline. A decade earlier, many of the members had also participated in the campaign "The petroleum is ours!" In March 1964, several members of the association had hoped to include a visit to Reduc as part of a planned rally to commemorate the second anniversary of its founding and to demonstrate solidarity among military and labor sectors of society.

The then president of Petrobras, Alves, supported the visit of the sailors to Reduc, even offering buses to transport them to Duque de Caxias. Pressed by the navy command, however, he later advised the association's leadership that the visit could not go forward. The entire program was ultimately canceled on order of the high command. Many defied the order and held a rally at the headquarters of the Sindicato dos Metalúrgicos (Metalworkers Union) in Rio de Janeiro on March 25, 1964. More than a thousand people attended. In an effort to link the rally to a history of righteous revolt, the organizers invited João Cândido, the leader of the 1910 Revolt of the Lash. Cândido, then eighty-four years old, attended. An escalation between the association and the military hierarchy over the next few days came to be known as the "Rebellion of the Sailors" and is considered one of the key fuses that set off the military coup against Goulart after he intervened on the sailors' behalf.[67]

Once the military ousted Goulart, a total of 1,123 who had taken part in the sailors' rebellion were named as subjects of internal investigations. More than 250 of them were subsequently convicted and sentenced to more than five years of prison. All of them were dismissed from military service for indiscipline.[68] After their petitions for amnesty were denied by the commission in the navy, a group of them filed a security measure with the Federal Supreme Court aiming to compel the military to reincorporate them. In a July 1981 decision, the judge ruled against them. Their attorneys complained that the judge opposed amnestying the sailors because they were not among "important sectors of society" and did not have any "political weight."[69]

Frustration and dissatisfaction with the efficacy of the amnesty continued for the remainder of the military regime and beyond. In one report concerning 407 military officers, only 38 had technically not been "amnestied" by 1985, but none had returned to active duty. A summary of other data as of May 1985 calculated that 11,434 individuals who had been sanctioned under the repressive acts had not yet been amnestied. In a partial report of 5,153 civilians among them, only 219 had returned to work by 1985, and 332 had been retired under the amnesty law. This left 4,730 designated as "unamnestied," many of whom were former petroleiros. An estimate by a group compiling data about the total number of individuals whose rights were impacted by the regime reached 54,000. The group acknowledged, however, the inability to substantiate the estimate since "the majority of those affected did not petition for amnesty."[70]

Luiz Greenhalgh, the former president of the Brazilian Committee for Amnesty in São Paulo and a sought-after attorney for matters related to the amnesty law, reported that 90 percent of purged civil servants in São Paulo had not been "amnestied" by late October 1985. The 10 percent who had were affiliated with universities and had gone back to work. Among military personnel, Greenhalgh said only 5 percent had been "amnestied," noting that they obtained their amnesty through the courts and not through any of the commissions. In fact, Greenhalgh complained, the armed forces denied all petitions, "no matter what the particular situation of a military member was," with the same stamp. The stamp came to be referred to as IPFAL, as shorthand for *Indeferido por falta de Amparo Legal*, which means "denied for lack of legal standing."[71] The União dos Militares Não-Anistiados (Union of Non-Amnestied Military Members) circulated a dossier at that same time naming the individuals who had been expelled by AI-1 but who were not yet amnestied, noting that under the amnesty law the lower-level personnel were the least likely to be reintegrated to the military. Perhaps matters were marginally better for officers; among nearly seven thousand low-level soldiers who had been expelled from the armed forces, just over four hundred had been amnestied, but only thirty-four had returned to duty.[72]

AMNESTY AS REINTEGRATION, 1985

Former petroleiros also continued to protest what they characterized as their virtual total exclusion from the guarantees of amnesty. In a letter to Figueiredo, they described the amnesty process in Petrobras as "humiliating and unacceptable." Accusing the amnesty commission of acting in bad faith, they enumerated a list of demands, which included reinstatement, promotions, and retirement benefits.[73] The former petroleiros quickly formed their own amnesty commission, the Comissão Nacional dos Anistiados da Petrobras (National Commission of the Amnestied of Petrobras, CONAPE), which was operating informally by 1979. After years of advocacy, the commission formalized itself as a civil society organization with a different name but with the same acronym.[74] Other collectives also established advocacy groups to secure rights through amnesty, including the Associação dos Militares Cassados (Association of Banned Military Members), which first formed in 1980 and then became the Associação Democrática e Nacionalista dos Militares (Democratic and Nationalistic Association of Military Members) in 1983.[75]

One of CONAPE's earliest and most formidable leaders was Mário Lima, the founder of the first union of petroleum workers in Salvador, Bahia. At the time of the military takeover, he was twenty-nine years old and serving as a federal deputy. Hearing that there had been scuffles in the occupation of the Petrobras refinery in Bahia, he reportedly asked security personnel there to let him confirm the safety of the workers. Instead, they detained him, alleging that he intended to sabotage the plant.[76] Lima spent the next eight months in prison. In August 1964, a notice appeared in the local paper announcing that Lima, together with eight others, had been "fired with just cause" from Petrobras. The notice appeared in the newspaper because the employees, many of whom were labor leaders, could not be located either at their job sites or at "the residence on record with the company."[77]

In September 1964, Lima was among the high-profile prisoners that Geisel, then the military chief of staff, visited in the northeast. Geisel reported that they did not hear any complaints about treatment from any of the prisoners and that no political prisoners were being tortured.[78] While incarcerated, Lima learned that he was doubly punished under AI-1. Together with more than 350 others (including Luis Carlos Prestes, whose name appeared first on a list that was published in the *Diário Oficial* in November 1965), Lima's political rights were suspended for a period of ten years. Lima was also one of more than one hundred who lost their legislative mandates at the same time. Lima was subsequently convicted for having led a work stoppage at Petrobras while he was president of the union, an act that constituted a national security crime under the dictatorship. He served another twenty-two months in prison, from August 1970 through October 1971.[79]

Within a decade Lima was representing CONAPE in meetings with high-level politicians to press for the benefits of amnesty for the 289 petroleiros whose petitions had been dismissed by the special commission. In 1980 he met with the minister of Mines and Energy, aiming to persuade this minister to press Figueiredo to readmit the petroleiros by decree. By February 1981 he had a commitment from the Ministry of Justice and the Ministry of Mines and Energy to work on a solution in the near term.[80] Lima argued that the 289 had been dismissed for political reasons and that Petrobras had said as much in a press release aiming to "clarify" to the public the "application of penalties" within the company in the months following the coup. Petrobras reported that, by October 1964, 526 employees had been fired, specifying that they were "incriminated by their participation in ideological-subversive activities or implicated in other grave irregularities contrary to the objectives of an industrial company of national security interest." All of those implicated from Bahia, Lima reported to the local press, had been cleared in subsequent investigations. "Only in rare cases," the company explained, "when the employee was a threat to the activities of Petrobras . . . was the Institutional Act applied."[81]

In the midst of this political advocacy, Lima also took his own case to court. In April 1982, a federal court granted him a security measure that enabled him to return to his former positions in Petrobras. Under the amnesty law, he had petitioned to return both as president of the Sindipetro union and to his post in the refinery in Bahia. Like those for whom he advocated, his petition was denied because he had not been fired under one of the institutional acts. When he asked that the ruling be reconsidered, he was made eligible for retirement. In his request for the security order, Lima noted that he was only forty-six years old and capable of doing the work both physically and mentally.[82]

Lima's lawsuit coincided with steps in the incremental transition from dictatorship to democracy in Brazil. Elections of state governors by popular vote were held later in 1982. Direct elections for mayors of state capitals were held in 1985. This phased return of elections by popular vote was part of the military's carefully engineered and tightly controlled plan to exit politics. Notably, the military plan rejected a popular election for the presidency. The insistence on the indirect election of the next president—via votes in Congress only—faced an impressive opposition

movement. Beginning in 1983 with a proposed constitutional amendment, the "Diretas, já!" (Direct elections now!) movement included many
of the same individuals and entities who had campaigned for amnesty.[83]

Efforts also continued to broaden the reach of the 1979 amnesty law.
One proposal, which became known as the Célio Borja project after the
representative who drafted it, seemed reasonable to most. Indeed, it had
been approved by the relevant committees in both the Chamber of Deputies and the Senate. The project would amend the 1979 law to facilitate
the return of civil servants and military personnel who had been prosecuted but ultimately absolved by the courts. Figueiredo vetoed it.[84] One
response letter appealed to Figueiredo as the son of the "illustrious General Euclydes de Figueiredo," although to no avail. The letter, in fact,
quoted from a 1946 speech in Congress in which the elder Figueiredo
declared that he was "in favor of broad and unrestricted amnesty." In his
speech, he criticized the incompleteness of the 1945 amnesty, which had
left "soldiers in misery, children of soldiers who don't go to school because they don't have shoes or even bread for lunch, [and] . . . humiliated
sergeants working as street sweepers." The rulings of the commissions
that followed the 1945 amnesty, the elder Figueiredo complained, had
left so many struggling to make ends meet and unable to "attend to their
families with dignity."[85]

Such was the climate in which Lima pressed for resolution of the
situation of the petroleiros. He had the ear of Tancredo Neves, the
emerging front-runner candidate for the presidency. Tancredo and Lima
had served together in the Chamber of Deputies prior to the military
regime.[86] In October 1984, Lima took the opportunity to press the issue
with Tancredo at a dinner in Brasília. Tancredo's running mate, the conservative José Sarney, also attended the dinner, as did Jorge Vianna, then
a representative representing the state of Bahia. Vianna remembered that
Lima expressed to Tancredo "the concerns of all those punished by the
military regime with the loss of employment . . . whose condition as amnestied had yet to be recognized by Petrobras and other institutions."
According to Vianna, Tancredo committed to focus on a solution for the
"problem of amnesty." By 1985 Tancredo had been elected, but he fell
seriously ill the day before his scheduled inauguration and died a short
time later. Lima met with Sarney after he assumed the presidency to ask
that he honor Tancredo's informal commitment to resolve the situation
of amnestied petroleiros. Sarney said he remembered the conversation
and intended to fulfill Tancredo's plan.[87]

During this first year under civilian rule, Congress also passed a
constitutional amendment to convoke a national constituent assembly.
The amendment convened the assembly for February 1987, and the new

constitution it drafted entered into effect in 1988. The fourth article of the 1985 amendment, however, had more immediate effect. It reaffirmed the terms of the 1979 amnesty as extending to civil servants and military personnel punished by the various acts of the regime and expanded it in two important directions. First, it included civil servants who had been fired for political reasons but based on legal mechanisms other than the institutional and complementary acts. Second, it explicitly included labor and student organizations. The amendment also—and importantly—stated that civil servants and military personnel would be granted promotions in their retirement to the post, position, or rank that they would have had the opportunity to achieve had they remained in active service. Also left open, but to the discretion of individual administrations, was the possibility of readmission and return to active duty.[88]

This accounting for not just what had been but for what might have been took fuller shape in an article of the Ato das Disposições Constitucionais Transitórias (Constitutional Transitional Provisions Act) of the 1988 constitution and would change the calculus of amnesty to make amends for lost opportunity. The measure aimed to remedy the situations of scores of civil servants and military personnel, like the petroleiros, who had lost their posts for political reasons but whose circumstances did not fit within the parameters of the 1979 law.[89] It was then further institutionalized in subsequent laws. In 1992 a decree provided for an "exceptional pension of the amnestied," which in practice reached sectors among former government employees. In 1995 another decree established the Comissão Especial de Anistia (Special Commission of Amnesty) in the Ministry of Labor, which was tasked with reviewing cases from the private sector, mixed-economy companies like Petrobras, and union representatives.[90] The same year, the Law of the Disappeared laid the groundwork for the establishment of a framework of reparations, first for surviving relatives of victims of the regime and then, with the establishment of the Amnesty Commission in 2001, for those who had been purged from their posts.[91]

Before the formulation of that new calculus, the right to return to one's former post was widely considered, in symbolic terms, the gold standard of amnesty. Everything short of readmission was deemed only partial amnesty—and most fell short. One exception was a group of former members of São Paulo's Força Pública (Public Force) and Guarda Civil (Civil Guard) who lost their positions in 1974 and 1975. Although those units had been disbanded by the time the amnesty law came into effect, the group of former employees were reincorporated into the Polícia Militar (Military Police). They did not, however, remain in their positions for long. Most, in fact, returned to duty for just a few weeks but nonetheless thought it important to obtain the full benefit of the law. The petroleiros also pursued "reintegration" as a matter of principle. As the contours of a deal to reconsider amnesty petitions were beginning to take shape, CONAPE reminded its members that "to return does not mean you have to stay."[92]

The deal that took shape had been facilitated by Aureliano Chaves, the minister of Mines and Energy. He established a new amnesty commission to review claims for readmission. By 1986, the average age of the petroleiros who had been under surveillance by the DOPS at Reduc was fifty-five. In the first instance, 436 petroleiros were readmitted, 77 to Reduc alone. Within months, the ranks of *anistiados*, as they could then consider themselves, reached 528, and only 15 petitions had been denied by the commission.[93] Within a year, the number of readmitted petroleiros reached 724, and included Francisco, Wilson, and Newton. Wilson would remain in his new post for just ten months, but Francisco and Newton stayed on for five years.[94] The majority of the others among the 46 that had been under surveillance at Reduc, as well as the executive who had sought asylum in the Paraguayan Embassy, were likewise among those that returned to positions at Petrobras.[95] At the event commemorating the return of these "*companheiros*," Chaves emphasized the conciliatory nature of amnesty, stating that, "amnesty is less in the law and more in the heart of each person."[96] But it is, of course, also in the law.

AMNESTY AS REPARATIONS

By the time Wilson, Francisco, and Newton were in or nearing their seventies in the early 2000s, the national Amnesty Commission had been established and was reviewing thousands of petitions for the benefits provided under the new law. In those earliest days, the commission issued its rulings on letterhead that read: *anistia, a comissão de paz!* (amnesty, the commission of peace!). Its various rulings specified that the amnesty granted represented "economic reparation of an indemnifying nature." Wilson, Francisco, and Newton all submitted their paperwork to the commission in 2002. Each submission included hundreds of pages of supporting documentation ranging from salary scales to tables outlining the recategorization of positions, and copies of previous agreements that had been reached within Petrobras over the question of amnesty. By August 2004, their cases, along with that of Mário Lima, were among a total of 932 involving former employees of state and mixed-economy companies, the majority of which were from Petrobras, that had been approved by the commission.[97]

By 2015 the directorate of CONAPE confirmed that 370 of their members had successfully petitioned to the Amnesty Commission, al-

though by then half were deceased.[98] The organization's website featured
a banner stating: "since 1979, in defense of the politically amnestied
and pensioners."[99] Their tally, more than fifty years after the coup and
thirty-five years after the amnesty law, included many who were among
the forty-some initially targeted at Reduc. The reparations approved
for these individuals typically provided and accounted for a promotion
within their particular career path. It also granted what previous amnesty laws had expressly denied—that is, retroactive payments. The law
establishing the commission, in fact, affirmatively guaranteed such payments dating back to October 5, 1988, when the new constitution came
into effect. These payments were paid in a lump sum and accounted for
any differential in the amount of monthly pension previously paid. For
those approved, their rulings from the Amnesty Commission explained
that any prior retirement arrangements were to be replaced with the new
"juridical framework" of reparations.[100]

In the intervening years, the work and vision of the Amnesty Commission evolved. It developed parallel to, but apart from, mechanisms
of transitional justice put in place elsewhere in Latin America. Human
rights related prosecutions became increasingly normative in the region,
but Brazil institutionalized and expanded forms of reparations. Over
time, the commission faced harsh criticism by both friend and foe, especially over the total value of some of the economic reparations granted.
The highest among the values caused a polemic and attracted acute and
lasting attention, much of which focused on former employees of Petrobras who had long been considered a privileged workforce. Of the 932
above-mentioned cases approved by August 2004, 35 involved former
Petrobras employees who had been found to have a right to retroactive
indemnity of more than one million reais, which was equivalent of between three hundred thousand and five hundred thousand US dollars at
that time. The retroactive payment was in addition to the "permanent,
continuing and monthly" reparations, which were themselves commensurate with pensions from high-salary jobs.[101]

By 2015, and amid the unfolding of the *lavo jato* ("car wash") investigation that was exposing staggering corruption at and through Petrobras, the newspaper *O Globo* reported that seventy of the one hundred
largest indemnities granted by the Amnesty Commission had been paid
to former Petrobras employees. Most had been approved between the
years of 2004 and 2005. The highest, a former senior engineer, had been
approved for thirty-eight thousand reais monthly, or the equivalent of
approximately fourteen thousand US dollars at that time. The sum, however, exceeded the ceiling for civil servants and was adjusted accordingly.[102] The criticism of the largest sums drew attention to the ways in

which the reparations replicated, and therefore exacerbated, economic disparities. At the same time, the criticism gave short shift to the many cases with more modest settlements and ignored altogether those that did not result in any economic reparation.

A related polemic brought attention to the dual tracks for reparations under the Amnesty Commission. One track handled the cases filed by those seeking restitution based on the impact that acts of repression by the dictatorship had on their economic livelihood, as the petroleiros had done. The other track handled the cases filed by those entitled to restitution for repression, often in its most egregious forms, but in ways not directly associated to their work. These cases included the scores of individuals who lost their political rights or who had been tortured and/or detained. In striking ways, the repression meted out under the infamous Fifth Institutional Act (AI-5), issued in late 1968, brings to the fore the distinct but simultaneous forms of repression during the dictatorship as well as the subsequent and parallel forms of reparations. Taken together, the two types of cases adjudicated by the Amnesty Commission show the extent to which Brazil relied on amnesty to remedy past injustices and the efficacy of the institution to do so.

CHAPTER 7

TWO LONG SHADOWS

AI-5 and the Federal Police in São Paulo, 1970s–2000s

A twenty-five-year veteran of police work, João was forty-seven years old on the day in August 1973 when he was fired under the infamous Fifth Institutional Act (AI-5). His name appeared in newspapers among forty-three employees of the federal police in São Paulo who were ousted by orders of the third military president of the dictatorship, Emílio Garrastazu Médici.[1] According to the press reports, João and the other agents had been dismissed because of their involvement in corruption and extortion. The purge followed a lengthy investigation that amassed hundreds of pages of materials, all of which was duly catalogued in a ten-volume case file. The lead investigator concluded that the group constituted a veritable criminal gang within the federal police and recommended that action be taken against them under AI-5.[2] What followed was one of a handful of such purges of federal police agents in the 1970s.

After Congress passed the amnesty law in 1979, João and dozens of his former colleagues filed petitions to a special commission within the Ministry of Justice requesting readmission to their former jobs, just as the petroleiros ousted in the earliest waves of repression had done. Unlike the petroleiros, the former federal police agents did not have a history of political or labor militancy. Indeed, they worked for one of the agencies that was complicit in political persecution during the military regime. Nonetheless, their situations more clearly fit the parameters of the amnesty law as they had been fired on the authority of one of the institutional acts instead of on ordinary labor regulations as the petroleiros had been. The outcomes of their petitions, however, had some similarities. The initial commission that reviewed the requests from the federal police following the amnesty, just as the one in Petrobras, determined that it was not in the interest of the department to readmit the former employees. A second review of their cases in 1986, following the affirmation and extension of the amnesty law through a constitutional amendment in 1985, came to the same conclusion, noting that their prior conduct made them unfit for police work. The petroleiros were denied on a technicality, but the commission reviewing the amnesty petitions of the former police agents recognized them as beneficiaries because of the manner in which they had been fired. Yet, rather than granting their readmission to the force, the commission placed them in retirement status. For some, adjustments to their pensions followed, often as the result of lawsuits.

In 2001, when the federal government created the Amnesty Commission, many of the former agents again filed petitions. A few, in fact, were among the earliest to file, out of what would eventually total more than seventy-five thousand cases.[3] Rather than reintegration as federal agents, as was requested to the commissions in the 1980s, this time many of the former agents requested adjustments to their retirement pensions and retroactive restitution at the top of their career track. The law establishing the commission permitted just such adjustments to account for what might have been had acts of repression not interrupted their lives and livelihoods. Although resolution of many of their cases took years (and in João's case extended beyond his death), the commission eventually affirmed their status as politically amnestied and, in some of the cases, also paid reparations. In 2010, though posthumously, João's case was finalized, and he joined the ranks of the then more than thirty thousand other Brazilians who had been, by then, officially "amnestied" by the Amnesty Commission.[4]

Federal police agents fired under AI-5 are, perhaps, surprising protagonists of a narrative of restitution for repression.[5] Yet their cases are not, on the face of it, unlike those of thousands of other individuals who also lost their jobs or mandate under an institutional act of the military regime. At the same time, their cases certainly contrast with those of the petroleiros, among others, who had been targeted early in the dictatorship because of their labor militancy and support for João Goulart. The jobs the federal police were fired from were also near the very center of the repressive apparatus. Indeed, the federal police, together with the military and other state forces, played a role in the machinations that targeted the political and ideological opponents of the dictatorship. They worked within the larger milieu of policing following the issuance of AI-5 in which torture of political prisoners was systematic and rampant.[6]

Some federal police agents, in fact, were among those who worked within the very agencies whose acronyms—DOPS, OBAN, and its successor DOI-CODI—are synonymous with torture in Brazil.[7]

Those same acronyms, which forever marked the lives of individuals who were tortured by the military regime, also appeared in the petitions to the Amnesty Commission filed by a few of the former agents who had been ousted under AI-5. Among them, one stated that he had been fired because he refused to participate in interrogations of political prisoners. He explained what everyone already knew: in their ongoing war against subversion the interrogators tortured prisoners to obtain information and confessions. Other officers, though not mentioning the repressive agencies, argued in their filings to the commission that they had been unjustly accused of corruption and denied any and all recourse to defend themselves against the accusations.[8] In more ways than one, therefore, their cases stand at a crossroad of two long shadows cast by AI-5. The former agents are among the thousands of Brazilians whose professional lives were, at a minimum, derailed by the arbitrary power instituted by and exercised under AI-5. Yet, they were fired under AI-5 in the context of an increasingly violent state of which they were part.

TWO LONG SHADOWS OF AI-5

Enacted on December 13, 1968, AI-5 was the swift and definitive answer of the then president, General Artur da Costa e Silva, to a vote of defiance by Congress a day earlier. Costa e Silva had been among the coup plotters of 1964 and was the first minister of war in the military regime that followed. From that post, he staunchly defended the interests of a hard-line contingent in the military. That contingent, it is worth noting, included Reserve Admiral Sílvio de Azevedo Heck—the son of Conrado Heck, who had been among the plaintiffs in the *Anistia Inversa* case of 1895 and who became the minister of the navy when Getúlio Vargas came to power in 1930. Maud Chirio describes the younger Heck as "something of a loose cannon." Within the decade leading up to the coup, he had attempted to prevent the inauguration of both Juscelino Kubitschek in 1955 and Goulart in 1961. He then plotted—albeit "amateurishly"—to topple Castelo Branco in favor of a more stridently "revolutionary" military government.[9]

In some ways, the jockeying for power within the military following the coup divided along one vision of the military as intervening in governance to "adapt Brazilian democracy . . . to the challenges of the Cold War" and another vision in which the government was more directly "answerable to the armed forces."[10] In October 1965, to stave off a brewing crisis, Castelo Branco issued the Second Institutional Act (AI-2), eighteen months after AI-1 had already resulted in widespread purges. For its part, AI-2 dissolved the existing political parties and extended exceptional powers to the executive. The restructuring of politics effectively ended an impasse the regime had found itself in with the conservative UDN political party, which had partnered with military leaders since the early 1950s in efforts to stamp out communism in Brazil.[11] Although it was a potent strike to civilian political participation, AI-2 did not eliminate it completely. Rather, it established a two-party system designed to provide a majority of support for the regime and a minority outlet for opposition.[12] The Aliança Renovador Nacional (National Renewal Alliance, ARENA) formed as the ruling, pro-regime party, and the Movimento Democrático Brasileiro (Brazilian Democratic Movement, MDB) formed, at least nominally, as the opposition party.[13] The following year, Costa e Silva won the ARENA nomination for president. An ARENA-controlled Congress then duly elected him. He took office in March 1967. A new constitution followed later that year. The constitution maintained some semblance of democratic procedures as a way to legitimize the government and provide an escape valve for dissent. The concern for democratic principles, however, was secondary to concerns for national security. With the issuance of AI-5 in December 1968, Costa e Silva gave the repressive apparatus a long-desired green light to act as it saw fit. With it, in the words of noted journalist Elio Gaspari, "they went on the hunt."[14]

The congressional vote to which Costa e Silva responded with AI-5 had rejected a pending request to suspend parliamentary immunity for Representative Márcio Moreira Alves. The vote was, in many ways, the culmination of a series of absurdities. The military wanted Alves to be prosecuted under national security law for a speech he had given a few months earlier, during a session (it is worth noting) that had been poorly attended by congressional representatives. While denouncing the use of repression, Alves was careful and evenhanded. He acknowledged and praised the members of the military who refused to support or tolerate repression. In the end, he appealed to mothers of servicemen and to young women who might attend social events or otherwise fraternize with military cadets to boycott the military and an upcoming Independence Day parade. The speech, which had been duplicated and circulated, offended military leaders. Their demand to prosecute Alves, in turn, offended many in Congress, including some ARENA representatives who were sympathetic to his predicament and concerned about what the military's request to suspend Alves's immunity might portend. Of the 216 total votes against lifting his immunity, 94 came from ARENA members.[15]

This vote against the military's wishes surprised and briefly buoyed the opposition. Alves knew, however, that it also made him a target. He immediately went into hiding, on his way to exile.[16] The next morning, Costa e Silva met with his National Security Council to definitely address what they saw as a challenge to the authority of the military and thus a serious threat to institutional stability. The resulting AI-5 consolidated power for the military. It gave the regime the authority to declare martial law, dissolve Congress (which it did immediately upon enactment), and cancel the mandates of elected officials. A full 20 percent of Congress was purged immediately, including 60 of 139 MDB representatives.[17] Alves was among those purged, as were many ARENA members who had voted against the request to lift his immunity.

AI-5 also suspended most civil liberties, including habeas corpus; permitted the military to fire, retire, and/or take away the political rights of any citizen; and allowed the military to confiscate goods. No actions taken under AI-5 were subject to review.[18] Under AI-5, the regime effectively instituted and endorsed tactics to be used in the war against subversion and inaugurated the structures necessary to wage it. Mariana Joffily characterizes the act as the "juridical entrance for a viable new repressive structure." Before AI-5, she explains, existing structures and political traditions to a certain extent limited the repression of the regime. After AI-5, the regime could and did operate both apart from and within legal frameworks. To obtain information, state agents tortured prisoners in interrogations not intended for legal purposes. Any subsequent legal phase began later. Often, as Joffily explains, transcripts from their first interrogations would be the starting point for a formal investigation and eventual appearance before the justice system.[19]

"A Government by Torture"

In hindsight, the issuance of AI-5 formalized and intensified repression that was already underway. Taken together, a string of incidents, especially during the year 1968 and against students, indicated that the military was taking a hard-line turn. In fact, Alves's speech occurred shortly after, and in response to, a telling episode in late August at the University of Brasilia, when nearly three thousand students assembled to protest the death of Edson Luis de Lima Souta, a teenager killed by military police during a protest in Rio de Janeiro in March of that year. The federal police entered the campus to break up the protest and arrested seven students.[20] Six months later, in October 1968, 920 students, including virtually all the leadership of the União Nacional dos Estudantes (National Student Union) were arrested during an underground congress held on a farm in Ibiúna, São Paulo. The police processed and photographed all of them. Victoria Langland describes the resulting documentation as "a veritable police gallery of student activists," many of whom would be hunted down in the years to come.[21] The regime also began a propaganda campaign designed to sow fear and to isolate the opposition. Critics of the campaign's slogan "Brazil: Love It or Leave It" offered the rejoinder: "and the last one turns off the lights."[22]

By June 1969, six months after the issuance of AI-5, the prototype of the secret police that would ultimately decimate the opposition was up and running in São Paulo. Dubbed Operation Bandeirantes (OBAN), in a nod to the seventeenth-century São Paulo campaigns to capture Indians and sell them into slavery, OBAN was to be a force multiplier, capitalizing on all of the security organs and centralizing information about subversion under the control of the Second Army in São Paulo.[23] Domestic and multinational corporations—including companies such as Ford, Nestlé, General Electric, Mercedes Benz, and Siemens—were rumored to have provided, or had been extorted to provide, financial and other support to OBAN and its pursuit of individuals identified as subversives.[24] It was, as Chirio describes, the "first attempt at civil-military collaboration for the sole purpose of combating 'subversion.'"[25] Costa e Silva's successor, Médici, nationalized the program in 1970 with the creation of the Destacamento de Operações de Informação (Department of Operations and Information, DOI) that functioned at the service of the Centro de Operações de Defesa Interna (Center of Operations of Internal Defense, CODI) under high military command. The resulting DOI-CODIs then collaborated with both DOPS and other forces, including the federal police.[26] State terror followed.

By July 1970, in a clear sign that word about the violations had permeated borders, *Look Magazine* dubbed Brazil a "government by torture."[27] By September 1972, Amnesty International published a detailed "Report on Torture in Brazil." The report was reprinted in 1973 (the year João was fired), with a second edition issued in October 1974 and a third in March 1976. It included a list of 1,081 prisoners who had been tortured, murdered, or disappeared under the military regime in Brazil. Separately, it listed 86 individuals who specifically had been tortured by or under the notorious chief of São Paulo's DOPS, Sergio Paranhos Fleury. The Amnesty International report also included, for limited distribution among international bodies and Brazilian officials, the names of 472 alleged torturers, several of whom most certainly would have worked in São Paulo. In the 1970s, citing the inability to "verify each case in loco" because Brazil would not permit the organization to conduct an investigatory mission, Amnesty International affirmed its willingness to "publish any documented evidence" contradicting this information. Amnesty International also suggested that Fleury could "rectify any inexact information by writing an open letter to the Secretariat of Amnesty International." In response, the regime banned the publication of any statements by Amnesty International in the Brazilian press.[28]

Of eleven torture victims who provided direct testimony to Amnesty International, seven had been arrested and detained in São Paulo between 1969 and 1971. Taken together, five of those seven named OBAN, four named the DOPS, and two specifically mentioned the address "921 Tutóia Street" in São Paulo.[29] Known as "grandma's house" to the agents who worked there, the Tutóia Street address was the headquarters of the Thirty-Sixth Police Station of the civil police and served as the home of OBAN and then the DOI-CODI. It was a site of torture.[30] The seven arrested and detained in São Paulo who provided testimony to Amnesty International (and many others in the years since) described torture by electric shocks, beatings, and the "parrot's perch," a much-used form of torture in Brazil in which an individual was hung, as if on a spit, from a pole that ran under his or hers knees and elbows. With wrists and feet tied, the position caused extreme pain, which was often intensified with electric shocks and beatings. For those working in OBAN under AI-5, as Marcelo Godoy has shown, torture was not seen as an aberration but, rather, as an effective weapon of war. The prisoners, in turn, were not seen as political opponents but mortal enemies. The idea that they were at war, Godoy explains, "made legal" in their minds what their prior police work had not allowed—namely, "ambush, a bullet through the back, and the death of the enemy."[31]

Statistics cited by the 2014 report of the Brazilian Truth Commission give an updated sense of the extent of torture practiced in São Paulo in the wake of AI-5. After six years of its being in force (that is, by the end of 1974), more than two thousand individuals had been detained and another three thousand questioned by the DOI-CODI in São Paulo. Of those detained, fifty were killed in custody. Well over a thousand prisoners held at the DOI-CODI, or transferred there from other state agencies, were then sent to the DOPS, which was run by the dreaded Fleury, and where further torture occurred, which resulted in additional deaths.[32] In March 2014, just months before the Truth Commission Report was published, a public event held in front of the DOI-CODI headquarters on Tutóia Street remembered the victims killed there and called for an end to amnesty for the state agents who had been complicit in torture and forced disappearance.[33]

One former agent also mentioned Tutóia Street in his paperwork submitted to the Amnesty Commission. When he explained that he refused to "participate in the interrogation of political prisoners in the

OBAN," he specified: "Operation Bandeirantes–Tutóia Street, São Paulo." The operation in São Paulo, "the first of its kind and the biggest of
all," had 250 men, the majority of which were military police, "its spine,"
because they had jurisdiction over first-line, street policing. Numbers
from the federal police, in comparison, were low.[34] The agent mentioned
no specific cases and may not have had direct knowledge of any, but the
events in the lives of one family of political prisoners underscore the climate at OBAN at that time. On a series of occasions during the months
just before João and the others were fired, state agents took two small
children to see their imprisoned parents who were being subjected to all
manners of torture at 921 Tutóia Street. Indeed, the visits of their children and the threats made to them involving their children were among
the tools of torture employed there.

The children, Edson Luis and Janaína Teles, were four and five years
old, respectively, at that time. Edson Luis was born in June 1968, six
months before the enactment of AI-5. He was named in homage to the
above-mentioned teenager Edson Luis de Lima Souta, who had been
killed by military police during a student protest in Rio de Janeiro three
months earlier. Their parents, César Augusto Teles and Maria Amélia
de Almeida Teles, were militants in the Partido Comunista do Brasil
(Communist Party of Brazil, PCdoB) and had been picked up in an
OBAN operation in late December 1972. The PCdoB had broken from
the PCB in 1962 and was attempting to foment a revolution against the
dictatorship through an armed guerrilla movement based in the Araguaia River basin in the state of Pará. By 1972, the military was conducting operations that would, over the next few years, completely wipe
out the guerrillas. The Teles children's aunt Criméia Alice Schimdt de
Almeida had been part of the guerrilla movement. She left Araguaia
earlier in 1972 on a mission to São Paulo and then was unable to return
both because of the ongoing military operations and because she was
pregnant. She was living with the Teles family when the parents were
picked up off the street and taken to the headquarters of the DOI-CO-
DI. Fleury's team also picked up Criméia and took her to OBAN. Soon
they transferred her to the DOI-CODI of Brasília where she was tortured under the command of General Antonio Bandeira, who was then
in charge of the operations in Araguaia. Her child was born in prison in
February 1973.[35]

The first time the police came to the Teles home to take the "children
of communists" to DOI-CODI headquarters, Edson had been watching
the children's program *Sesame Street*. If events on Sesame Street teach
children about life as it should be, what Edson witnessed at the Tutóia
Street address was a world undone. He recalls not recognizing his moth-

er the first time he was brought to her because she was purple and disfigured from torture. She called to him, and he was happy to hear her voice but was confused because the person who had the voice of his mother and the same way of talking to him looked nothing like her.[36] Years later, retired Colonel Carlos Alberto Brilhante Ustra, who commanded the DOI-CODI in São Paulo from 1970 to 1974, described the practice of taking children to see their parents who were prisoners not as a tool of further torture but rather as a merciful act.[37] The Teles family disagreed. They filed suit against Ustra in 2002, just as the Amnesty Commission was receiving its first petitions.[38] In 2006, a judge in São Paulo accepted the case, finding that the statute of limitations did not apply to crimes involving violations of human rights. In October 2008 Ustra was declared "responsible" for torture and was "morally and politically condemned."[39] Because of the amnesty, Ustra could not be criminally convicted or sentenced for the crime.[40]

What Was Written Down

In 1973 João learned he had been fired when his name appeared in the *Diário Oficial*. The newly appointed director general of the federal police, General Bandeira, who had been commanding the military operation in Araguaia, brought João and his colleagues to the attention of Médici. Nearly forty years earlier, in November 1935, a nineteen-year-old Bandeira, then a cadet in the Realango military school, took part in putting down the barracks revolt, the Intentona Comunista, in Rio de Janeiro. He was also among troops that defended Vargas in May 1938 against the integralista uprising. He had, as well, taken part in the 1964 coup to depose Goulart and in the events that led to the arrests of hundreds of politicians and unionists in the Northeast in the earliest days of the military regime. During his tenure at the helm of the federal police, from May 1973 to March 1974, he is perhaps most known for his role in the strict censorship of print, film, and theater.[41] Before the dictatorship would cede governance back to civilians, his name would be directly linked to the torture of political prisoners, including in São Paulo during his tenure in this post.[42]

Bandeira provided the information to Médici based on a ten-volume case file compiled by Walter Dias of Internal Affairs, who conducted the inquest within the federal police. Dias's investigation of dozens of agents and other personnel in São Paulo began in 1972 and followed on the heels of an investigation that had resulted in the firing or retiring of twenty-six agents operating along the Belem to Brasília highway.[43] All the names of these individuals, together with fifteen others likewise fired from the federal police since 1970, appeared in a July 1973 confidential report from the federal police to the intelligence apparatus of the branches of the armed forces. The report explained that the "sanitizing measures" had been undertaken to "expunge undesirables" who had been complicit in corruption that compromised the good name of the police force.[44]

Among the men identified in the report, one later described Dias's investigation to the Amnesty Commission as a "veritable administrative massacre," targeting at all costs anyone who did not fall in line. The allegations that led to this man's dismissal also resulted in criminal charges in federal court. The presiding judge, however, closed the case. Comet tails of having been fired nonetheless followed him. He later qualified in the exam for a post with the Brazilian telecommunications company but was never hired, he assumed, because the information services maintained derogatory information on him, likely including the July 1973 report to the intelligence agencies. Another agent described "systematic persecution" within the federal police by military authorities that held command positions in all sectors. This agent noted to the Amnesty Commission that AI-5 had denied him the right to defend himself against the allegations that led to his firing.[45]

The same July 1973 report also named another seventy-eight employees who were on their way to being fired or retired, including all but two of those who would be purged with João a month later. The report aimed to get in front of a "defamatory campaign" orchestrated by those, especially in São Paulo, for whom action under AI-5 was imminent. According to the report, these soon-to-be-former employees had sought in every way to "denigrate the names of not only those directly responsible for bringing the corruption to light but all of those who, in whatever way, had been linked to or ostensibly supported this purifying process in the Federal Police." The efforts included sending "apocryphal" materials to the various intelligence organizations in attempts to discredit individuals ranging from the chief of staff of the federal police, Alceu Andrade Rocha, to the DOPS director, Firmiano Pacheco de Arruda and (not surprisingly) Walter Dias from Internal Affairs.[46] Attention continued even after they were fired. In June 1974 the department circulated a photo book internally, complete with identifying information regarding João and the others who had been dismissed. The purpose was to "facilitate the immediate identification and recognition of any who might come, for whatever reason, seeking to make contact" with the federal police.[47]

The case file itself included witness statements alleging that the agents participated in a blitz that extorted money from businesses in exchange for looking the other way on foreign counterfeit merchandise. One witness offered hearsay, explaining that he had heard that an agent had bragged about having extorted someone.[48] Bandeira, in statements regarding the dismissals and retirements, explained that additional witnesses and personnel in a position to possibly defend those under investigation had also been interviewed but to no avail because of the flagrant nature of the violations. Of the forty-three employees, twenty-one were fired because of their alleged involvement in illicit activities and the other twenty-two were retired because, through acts of omission, they enabled the criminal behavior of those that had been fired.[49] The distinction mattered. Those who had been retired retained pensions commensurate with their length of service, while those who had been fired did not.[50] João, as mentioned above, was fired. Some also faced criminal proceedings that resulted from the police inquiry. One agent reported that charges against him were thrown out by the presiding judges who "criticized the Federal Police Department, between the lines, for bringing cases without merit." On the day they were fired, an editorial in *Jornal do Brasil* lamented the criminal behavior more generally of the police in Brazil, citing the infamous cases of Mariel Mariscot and Nélson Duarte who had meted out vigilante justice and revenge and built empires of corruption. The purge in the federal police occurred at the same time as the firing of eleven state police officers from an impoverished area outside of Rio de Janeiro for alleged involvement in torture and rape. They were fired by the governor, who reportedly was seeking federal intervention to have them dismissed under AI-5 so as to deny them any recourse or review of the decision.[51]

Indeed, being fired under AI-5 did just that. One federal police agent fired in a subsequent purge had been among a group of agents who, he later learned, had been reported to a police investigative commission by Fleury. Knowing that he was under investigation, this agent filed a security measure to compel the police commission to allow him to review the allegations against him. In response, the president of the police commission simply cited the authorities provided under article 11 of AI-5—namely, that acts taken under AI-5 "are exempt from any judicial review" and that such exemptions applied to "any examination of the intrinsic formalities or the substance." The president further explained that the particularities of the investigation and matters of witness security required that the documents be classified as confidential. The classification, in turn, prevented the commission from providing copies to the accused or his attorneys. The security measure was denied.[52]

Amnestied but Unfit to Return, 1980 and 1986

The action of August 1973 that expelled João, among forty-three employees from the São Paulo department, was the largest single purge in the federal police during the dictatorship, accounting for more than one-third of a total of 122 federal police officers ousted under AI-5 between 1970 and 1978. Twenty-six were fired between the months of March and August 1972, and another twenty-two all on the same day in January 1978. A smaller group of eight were fired in May 1977. With the decreeing of amnesty in August 1979, these and other civil servants and military personnel had the opportunity to potentially return to their formerly held posts, if they applied to ad hoc committees within their department, agency, or company. Internal documents related to the special commission in the Ministry of Justice, the ministry to which the federal police belong, read like the minutes from the council meeting that resulted in the rescinding of the contract of Bernardo Kucinski's sister from the University of São Paulo. The commission relied on the Division of Security and Information within the Ministry of Justice for personnel information, which produced a list with details concerning the 146 individuals who had petitioned to return. The resulting confidential report by the commission, dated July 17, 1980, included a stamp just below the signature affirming one of the primary refrains of the military regime: "the revolution of 1964 is irreversible and consolidated democracy in Brazil."[53] The regime had long referred to its 1964 coup as a "revolution."

Of the 146 former employees who petitioned to the commission in the Justice Ministry in 1980, thirteen had lost their jobs outside of the temporal scope of the amnesty and another seven had been employed by a different ministry and thus likewise were outside the commission's purview. Of the remaining 126 petitions, former employees of the federal police had filed 101 of them, most of whom were among the 122 who had been fired under AI-5. The other twenty-five were primarily prosecutors and judges, many of whom had been ousted in the early waves of repression following the coup in 1964. Of those 126 applicants who fit the scope of the mandate of the special commission and whose cases were reviewed by July 1980, only nine were approved to return to active duty. Five of the nine were federal prosecutors, three were judges, and one was a notary. The remaining 117 individuals, including all of the former agents, were either retired under the amnesty or—if they had been retired by the regime—had their time of service recalculated for their retirement. Three requests for pensions, including from two widows, were approved. A total of thirty-five of the forty-three purged together with João in August 1973 were among those that petitioned to return. The original stratifications in 1973 were replicated in the results of the commission. Those who had been fired were then considered retired; those who had been retired received an adjustment to the length of their active service for pension purposes. The other purges in the federal police had similar outcomes.[54] For João, the commission officially retired him as a

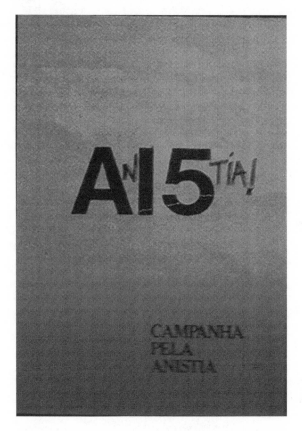

Figure 7.1. From AI-5 to Amnesty. Campaign for Amnesty. Courtesy of Armazém Memória, digital archive.

special class agent, which was the highest level in his particular career track. He did not return to work, but the act of retiring him in 1980 was considered "reintegration" under the amnesty.

In March 1986, following the constitutional amendment in 1985 that affirmed and expanded the 1979 amnesty, the petitions to return to active duty from civil servants who had specifically been fired under AI-5 were reviewed anew by a commission.[55] As before, those not readmitted to their posts would be considered retired. Again, it would be up to the agency to determine the appropriateness, or not, of the return of any and all employees. The Ministry of Justice completed its review and filed a report in September 1986. The text began with characterizing AI-5 as part of the regime's efforts to instill "a political and juridical system . . . based in liberty [and] respect for the dignity of the human person." It further justified the act as necessary "in the search for economic, financial, political, and moral reconstruction," to secure "democratic order" in the face of corruption, subversion, and "ideologies contrary to the traditions of the [Brazilian] people." As framed, nothing less than the "restoration of internal order and international prestige" had hung in the balance.[56]

The commission reviewed the situation of the 101 former federal police agents who had previously petitioned, all of whom had been fired under AI-5, as well as 21 other former Ministry of Justice employees likewise ousted under AI-5. Of the 122, the commission found that twelve were deceased and twelve were over the age for compulsory retirement. Another ten were more than sixty-five years old, and forty-nine had years of service greater than required for voluntary retirement. That left thirty-nine who in theory could return to active service. The commission members, however, were of the same mind as commission members six years earlier. They emphasized the likely negative public perception concerning federal police who had been fired for disciplinary reasons returning to the force. They also mentioned the potential threat of some returning with "feelings of revenge." And, finally, they raised potential issues of employees returning after more than ten years away who would most certainly be behind on technical and operational advancements and would therefore require extraordinary resources to train them. The committee recommended, therefore, that all petitions be denied, placing everyone into retirement status.[57] In an echo of the arguments surrounding the situation for the petroleiros, the announcement that followed in the *Diário Oficial* explained the rational: they had been forced out for disciplinary rather than political reasons.[58]

REPARATIONS AND THE ASYMMETRY OF OUTCOMES

Fifteen years later, scores of individuals who had been subjected to AI-5 and other repressive measures were eligible to petition for reparations to the Amnesty Commission. Created in 2001 and formalized by law in 2002, the commission addressed the rights of two groups: those persecuted in what was described as the "most classic sense"—that is, "the citizen violated in his or her public liberties and physical integrity"—and those that lost their jobs during the military regime.[59] For the former, in which the repression was neither linked to nor directly impacted the individual's professional life (including those targeted and tortured by OBAN, DOI-CODI, and DOPS), the commission could approve lump sum payment equivalent to the value of thirty minimum wages per year of repression but not to exceed one hundred thousand reais. For the latter, in which the repression was linked to the individual's professional or economic life (including those fired under AI-5), the commission could approve "monthly, permanent and continuing," indemnity in an amount corresponding to the salary they would have had, reflecting progress in their career track as if they had never been removed.[60] In many cases, such individuals were also eligible for retroactive payments.

At the time of the establishment of the Amnesty Commission, Brazil stood as an outlier in the region in terms of transitional justice mechanisms, especially for the absence of any accountability for torture, executions, and forced disappearances committed by state agents. In 2001, there was no truth commission, almost no access to official records, and certainly no trials. Brazil did have, however, a program of reparations operating since 1995 following the passage of the Law of the Disappeared and the establishment of the Special Commission on Political Deaths and Disappearances. An annex to the law itself recognized 132 individuals as having been forcibly disappeared.[61] The subsequent commission, which was framed as grounded in the amnesty of 1979, could grant reparations payments totaling 3,000 reais per year for the number of years corresponding to the life expectancy at the time of death, with a minimum value of 100,000 reais.[62] The commission reviewed a total of 475 cases and recognized 353 victims. All told, the Special Commission on Political Deaths and Disappearances granted indemnities totally approximately 40 million reais, with a median value of 120,000 reais.[63] As would happen in the Amnesty Commission (itself viewed as an extension of the reparations program administered under the Law of the Disappeared), the burden largely fell on the families to prove their loved ones' deaths or disappearances and thus how they qualified for the indemnity.[64]

In expanding the reparations program beyond those who had been killed or disappeared, the law establishing the Amnesty Commission largely replicated the calculus for cases of those individuals who had been violated in their "public liberties and physical integrity" by establishing a ceiling on reparations that could be paid to those who had lost their political rights or been detained and tortured. There was no upper limit on reparations, however, for career loss. The commission acknowledged that in "some extreme cases . . . individuals brutally tortured receive[d] much less than someone who lost their job." They took steps to apply what they described as a "principle of reasonability."[65] The formula in the law itself, however, favored those who had been impacted professionally and, even more so, those from the more privileged professional sectors whose earning potentials were higher. In fact, the compensation was "a way to reestablish the previous status quo."[66]

The disparity among reparations was, for some, another seeming inversion of what amnesty should be. In a sharp critique Glenda Mezarobba argued that basing reparations on the professional trajectory of the victim "not only reaffirms [Brazil's] historic social inequality but sanctions it." She further noted that, because the indemnity was often less for families of the "principle victims" of the regime (that is, those who had been killed and disappeared), the process gave the impression that the "professional losses represent a greater prejudice than torture."[67] In 2004 the secretary of human rights, Nilmário de Miranda (who would himself be a recipient of reparations, although of a comparably modest sum), shared frustration expressed over large sums that had been approved by the commission. Amnesty, he said, was meant to be "reparation for an injustice" and not "an economic boost." He explained, however, that Congress had passed the law setting forth the parameters for reparations and the commission had simply applied them.[68] In a 2007 interview during his term as president of the Amnesty Commission, Marcello Lavenère likewise acknowledged that reparations from the Special Commission on Political Deaths and Disappearances for those killed were small in comparison with some of those granted by the Amnesty Commission for loss of employment. The discrepancies, he said, were a product of the incrementality of such laws in Brazil. He surmised, in fact, that "if we were to propose a law now to benefit the surviving relatives of those killed or disappeared, the sums would probably be much higher."[69]

The Amnesty Commission divided the caseload among three chambers.[70] One of the earliest cases was filed by a man named Luís Carlos Prestes de Lima who asked for compensation for "moral damages / pain and suffering" endured for having the same name as the communist leader and revolutionary. He claimed that his wish to work for the electric company in Rio de Janeiro never came through as a result of his name. The commission, however, did not receive the requisite biographical informational, including details of any military service and his professional life. The commission sent word that his application lacked the information it would need to receive before a determination could be made.[71]

   In 2005 the commission partially, and posthumously, granted amnesty to Luís Carlos Prestes himself. Prestes had died in 1990; his surviving companion and beneficiary of his military pension filed the paperwork. It noted that he had first entered the army in 1916 and was discharged and then readmitted during and following the Long March. He had reached the rank of captain before ultimately being ousted in 1936 following his role in the Intentona Comunista the year before. A prior settlement based on the amnesty in the 1988 constitution had granted Prestes a pension associated with the rank of colonel. Under the new framework, in addition to an official declaration that Prestes had been politically amnestied, the commission approved "economic reparations of an indemnifying nature, in permanent and continuing monthly payments," equivalent to the rank of general to his surviving dependents.[72]

In 2010, the commission also declared one of his sons, Luís Carlos Ribeiro Prestes, politically amnestied and, on behalf of the state, asked for forgiveness (see below). The younger Prestes, born in 1959, had spent his earliest years underground. By the time he was ten years old, he was living in exile in the Soviet Union where he later completed a degree in cinematography. He returned to Brazil following the amnesty of 1979. The reparations for the younger Prestes, a minor during the dictatorship, took into consideration his nearly ten years in exile (from early 1970 until the enactment of the amnesty in 1979), as well as the years from his fourteenth birthday to the date of the amnesty law, which could be counted as time in which he was prevented from exercising professional activities. The amnesty also included the registration and recognition in Brazil of his diploma earned in the Soviet Union.[73]

Among the earliest petitions filed and granted based on repression meted out under AI-5 were from two elected officials who, in addition to the cancelation of their electoral mandates, had lost their political rights for a period of ten years. Fausto Thomaz de Lima, catalogued as the twenty-ninth petitioner before the commission, was a state representative in São Paulo. He was forced underground and then used a false name following the loss of his mandate and the suspension of his political rights under AI-5 in July 1969. In October 2001 the commission recognized him as a beneficiary of amnesty and approved a single payment of fifty-four thousand reais, the equivalent at the time of the payment of three hundred minimum wages, or thirty per year for the ten years that he had his rights suspended.[74] A month earlier, the same had been granted to Nysia Coimbra Flores Carone, whose petition was the thirty-seventh recorded. Like Fausto, Nysia lost her political mandate, in her case as a representative in the Chamber of Deputies, as well as her political rights for a period of ten years under AI-5.[75]

Some caught in the web of the security forces had similar outcomes before the commission. The above-mentioned Nilmário de Miranda had been detained and tortured both before and after AI-5. In 1972 he spent forty days imprisoned and tortured by the DOPS under Fleury in São Paulo. In 2008 the commission approved economic reparations for an eight-year period—from April 1968, when he was arrested for the first time and before the issuance of AI-5, through June 1975, when he was ultimately released from prison—for a total of the equivalent of 240 minimum wages.[76] Others who had been similarly targeted by AI-5 opted to seek reparations under the formula for employment loss. Alpírio

Raimundo Viana Freire, a member of the PCdoB, had been picked up by OBAN in August 1969 and was ultimately convicted by a military court and sentenced to ten years in prison. Rather than petition for lump sum reparations for having been targeted by OBAN and imprisoned, he petitioned for restitution for having lost his livelihood as the result of having been arrested, detained, and imprisoned. Prior to his detention, Alpírio worked as a journalist. The commission resolved his case in 2004, granting him reparations to account for the loss of his professional life. He was approved for monthly reparations payments of nearly seven thousand reais, the equivalent at the time of the salary of an editor.[77] Within a year, his reparations would outpace those granted to others for whom the repression did not directly implicate their working life.

The earliest years of the commission also dealt with a number of cases of former military members. By August 2005, 5,540 cases had been approved by the commission, of which 3,887 involved former military personnel, primarily from the air force.[78] In one session in July 2002, the commission found that a specific ordinance expelling cadets, issued by the air force on October 12, 1964, had been "of an exclusively political nature." The commission determined that the ordinance had sought to "arbitrarily punish" cadets, especially those with links to an association of air force cadets, who participated in the rally at the Metalworkers Union in Rio de Janeiro in late March 1964.[79] In its ruling thirty-eight years later, the commission recognized the former cadets as beneficiaries of political amnesty and granted them promotion to the rank of second lieutenant, which would have been the rank achieved upon completion of their studies. The promotion initially applied to nearly seventy former cadets.[80] Individual economic reparations were handled in subsequent hearings, such as that for José Soares Rodrigues, who would receive, as would the others, the equivalent of the salary and benefits of a second lieutenant as well as five years of retroactive payments, which totaled more than 200,000 reais.[81] Many among ousted military members, however, would not be amnestied. Indeed, by August 2005, more than twice as many petitions from military members (7,837 in total) had been denied.[82] Moreover, the "declaration of amnesty" that was extended to the former cadets by the commission between 2002 and 2005 had been annulled by late 2020. The decision to "unamnesty" the air force personnel was based on a reevaluation of the existence of political motivations behind the ordinance that resulted in their expulsion.[83]

No single case before the commission was more controversial than that of former army captain Carlos Lamarca. In late January 1969, roughly five weeks after the issuance of AI-5, Lamarca stole weapons and ammunitions from a military base and took command of an armed

guerrilla group, the Vanguarda Popular Revolucionária (Popular Revolutionary Vanguard). His defection from the army and allegiance to
the guerrillas infuriated the regime. They went after him, eventually
shooting and killing him in September 1971 in the state of Bahia. The
operation involved more than two hundred men from the military and
federal police. In 2007, the commission issued a posthumous declaration that Lamarca had been amnestied, granted a promotion to the rank
of colonel, and approved monthly reparations at the rank of general for
his widow.[84] In short order, the military clubs from the army, navy, and
air force filed a lawsuit contesting the promotion and the concession of
a reparation that reportedly totaled more than nine hundred thousand
reais.[85] By 2015 and following additional court battles, the decision of
the Amnesty Commission in his case had also been annulled, the reparations granted to his widow suspended, and the family required to repay
what they had already received.[86] A statement issued by the president
of the commission, Paulo Abrão, expressed "grave concern" about the
"judicialization of the right to amnesty" and the risk it posed to the long
struggle to reckon with the legacy of authoritarianism in Brazil.[87]

Many cases took years to resolve, including that of João and some of his
former colleagues. João had filed in 2001, but the commission did not
issue a decision until 2008, when he was more than eighty years old. The
decision ratified his status as amnestied and granted economic reparations both as permanent and continuing monthly indemnity going forward, as well as a retroactive payment. The commission approved, essentially, an upward adjustment to his pension commensurate with that of a
police chief, a post he could have arrived at if he had not been removed
from the force. The math, however, was a bit off. A few months later, a
technical note signed by the president of the commission returned the
petition for a new judgment based on an error of roughly twenty reais
per month in the original calculation. At a meeting in late July 2009, the
commission approved the adjustment, which happened to have occurred
just hours before João's death. A subsequent ruling the following year
noted that he had been "posthumously" amnestied.

For João and other former federal police officers, many of whom received rulings between 2008 and 2010, the commission found, variously,
that they had "suffered persecution during the period of the military regime," that the state "had interfered in their lives—removing them from
their jobs for political reasons," and that they had "overcome the burden
of showing exclusive political motives" for the repression for which they
sought restitution.[88] Although decisions in some cases noted, for example, that charges related to corruption or other crimes were later dropped,

the rulings tended primarily to acknowledge that individuals had been fired under AI-5 and then to apply the framework of reparations to their particular cases. In assessing the cases, the "political reasons" and "political motives" rested on the side of the military regime itself, which had taken action against those individuals based on the most notorious of its repressive acts. The commission did not examine or weigh the politics of the individual agents, nor did it—in these cases or in cases of political militants—comprehensively review any of the allegations that precipitated actions against them under AI-5.

Several of João's former fellow agents were recognized by the commission as amnestied but did not qualify for economic reparations beyond the value of retirement settlements previously reached. One former agent, perhaps knowing he had already exhausted the possibilities within the framework for those impacted professionally by the regime, made an argument for lump sum reparations designed for those "violated in his or her public liberties and physical integrity." He argued that his ousting under AI-5 rendered him "nonexistent," and, in fact, "dead to the regime." As such, he was unable to defend himself in the face of discrimination and accusations that followed. He requested reparations for material and moral damages. The commission, however, denied his petition, finding that he had already been amnestied under the framework of professional impact and was receiving monthly indemnity, which was "incompatible" with the application of the framework for lump sum reparations.

The commission's practice of ratifying individuals' status as beneficiaries of political amnesty, whether they qualified for economic reparations or not, aimed to acknowledge the individuals' "right to resistance" as well as the "wrongdoing of the state against its citizens."[89] For some, but not uniformly, the commission also extended a *pedido de desculpas*, or an official apology.[90] The practice of apologizing began in earnest in 2008, under Abrão's leadership of the commission. The commission expressed remorse on behalf of the state for "having persecuted citizens that it had an obligation to protect." An apology had not been part of the majority of cases of the petroleiros, which largely had been resolved earlier in the work of the commission and before Abrão's term as its president. The institution of the new practice was described by members of the commission as "a hermeneutical turn" in their work and in the evolution of transitional justice in Brazil.[91] By 2009, just as it was finalizing João's case, the commission had conceded "a declaration of amnesty" (by which it meant official recognition of having been politically persecuted) to 30,967 individuals. Of those, roughly one-third (10,578 individuals) also received some form of economic reparation.[92]

Reversing the Gaze

Under the leadership of Abrão, the Amnesty Commission took steps to further institutionalize itself, especially in the development of educational and related projects on citizenship and memory. Chief among these was a program called the "Caravans of Amnesty." As traveling public sessions, the caravans aimed to give more visibility to the work of the commission as well as to expand the scope of the reparations extended by the commission to include elements of collective memory. The various sessions held throughout Brazil were veritable performances of transitional justice. Abrão would later comment that what sets transitional justice apart from ordinary justice is the lack of "antagonism between the parties." Rather than a situation in which the state defended itself against claims by the victims, the Amnesty Commission recognized "without opposition" those who met the legal threshold. Doing so, Abrão explained, restored the "civic confidence of the victims in the institutions of the state."[93]

The Caravans of Amnesty projected a vision of the transformative possibilities in witnessing acts of reparations. In partnership with state and local government as well as with professional associations, civil society organizations, and human rights groups, the caravans sought to raise awareness and recover memory about repression in the locations where it had occurred. Between April 2008 and December 2010, in forty-seven public hearings held in eighteen different states, more than one thousand Brazilians were officially amnestied during sessions of the caravan. These acts of extending moral and economic reparations to individuals were witnessed by another fifteen thousand Brazilians.[94] The individual cases in such public settings were viewed as adding to the more collective aspects of transitional justice.

The caravans resulted in an increase in reports and testimonies about repression in Brazil. In response, the Amnesty Commission once again expanded its work beyond the confines of applying a formula for indemnity to individual cases. The resulting Marcas de Memória (Marks of Memory) project sponsored public hearings, oral history interviews, and calls for memory and justice-related initiatives.[95] The commission also sought to establish itself in the very landscape of Brazil, with a monument and a museum dedicated to political amnesty in Brazil. Planned for the city of Belo Horizonte in the state of Minas Gerais, the memorial, as it was called, had the "mission to preserve the memory of repression in Brazil." It was to stand as an "affirmation of democracy and human rights to overcome the traumas of the past."[96] The very idea of a memorial to amnesty turned the long-standing trope about amnesty on its head. Rather than a path to forgetting, it would be the route to memory.[97]

In the absence of other mechanisms of transitional justice at that time, especially a truth commission and trials of perpetrators, great hope was placed in the ability and viability of the institution of amnesty, such as it had been in Brazil, not only to provide reparations but to address demands for truth and accountability as well. Abrão and his colleague Marcelo Torelly expressed just such an operational vision of the work of the commission. They argued, in fact, that its implementation of a "policy of reparations to victims" served as "the lynchpin of the Brazilian transitional justice agenda." They then identified how the work of the commission had "fostered progress in the recovery of truth and memory, and more recently, in the pursuit of justice." The very linking of amnesty to reparations, they argued, did the work of legitimizing amnesty for the victims while delegitimizing it for perpetrators. Similarly, the manner in which the work of the commission acknowledged that violations "really happened" opened the door for "the development of other transitional justice dimensions . . . through which greater accountability might be possible in the future."[98]

Perhaps among the most symbolic shifts instituted by the Amnesty Commission was the act of asking for forgiveness. Doing so reversed the gaze. Amnesty was no longer the state "forgetting a crime" but the state asking for forgiveness. In a way, therefore, no longer was the state extending amnesty but, rather, it was receiving it from the citizen.[99] This idea of the fulfillment of amnesty as the recentering of aggrieved citizens reinforced a sense of the potential of amnesty to effectuate meaningful transformations. There were, however, limits to the transformational possibilities, including the stubborn, if paradoxical, impunity guaranteed under the same amnesty law that over time had given rise to the program of reparations.

CHAPTER 8

CONNECTED TO AMNESTY

From a Clandestine Life to the Inter-American Court of Human Rights, 1964–2010

On December 10, 1981, a unanimous decision of a commission within Rio de Janeiro's Secretariat of Education authorized the correction and reissuance of an eighth-grade graduation certificate of a student named Jorge Freitas. Jorge had earned the diploma in 1980 and was, according to school records, the son of Teresa da Rosa Freitas. Based on an action before a federal court in São Paulo, however, the commission concluded that "the student Jorge Freitas . . . was, in reality, Igor Grabois Olímpio, the son of Victória Lavínia Grabois Olímpio and Gilberto Olímpio Maria."[1] This was not, as one might imagine, a matter of a gross administration error or even a nefarious case of a stolen baby. Igor's mother, Victória Grabois, filed the request to change the graduation certificate. Her petition explained that her father, her husband, and her brother had been part of a guerrilla movement and were disappeared in apparent confrontations with federal troops in 1972 and 1973 in a remote area of the Amazon region, near the Araguaia River in the state of Pará. Years earlier, she had assumed a false identity as Teresa da Rosa Freitas and then obtained a birth certificate for her son Igor in the name of Jorge Freitas. She did so to avoid detection by the military and police who most certainly would have been looking for her.[2]

Following the amnesty in 1979, Victória made the decision to exit her clandestine life lived as Teresa and to resume living openly as Victória Grabois. Her efforts would test the interpretation of a clause in the law extending amnesty not just to political crimes but also to crimes "connected to" them. Victória had obtained and then used a false identity to

189

do things like rent a house, register her son for elementary school, earn a university degree, and get a job. Those acts were technically crimes of *falsidade ideológica* (ideological fraud) but were not in themselves overtly political. She made the case, however, that the illegal steps she took to live clandestinely were connected to the Guerrilha do Araguaia (Guerrilla Movement of Araguaia). This movement, quite explicitly political, aimed to foment a revolution against the dictatorship in Brazil.

In a war waged against them in near secrecy, the Brazilian military decimated the small band of guerrillas by 1974. Only in the earliest stages did the military take prisoners, many of whom, including local residents, were tortured. A final operation disappeared the bodies of those killed. For the years and decades that followed, the military either denied outright anything related to their incursion against the Araguaia guerrillas or sought to obfuscate information about the events that had transpired in the remote region. When such an approach became largely untenable, the military then denied the existence of, or obfuscated information about, any records of the operations. This well-worn tactic of denial and obfuscation, straight from the playbook of authoritarian regimes, was part and parcel of the repressive apparatus not only in Brazil but elsewhere in Latin America too. In opting for truth commissions, other countries in the region put the lie to such false narratives propagated by the dictatorships in an attempt to ensure a right to truth, if not accountability, for the victims.

In Brazil, however, an official truth commission would not be established as part of the transition from military to civilian rule. Indeed, it would take more than a generation, and it happened only after a 2010 Federal Supreme Court ruling reified a long-standing interpretation of the 1979 amnesty that it was "bilateral" and extended to state agents who had been complicit in abuses. The abuses were covered by the same "connected crimes" clause through which Victória sought to avoid criminal liability for having assumed a false identity during the dictatorship. What allowed her to exit clandestine life in the early 1980s would also, in the decades that followed, stand firmly as an obstacle to obtaining official information about, and accountability for, the disappearances of her family members during the Araguaia guerrilla war.

Following the enactment of the amnesty in 1979, Victória struggled both to secure its guarantees for herself and to deny them to the agents of repression. She filed paperwork to the federal court in São Paulo and before the Rio de Janeiro Secretariat of Education to have her official documents and those of her son reissued under their true names. Soon after, she began what would be a lifelong struggle on behalf of the disappeared of Araguaia. In 1980 she was part of a caravan of families, accompanied by the Brazilian Bar Association and others, who visited Araguaia on a fact-finding mission. In 1982 she joined a group of twenty-two family members in a civil suit to obtain information about the circumstances of the deaths of their loved ones and the location of their remains. For Victória, her role and participation in these events would not have been possible if not for the birth of her son, whom she credits with saving her life. Indeed, had it not been for Igor's birth, she likely would have been among the disappeared of Araguaia. In her reflections, years later, she also credits her time lived as "Teresa" for developing in her a new identity in another sense. In her clandestine life, she had become a "strong women, a fighter, who would contribute to continuing the struggle for a more justice and equal society."[3]

Victória's efforts on Araguaia reached a pinnacle of sorts in 2010 with a ruling from the Inter-American Court of Human Rights. A regional human rights tribunal, the Inter-American Court of Human Rights was established through a treaty in 1978 and is an autonomous body within the Organization of American States. Victoria's journey to the court had begun in 1995, with a complaint filed before the court's sister entity in the Organization of American States, the Inter-American Commission on Human Rights. The complaint addressed the failure of the Brazilian state to adequately respond to lawsuits filed by surviving relatives of the disappeared of Araguaia and other requests for information about their loved ones. Unable to reach a satisfactory resolution of the issues, the Inter-American Commission on Human Rights referred the matter to the court. The court's decision in 2010 found that the application of provisions in the 1979 amnesty to prevent the investigation and prosecution of crimes such as torture and forced disappearance was incompatible with Brazil's treaty obligations. The condemnation from the regional court was forceful and in line with the its expanding jurisprudence on amnesty in the Americas, but the impact of the ruling was tempered by Brazil's Federal Supreme Court decision that preceded and contradicted it.

A CLANDESTINE LIFE

In November 1979, less than three months after the passage of the amnesty law, Victória appeared in the office of attorney Luis Eduardo Greenhalgh in São Paulo. She told him that she was Victória Grabois, the daughter of Mauricio Grabois, and that she was living a clandestine life. Greenhalgh had played a role in the founding of the Brazilian Committee for Amnesty and would take part in the *Brasil nunca mais* project that soon followed. At the time, he was also busy defending Luiz Inácio Lula da Silva, the labor leader and future president known as "Lula," in matters stemming from general strikes in 1978 and 1979.[4]

Victória, in her previous life as Teresa, had led a teachers' union in some of those strikes. She did not, however, seek Greenhalgh's counsel in labor matters. Rather, she needed his advice about how to exit her clandestine life and live again as Victória Grabois.

Her transition to clandestine life sixteen years earlier began undeniably on the morning of April 1, 1964. On that fateful morning, at the age of twenty, Victória was scheduled to take a makeup exam at the National Philosophy Faculty of the University of Brazil, today the prestigious Institute of Philosophy and Social Sciences at the Federal University in Rio de Janeiro.[5] The makeup exam had been part of a special arrangement made for Victória and fourteen classmates, all of whom had been suspended previously. Police documents at that time identified Victória as a member of the Communist Party and considered her "highly politicized" and "highly dangerous." She had been involved in a student strike in August 1963, reportedly even appearing in a photo in the *Jornal do Brasil* newspaper "standing atop a ping-pong table . . . with a hostile attitude." She had also "collaborated in the invasion" of the university director's office after he prohibited Wanderley Guilherme dos Santos, a prominent political scientist, from speaking at an event. In 1962, it is worth noting, Dos Santos had published the prescient essay "Quem dará o golpe no Brasil?" (Who will stage a coup in Brazil?)[6]

A DOPS report on these matters noted accurately that Victória's father had been a leader of the PCB for years and that she had close ties to deeply rooted political resistance in Brazil. Her father, Mauricio Grabois, was a descendant of a Russian Jewish family that fled Ukraine in 1905 during the war between Japan and Russia. The family lived first in Argentina before settling in Brazil where Mauricio was born in 1912. When his daughter was born in November 1943 in Rio de Janeiro, he named her Victória in homage to the Russian army's victory over Nazi Germany in the decisive Battle of Stalingrad earlier that year. During the first years of her life, the family would witness and be part of dramatic changes in Brazil, including the PCB's renewed legality, Mauricio's election as a representative from the PCB in December 1945, and his role at the head of the party's block at the 1946 constituent assembly that drafted a new constitution.[7]

By 1962 Mauricio had joined other dissenters in breaking with the PCB. Long led by Luis Carlos Prestes, the Moscow-aligned PCB had taken a position opposing armed struggle and advocating a peaceful road to socialism.[8] During the dictatorship that would soon follow, Prestes and others among the leadership were nonetheless among those who immediately lost their political rights and were banished from Brazil.[9] Operating clandestinely, the PCB denounced the regime but maintained its position against armed struggle. Thomas Skidmore credits their cautionary approach to the experience of its older guard who remembered well the failed 1935 barracks revolts (the Intentona Comunista) and the persecution and imprisonment that followed. The older members of the PCB, however, would not be the only ones with long memories. Indeed, after largely decimating the armed opposition, the dictatorship began to target the clandestine PCB. Between March 1974 and January 1976, eleven members were disappeared, another eight were killed, and dozens of others were imprisoned and tortured.[10]

Yet before the deadly events of the dictatorship would transpire, in fact even before the dictatorship began, Grabois and others broke with the party and formed the Maoist-line PCdoB whose members considered the PCB's defense of a peaceful transition to socialism to be naïve. Once the coup took place, they resolved to mount armed resistance against the military regime. Other PCB defectors who likewise rejected the party's cautionary approach formed guerrilla groups too.[11] Chief among them was Carlos Marighella, who, together with fellow Bahians Mauricio Grabois and Jorge Amado, also had been elected and served in the 1946 constituent assembly. In 1967 Marighella founded the ALN, the organization to which Bernardo Kucinski's sister belonged when she was disappeared in 1974. He soon became the intellectual leader of urban guerrilla warfare in Brazil and thus one of the principal targets of the regime. In 1969, as part of the intense crackdown following the issuance of AI-5, Marighella was gunned down in an ambush that was planned from information obtained under torture. Among the armed groups, the PCdoB was the only one to take the fight to a rural area. The ranks of both the PCdoB and the more urban guerrilla organizations were composed primarily of young people, most of whom were middle-class students who had been active in university politics, like Victória.[12]

Well before she could imagine that her family would perish in a guerrilla war against a military regime, the twenty-year-old Victória prepared for a makeup exam and her return to the university that was to take place on the morning of April 1, 1964. In the time during her suspension, Victória had been working for the Programa Nacional de Alfabetização (National Literacy Program) within the Ministry of Education and Culture. The program had been formally instituted in January 1964 under the administration of João Goulart, nationalizing a literacy program in place since 1961. The agency employed the methods of Paulo Freire who had developed a "pedagogy of the oppressed" to pair basic literacy training with consciousness raising.[13] Victória had been a group supervisor of tutors. In May 1965, more than a year after she entered clandestine life,

Victória's name appeared in the military police inquest of the literacy program. It accused the program of being overrun with communists, "intent on indoctrinating people on a national scale and turning the country into a dictatorship of the proletariat."[14]

With the coup against Goulart underway on the morning of April 1, 1964, instead of appearing for an exam that would not take place, Victória joined three hundred other students, mostly from the PCB, who had assembled at the National Law School. The military soon surrounded the building and used teargas against those assembled. In the standoff that followed, seven students were injured and one was killed. As Victória fled for home, she passed the National Student Union's building and saw it was in flames, set on fire by supporters of the coup who were pleased to destroy the headquarters and thus symbolically the stature and influence of the student union. It was then, she said, that she understood the military had taken power and there was no turning back.[15]

The other students who were to sit for the exam on that fateful morning included three from the chemistry department who were suspected of making Molotov cocktails for student militants and the now noted journalist and author of a five-volume series on the dictatorship, Elio Gaspari. They had been suspended in late 1963 following their unsuccessful campaign to remove Eremildo Luiz Viana as chair of the philosophy department. A recurring personality in Gaspari's newspaper columns at the time was named "Eremildo, the Idiot."[16] By July, three months after the coup, Eremildo had expelled Gaspari, as well as Victória and a total of seventeen other students.[17] Such expulsions were not uncommon as the regime consolidated itself. In fact, radicalized students—and the potential for radicalization in the universities—were matters of particular concern for the regime.[18]

In interesting ways, the processes behind the expulsion of Victória and the other students in 1964 were similar to those that Kucinski described in the firing of his sister from the chemistry department of the University of São Paulo a decade later. In a vote, the council terminated Ana Kucinski's contract because she had not shown up to teach her classes. The obvious if unspoken fact that her absences from work were the result of her having been disappeared by the São Paulo police did not matter, at least not in what was discernible from the cursory notes he found documenting the event. Ten years earlier, before the devastation of forced disappearances committed by the military, a university council met to review a request made by a disciplinary commission to expel Victória and the other students. Two votes opposed the recommendation. A subsequent vote to commute the expulsion to a one-year suspension likewise received just two votes.[19] The official bulletin of the university announced the expulsions the next day on its front page, citing "serious misconduct uncovered in an investigation conducted by . . . that department." The students learned they had been expelled through this notice.[20]

Thirty-five years later, in August 1999, Victória and eighteen other students received word that a unanimous decision of the university council had annulled their 1964 expulsion. A ceremony held a few months later formally welcomed them back as an act of "symbolic reintegration."[21] The university rector explained that he considered the expulsion to be "a stain" and "a shameful episode" in the history of the university. The symbolic act itself, he said, was a form of reparation. Of the nineteen expelled, two were by then deceased. The majority of the rest had careers in academia as university professors, including abroad. Among them, Raquel Teixeira, explained that it had not been particularly difficult for most of them to complete university studies elsewhere. What was difficult, she said, was "overcoming the trauma of the expulsion and that horrible period" in Brazilian history.[22] Notably, a headline in the *Jornal do Brasil* about the ceremony conflated the event with amnesty, explaining that "19 students are amnestied and will be symbolically reintegrated."[23]

Beginning in the days following the coup, Victória took a series of precautions to avoid detection by police, including dying her dark hair a shade of blonde. Given her father's life after the PCB was declared illegal in 1947, she explained, she knew what to do in such situations: "I never kept a diary, never took notes. I was raised to memorize details, addresses, situations."[24] She postponed her plans to marry her boyfriend, Gilberto, later that month. (In late December 1964, Victória would marry Gilberto in a small town in São Paulo.) In the early days after the coup, she and her family stayed with friends and relatives in Rio de Janeiro, but they soon moved to São Paulo. That is where she began using a false name. To make things easier for them, her father wanted their new names to be similar to their real names so Victória became Virginia.[25] Lacking official documents to substantiate the new identity, however, posed a risk. Within a short time, her father gave her a birth certificate belonging to the niece of a contact who lived in the interior of Brazil. The woman's name was Teresa da Rosa Freitas; she was eight years older than Victória.

On the day of Victória's twenty-first birthday in November 1964, she used that birth certificate in Porto Alegre, the capitol of the state of Rio Grande do Sul, to obtain an ID she could use to live clandestinely. Victória, fearful that the eight-year age difference between her and Te-

Figure 8.1. Victória Grabois and her young son, Igor Grabois Olímpio. Courtesy of Victória Grabois.

resa would arouse suspicion, went first to a salon to get her hair styled to make her look older. She fretted that her obvious accent from Rio de Janeiro would give her away once she had to present herself in the office in Porto Alegre. Obtaining and using this ID would be among the crimes that Victoria would successfully argue were "connected" to political crimes and therefore covered in the amnesty. By the time Victória sought Greenhalgh's counsel in São Paulo years later, many who had known her in Rio de Janeiro before the dictatorship assumed she was dead. With her false documents as Teresa, Victória had rented homes, raised her son, earned a degree, became a teacher, bought a car, and even participated in teacher strikes. She also traveled, including abroad.[26]

In the early days, Victória worked alongside Gilberto and other party operatives in Guiratinga, western Mato Grosso, in what they would later understand to be groundwork for a possible *foco* war against the dictatorship. Accustomed to city life, Victória said the silence and calm of Guiratinga depressed her. She passed the long spells when Gilberto was away by teaching neighborhood children and reading the works of Jorge Amado and Graciliano Ramos from the local public library. When he was home, she remembered that they would dance to the music of the Beatles and the Rolling Stones when it played on the radio. By September 1965, Victória was pregnant. Before year's end, the couple was forced to leave Mato Grosso because of "questions of security." As Victória tells it, one day her father appeared and announced that plans had changed: Guiratinga would not be the site for a guerrilla movement. She was to return to São Paulo to begin a nursing program and the men would go on party missions elsewhere. (She did not want to be a nurse.) Her son Igor was born in June 1966. Shortly after Igor's birth, Gilberto traveled to China for training in guerrilla warfare.[27] With the assistance of an aunt, Victória obtained a birth certificate for Igor. It named his two parents: Victória Lavínia Grabois Olímpio and Gilberto Olímpio Maria. Between the years 1966 and 1969, her father, brother, and husband all went to Araguaia while Victória settled into motherhood, albeit an unusual one.

THE GUERRILLA MOVEMENT OF ARAGUAIA

The idea that a small band of armed guerrillas could foment a revolution against a repressive regime had its root in foco theory. The theory gained ground in Latin America following Fidel Castro's successful ousting of the Cuban dictator Fulgencio Batista in 1959. The case of Cuba, however, proved to be an outlier. Those who attempted similar revolutionary movements elsewhere, including in Araguaia, met an entirely different fate. The first guerrillas to Araguaia arrived in 1966 and worked to win the confidence of the community. Victória's brother, André, was among them.[28] As Joan Dassin describes, their "subversive activities" at that time "included building a school, providing health care, and giving agronomy lessons to the local population while training in the jungle at night." The local residents were reportedly unaware of their guerrilla training, at least initially. The decreeing of AI-5 in December 1968, however, would harden a conviction that armed revolt was the only viable avenue for resistance and opposition.[29]

The Araguaia guerrillas did not espouse a pure Cuban form of *foquismo*, consisting of "a military vanguard in armed action via small columns" but, rather, attempted a Chinese-influenced path of broad popular mobilization wherein the guerrillas complete just one phase. In fact, they opted for a rural agrarian base that would begin with a small group of guerrillas who could avoid direct confrontation with state forces as the revolutionary movement expanded. Over time, some local residents joined the guerrilla movement, just as PCdoB members continued to fill the ranks. Those ranks soon included Victória's father and her husband. By April 1972, the best estimates tally approximately 90 members in the Araguaia guerrilla movement, including both militants of the PCdoB and local residents. One source registered the support of 194 from the local population, of whom 26 took up arms or performed a strategic role.[30]

Inhabited by Indians and peasants, Araguaia is an area of tropical rain forest in the Amazon basin, in the state of Pará. There was little state presence, although local police maintained the status quo in near constant conflict between the poor and the large landowners. The region, therefore, combined factors deemed favorable to a guerrilla movement, including a local population that had been oppressed by the state and a rural location where the militants could operate clandestinely without the risk of capture by the police that was ever present in urban centers.[31] The dense forest of the region also seemed ideal for evading direct confrontation once the revolutionary movement was afoot.

General Emílio Garrastazu Médici, who became the third president of the regime in late 1969, assumed control of the military campaign against the Araguaia guerrillas. By 1971 military intelligence had information on the foco in gestation. A series of operations followed. The initial operations focused mostly on intelligence gathering. Intelligence personnel attempted to integrate with the local communities, some even bought parcels of land and set up little shops and bars where they could interact more closely with residents and obtain information on the guerrilla movement. Over the course of the military operations, approximately three hundred members of the local population were detained, and the majority of them were also tortured. Former members of the movement who had left were also captured and tortured in the attempt to obtain further information.[32]

The guerrillas tried to subvert the military campaigns with direct appeals to the soldiers involved. They sent messages telling the soldiers that a short distance from where they were was the largest iron deposit in the world, the profits of which flowed to American companies. In contrast to the economic program of the dictatorship, they described themselves as "young patriots . . . [who] want to end the dictatorship and construct a free and prosperous nation, for the well-being of all Brazilians." The guerrillas also emphasized the loss of democracy in Brazil and the lack of political space for any sort of criticism. They asked, "Is it worth sacrificing yourself for such an ingrate cause?" and pleaded that the soldiers not allow the military to "turn [them] into automatons and murderers of [their] brothers."[33] The appeals, however, could not stave off the coming onslaught.

The first military campaign, from March to June 1972, involved two thousand troops who occupied the cities of Marabá and Xambioá. Covert operations employed during the campaign aimed to confirm intelligence previously obtained and then to capture the leadership of the guerrilla movement. The first direct confrontation between the military and the guerrillas occurred during this operation, in April 1972. At that time, sixty-nine of the guerrillas were organized in three detachments. Victória knew by then about the existence of the guerrilla front in Araguaia and that it was under the command of her father. She soon learned that her brother, André, had been in the region of Marabá and was killed in an ambush.[34]

A second military campaign began in September 1972 and involved troops estimated to number from three thousand to five thousand. By December 1972, in fact, Brazilian newspapers reported that "5,000 troops were hunting for guerrillas near the Araguaia River." Thousands of miles away, the *Los Angeles Times* noted that "the armed forces never confirmed this but the fact that the story was allowed to run in a paper constantly under the eyes of government censors indicated it was probably true."[35] That same month in São Paulo, the dreaded OBAN detained and tortured Victória's pregnant sister-in-law, Criméia Alice Schmidt de Almeida, who had previously been part of the guerrillas in Araguaia but was then living with the Teles family. During her interrogations she was asked about her husband, André, as well as about Victória's father and husband. Victória feared she too might be discovered and hunted by OBAN. With those fears hanging over her, Victória and her mother left the house they were renting and moved to a different neighborhood where Victória signed a lease using her documents in the name of Teresa. The following July, and posing as Teresa, Victória obtained a birth certificate for Igor in the name of Jorge. No father was named. She registered Igor for his new school using the new birth certificate.[36] She explained to the child, nearly six years old, that his new school did not allow students to have foreign names. So instead of Igor, a Russian name, he would use the Portuguese equivalent: Jorge.

The third and final military campaign against the guerrilla movement began in October 1973 and added to the forces already in place an additional 750 soldiers trained in direct combat. In the military headquarters, photos of the guerrillas lined the walls. When confirmed killed, the photo was marked with a red X. There were reports that the military decapitated guerrillas and displayed their heads. Both Victória's father and husband were killed and disappeared in a military ambush carried out on a rainy Christmas morning in 1973. By October 1974, local residents witnessed the remaining PCdoB militants detained in military bases. They were never seen again. A January 1975 "cleansing operation" disappeared the bodies.[37]

Of the seventy guerrillas disappeared between 1972 and 1975, little is known about eight of them, all of whom came from the local population. The others, in large part, were young; the majority were under the age of thirty. Nearly one-quarter of those killed were under the age of twenty-five. They were also largely middle class, having completed degrees or studied in diverse fields including medicine, nursing, engineering, psychology, law, agronomy, education, geology, philosophy, economics, the humanities, geography, architecture, pharmacy, biology, chemistry, and music. Most had experience in militancy, especially in the student movement. Two of them had been directors of the National Student Union, and a total of seven had been imprisoned during a mass arrest of more than one thousand students at the secret meeting of the National Student Union in Ibiúna in October 1968. Several had also previously been imprisoned and, like Victória, had lived under false identities. Five of the seventy had children of their own, and there were ten couples among them.[38] The remains of only three of the guerrilla fighters—Maria Lúcia Petit da Silva, Lourival Moura Paulino, and Bérgson Gurjão Farias—have been located and identified.[39]

Two decades after the military incursions, in the dearth of information about what transpired in Araguaia, one military member involved in the operations spoke out, perhaps to exorcise demons that haunted him. He did so not through sworn testimony—at least not initially—but through fiction. In 1993 the former air force pilot, Pedro Corrêa Cabral, published *Xambioá: Guerrilha no Araguaia*. The cover billed the book as a "novel based on real facts." Cabral had been a pilot for the "operation clean-up," transporting bodies that had been disinterred to where they would be incinerated.[40] In explaining why he had written a work of fiction, he said that a factual account would have been discredited by "defenders of the military regime" who would have "pointed out all the gaps in memory and knowledge." Writing his account as fiction, he maintained, shielded him from any such challenges. As a novel, "no one could deny what he had experienced or the impact it had on his life." In step with the larger paradox that much of what Brazilians knew about the violence of the dictatorship at that time had come from fiction, he mused that "audiences could use his emotional truth to assert the need for investigation and the facts behind his story."[41] Cabral also wrote as someone with twenty more years of life and experience. He explained, "when I refer to the young people, I am not assuming they were all angels. I know that many went there already well-trained with courses in Cuba and China, but others were very naïve. The majority wanted the best for Brazil, although in a different way than ours."[42]

Cabral followed up with an interview published in the newsweekly *Veja* in October 1993 that ran under the cover title "Eu vi os corpos queimados" (I saw the burned corpses). The journalist who interviewed Cabral, Rinaldo Gama, likened the military campaigns in Araguaia to those of the 1890s that resulted in the extermination of the settlement at Canudos. In fact, he framed the events in reference to Mario Vargas Llosa's recently published fictionalized account of Canudos, describing Araguaia as "the end of the war at the end of the world." He also argued that, at some determined point, what happened in Araguaia ceased to be a war and became "an extermination, an atrocity." In the course of the interview, Cabral identified Sebastião Curió Rodrigues de Moura, known as Major Curió, as the leader of the extermination teams. In a letter to the editor in the subsequent edition of *Veja*, Curió responded to the allegations and stated that he had "taken steps to criminally investigate the lies and insanity of Cabral."[43]

Years later, Curió allowed journalist Leonencio Nossa to interview him and provided access to documentation about what had happened in Araguaia. In 2012 Nossa published a book based on those interviews and documents. He entitled it *Mata!*, a word in Portuguese that encapsulates the two overshadowing realities of the Araguaia conflict: kill and jungle. Nossa twice asked Curió, "Why kill the prisoners?" The first time, Curió responded obliquely: "that's the delicate part." The second time he responded with a counterfactual: "had there not been such determination and a strong impulse to eradicate the guerrillas, today they would have [in Brazil] a movement similar to the FARC" in Colombia. Nossa's analysis emphasized the secrecy surrounding the military operations, noting that "the officers of Araguaia had participated in a war that the country had never heard of." The accompanying "censorship of the press and the code of silence" within the military then prevented the conflict from "entering into the collective imagination and the national debate."[44]

The Truth Commission, which followed soon after the publication of Nossa's book, held three public hearings about Araguaia precisely "to address the prevailing silences."[45] In its investigation, the commission found that the events that transpired in Araguaia were emblematic of the "structures of political repression in Brazil." The commission's report described what happened in Araguaia as the height of the "maturation" of "a system of information and later of extermination" that was used by the regime against its enemies. In less technical language, one officer who had been involved in the disappearances explained in testimony to the Truth Commission that the military had taken the extra step to dig up the bodies and "transfer them" because if the bodies were to be found, "they will canonize them."[46]

AMNESTY FOR VICTÓRIA'S CONNECTED CRIME

Although the guerrilla movement was decimated and all the men in her family were disappeared, life nonetheless went on for Victória and her young son Igor. In 1975 Victória took entrance exams as Teresa and was accepted at both the prestigious University of São Paulo and the Catholic University of São Paulo, among other universities. Fearful that her documentation as Teresa may come under scrutiny in the university bureaucracy of the more elite schools, she opted to attend a second-tier school, the University of Moema. By 1976 she was working as a substitute teacher and began to take part in professional associations.[47] That same year, in a terrifying moment for Victória, the military moved against the leadership of the PCdoB, which had been operating secretly in the neighborhood of Lapa in São Paulo.[48] Three leaders were killed, and another five were detained and tortured. Fearing the worst Victoria took Igor to a neighbor she had been friends with since 1972. The neighbor knew the mother and son only as Teresa and Jorge. Victória told her friend that she had to travel unexpectedly for a few days and asked that she care for Jorge in her absence.

By the time the regime sent its proposed amnesty to Congress in 1979, Victória had earned a university degree in Portuguese and French literature and had become a main organizer in the teachers' union in São Paulo state, taking on a leadership role in union strikes.[49] She had also worked with the Brazilian Committee for Amnesty. In November 1979, Victória made the decision to get Greenhalgh's help in resuming her true identity. Greenhalgh advised her to leave São Paulo for Rio de Janeiro where she should stay with family. He told her not to renew her teaching contract she had in the name of Teresa, and he helped her sell her car to finance the move. In Rio, now thirty-six years old, Victória got an ID in her real name and through a contact got a job managing a cosmetic store. Victória is quick to point out that she made a higher salary in that position than she had as a teacher. She also entered into the amnesty process to transfer aspects of the life she had as Teresa for sixteen years— her college degree, her work experience, and the like—to her real name.

In her case before the court, aiming to have her administrative and bureaucratic life lived as Teresa transferred to her real name, Victória requested the reissuance of her son's academic certificate too.[50] Her subsequent petition to the commission within Rio de Janeiro's Secretariat of Education explained that her father, her husband, and her brother had taken part in the guerrilla movement in Araguaia and confirmed that they were among the disappeared. Victória argued that she and her child were beneficiaries of the 1979 amnesty via the clause including "connected crimes." The amnesty extended to those punished under institutional and complementary acts decreed by the regime and to all who committed political crimes or crimes "connected" to them. A subsection defined (obliquely) the term "connected crimes" as "crimes of whatever nature related to political crimes or practiced for political motivation." Victória explained that her crime—namely, utilizing false documents and the identity of another—had been committed because she was a target of political persecution.

At a hearing in February 1981, still under the military regime, a number of individuals testified on Victória's behalf, some of whom had long known her family and others who had only known her as Teresa. Among them, the friend in whose care Victória had left Igor following the assault on the leadership of PCdoB explained that she only learned of Victória's real identity after the amnesty became law, in spite of the fact that they had been close friends and neighbors for years. One of the survivors of the operation conducted against the PCdoB leadership, Elza de Lima Monnerat, also testified. She explained that she had known Victória's family since the amnesty of 1945, when Mauricio Grabois exited a long period of living clandestinely. A survivor among the Araguaia guerrillas testified as well. José Genoíno had been captured in April 1972, around the time Victória's brother was killed, and spent the next five years in prison. Prior to his involvement in Araguaia, he had been a leader of the student movement and, like Victória, had lived under an assumed identity.[51] Once captured, Genoíno was tortured in a way "that went from savage to scientific."[52]

The judge found in Victória's favor, allowing her to transfer her diploma and similar documentation from her assumed name to her real name, without risk of prosecution for the crime of having used an identity not her own. He based his decision on the 1979 amnesty law and the inclusion of "connected crimes." The education commission in Rio de Janeiro then followed suit and reissued her son's academic certificate in his real name.

In the absence of an official truth commission following the transition to civilian rule in March 1985, civil society actors stepped in, and Victória was among them.[53] In July 1985, just a few months after the military exited power, copies of the *Brasil nunca mais* report suddenly and without explanation appeared in bookstores. Directed by the archbishop of São Paulo, the report compiled and analyzed details and information about torture that had been derived from testimony in military court records. Access to those records had been provided, on a limited basis, to lawyers preparing amnesty petitions for clients in prison or exile. The report included an annex listing the names of 125 individuals who had been disappeared since 1964. The letter "A" appeared next to sixty of the names; a key noted that "A = Araguaia."[54]

In September 1985, torture survivors and family members of the disappeared joined together to form Grupo Tortura Nunca Mais in Rio de Janeiro. The members began their advocacy denouncing the appointment to public positions of individuals who were recognized as torturers by torture survivors. They would soon lobby for the revocation of medical licenses of doctors who oversaw torture sessions or who falsified autopsy reports to cover up torture.[55] In the 1990s, and by the time Victória had joined their ranks, the group was involved in investigations that led to the discovery of the remains of fourteen political militants who had been secretly buried in graves used for the bodies of unidentified indigent people in cemeteries in Rio de Janeiro. The group was also involved in a prolonged struggle to locate and identify the remains of additional militants similarly buried in a collective grave in São Paulo. Leveraging this proof of the regime's use of forced disappearances, members then increased their pressure to open the archives of the dictatorship so that all the remains of the disappeared could be located, identified, and returned to their families for a proper burial.[56]

Victória pursued other forms of amnesty and acknowledgment as well. Following the constitutional amendment passed in 1985 that expanded the contours of the 1979 amnesty, she applied for reinstatement to the job she had held in the early 1960s with the National Literacy Program in the Ministry of Education and Culture. Her amnesty in this matter was formalized in March 1994, and she was reinstated as a mid-level supervisor. (In 2010, the Amnesty Commission approved a further adjustment to her pension based on the new calculus for reparations.)[57] In 1995, the same year that she and others filed the initial petition to the Inter-American Commission on Human Rights, Brazil enacted the Law of the Disappeared, through which the government recognized its responsibility for the "murders of the political opposition" from September 2, 1961, to August 15, 1979. Of the 132 individuals identified as disappeared in an annex to the law, 60 had been part of the guerrilla movement in Araguaia and included Victória's father, brother, and husband. Through the Special Commission on Political Deaths and Disappearances, which had been established under the Law of the Disappeared, Victória obtained a death certificate for Gilberto. The certificate only confirmed his death; the date, location, and cause of his death, as well as the location of the burial of his remains, are noted as "unknown."[58]

Figure 8.2. Victória Grabois at the Inter-American Court of Human Rights, San José, Costa Rica, 2010. Courtesy of Victória Grabois.

IMPUNITY FOR STATE AGENTS

In 2010 Victória testified before the Inter-American Court of Human Rights. A total of 117 family members of 48 of the victims provided power of attorney to the organizations involved in the case including Grupo Tortura Nunca Mais, which was represented by Victória, among others. The majority of the family members were siblings of one of the victims. There were also two partners/spouses, ten parents, five children, and four nieces and nephews. Victória fell in three of these categories, as spouse, child, and sibling.[59]

In 1982, nearly three decades earlier and still under the dictatorship, twenty-two of those families had brought a case before the federal court in Rio de Janeiro. They were represented by Greenhalgh, the same attorney Victória had gone to for advice on how to exit clandestine life. In their case, a civil matter, they requested that the state be compelled to disclose the following information: who had been taken prisoner by the military, what happened to them after their capture, who was killed in combat, what documents existed to confirm their deaths, and the location where the bodies are buried. The case followed what had been a frustrated fact-finding mission to Araguaia in 1980 by family members of the disappeared in Araguaia, including Victória, with the accompaniment of representatives of the Brazilian Bar Association. Rumors reportedly circulated that the local populations had been threatened by the police prior to the arrival of the families.[60]

Their complaint proceeded initially. The presiding judge called witnesses and requested official documents. The military regime, however, denied everything, including that there had been confrontations between guerrillas and state forces. In 1989, after the transition to civilian government, a new judge assigned to the matter dismissed it outright. He ruled that the request of the families for clarification of the events and for recovery of the bodies was impossible in both physical and legal terms. Physically, he emphasized the difficulties in locating bodies in the Amazon region more than a decade after death. On the legal front, he cited the lack of any mechanism to compel the state to provide information about where anyone is buried. The judge also cited the 1979 amnesty as an existing remedy for the family's demand to obtain an official death certificate for each of their loved ones because the law allowed families of disappeared persons to obtain a "declaration of absence," which was to function as a death certificate.[61]

When the regime sent its proposed amnesty to Congress in 1979 including the language of "connected crimes," families of disappeared persons wrote to Senator Teotônio Vilela, the chairperson of the committee responsible for reviewing the legislation and any proposed amendments. Signed by twenty-three individuals, including Bernardo Kucinski, the letter expressed their concern that the "connected crimes" clause was an attempt to preemptively "amnesty the crimes committed by torturers." As such, the clause robbed them of the chance to make progress in their "struggle to clarify the deaths that occurred [and] to hold those responsible to account."[62] Family members also provided the senator with a file containing information about cases of deaths and disappearances, which would be further organized and expanded and then published in 1984 as the *Dossiê dos mortos e desparecidos* (Dossier on death and disappearances).[63]

The primary focus of the congressional debates that followed was on those among the opposition who would be excluded from the amnesty, a cause made urgent by the hunger strike of remaining prisoners (see chapter 6). Indeed, the rally cry of an unrestricted amnesty, coupled with the unexpected and suspicious death of Sergio Fleury, the notorious torturer from the São Paulo DOPS—just weeks before the proposed amnesty had been sent to Congress—seemed to have taken the teeth out of parallel arguments to exclude state actors from the amnesty.[64] The efforts put forth largely applied the regime's logic for the exclusion of "terrorist" crimes committed by the armed opposition to that of state agents who tortured and killed.

The São Paulo section of the Brazilian Bar Association, for example, drew an equivalence between the acts described as terrorism that the regime sought to exclude from the benefits of amnesty and the acts of torture committed by state agents that would be included under "connected crimes." The argument emphasized that the majority of those involved in the excluded "terrorist" crimes had subsequently been tortured by state agents and then concluded that "either you exclude the torturers, taking away the 'connected crimes' from among those amnestied, or you extend amnesty to all, without restriction."[65] In similar advocacy for those excluded, the vice president of the Brazilian Bar Association, José Paulo Pertence (who had himself been targeted under AI-5), stated that if, as it appeared, the "universal ethical condemnation of torture" was no obstacle to extending legal impunity to those crimes under the proposed amnesty, than the ethical condemnation of terrorism must also not serve to exclude those in the opposition even though they acted violently.[66]

Only seven of more than three hundred amendments proposed by legislators aimed to explicitly prevent the application of amnesty to state agents complicit in torture, forced disappearance, and other egregious violations.[67] Among them, one proposed adding a section to further clarify that "connected crimes" did not include "crimes committed against persons that were imprisoned, unarmed or otherwise incapable of defending themselves." Another specified that "acts of cruelty or torture, which may or may not have resulted in death, practiced against political prisoners" were not covered by the amnesty. A third noted that such "acts of intimidation, cruelty or torture" constituted common crimes and thus were excluded. And yet another specified that any "abuse of power committed by state agents, whether civilian or military, against persons who were detained, accused or convicted of national security crimes" could not be amnestied.[68] None of them was adopted. The proposed law passed with minimal adjustments and with the "connected crimes" clause intact.

In the years following the dismissal of the civil case brought by surviving family members, more information emerged, advocacy continued, and the demands surrounding Araguaia expanded. For example, documents provided by the navy to a special commission in the Chamber of Deputies recognized for the first time the death of more than forty Araguaia guerrillas. Relatives of the disappeared also conducted additional missions to the region in 1991 and 1993. In 1995, with no resolution in Brazilian courts, the families sought recourse through the Inter-American Commission on Human Rights.[69] In response to the allegations made by the families, the government of Brazil asked the commission to dismiss the petition, explaining that the recent enactment of the Law of the Disappeared provided reparations to relatives of those killed and disappeared and thus satisfied any obligations in the matter. While recognizing the importance of the new law, the families responded with the argument that "indemnification is not full reparation . . . as those responsible for it have yet to be identified and punished."[70] Their demands had evolved since 1982. Beyond information about the circumstances of the deaths of their loved ones and the location of their remains, their petition to the Inter-American Commission on Human Rights argued that the government of Brazil could not utilize the amnesty or other measures "to impede the investigation of the facts," or to prevent "sanction[ing] those responsible for grave violations of human rights."[71]

The next year, in 1996, the renowned Equipo Argentino de Antropología Forense (Argentine Forensic Anthropology Team), which had recently worked on exhuming remains from the site of the El Mozote massacre in El Salvador, conducted a mission to Araguaia. Their work resulted in the location of the remains of two PCdoB militants—namely, those of Maria Lucia Petit, which were positively identified that same year, and those of Bergson Gurjão Farias, which were uncovered on that mission but only identified in 2009. In 2001, statements were taken from fifty-five local residents who had had contact with the guerrillas. Those interviews resulted in information about the existence and location of military bases, including in the city of Xambioá, which operated as a prison and an interrogation center. Further excavations, however, did not result in the location of any additional human remains.[72]

During these same years, from 1996 to 2001, the Inter-American Commission on Human Rights held three hearings and requested and reviewed a number of responses from both the petitioners and the state. On matters specific to the amnesty, the government argued that the law "extinguished the individual criminal responsibility of persons involved on both sides of the conflict," noting that the law itself was "the result of broad national consensus in the sense that it enabled democracy to be restored in the early 1980s."[73] The petitioners disagreed, arguing that the amnesty law had effectively "institutionalize[d] impunity" in Brazil. By 2004, under mounting pressure for fuller accounting and transparency, the Ministry of Defense announced that "all archival documents related to historic events had been destroyed," claiming that the records had been "incinerated or shredded" along with the terms that authorized their destruction.[74] Some such documents, however, were subsequently reproduced in books about Araguaia.

In 2008, the Inter-American Commission on Human Rights published a report finding not only that the Brazilian state had arbitrarily detained, tortured, and disappeared members of the PCdoB and local residents but also that the amnesty law had impeded the state from conducting an investigation so that those responsible could be punished.[75] The following year, the commission referred the matter to the Inter-American Court of Human Rights for a decision on the issue of whether the amnesty in Brazil had "establishe[d] a regime of impunity" that prevented the prosecution and punishment of the perpetrators of forced disappearances in Araguaia.[76] The case was framed as an "important opportunity for the Court to consolidate the Inter-American jurisprudence on amnesty laws" that had enforced the obligation of governments to investigate and prosecute egregious violations of human rights. The Inter-American Commission on Human Rights had concluded that the measures put in place in Brazil to guarantee access to information about what happened to the Araguaia guerrillas had proved ineffective, and the "lack of access to justice, the truth, and information ha[d] negatively affected the personal integrity of the next of kin." In their subsequent filing to the Inter-American Court of Human Rights, the families affirmed the commission's conclusions about the Brazilian amnesty, saying that "all those responsible remain in the most absolute impunity, principally owed to the prevailing interpretation of the . . . amnesty law."[77]

The inter-American human rights system, both the commission and the court, had developed a clear and long-standing jurisprudence on the issue of amnesty. The position on amnesty dated back to 1992 when the commission concluded that the amnesties granted in Argentina and Uruguay were incompatible with the Inter-American Convention on Human Rights. The same conclusion was echoed by the Inter-American Court of Human Rights in decisions in *Barrios Altos v. Peru* in 2001, and two subsequent decisions in 2006—namely, *La Cantuta v. Peru* and *Almonacid v. Chile*. The court took issue with the amnesty laws in so far as they were "intended to prevent the investigation and punishment of those responsible for serious human rights violations." Such "perpetuation of impunity," moreover, "contributed to the defenselessness of victims."[78] The court also argued in the 2006 cases that the violations constituted crimes against humanity. Doing so rendered the failure to investigate and punish not only incompatible with the Inter-American Convention on Human Rights but, more broadly, with the norms of international law.[79]

As in its earlier decisions related to amnesty in other countries, the Inter-American Court of Human Rights faulted Brazil. In the resulting decision, *Guerrilha de Araguaia v. Brazil*, the court declared that "the provisions of the Brazilian Amnesty Law that prevent the investigation and punishment of serious human rights violations are not compatible with the American Convention, lack legal effect, and cannot continue as obstacles for the investigation of the facts of the present case." The decision further specified that the amnesty provisions could not prevent the "identification and punishment of those responsible, nor can they have equal or similar impact regarding other serious violations of human rights enshrined in the American Convention which occurred in Brazil." The court ruled that Brazil must investigate the Araguaia case to determine the facts about what had occurred and who was criminally responsible. Brazil must also "effectively apply the punishment and consequences which the law dictates."[80] The decision stood as a clear vindication for the families of the disappeared who had met resistance, obfuscation, and harassment at every turn in their search both for information about what happened to their loved ones and for justice for the crimes committed against them.

Brazil's Federal Supreme Court, just months before the Inter-American Court decision, stated that it could not and would not change the interpretation of the "connected crimes" clause that effectively guaranteed impunity for crimes such as torture, extrajudicial execution, and forced disappearance.[81] Its decision held that the Brazilian courts lacked jurisdiction over the interpretation of the clause in the amnesty law since it had been arrived at in a legislative process. As such, any review belonged as well to the legislature and not to a constitutional court. Furthermore, the Federal Supreme Court noted that the 1979 amnesty law preceded the 1988 constitution, included its prohibition of torture, as well as Brazil's commitment to the Inter-American Convention on Human Rights. The court found that any ruling on the amnesty, therefore, was beyond its reach.[82]

The case before the Federal Supreme Court began when the Brazilian Bar Association submitted a "claim of non-compliance with a fundamental precept." The claim argued that the interpretation of "connected crimes" to include state agents complicit in what were in fact "common crimes" committed against political opponents of the regime "offends various fundamental precepts inscribed in the Federal Constitution." The Brazilian Bar Association called out what it described as an intentional and surreptitious inclusion of torture and other cruel treatment committed by state agents within the ambit of crimes "connected" to political crimes. They argued that a connection between political and other crimes can only be recognized in cases where such crimes "were committed by the same person or other co-authors," underscoring that the amnesty applies only to "authors of political crimes or crimes against national security and, sometimes, to common crimes linked to the political crimes through a shared objective."[83] Therefore, the amnesty categorically excluded state agents. In practice and in the opinion of the Federal Supreme Court, however, it did.

Rather than argue about the interpretation in place since the decreeing of amnesty in 1979, the Brazilian Bar Association had asked the court to apply an interpretation that "conforms with the constitution" that followed in 1988. The court declined to do so. Rather, it emphasized that the 1979 law was the result of a political agreement that involved a conscious trade-off. In spite of "heroic" efforts on the part of those who campaigned for amnesty for all those opposed to the regime, no matter their tactics, the law that ultimately passed excluded some of them. The court found that while not as "broad" as was sought, the law was nonetheless, and undeniably, "bilateral."[84] In some ways, the ruling appeared to come full circle. It was not so different from the findings of the Federal Supreme Court more than a century earlier that had responded to arguments posed by Rui Barbosa about an apparent punishment imposed in an amnesty. Although framed as a case about the balance of power and the role for judicial review, the 1890s court had found that amnesty was fundamentally a political mechanism and the product of a political process.

THE UNANSWERED QUESTIONS

An article in the *New York Times* in December 2011 featured a photo of Victória, then sixty-eight years old, under a title referencing "ghosts" from the period of the military rule that had begun to "stir" amid an "uneasy search for truth." The article appeared more than a year after the opposing decisions of the Federal Supreme Court and the Inter-American Court of Human Rights. It was just after President Dilma Rousseff signed a law that would institute a truth commission in Brazil. The article reported on the criticisms the commission faced from multiple sides. Some victims saw the truth commission as a "token effort," since the amnesty still protected those identified as responsible for and complicit in human rights violations. One human rights advocate stated succinctly that the law reflected "what's possible in today's Brazil . . . shamefully behind other countries in coming to terms with our past." Some in the military, on the other hand, went on the defensive. The truth commission, in fact, immediately faced a lawsuit filed by Pedro Ivo Moézia de Lima, who had overseen interrogations in the 1970s. He explained that there was "rigor" in the interrogations, but he dismissed allegations of torture as exaggerations and inventions. He stated that he was "very proud of what he did."[85]

The last word in the article, however, was given to Victória. More practical than pessimistic, she noted frankly that most of the individuals complicit in torture and forced disappearance were "either in their 80s . . . or dead." Yet, in the years that followed, efforts nonetheless continue to hold them to account. In her last words of the biography she wrote of her father, which was published in 2012, Victória stated that she had the "duty to continue . . . and to demand of the Brazilian state answers to the questions of how, where, when, and who assassinated Mauricio, Gilberto, André, and their companions and then disappeared the bodies?" Her words echoed those used to describe the father known as "K" in Bernardo Kucinski's novel. As he searches, "the weeks become months, he gets tired and does less, but doesn't stop. The father seeking his disappeared daughter never stops. His hope dies but not his persistence."[86]

Long before the Federal Supreme Court demurred on the question of amnesty, neighboring countries had already largely dismantled amnesty laws that had protected state agents from the prospect of individual criminal accountability.[87] Faced with similar prohibitions on investigations and prosecutions, courts elsewhere found that not all claims to amnesty were absolute. Notably among them, a 1999 decision by a Chilean appeals court did not expressly challenge the amnesty in connection with alleged crimes of the infamous "Caravan of Death" that killed and disappeared dozens of political prisoners in the weeks following the 1973 military coup in Chile. Rather, it categorized cases of disappearances—where no body had ever been located—as kidnappings that were to be understood as ongoing or continuing.[88] In a clever twist, it required those accused, should they wish to appeal to the amnesty, to provide proof that the crime had been fully committed during the period covered by the amnesty. Thus, in the absence of a body or of credible information about the whereabouts of the person, the court had to assume that the crime of kidnapping was still in progress. Application of the amnesty to evade criminal liability in Chile would therefore ostensibly be predicated on information about the whereabouts of the disappeared.[89]

The argument held sway in Chilean courts, but a Brazilian judge was not similarly persuaded. In March 2012 in a criminal court in the state of Pará, the judge rejected a complaint filed against Major Curió for the aggravated kidnapping of five guerrillas who were captured between January and September 1974 and never seen again. He did so based on the 1979 amnesty. With a sentiment of let bygones be bygones, he argued that it would be a travesty to ignore the "historical circumstances that [brought the law into being] in a great effort for national reconciliation." As in Chile, the argument in the case relied principally on the "permanent character of the crime" because no remains had ever been recovered.

The judge, however, ruled both that the amnesty applied and that the statute of limitations had expired. The logic for the latter, odd as it might seem, was that the facts in the case were not constitutive of a kidnapping. It defied logic, the judge said, that "the disappeared, thirty-some years later, remain in captivity imposed by the defendant." Rather, all signs point to the "extreme probability of the death of the disappeared, even the assumption of the event of death." Besides, he continued, the victims named in the case had been official recognized by the 1995 Law of the Disappeared as among those killed by the military regime.[90]

Other cases related to Araguaia would be filed in Brazilian courts. As a result of the Inter-American Court of Human Rights decision, in fact, a working group on Araguaia was formed in the Public Ministry. To date, however, no complaints have reached the trial phase. Regionally, the lack of accountability for such crimes is increasingly a Brazilian phenomenon.[91] Indeed, in a 2014 study of the implementation and outcomes of transitional justice measures in Latin America, Brazil consistently ranked either as the lowest, or second only to El Salvador, in a number of assessments regarding accountability.[92] An updated analysis, however, would likely put Brazil uniformly on the bottom. By 2016 El Salvador had annulled its amnesty law, and in short order a regional court charged members of the high command and battalion commanders with crimes associated with the notorious 1981 El Mozote massacre.[93]

Nothing comparable has occurred in Brazil to date. In accountability terms, as the authors of the 2014 study stated, "Brazil's lack of meaningful trials continues to hold it back," as does its lack of compliance with the Inter-American Court of Human Rights verdict in the Araguaia case.[94] Brazil did better, relatively speaking, on a ranking of the "reparations dimension of accountability," and albeit somewhat surprisingly, the "truth-finding dimension of accountability." Although noting the controversy in procedures of the reparation programs, which essentially placed the "onus of proof" on the victims, the study's authors credited the Special Commission on Political Deaths and Disappearances, the Amnesty Commission, and the "grassroots momentum" surrounding the creation of the Truth Commission for their roles in acknowledging state-sponsored violations.[95] Amnesty, as it developed in Brazil, formed the roots running under both these shortcomings and successes.

THE *POLÍTICA* OF AMNESTY IN BRAZIL

In May 2019, in response to the nomination of seven military officers as new advisors to the Amnesty Commission, Rita Sipahi, a long-standing advisor, echoed the argument Rui Barbosa had made more than a century earlier. Sipahi called the move "the inversion of the *política* of amnesty." She expressed her condemnation in an open letter to Damares Alves, the minister of women, family and human rights in the administration of Jair Bolsonaro. Sipahi had served as an advisor, representing the "amnestied" and "amnesty-ing" for a decade before the commission. The open letter served as her resignation made in protest.[1]

The nomination of the military officers was but the latest move by the Bolsonaro administration to sideline, if not hamstring, the Amnesty Commission. The first, made shortly after he took office in January 2019, was to remove the commission from the auspices of the Ministry of Justice, where it had operated since 2001. Placing it in the newly created Ministry of Women, Family and Human Rights seemed part of a larger gesture intent on relegating those matters to the periphery. Bolsonaro, long known for his misogynistic, homophobic, and racist comments, had proudly served as an apologist for the abuses of the military regime when he dedicated his 2016 impeachment vote against Dilma Rousseff to Carlos Brilhante Ustra, the man responsible for her torture, and that of scores of others, during the dictatorship.[2]

In her May 2019 resignation, Sipahi is careful to note that the degradation of the commission did not begin with Bolsonaro. Indeed, following the impeachment of Rousseff, under the brief and tumultuous tenure of Michel Temer, the Amnesty Commission abandoned the practice of extending an apology on behalf of the state, which had served as a form of symbolic or moral reparation in recognition of the "right to political resistance against authoritarian acts." Instead, the commission returned to a simple analysis of the material and economic aspects of each case, as it had done in its earliest days. By 2014, before this reversal, the commission had received approximately seventy-five thousand individual petitions. Those cases, Sipahi argued, represent seventy-five thousand "narratives of political persecution," which comprise "the largest collection in first-person about political persecution in Brazil." The sum of these individual narratives, like individual stars in a constellation, had begun to enter into the "collective memory" of Brazil.[3]

Alves, an evangelical pastor before taking over the new ministry, saw things differently. By 2019 a total of seventy-eight thousand petitions had been filed with the Amnesty Commission, of which eleven thousand remained pending review. She noted, with apparent exasperation, that the commission had by then granted ten billion reais in indemnity, which had already been paid, and had approved another fourteen billion reais for payment. In March 2019, when she placed the new advisors on the commission, Alves announced that prior "suspicious" acts of the commission would be reviewed.[4] It appeared that reparations granted in relation to the events in Araguaia might be among them. The new president of the commission, João Henrique Nascimento de Freitas, had previously filed an injunction against the payment of indemnity to forty-four local residents recognized as victims of torture during the Araguaia guerrilla movement. Less than a year later, he tweeted an article announcing that the commission had collectively denied three hundred petitions related to Araguaia.[5]

In August 2019, just a few months after reorganizing and reorienting the Amnesty Commission, Alves cancelled a project underway in Belo Horizonte to build a memorial site to and for amnesty in Brazil. The project included space to house the archive of the Amnesty Commission.[6] That same month, reports emerged that the commission had referred to petitioners as "terrorists" and relied on memoirs of military officers as evidence in proceedings. In a case involving a former university student who had been a member of a clandestine organization imprisoned by the DOPS in São Paulo, one of the new military advisors, General Luis Eduardo Rocha Paiva, found that "what happened to her was not political persecution." He then called for her to be investigated "because she was a militant in a terrorist organization." Another representative on the commission protested, saying that the job of the commission was not to "re-judge the political militants from the time of the dictatorships." If it were, he said, the commission would also need to call the torturers and "debate their situation" too, but "amnesty is not this."[7] By September 2019, with a foreboding sense of fait accompli, one representative of petitioners alleged that Alves had oriented the commissioners to deny, en masse, the remaining petitions.[8]

Sipahi did not reference Rui Barbosa by name in her letter of resignation. Her condemnation of the changes imposed by Alves as "the inversion of the *política* of amnesty" nonetheless linked her arguments to the longer history of amnesty in Brazil. In obvious ways, the use of the term "inversion" harked back to the arguments made by Barbosa in the *Anistia Inversa* case in the 1890s. More than a century after those arguments, Sipahi did not denounce so much the inversion of amnesty itself but, rather, that of the *política*, or policy, of amnesty that had been developed and implemented in Brazil. Without wanting to make more of this distinction than she perhaps intended, the remark nonetheless assumed an established practice related to amnesty in Brazil—and that practice had to do with amnesty as recompense.

The linkage of amnesty to restitution and reparations in Brazil can be traced back to Rui Barbosa, a central figure in the founding of the republic in the late nineteenth century. His arguments about the purposes and effects of amnesty, especially in the *Anistia Inversa* case, conspicuously shaped subsequent debates in Brazil. This fact is striking, given that those same arguments failed to persuade the Federal Supreme Court at the time he made them. Nonetheless, throughout the twentieth century, his litany about amnesty—delivered in the moment of the consolidation of republican rule in the 1890s—was quoted verbatim by others to argue in favor of amnesty for the sake of democratization, citizenship rights, and reconciliation. These moments include the large-scale political transformations in the twentieth century: from the oligarchy of the early decades to the centralized state in the 1930s; from the dictatorial Estado Novo to mass-based democracy in the 1940s; and from the military regime of the 1960s and 1970s to civilian rule in the 1980s. In those moments, the granting of amnesty went hand-in-hand with promises of liberalization or democratization and often with the expressed intent to serve restorative ends. The Amnesty Commission, instituted more than a century after the *Anistia Inversa* case, also emphasized, at least until recently, these same notions of amnesty as a step toward deeper democratization, a recognition and restoration of rights, and over time, a sign of national reconciliation.

To be sure, this conflation of restitution and reparations with amnesty has a particular history. In the 1890s *Anistia Inversa* matter, the issue was the constitutional protection of rights associated with the acquired status and station of military officers. As their attorney, Barbosa argued that the amnesty under question had imposed a punishment and was thus not truly amnesty. True amnesty instituted "legal amnesia," which would restore its beneficiaries to their formerly held positions and any corresponding rights. The legacy of the *Anistia Inversa* case supported arguments in favor of unrestricted general amnesties during the twentieth century, but the actual stakes in the case were much narrower. The offense or injury, as Barbosa laid it out, was less in the action of forcibly retiring rebel military officers and more in the amnesty decree itself, which targeted a class of people with constitutional protection. When Barbosa exclaimed that "there are jobs, and then there are jobs," he reinforced prevailing notions that some rights in Brazil derived from positions of honor. He might have said that there are citizens, and then there are citizens.

And, indeed there were. The 1910 revolt of Black sailors underscored the boundaries of tolerance for political opposition. The spectacle of a revolt by Black enlisted men in the navy proved too threatening to the elites. The sailors' demands for an end to corporal punishment and an amnesty were not regarded as political. The amnesty granted, in turn, was not enforced and therefore afforded them no protection. The rebel sailors won one battle in securing a grant of amnesty but then lost the war. Unlike the officers in the *Anistia Inversa* case, the sailors had no firm ground, constitutional or otherwise, from which to contest their claims for protection of basic human dignity. The contrast of the two cases in the space of one generation brings to the fore the dominant ideas about the appropriate price to be exacted for political opposition. There is something there of the paradoxical "double code" from Roberto DaMatta's "Brazilian dilemma": Brazilian society permitted exceptions and adjustments to laws based on hierarchy and privilege.[9]

For many reasons, the sailors' history is poignant in comparison. Rather than specific monetary entitlements, they asked for an end to corporal punishment in the navy. While the higher-ranking officers in the 1890s ultimately reversed the restrictions placed on them by the amnesty, the sailors endured, virtually without recourse, the full blunt force of the state's hand in retribution in spite of the amnesty that had been granted. Indeed, the extension of amnesty to them seemed to have sullied it as a political tool for many years to come.

With the installation of the era of Getúlio Vargas in 1930, amnesty returned as a key political recourse. It was accompanied by the institution of ad hoc bureaucracies to adjudicate any subsequent claims for restitution. A little over a generation after the officers of the *Anistia In-*

versa case made arguments about exceptional constitutional guarantees, another sector of the military laid claim to special rights via amnesty. The tenentes, like the officers of a generation before, had political ambitions that had been thwarted in the reordering of politics following the revolutionary movement that brought Vargas to power. The amnesty promised to restore if not the political possibilities at least the economic security and social mobility of a military career. The outcomes of their cases and those of other military personnel, however, were much more mixed. Some fared well, while others remained outside the benefits of amnesty for the better part of their working years. The civilian bureaucrats who had been purged from their positions, for their part, received a benevolent gesture of a would-be dictator: the opportunity to petition to a commission for reinstatement to their positions. The actual outcomes for them were also mixed.

By the 1940s, and in the waning months of the Second World War, the emphasis on political prisoners in the widespread social mobilization for amnesty associated it closely with democracy. The campaign was potent and Vargas's situation was urgent. If in the earlier cases, the restoration of rights was based on status and something akin to paternalism, claims for the restoration of rights in the 1945 amnesty drew more from the expanding expectations about universal rights. More acutely than before, the figure of the political prisoner inspired sympathy and resonated in Brazil. Behind the scenes, however, the specter of the communist-backed barracks revolt in 1935 beleaguered the committees charged with ruling on the reinstatement of military personnel—so much so that the whole process ground to a halt. Although the civilian hearings made more progress, they also reflected the constricting of political life and the renewed repression that characterized the coming of the Cold War.

In the 1970s and 1980s the stakes in the campaign for amnesty were framed in the language of human rights, especially in light of the prevalence of torture by the military regime. As in 1945, the amnesty law enacted in 1979 provided for possible restitution through bureaucratic commissions that would review individual petitions. And, as in 1945, the rulings of those commissions did little to satisfy expectations of the restorative imperatives of amnesty. Moreover, the 1979 amnesty also effectively shielded state agents of terror from the prospect of criminal accountability for their actions. So, while Brazil's southern cone neighbors increasingly submitted to demands for individual accountability and justice, impunity reigned in Brazil. In the absence of accountability, Brazil relied on a model of reparations and memory—referenced as amnesty—in its paradigm of transitional justice.

The cases examined here have given a glimpse of a century of amnesties in Brazil. They reflect the implementation of new ideas and old assumptions about rights over time, showing that any footing of the amnestying in seeking or securing recompense was often shaky and subject to sudden shifts. These cases also call attention to the contingencies that affected the outcomes. By focusing on the outcomes of the petitions, the cases bring to the fore the foundations for claims to restitution and mark the moments in which those claims were adjudicated, affirmed, denied, or adjusted. In the end, what stands out is the fact that there were such contingencies involved in adjudicating amnesty, the very measure that aimed in all the cases to effect some sort of finality. Indeed, in some ways, this is the history of those who persisted, who left a paper trail, who had access to political brokering or sufficient social and political weight, or who continued in their political militancy. It is a history whose urgency ebbed and flowed, in which opportunities opened and closed and new stakes appeared while others faded. The cases, in fact, highlight more than anything else how unsettled and uneven the settlements were. These details add something to our understanding of the ways in which transitional justice works.

If the history of amnesty in Brazil began in earnest with the *Anistia Inversa* case, the history of the amnestied likewise began with the forty-seven military members who were the plaintiffs in that case. In simple numerical terms, the total number of individuals who filed suit or applied to special commissions for some sort of material restitution has shown a steady upward trajectory during the twentieth century, from the forty-seven in the *Anistia Inversa* case in 1895, to the nearly eight hundred who petitioned the centralized Review Commission in 1935, to the thousands upon thousands in the 1945 and 1979 atomized bureaucratic hearings, to the tens of thousands who have filed petitions to the Amnesty Commission since 2001. As of February 2020, nearly thirty-nine thousand of them have had their petitions approved by the commission and thereby have joined the ranks of the amnestied of Brazil.[10]

Clearly, something happened with the institution of amnesty and expectations about restitution during the long twentieth century. On a more symbolic and discursive plane, grants of amnesty were collective and reconciling measures. As things played out, however, amnesty and any accompanying recompense was awarded largely on a case-by-case basis and was constrained by old and new political realities. Attempts by individuals to seek and secure the benefits or guarantees outlined in various decrees and laws, both immediately after their enactment and in the years and decades that followed, reflected prevailing—and often shifting—perceptions about just and unjust repercussions for political opposition and resistance. The results of those attempts, in turn, reveal the parameters and limits of amnesty as a recourse to secure rights and entitlements over time. The sum of the century-plus history of amnesty, in some ways, ends as it first began, as something not yet fully realized.

NOTES

INTRODUCTION: THE CALCULUS OF RESTITUTION IN BRAZIL

1. In one oral history project involving women who were former militants in Brazil, all were either still in high school or first-year university students when they began their political militancy. See E. Ferreira, "Oral History," 17.

2. The Amnesty Commission was created under Provisional Measure no. 2,151 on August 28, 2001, a date that marked the twenty-second anniversary of the enactment of the 1979 amnesty law in Brazil. The commission was formalized under Law no. 10,559 on November 13, 2002.

3. Barkan, *Guilt of Nations*, xv; for further discussion of the Swiss case, see 88–111.

4. Roht-Arriaza, "Reparations," 124; Helen Hughes and Kevin G. Hall, "Soul-Searching Chile Creates a Stir with Torture Testimonies; Leaders All Over South America Are Taking a Hard Look at Past Abuses by Right-Wing Regimes," *Philadelphia Inquirer*, November 14, 2004, A10.

5. Prates, Loup, and Gois, "Cemitério São João Batista."

6. For a brief background on Grupo Tortura Nunca Mais, see Salgado and Grabois, "O Grupo Tortura Nunca Mais," 61–66; A. Schneider, "Unsettling and Unsettled Monument," 497–99.

7. In her analysis of amnesty, Agata Fijalkowski succinctly states that "the measure has come to epitomize an obstacle to justice" because it has been politicized "to silence the crimes and protect the perpetrators under the guise of policies that claim to address the past injustices of the predecessor regime." See Fijalkowski, "Amnesty," 116.

8. The general amnesty covered crimes committed between September 11, 1973, and March 10, 1978, and included accomplices and people involved in covering up crimes. See Ensalaco, *Chile Under Pinochet*, 129.

9. Roht-Arriaza, *Pinochet Effect*, 70, 74–86.

10. Bois-Pedaín, "Accountability through Conditional Amnesty," 239–41.

11. Teitel, "Transitional Justice Genealogy," 79. See also Wilson, *Politics of Truth*.

12. Desmond Tutu reportedly commented to President Fernando Henrique Cardoso, on the occasion of an official visit to South Africa, that "we have much to learn from Brazil" about amnesty and reconciliation. See Lemos, "Anistia e crise política," 295. For a comparison of the Brazilian and South African cases, see E. Teles, "Entre justiça e violência."

13. A. Schneider, "Legislative Efforts," 24–29; Fico, "A negociação parlamentar," 324–27.

14. Abrão, Bellato, Alvarenga, and Torelly, "Justiça de transição," 17.

15. R. Martins, *Liberdade para os brasileiros*. See also Câmara dos Deputados, *Anistia*. Some sources reference as many as forty-eight amnesties granted from 1895 to 1979 in Brazil. See P. da Cunha, "Militares e anistia no Brasil," 15.

16. Ricoeur, *Memory, History, Forgetting*, 453.

17. In their seminal works in the 1930s, Gilberto Freyre and Sérgio Buarque de Holanda described a seemingly essential uniqueness about Brazil that, they argued, derived from a divergent colonial experience. Freyre applied the term "lusotropicalism" as a shorthand to describe the distinct attributes of this particularized system, which was milder and more informally transactional. Holanda's conception of the *homem cordial* (cordial man) similarly explained a blurring of distinctions between public and private realms in the development of Brazilian institutions. See Freyre, *Masters and the Slaves*; Holanda, *Raízes do Brasil*.

18. Dain Borges described one such pattern of paternalism among late nineteenth- and early twentieth-century elites as a "ritual of punishment, *castigo*." In the context of slavery and its aftermath, he explained, patrons "knew in their hearts that they had coerced," so they could never trust the apparent loyalty of their clients. To exorcise the demons of doubt, they followed a "scripted ritual involving stages of accusation, passing judgment, defiance or reveling, corporal punishment or the suspension of sentence, and then often pardon and reconciliation." See Borges, "Salvador's 1890s," 53.

19. José Honório Rodrigues framed conciliation as a "tradition" in Brazil and situated it as the antithesis of democratic reform, arguing that political elites utilized forms of conciliation as a strategy to preserve the status quo and derail revolutionary momentum in politics. See J. Rodrigues, *Conciliação e reforma*.

20. He viewed this dynamic through the lens of dependency theory, explaining that, through "certain advantages afforded to the weakest pole, conciliation consolidated the position of the strongest pole." See Debrun, *A "conciliação" e outras estratégias*, 52, 124.

21. Fijalkowski, "Amnesty," 115. The phonetic similarity between "amnesty" and "amnesia" is even closer in Portuguese prior to the orthographic change from *amnistia*, used in the sources related to the cases from the 1890s through 1930s, to *anistia*, used in the sources beginning in the 1940s. The word *amnesia*

in Portuguese did not undergo any orthographic change over the period considered here.

22. Rebecca Atencio notes a slippage in Brazil, especially in relation to reckoning with the crimes of the Cold War–era dictatorship, that equates the pursuit of accountability with revenge-seeking. This perceived revenge, in turn, is cast as un-Brazilian, in the sense that it rejects the celebration of "conciliation and cordiality . . . as a defining characteristic of national identity." To some extent, a similar tension emerges in relation to those seeking indemnity through the Amnesty Commission. See Atencio, *Memory's Turn*, 87.

23. Paulino, *O Julgamento dos anistiados políticos*. Unless otherwise noted, all translations from the Portuguese are my own.

24. In distinguishing the simpler concept of restitution from the "messier" one of reparation, Charles Maier notes that the former refers to a "specific material good [that] is restored to a previous owner" while the latter demands putting "a price on [a] priceless loss." In so doing, the payment of reparations requires "remov[ing] the losses from the realm of the sacred, the never-to-be-forgotten, into the realm of the politically negotiated." See Maier, "Overcoming the Past?," 296–97.

25. Abrão and Torelly, "Mutações do conceito de anistia." In brief, the phases of amnesty outlined include: (1) the paradox of amnesty as signifying both liberty for political prisoners and impunity for perpetrators of human rights violations; (2) the association of amnesty with reparations, beginning with the Amnesty Commission; and (3) the development from Brazil's paradigm of reparations, through amnesty, to a broader recognition of truth and justice about past state atrocities.

26. Luiz Felipe Barbiéri, "Damares amplia número de integrantes e determina auditoria em atos da Comissão de Anistia," *O Globo*, March 27, 2019, https://g1 .globo.com/politica/noticia/2019/03/27/damares-amplia-numero-de-inte grantes-e-determina-auditoria-em-atos-da-comissao-de-anistia.ghtml.

PART I: AMNESTY AS RECOURSE, 1890S–1910

1. Letter from Eduardo Wandenkolk, June 19, 1892, correspondence 1526, Rui Barbosa Archive, Fundação Casa Rui Barbosa (Rui Barbosa House Foundation), Rio de Janeiro.

2. Unless noted, biographical details about Wandenkolk are derived from the biographical information contained in the *Dicionário Histórico-Biográfico Brasileiro* (*DHBB*). See Izabel Pimentel da Silva, "Eduardo Wandenkolk," *DHBB*, Centro de Pesquisa e Documentação de História Contemporânea do Brasil, Fundação Getúlio Vargas (Center for the Research and Documentation of Contemporary Brazilian History, Getúlio Vargas Foundation), hereafter cited as CPDOC/FGV, http://cpdoc.fgv.br/sites/default/files/verbetes/primeira -republica/WANDENKOLK,%20Eduardo.pdf.

3. Nine individuals were exiled to Cucuhy. Wandenkolk, four other officers, and a dental surgeon were exiled to Tabatinga. See notices in *Gazeta de Notícias*, April 8, 13, 1892.

4. Supremo Tribunal Federal, *Acórdão, Habeas Corpus no. 300*, April 27, 1892, http://www.stf.jus.br/arquivo/cms/sobreStfConhecaStfJulgamentoHisto rico/anexo/HC300.pdf.

5. Barbosa, "Os atos inconstitucionais," 183.

6. Barbosa, "O caso Wandenkolk," 289–90.

7. During his imprisonment Wandenkolk wrote the fourth volume of his diary. See Jesus, "O diário do almirante."

8. Centro de Instrução Almirante Wandenkolk, https://www.marinha.mil .br/ciaw.

9. Love, *Revolt of the Whip*, 97–99. On the revolt, see also Nascimento, *Cidadania*; Morgan, *Legacy of the Lash*; H. da Cunha, *A revolta na esquadra brasileira*.

10. J. M. de Carvalho, *Pontos e bordados*, 22–32. See also Love, *Revolt of the Whip*, 108–9.

11. João Cândido later referred to his assumed rank in quotation marks. See Love, *Revolt of the Whip*, 31.

12. Love, *Revolt of the Whip*, 99–100, 103–4.

13. Love, *Revolt of the Whip*, 66.

Chapter 1: Linking Restitution to Amnesty, "Even though Superfluous," 1890s

1. Seabra made these statements on September 21, 1892. See Moraes Filho, *Um estadista da república*, 40–41.

2. Decree no. 791, 1892. Unless otherwise noted, all decrees and laws cited can be located in the Chamber of Deputies database of federal legislation, https://www2.camara.leg.br/atividade-legislativa/legislacao. See discussion of this decree in Lago, *Rui Barbosa*, 19–20.

3. Barbosa, "Os atos inconstitucionais," 21.

4. Barbosa, "Os atos inconstitucionais," 183.

5. Unless noted, biographical details about Almeida Barreto are derived from information contained in Cláudio Beserra de Vasconcelos, "Barreto, Almeida," *DHBB*, CPDOC/FGV, http://cpdoc.fgv.br/sites/default/files/verbetes/primei ra-republica/BARRETO,%20Almeida.pdf.

6. Simmons, "Deodoro da Fonseca"; E. da Costa, *Brazilian Empire*, 233.

7. Schwarcz, *Emperor's Beard*, 301.

8. The quote by Aristides Lobo—that the people watched the parade "*bes-tializado*"—appeared in the *Diário Popular* of São Paulo. The term *bestializado* connotes a sense of surprise. For discussion of the historiography, see Mello, *A*

República Consentida, 9–10. See also J.M. de Carvalho, *Os Bestializados*, 140–42. On the conspirators, see Fausto, *Concise History*, 139.

9. Lacombe, *A Sombra de Rui Barbosa*, 36–37.

10. Constant also shaped the new republican institutions that would follow, serving as the first minister of war in 1889, then as the minister of education until his death in 1891. Positivism in Brazil was both a religion and a political ideology. While Comtean positivism was prevalent in the military, some adherents in the military and elsewhere looked more toward a Spencerian version or an eclectic approach. See Lins, *História do positivismo*.

11. Lins, *História do positivismo*. See also Costa, *Contribuição à história*.

12. Queiroz, "Reflections on Brazilian Jacobinism," 189–90.

13. See discussion in the introduction of Freyre, *Masters and the Slaves*.

14. Queiroz, "Reflections on Brazilian Jacobinism," 181–82.

15. Constitution of the Republic of the United States of Brazil, February 24, 1891.

16. Galvão, *Rui Barbosa*, 23.

17. Galvão, *Rui Barbosa*, 21–22.

18. The amnesty provision can be found in article 34, section 27 of the 1891 constitution.

19. The legislature passed three amnesties, two in 1835 and one in 1836. Amnesties were decreed via the moderating power in 1831, 1840, 1841, 1844, when there were three, and in 1849. On the moderating power and amnesty, see Santos, *Repertorio enciclopédico*, 281.

20. R. Martins, *Liberdade para os brasileiros*, 34.

21. Barbosa, "Os atos inconstitucionais," x. The assembly drafted and passed the 1891 constitution and elected Deodoro as president with 129 votes to 97 votes for Prudente de Morais. They also elected Floriano Peixoto as vice president with 157 votes. Wandenkolk was runner-up, but with a hundred less votes. Almeida Barreto received 4 votes to be vice president.

22. E. da Costa, *Brazilian Empire*, 243, 265.

23. Queiroz, "Reflections on Brazilian Jacobinism," 182–83.

24. Fausto, *Concise History*, 148–53.

25. R. Martins, *Liberdade para os brasileiros*, 53–54.

26. Freyre, *Order and Progress*, 172–73.

27. Topik, "Brazil's Bourgeois Revolution?"

28. Gonçalves, "Judiciabilidade dos atos políticos," 197–98.

29. Barbosa, "Os atos inconstitucionais," 140.

30. Session on May 26, 1892. See *Annães do Senado Federal*, 97–98.

31. The petition for habeas corpus was filed on April 18, 1892. See Barbosa, "Estado de Sítio," 11–13.

32. José Libânio Lamenha Lins de Sousa, Antonio Carlos da Silva Piragibe,

and Sebastião Bandeira were also among those named in the habeas corpus petition who would be a party to the lawsuit over the 1895 amnesty.

33. Barbosa, *Martial Law*, 5.

34. Barbosa, "Acórdão," 355–61.

35. The slave trade was abolished in 1851 but continued illicitly.

36. Barbosa, *Martial Law*, 7.

37. Barbosa, *Martial Law*, 6–7.

38. Carvalho, *Cidadania no Brasil*, 64, 75. Other examples contemporaneous to the 1892 petition for habeas corpus include the millenarian movement in Canudos later in the 1890s and the revolt against obligatory vaccinations in Rio de Janeiro in 1904.

39. Barbosa, *Martial Law*, 10–18.

40. Barbosa, *Martial Law*, 25.

41. Barbosa, *Martial Law*, 31–32.

42. Barbosa, *Martial Law*, 60.

43. Barbosa, *Martial Law*, 58.

44. Barbosa, *Martial Law*, 30.

45. See Haskins and Johnson, *Foundations of Power*; Dewey, *Marshall versus Jefferson*.

46. The date of the judgment was April 27, 1892; the petition for habeas corpus was denied by a ten-to-one majority. Minister Costa Barradas wrote the majority opinion.

47. L. Rodrigues, *História do Supremo Tribunal Federal*, 61–66.

48. Barbosa, "Os atos inconstitucionais," 21.

49. Barbosa, "Os atos inconstitucionais," 36.

50. Barbosa, "Os atos inconstitucionais," 20, 19, also 24–25.

51. Barbosa, "Os atos inconstitucionais," 19–28. The petition is dated May 8, 1893. The monthly total was tallied as follows: *Sôldo*, 750$000; *Etapa*, 300$000; *Gratificação do exercício*, 370$000; *Criado*, 370$000. With the forced retirement, Almeida Barreto received the *sôldo* of 750$000 and a *cota de reforma* of 213$000.

52. The original quote by Rui Barbosa in Portuguese reads: "*Distingo. Há emprêgo e emprêgo.*" See Barbosa, "Os atos inconstitucionais," 191.

53. Barbosa, "Os atos inconstitucionais," 30.

54. Barbosa, "Os atos inconstitucionais," 26.

55. Barbosa, "Os atos inconstitucionais," 184, 184, 186, 185.

56. Barbosa, "Os atos inconstitucionais," 27.

57. "Apelação Civel no. 112, Acórdão, September 19, 1895," in Barbosa, "Os atos inconstitucionais," 225–28. See also L. Rodrigues, *História do Supremo Tribunal Federal*, 61.

58. Nogueira, *O advogado Rui Barbosa*, 142–43.

59. A fourth book was published decades later, in 1999, when Nogueira was eighty-six years old. When the military regime began its gradual return to civil-

ian government, Nogueira served as a consultant to the minister of justice and wrote an opinion that served as the basis for the 1979 amnesty law. He would live another decade, dying at ninety-six years of age in 2010. See "Rubem Rodrigues Nogueira," *DHBB*, CPDOC/FGV, http://www.fgv.br/cpdoc/acervo/dicionarios/verbete-biografico/rubem-rodrigues-nogueira.

60. Nogueira, *O advogado Rui Barbosa*, 144.

61. Barbosa, "Os atos inconstitucionais," 187.

62. *Diário Oficial*, no. 310, November 15, 1895, 7601.

63. *Diário Oficial*, no. 310, November 15, 1895, 7601.

CHAPTER 2: AMNESTY AS PENALTY

1. As explained in L. Rodrigues, *História do Supremo Tribunal Federal*, 63.

2. The poem, by Aprigio Mendonça, "a worker at the War Arsenal," was published on the front page of the *Jornal do Comercio* on September 20, 1895. See Fundo SF, Prudente de Morais, Codices, Livro 6, #1043, Arquivo Nacional (National Archive), Rio de Janeiro and Brasília (hereafter cited as AN).

3. Barbosa, "Anistia inversa," 1–196.

4. L. Rodrigues, *História do Supremo Tribunal Federal*, 68, 70.

5. The initial filing of the *Anistia inversa* case was subtitled "Defense . . . of those *condemned* by the amnesty of 1895" (emphasis mine).

6. Borges, "Puffy, Ugly," 235.

7. Lima Barreto, *Triste Fim de Polycarpo Quaresma*; Da Cunha, *Rebellion in the Backlands*.

8. "Lima Barreto," O Museu Afro Brasil, http://www.museuafrobrasil.org.br/pesquisa/hist%C3%B3ria-e-mem%C3%B3ria/historia-e-memoria/2014/07/17/lima-barreto. On his life and works, see also Schwarcz, *Lima Barreto*.

9. Wasserman, "Lima Barreto," 55.

10. Derik Badman, "Bouvard and Pecuchet," *Quarterly Conversation*, accessed November 10, 2019, http://quarterlyconversation.com/bouvard-and-pecuchet-by-gustave-flaubert-review (no longer available). See also Nicholas Lezard, "The Sad End of Policarpo Quaresma by Lima Barreto," *The Guardian*, July 15, 2014, https://www.theguardian.com/books/2014/jul/15/sad-end-policarpo-quaresma-lima-barreto-review.

11. Madden, "Canudos War," 6–8, 17. On Canudos, see also Levine, *Vale of Tears*; Della Cava, "Brazilian Messianism."

12. Levine, "Mud-Hut Jerusalem," 526.

13. Williams and Vargas Llosa, "Boom Twenty Years Later," 204–5.

14. Borges, "Puffy, Ugly."

15. On the civil war in Rio Grande do Sul, see Love, *Rio Grande do Sul*, 1–105; Chasteen, "Background to Civil War"; Chasteen, "Fighting Words"; and Lourdes and Janotti, "Monarchists Response," 228. See also Izabel Pi-

mental da Silva, "Castilhos, Julio de," *DHBB*, CPDOC/FGV, https://cpdoc
.fgv.br/sites/default/files/verbetes/primeira-republica/CASTILHOS,%20
J%C3%BAlio%20de.pdf.

16. See Decrees nos. 174, 175, 176, September 12, 1893.

17. Ribeiro, *Sonho no cárcere*.

18. "Amnesty in Brazil," *Washington Post*, January 10, 1895, 4.

19. H. Martins, *A Revolta da Armada*, 438, 439 (Bocaiúva from June 5, Campos Sales from June 6, 1895).

20. Those in the navy would be placed *em disponibilidade* and those in army would be assigned to a *quadro extraordinario*. For the purposes here, I have translated both technical Portuguese terms as "reserve" status. See Parecer 6/895 in H. Martins, *A Revolta da Armada*, 437–38.

21. Barbosa, "Anexos," 319–37.

22. Decree no. 310, October 21, 1895. See also Barbosa, "Anistia inversa," 63–64.

23. Barbosa, "Anistia inversa," 15, 16.

24. Constitution of the Republic of the United States of Brazil, February 24, 1891.

25. Juizo Seccional do Districto Federal, "Acçao summaria especial, Jul. 26, 1896."

26. Barbosa, "Anistia inversa," 177–79.

27. Barbosa, "Anistia inversa," 180–81.

28. Câmara dos Deputados, "Sessão em 14 de agosto de 1896," *Annaes de Camara*, 313–14.

29. Letter from First Lieutenant João da Silva Retumba, February 12, 1897, correspondence 1235 (6), Rui Barbosa Archive, Rui Barbosa House Foundation, Rio de Janeiro.

30. Decree no. 2,673, November 16, 1897.

31. Decree no. 2,674, November 16, 1897.

32. Project no. 12/1898. See Congresso Nacional, "Suppresão de restricções a amnistia decretada em 1895," 224–25.

33. The criticism came from Belfort Vieira. See Congresso Nacional, "Suppresão de restricções a amnistia decretada em 1895," 233.

34. Barbosa, "Anistia inversa," 107–30.

35. "A anistia constitucional de 1934 não abrange apos já compreendidos pelas anistias anteriormente decretadas," *Diário de Notícias*, February 16, 1941, 4. Unless noted, all articles cited from historical Brazilian newspapers can be located in the Brazilian National Library's Hemeroteca Digital database, http://bndigital.bn.gov.br/hemeroteca-digital.

36. The decision by the Federal Supreme Court on "Apelação Civil no. 7.748, August 4, 1947," is discussed in the introduction to the *Anistia inversa* case. See Barbosa, "Anistia inversa," 9.

CHAPTER 3: THE SHAME OF AMNESTY

1. "Brazilian Sailors Had Been Tortured," *New York Times*, November 28, 1910, 3. See also Love, *Revolt of the Whip*, 75.

2. "Tells of Brazilian Mutiny," *New York Times*, December 6, 1910, 11.

3. Love, *Revolt of the Whip*, 34, 67.

4. Cited in various sources, including H. da Cunha's *A revolta na esquadra brasileira*, 42; Love, *Revolt of the Whip*, 31.

5. Leão, *Relatório*, 9.

6. For a concise narrative of the revolt, see Morel, *A revolta da chibata*, 73–113; Love, *Revolt of the Whip*, 27–47; Nascimento, *Cidadania*, 25–71; Morgan, *Legacy of the Lash*, 194–227.

7. Love, *Revolt of the Whip*, 28–30.

8. Love, *Revolt of the Whip*, 33.

9. The amnesty is Decree no. 2,280, November 15, 1910. The removal of enlisted men was authorized in Decree no. 8,400, November 28, 1910.

10. Love, *Revolt of the Whip*, 89–90.

11. Freyre, *Order and Progress*, 402, 400.

12. R. Graham, *Patronage and Politics*, 23–42.

13. Borges, "Puffy, Ugly," 235.

14. DaMatta, *Carnivals, Rogues, and Heroes*, 141.

15. Lima Barreto, *Triste Fim de Policarpo Quaresma*, 172, 207.

16. Borges, "Puffy, Ugly," 240.

17. For this period, see Needell, *Tropical Belle Epoque*; Meade, *"Civilizing" Rio*.

18. The term "Belle Époque" refers to the period when the oligarchic power was consolidated under President Campos Sales, beginning the *política dos governadores* in which executive power alternated between the states of São Paulo and Minas Gerais. See Needell, "Revolta Contra Vacina," 241–43.

19. Romero, *Latinoamérica*, 251.

20. José Murilo de Carvalho explained that Cruz's program reformulated existing legislation that required universal vaccination. See J.M. de Carvalho, *Os bestializados*, 95–96.

21. Needell, "Revolta Contra Vacina," 244.

22. Beattie, "House, the Street, and the Barracks," 454; also cited in J.M. de Carvalho, *Os bestializados*, 100–101.

23. J.M. de Carvalho, "Brazil 1870–1914."

24. Needell, "Revolta Contra Vacina."

25. Facsimile of the manifesto is reprinted in Morel, *A Revolta da Chibata*. See also Love, *Revolt of the Whip*, 33.

26. J.C. de Carvalho, *O livro da minha vida*, 348.

27. "The Naval Situation: Foreign Powers," *London Times*, March 4, 1911.

28. Morel, *A revolta da chibata*, 37, 59.

29. Granato, *O negro da chibata*, 20; Morel, *A revolta da chibata*, 74.

30. Silva, *Caricata República*, 41–43.

31. Barbosa, "Anistia para os marinheiros," 167.

32. Borges, "Intellectuals and the Forgetting of Slavery in Brazil," 30.

33. Beattie, "Conscription versus Penal Servitude."

34. Robert A. Hayes discusses how the various exemptions led to accusations that citizens lacked patriotism. At the same time, the crisis served as a "benchmark" in the military's search for its role and thus provided a deep sense of "corporate solidarity." See Hayes, *Armed Nation*, 62.

35. Data derived from the 1888 navy minister's report, cited in Nascimento, *A ressaca da marujada*, 75.

36. Ministério da Agricultura, *Annuario Estatístico do Brazil*, 248.

37. F. McCann, "Formative Period," 739. See also F. McCann, "Brazilian General Staff."

38. DaMatta, *Carnivals, Rogues, and Heroes*, 152–53.

39. Peter Beattie described the army as the "primary institutional bridge between the state and the criminal underworld." See Beattie, "Conscription versus Penile Servitude," 847.

40. Beattie, *Tribute of Blood*, 181.

41. Caminha, *Black Man and the Cabin Boy*, 42. Peter Beattie explained that the title *Bom Crioulo* was "likely intended as an ironic evocation of Bom Selvagem (the noble savage)." See Beattie, "Adolfo Ferreira Caminha," 99. See also Azevedo, *Adolfo Caminha*, 117.

42. Caminha, *Black Man and the Cabin Boy*, 35.

43. On the significance of homosexuality, race, and violence in the novel, see Beattie, "Adolfo Ferreira Caminha," 99–101.

44. Caminha, *Black Man and the Cabin Boy*, 102.

45. Borges, "Puffy, Ugly," 242.

46. Berger, "On the Obsolescence of the Concept of Honor," 177.

47. The contradiction is not unlike Lima Barreto's character, Policarpo Quaresma, who is hardly an "honorable" man, but his conviction and gentleness contrast sharply with the machinations of politics and the actions of self-serving elites.

48. Leão, *Relatório*, 22–24.

49. Barbosa, "Os castigos corporais," 209.

50. For discussion of this code, see Nascimento, *Cidadania*, 153–54.

51. Official da Armada, *Política versus Marinha*, 85, also 88–89.

52. Nascimento, *A ressaca da marujada*, 36.

53. For discussion of this and other cases, see Nascimento, *A ressaca da marujada*, 31–47.

54. Beattie, "Conscription versus Penal Servitude," 847.

55. Machado de Assis, "Rod of Justice." See also Borges, "Relevance of Machado de Assis," 236, 239–40.

56. J.C. de Carvalho, *O livro da minha vida*, 348–49.

57. Barbosa, "Anistia para os marinheiros," 161.

58. Leão, *Relatório*, 6.

59. Love, *Revolt of the Whip*, 35–36.

60. Love, *Revolt of the Whip*, 38, 42.

61. Barbosa, "Anistia aos marinheiros rebeldes," 179. This was the point that Senator Pinheiro Machado made repeatedly during the congressional debate over amnesty.

62. H. da Cunha, *A revolta na esquadra brasileira*, 58.

63. From *Careta*, no. 131, December 3, 1910, reproduced in Silva, *Caricata República*, 44.

64. From a 1910 edition of *Careta*, reproduced in Roland, *A revolta da chibata*, 30.

65. H. da Cunha, *A revolta na esquadra brasileira*, 38.

66. "A revolta da marinhagem brasileira e a impressão causada na Europa," *Correio da Manhã*, December 22, 1910, 1.

67. "Brazil Gives Way; Rebel Fleet Gone, Congress, After Fisticuffs, Votes Amnesty to Mutineers—Then, Can't Find Ships," *New York Times*, November 26, 1910.

68. "Disgraceful Affair in Brazil's Navy Has No Parallel in American Services," *Washington Post*, December 25, 1910.

69. GH Vidal, "Graça e amnistia," *Correio da Manhã*, January 5, 1911, 1.

70. Presidential Decree no. 8,400, November 28, 1910. See also Love, *Revolt of the Whip*, 89.

71. Love, *Revolt of the Whip*, 90–91. See also Morgan, *Legacy of the Lash*, 228–51.

72. Love, *Revolt of the Whip*, 94–95, 97–98.

73. GH Vidal, "Morticinio horroroso," *Correio da Manhã*, January 20, 1911, 1.

74. Love, *Revolt of the Whip*, 101.

75. Cândido and others who had survived the repression following the second revolt were put on trial and acquitted in mid-1912. An amnesty granted in December 1912 then extended the 1910 decree to include anyone who had taken part in the second revolt. Morgan, *Legacy of the Lash*, 250; Decree no. 2,687, December 13, 1912.

76. Law no 11,756, July 23, 2008.

77. Alessandro Soler, "Marcha rumo ao reconhecimento de um herói," *O Globo*, November 20, 2005, 29.

78. Mário Magalhães, "Lula elogia marinheiro, e Marinha volta a criticar revolta liderada por ele," *Folha de São Paulo*, November 21, 2008. Milton Teixeira explained that the navy continued to consider Cândido a criminal (*bandido*) and an anti-patriot. See also Alessandro Soler, "Marcha rumo ao reconhecimento de um herói," *O Globo*, November 20, 2005, 29.

PART II: THE BUREAUCRATIZATION OF AMNESTY, 1930S–1940S

1. Da França, "Instituto jurídico da graça," 247.

2. Emphasis mine. Da França, "Instituto jurídico da graça," 250.

3. Da França, "Instituto jurídico da graça," 250.

4. Amado, *Vida de Luís Carlos Prestes*, xi.

5. Chirio, *Politics in Uniform*, 40.

6. Amado, *Vida de Luís Carlos Prestes*, xvi.

7. Freyre, *Masters and the Slaves*.

8. Dulles, *Anarchists and Communists*, 102, 107. On the dates of his service, see L. Galvão, *História constitucional*, 156.

9. Caulfield, *In Defense of Honor*, 66–67.

10. L. Galvão, *História constitucional*, 105.

11. Decree no. 19,711, February 18, 1931.

12. Needell, *Tropical Belle Époque*; Meade, *"Civilizing" Rio*.

13. Da França, "Instituto jurídico da graça," 251–52.

14. Da França, "Instituto jurídico da graça," 248–49, 373.

15. Oliveira, "Early Jorge Amado," 164.

16. Duarte, "Jorge Amado," 390. See also Melo, "Jorge Amado," 185, 192–93; Oliveira, "Early Jorge Amado," 159–60.

17. Oliveira, "Early Jorge Amado," 160, 168.

18. Amado, *Vida de Luís Carlos Prestes*, xi.

19. Duarte, "Jorge Amado," 391.

20. Duarte, "Jorge Amado," 387, 393.

CHAPTER 4: REVOLUTIONARIES AND BUREAUCRATS

1. Unless otherwise noted, biographical details about Herculino Cascardo are derived from information contained in the *DHBB*. See Renato Lemos, "Cascardo, Herculino," CPDOC/FGV, http://www.fgv.br/cpdoc/acervo/dicionarios/verbete-biografico/cascardo-herculino.

2. Duff, "Luis Carlos Prestes," 6.

3. Duff, "Luis Carlos Prestes," 6.

4. Fausto, *Concise History*, 184–88.

5. Duff, "Luis Carlos Prestes," 12.

6. Duff, "Luis Carlos Prestes," 10–11.

7. "A Revolta do São Paulo: O julgamento dos implicados—sete oficiaes foram condemnados a 11 annos e 8 mezes de prisão," *Jornal do Brasil*, April 29, 1927.

8. Decree no. 19,395, November 8, 1930.

9. Once established, the only exceptions to this general rule included the 1909–1910 administration of Nilo Peçanha, the 1910–1914 administration of Hermes Rodrigues da Fonseca, and the 1918–1922 administration of Epitácio Pessoa.

10. R. Graham, *Patronage and Politics*, 1–6.

11. R. Martins, *Liberdade para os brasileiros*, 77.

12. Fausto, *Concise History*, 194.

13. Decree no. 19,395, November 8, 1930.

14. R. Martins, *Liberdade para os brasileiros*, 78.

15. Decree no. 19,395, November 8, 1930. See also R. Martins, *Liberdade para os brasileiros*, 78.

16. Decree no. 19,406, November 15, 1930.

17. Decree no. 19,526, December 24, 1930.

18. Decree no. 19,616, January 22, 1931.

19. "Novo ajudante de ordens do Ministro da Marinha," *O Jornal*, January 10, 1931, 5.

20. Letter from Herculino Cascardo to Getúlio Vargas, Getúlio Vargas Archive, c 1931.01.31, CPDOC/FGV.

21. Decree no. 19,654, February 2, 1931; Decrees no. 19,696 and no. 19,699, February 12, 1931.

22. Decree no. 21,461, June 3, 1932.

23. "Um pacto de solidariedade integral entre os tenentes," *Diário da Noite*, June 1, 1932, 3.

24. "O caso dos tenentes amnistiados," *Correio da Manhã*, May 26, 1932, 2.

25. Decree no. 21,461, June 3, 1932.

26. "O caso dos tenentes amnistiados," *Correio da Manhã*, June 1, 1932, 3.

27. Decree no. 19,551, December 31, 1930.

28. Gallotti, "Alcance e efeitos da anistia."

29. Skidmore, *Politics in Brazil*, 17–19.

30. Letter from Flores da Cunha to Getúlio Vargas, September 17, 1932, Getúlio Vargas Archive, c 1931.01.31, CPDOC/FGV. On Flores da Cunha, see R. Martins, *Liberdade para os brasileiros*, 77; Vilma Keller, "Cunha, Flores da," in *DHBB*, CPDOC/FGV, http://cpdoc.fgv.br/sites/default/files/verbetes/primeira-republica/CUNHA,%20Flores%20da%20red.pdf.

31. "Relação dos officiaes do Exército, reformados administrativamente, nos movimentos revolucionários de 1930 e 1932," Arquivo Público do Estado do Rio de Janeiro (Public Archive of Rio de Janeiro State), Rio de Janeiro (hereafter cited as APERJ).

32. Fausto, *Concise History of Brazil*, 211.

33. Decree no. 23,674, January 2, 1934.

34. Letter to Vargas from Infantry Major, Reserve First Class, Alcide Rodrigues de Souza, December 12, 1938, Oswaldo Aranha Archive 1938.12.12, rolo 16, 52, CPDOC/FGV.

35. Decree no. 24,297, May 28, 1934.

36. "Em torno de amnistia," *A Noite*, May 31, 1934, Prontuários, #684, Euclides de Oliveira Figueiredo, Fundo Delegacia Especial de Segurança Política e Social (hereafter cited as DESPS), 1933–1944, APERJ.

37. Articles nos. 18, 19, *Disposições Transitórias*, Constitution of the Republic of the United States of Brazil, July 16, 1934.

38. "Comissão Revisora realizou-se ontem a sua primeira reunião," *Jornal do Brasil*, September 18, 1935, 8; "Agradecimentos a extinta Comissão Revisora," *Jornal do Brasil*, November 25, 1937, 7.

39. Comissão Revisora, *Pareceres*, 6.

40. Comissão Revisora, *Pareceres*, 3.

41. Comissão Revisora, *Pareceres*, 6–7.

42. Bethell, *Brazil Essays*, 198–99. On the ANL, see also Skidmore, *Politics in Brazil*, 20–21; Hilton, *Brazil and the Soviet Challenge*, 53–59.

43. Bethell, *Brazil Essays*, 199.

44. Chirio, *Politics in Uniform*, 40. On the mythification, see also Motta, "Intentona Comunista," and Skidmore, "Failure in Brazil," 151–53.

45. Bethell, *Brazil Essays*, 200.

46. Of the 3,000 arrested, 2,644 had been released by early 1936, while 401 remained incarcerated. A year later, roughly 7,000 had been arrested of which 1,000 were still in prison. Hilton, *Brazil and the Soviet Challenge*, 79, 83.

47. Bethell, *Brazil Essays*, 200.

48. Skidmore, *Politics in Brazil*, 23.

49. Hilton, *Brazil and the Soviet Challenge*, 76–77.

50. Skidmore, *Politics in Brazil*, 23.

51. Robert Levine suggested that it is more accurate to characterize the Estado Novo as fascist-like, rather than fascist. He argues that the 1937 Brazilian constitution was modeled on the Italian *carta del lavoro*, but the regime could have gone decidedly more fascist and that outright military fascism was rejected all together. See Levine, *Father of the Poor*, 50–59.

52. Article no. 177, Constitution of the United States of Brazil, November 10, 1937.

53. Skidmore, *Politics in Brazil*, 27.

54. Comissão Revisora, *Pareceres*.

55. "Para reintegrar os demitidos pela revolução: reuniu-se a Comissão Revisora," *Jornal do Brasil*, February 13, 1936, 7. See also articles on the commission in *Jornal do Brasil*, November 13, 1935, 14, and April 1, 1936, 8, among others. The ministers included Antônio Bento de Faria, Fernando Antunes, Eugenio do Lucena, Filadelfo Azevedo, Luís Gallotti, and Alberto de Abreu Filho.

56. Comissão Revisora, *Pareceres*, 10.

57. "A Comissão Revisora trabalha: Avoluma-se o número de processos conclusos aos relatores," *Jornal do Brasil*, October 24, 1935, 7.

58. "A Comissão Revisora," *Jornal do Brasil*, November 16, 1935, 5.

59. "Comissão Revisora de S. Paulo," *Jornal do Brasil*, December 7, 1935, 11; "Comissão Revisora de S. Paulo: vão ser examinados 641 processos ate agora

apresentados" *Jornal do Brasil,* December 12, 1935, 8; "A Comissão Revisora Fluminense" *Jornal do Brasil,* January 4, 1936, 33.

60. Comissão Revisora, *Pareceres,* 392. "Atos do governo," *Jornal do Brasil,* March 12, 1937, 8.

61. On the ruling of the commission, see "As deliberações da Comissão Revisora," *Jornal do Brasil,* June 14, 1936, 6. For the letter, see "Pela prestígio da constituição," *Jornal do Brasil,* August 14, 1936, 5.

62. Mozart Lago, "O parag. único do artigo 18 das 'Disposições Transitórias,'" *Jornal do Brasil,* June 25, 1936, 7.

63. "Comissão Revisora," *Jornal do Brasil,* October 3, 1936, 23.

64. "Uma medida justa," *Jornal do Brasil,* November 29, 1936, 5.

65. "Os funcionários readmitidos não têm direito ao pagamento de vencimentos atrasados ou indenizações," *Jornal do Brasil,* October 7, 1936, 11.

66. "O governo e os demitidos," *Jornal do Brasil,* December 12, 1936, 5.

67. "Os demitidos, que esperem!" *Jornal do Brasil,* December 27, 1936, 5.

68. "Justiça completa," *Jornal do Brasil,* January 7, 1937, 5.

69. "Reparações prometidas," *Jornal do Brasil,* March 7, 1937, 5. See also "A Divisão dos Cartórios: observações de um antigo escrivão que teve parecer favorável da Comissão Revisora," *Jornal do Brasil,* February 3, 1937, 24; "E o Ministério Publico?" *Jornal do Brasil,* February 7, 1937, 3; "Vai encerrar os seus trabalhos a comissão revisora," February 26, 1937, 6.

70. "O projeto de lei criando cargos de Justiça," *Jornal do Brasil,* June 4, 1937, 24; "Reparação de injustiças," *Jornal do Brasil,* June 25, 1937, 5.

71. Law no. 441, June 3, 1937.

72. "Decretados assinados nas pastas da Justiça e das Relações Exteriores," *Jornal do Brasil,* June 22, 1937, 5.

73. Da França, "Instituto jurídico da graça," 373.

CHAPTER 5: A DEMOCRATIZING AMNESTY UNDER RENEWED REPRESSION, 1945–1960S

1. Processo no. 20,568/1946, Braz Antônio da Silva, caixa 2300, Fundo 4T, Ministério de Justiça e Negócios Interiores (hereafter cited as MJNI), AN. Da Silva was arrested by the DESPS. His dismissal was based on amendment no. 3 of the 1934 constitution, for the "exercise of activities subversive to political and social institutions."

2. Fausto, *Concise History of Brazil,* 237–79.

3. Bethell, *Brazil Essays,* 201.

4. Laurence Whitehead characterized democratic transitions as a drama in which complex periods of time, both past and future, are condensed and narrated. See Whitehead, *Democratization,* 36.

5. On bureaucratic reform, see Siegel, "Strategy of Public Administration Reform." See also L. Graham, *Civil Service Reform;* A. Viana, *D.A.S.P.*

6. Jorge Miguel Mayer, "Euclides de Oliveira Figueiredo," in *DHBB*, CPDOC/ FGV, http://www.fgv.br/cpdoc/acervo/dicionarios/verbete-biografico/euclides -de-oliveira-figueiredo. On the events surrounding the 1930 election and subsequent revolution, see Skidmore, *Politics in Brazil*, 3–12.

7. Skidmore, *Politics in Brazil*, 334n16, also 334n15.

8. Mayer, "Euclides de Oliveira Figueiredo," *DHBB*, CPDOC/FGV.

9. Skidmore, *Politics in Brazil*, 9–12.

10. On the "Constitutionalist Revolution" by the revolutionaries, see Figueiredo, *Contribuição*; Klinger, Figueiredo, Franco, Lôbo, and Brasil, *Nós e a Ditadura*.

11. Hilton, *Brazil and the Soviet Challenge*, 75.

12. On the integralistas, see Skidmore, *Politics in Brazil*, 20–21; R. Martins, *Liberdade para os brasileiros*, 83–86.

13. Mayer, "Euclides de Oliveira Figueiredo," *DHBB*, CPDOC/FGV.

14. Hilton, *Brazil and the Soviet Challenge*, 53–65.

15. Dulles, *Sobral Pinto*, 50–59, 95–98.

16. On the fate of the two women, see Dulles, *Sobral Pinto*, 228. See also Bethell, *Brazil Essays*, 200–201.

17. A total of 5,986 cases were filed, which named 19,018 defendants. Among those, 3,066 were convicted; 7,658 were acquitted; and 8,294 had their cases dismissed, were excluded from the case, or were transferred to another court. "Relatório: Tribunal de Segurança Nacional," Notação 4, caixa 1037, Fundo Polícias Políticas, APERJ.

18. Hilton, *Brazil and the Soviet Challenge*, 88. Prestes would later have thirty years added to his sentence for his conviction in connection with the murder of Elza Fernandes, a former Communist Party member suspected of being a police agent. See Alzira Alves de Abreu and Alan Carneiro, "Luís Carlos Prestes," *DHBB*, CPDOC/FGV, http://www.fgv.br/cpdoc/acervo/dicionarios/ verbete-biografico/prestes-luis-carlos.

19. Mayer, "Euclides de Oliveira Figueiredo," *DHBB*, CPDOC/FGV.

20. Announcements from the "C.R. do P. Comunista do Brasil," September 1939, pamphlets 31, 134, 437, Fundo DESPS, APERJ.

21. Letter to Oswaldo Aranha, November 20, 1939, Oswaldo Aranha Archive, 1939.04.02, rolo 16, 800, CPDOC/FGV.

22. Letter to Oswaldo Aranha, November 4, 1939, Oswaldo Aranha Archive, 1939.04.02, rolo 16, 798–99, CPDOC/FGV.

23. Open letter from Honorio Hermeto Bezerra Calvacanti to Getúlio Vargas, published in *O Jornal*, July 29, 1938, pamphlet 736, Fundo DESPS, APERJ.

24. Processo no. 17,978/1941, Guida Camargo Carone, caixa 1013, Fundo 4T, MJNI, AN.

25. Processo no. 22,478/1941, Maria Grill, caixa 1047, Fundo 4T, MJNI, AN.

26. Amado, *Vida de Luís Carlos Prestes*, xv.

27. Letter to Eurico Dutra, May 11, 1944, Eurico Dutra Archive, vp 1944.04 .28, 127–31, CPDOC/FGV.

28. Letter from V. Benício da Silva to Dutra summarizing previous conversations, April 28, 1944, Eurico Dutra Archive, vp 1944.04.28, 125–26, CPDOC/FGV.

29. Letter dated May 11,1944, Eurico Dutra Archive, vp 1944.04.28, 127–31, CPDOC/FGV.

30. Letter dated May 23, 1944, in processo no. 32,053, caixa 2377, Fundo 4T, MJNI, AN.

31. Cited in R. Martins, *Liberdade para os brasileiros*, 87.

32. "Poema de 45," Carlos Drummond de Andrade, March 26, 1945, pamphlet 1586, Fundo Divisão de Polícia Política e Social (hereafter cited as DPS), APERJ.

33. Pamphlet 53, caixa 460, Fundo DPS, APERJ.

34. Pamphlet 1807, Fundo DESPS, APERJ.

35. Decree-law no. 7,474, April 18, 1945.

36. A total of ninety-seven political prisoners were detained on Ilha Grande of which ninety-three were immediately released following the amnesty. The remaining four were hospitalized, which delayed their release. See "Anistia," dossiê 1, pasta 3, Fundo Polícias Políticas, APERJ. On amnestied political prisoners, see also "Relação dos Presos Políticos Anistiados, 18 Abril 1945," dossiê 65000, Fundo DPS, APERJ.

37. Decree-Law no. 7,474, April 18, 1945.

38. Thomas Skidmore described this period as "an experiment in democracy." On the election, see Skidmore, *Politics in Brazil*, 54-64.

39. French, "Populist Gamble of Getúlio Vargas," 153–54.

40. Abreu and Carneiro, "Luís Carlos Prestes," *DHBB*, CPDOC/FGV. On Vargas and Prestes, see also Bethell, "Brazil," 48; Skidmore, *Politics in Brazil*, 50.

41. Bethell, "Brazil," 45. See also French, "Populist Gamble of Getúlio Vargas," 155–56.

42. Skidmore, *Politics in Brazil*, 52–53. See also B. McCann, "Carlos Lacerda," 669.

43. Mayer, "Euclides de Oliveira Figueiredo," *DHBB*, CPDOC/FGV.

44. "Anistia aos presos políticos," March 3, 1946, dossiê 1899, Campanha Pro-Anistia, Fundo DPS, APERJ.

45. "Anistia aos presos políticos," March 3, 1946, dossiê 1899, Campanha Pro-Anistia, Fundo DPS, APERJ.

46. "Anistia aos presos políticos," March 3, 1946, dossiê 1899, Campanha Pro-Anistia, Fundo DPS, APERJ. Thomas Skidmore noted that the claim officers had been killed *while sleeping* was a manufactured myth, and one he himself

had mentioned in earlier publications. See Skidmore, "Failure in Brazil," 153; Skidmore, *Politics in Brazil*, 23.

47. The amnesty for military deserters passed with 138 votes in favor against 114 opposed. Amnesty for those involved in labor strikes passed with 127 votes in favor against 109 opposed.

48. "Anistia política," September 12, 1946, dossiê 1899, Campanha Pro-Anistia, Fundo DPS, APERJ.

49. Processo no. 25,394/1945, Nelson Dimas de Oliveira, caixa 932, Fundo 2C, Departamento Administrativo de Serviço Público (hereafter cited as DASP), AN.

50. Decree no. 20,401, January 15, 1946.

51. "Relação dos Presos Políticos Anistiados, 18 abril 1945," dossiê 3, Fundo DPS, APERJ.

52. Processo no. 5,761/1946, Manoel Miguel de Melo Filho, caixa 2175, Fundo 4T, MJNI, AN.

53. "Não voltará ao Exército o Sr. Luiz Carlos Prestes," *Diário de Notícias*, May 24, 1946, 2.

54. "Oficiais anistiados, que não podem mais voltar às fileiras do Exército," *Diário de Notícias*, June 4, 1946; "Não podem voltar as fileiras," *Diário de Notícias*, June 7, 1946, 5; "Os oficiais comunistas anistiados não voltarão ao Exército," *Diário da Noite*, May 23, 1946, 5.

55. "O sr. Carlos Prestes julgou-se injuriado por um vespertino," *Diário de Notícias*, June 13, 1946, 5.

56. Processo P.R. no. 14,175-53, *Revista de Direito Administrativo* 35 (January–March 1954), 388–90.

57. Processo no. 36,465/1946, caixa 2411, Fundo 4T, MJNI, AN. Approved by Dutra on November 14, 1947. He was convicted under Decree-law no. 431, May 18, 1938.

58. "Anistia," dossiê 1, Pasta 3, Fundo DPS, APERJ.

59. Processo no. 36,465, caixa 2411, Fundo 4T, MJNI, NA.

60. Secret circular from Gabriel Monteiro da Silva, secretary of the presidency, to the president of DASP, May 14, 1946, caixa 1049, Fundo 2C, DASP, AN.

61. "Reservado 1015-A em 10 de 6 de 1947 P.R. 12528/4 arquiva-se 22.6.47," caixa 964, Fundo 2C, DASP, AN.

62. Secret circular from Gabriel Monteiro da Silva, secretary of the presidency, to the president of DASP, May 14, 1946, caixa 1049, Fundo 2C, DASP, AN.

63. Processo no. 20,568/46, Braz Antônio da Silva, caixa 2300, Fundo 4T, MJNI, AN.

64. Bethell, "Brazil," 61.

65. R. Martins, *Liberdade para os brasileiros*, 91.

66. Processo no. 5,761/1946, Manoel Miguel de Melo Filho, caixa 2175, Fundo 4T, MJNI, NA.

67. For a similar case, see Processo no. 44,747/1946, Manoel José Pães, caixa 2468, Fundo 4T, MJNI, AN.

68. Processo no. 38,125/1946, Thomas Ribeiro de Carvalho, caixa 2422, Fundo 4T, MJNI, AN.

69. Law no. 171, December 15, 1947, created such a commission.

70. See, for example, Law no. 500, November 29, 1948.

71. Decree-legislation no. 18, December 15, 1961.

72. Processo no. 38125/1946, Thomas Ribeiro de Carvalho, caixa 2422, Fundo 4T, MJNI, AN.

73. Processo no. 20568/1946, Braz Antônio da Silva, caixa 2300, Fundo 4T, MJNI, AN.

74. R. Martins, *Liberdade para os brasileiros*, 192.

75. Pontes de Miranda, *Comentários à Constituição*, 424–28.

76. Maximiliano, *Comentários à Constituição brasileira*, 161, 171.

77. Pontes de Miranda, *Comentários à Constituição*, 432.

PART III: AMNESTY AND TRANSITIONAL JUSTICE, 1979–2010

1. Kucinski, *K*, title page, 162.

2. Levi, *Survival in Auschwitz*, 9–10.

3. Atencio, "Toward a Culture of Memory," 122.

4. Comisión Nacional sobre la Desaparición de Personas, Argentina, *Nunca Más*; Comisión Nacional de Verdad y Reconciliación, Chile, *Informe*. See also Hayner, *Unspeakable Truths*, 45–48.

5. Sikkink, *Justice Cascade*, 70–76. See also Malamud-Goti, *Game without End*. There is a contemporaneous debate about the trials in the *Yale Journal of International Law*. See Mignone, Estlund, and Issacharoff, "Dictatorship on Trial"; Nino, "Human Rights Policy."

6. Linz and Stepan, *Problems of Democratic Transition*, 66–68.

7. Huntington, *Third Wave*, 231.

8. Teitel noted that in the post–Second World War context, amnesty was antithetical to the rule of law. In the post–Cold War era, the concept of amnesty "broadened" to include reconciliation. Teitel, "Transitional Justice Genealogy," 75, 80, 82.

9. Roht-Arriaza, "New Landscape," 2–3. See also Teitel, "Transitional Justice Genealogy," 78.

10. Comissão Nacional da Verdade (the National Truth Commission, hereafter cited as CNV), *Relatório*.

11. Skidmore, *Politics of Military Rule*, 217–19.

12. Teitel, *Transitional Justice*, 53.

13. Skaar, Collins, and García-Godos, "Uneven Road towards Accountability," 287.

14. Teitel, *Transitional Justice*, 48, 53.

15. A. Schneider, "Truth Commissions," 268–69.

16. See Lessa and Payne, *Amnesty in the Age of Human Rights Accountability*; Binder, "Prohibition of Amnesties."

17. Arguição de descumprimento de preceito fundamental (ADPF) 153, Acórdão, Supremo Tribunal Federal (2010). See also N. Schneider, "Impunity in Post-authoritarian Brazil"; Serbin, "Ghosts of Brazil's Military Dictatorship."

18. On the kidnapping of US ambassador Charles Elbrick, see Serbin, *From Revolution to Power*, 27–50.

19. Archdiocese of São Paulo, *Brasil nunca mais*, 93–95; Serbin, *From Revolution to Power*, 63–74, 115–21.

20. CNV, *Relatório*, 1:344, 543.

21. Kucinski, *K*, 169.

22. Kucinski, *K*, 137–38.

23. Archdiocese of São Paulo, *Brasil nunca mais*.

24. Comissão de Familiares de Mortos e Desaparecidos Políticos, *Dossiê dos mortos e desaparecidos políticas a partir de 1964*; "Ana Rosa Kucinski/Ana Rosa Silva," in CNV, *Relatório*, 3:614–23.

25. The reparations payments ranged from the equivalent of approximately $100,000 to $150,000 US. See Mezarobba, "Between Reparations, Half Truths and Impunity," 14; N. Schneider, "Breaking the 'Silence'," 203.

26. Law no. 9,140, December 4, 1995.

27. Mezarobba, *Um acerto de contas com o futuro*, 150.

28. Mezarobba, "Between Reparations, Half Truths and Impunity," 16.

29. "IQ anula demissão de Ana Rosa Kucinski e pede desculpas à família da professora," *Associação dos Docentes da Universidade de São Paulo (ADUSP)*, April 25, 2014, https://www.adusp.org.br/index.php/ditadura-militar/1918-iq-anula-demissao-de-ana-rosa-kucinski-e-pede-desculpas-a-familia-da-professora. See also "Comissão da Verdade aplaude reparação histórica a Ana Rosa Kucinski Silva," *Jornal GGN*, April 22, 2014, https://jornalggn.com.br/noticia/comissao-da-verdade-aplaude-reparacao-historica-a-ana-rosa-kucinski-silva.

CHAPTER 6: PREEMPTING AN INEVITABLE AMNESTY

1. "Canavarro: ativista que colocou o 'sino no pescoço do gato,'" *Conape*, July 12, 2014, http://conape.org.br/canavarro-ativista-que-colocou-o-sino-no-pescoco-do-gato.

2. See the request from Ademar de Queiroz, president of Petrobras, for funding for security work, May 19, 1964, Artur Levy Archive, Repercussões

do Golpe de 1964 na Petrobras, 1964.01.30, 117, CPDOC/FGV. For April and May reports, see 1964.01.30, 107–9, 114, CPDOC/FGV.

3. Law no. 6,683, August 28, 1979.

4. *Jornal Petrobras* 6, no. 68 (November 1985): 3; *Jornal Petrobras* 7, no. 71 (March 1986): 2.

5. Skidmore, *Politics in Brazil*, 97–99; Bethell, *Brazil Essays*, 181–82. On the founding of Petrobras and industrialization in Brazil, see Alveal Contreras, *Os desbravadores*, 71–73.

6. Scaletsky, *O patrão e o petroleiro*, 43–45. See also Smith, "Petrobras"; Moura, *A campanha do petróleo*. The revolution had upset the ruling oligarchy and catapulted Vargas onto the national political scene, which he dominated until, and even after, his death by suicide in 1954.

7. Smith, "Petrobras," 199.

8. Skidmore, *Politics of Military Rule*, 5. On the growing consensus among military officers to stage a coup, see Chirio, *Politics in Uniform*, 17–18.

9. Bethell, *Brazil Essays*, 182; B. McCann, "Carlos Lacerda," 672, 680.

10. B. McCann, "Carlos Lacerda," 680.

11. Skidmore, *Politics of Military Rule*, 5–6. See also Chirio, *Politics in Uniform*, 36–37; B. McCann, "Carlos Lacerda," 689.

12. Skidmore, *Politics of Military Rule*, 6.

13. At that time, the refinery was known as REFRIO (Refinery of Rio de Janeiro). On the history of the labor movement in Petrobras, see G. Carvalho, *Petrobrás*, 115–29; Randall, *Political Economy of Brazilian Oil*, 194–201.

14. "Síntese histórica movimento 2004 1964/66," caixa 1065, Petrobras, Fundo Polícias Políticas, APERJ.

15. Some supporters expected that he would "use his famous broom" to clean up Petrobras or rid Brazil of the company entirely. See Smith, "Petrobras," 190.

16. Skidmore, *Politics of Military Rule*, 7–8.

17. Skidmore, *Politics of Military Rule*, 8–9.

18. By 1986, shortly after the amnestied petroleiros returned to work, the number of Petrobras employees totaled 60,241. See Randall, *Political Economy of Brazilian Oil*, 189. On levels of unionized workers, see "Quadro de Empregados Sindicalizados," Artur Levy Archive, 1964.01.30, 92, CPDOC/FGV. On the corporatist structure of union organization, which operated under federal government control beginning in the Vargas era, see Skidmore, *Politics of Military Rule*, 33–34.

19. Smith, "Petrobras," 191–92; Chirio, *Politics in Uniform*, 44; Decree no. 53,701, March 13, 1964; Bethell, *Brazil Essays*, 187.

20. Scaletsky, *O patrão e o petroleiro*, 19. On Castelo Branco and his arrival to lead the military government, see Chirio, *Politics in Uniform*, 49–54.

21. Institutional Act no. 1, April 9, 1964. In the earlier days of the regime, the *cassação* referred only to the taking away of political rights; *destituição* was the

term used in reference to the firing, relieving of duties, retiring, or transferring to reserve status of military or public employees. See Raymundo Faoro, "Revisão ou Anistia," Fundo Comitê Brasileiro pela Anistia, 50, Arquivo Edgard Leuenroth (Edgard Leuenroth Archive), Campinas, São Paulo.

22. Vera Calicchio, "Atos Institucionais," *DHBB*, CPDOC/FGV, http://www.fgv.br/cpdoc/acervo/dicionarios/verbete-tematico/atos-institucionais. On the tally for military members, see F. Machado, "As Forças Armadas," 117. Maud Chirio cites in total (that is, not just through the end of 1964), 1,013 troops and 264 officers who were disciplined through AI-1, which amounts to 0.4 and 3.3 percent, respectively, of the total force at that time. See Chirio, *Politics in Uniform*, 19–20.

23. "Ordem de Serviço no. 24/64," Artur Levy Archive, 1964.01.30, 62, CPDOC/FGV. Mendes was named superintendent of Reduc on April 7, 1964.

24. Artur Levy Archive, 1964.01.30, 109, CPDOC/FGV.

25. Artur Levy Archive, 1964.01.30, 94, 119, CPDOC/FGV.

26. The second list of employees to be fired from Petrobras was issued on April 8, 1964. Letter from Roberto Coimbra, May 29, 1964, Artur Levy Archive, 1964.01.30, 118A, CPDOC/FGV.

27. Artur Levy Archive, 1964.01.30, 113-A, 123, CPDOC/FGV.

28. Letter to General Ademar de Queiroz, April 6, 1964, Artur Levy Archive 1964.01.30, 61, CPDOC/FGV.

29. Ademar de Queiroz took over on April 7, 1964, replacing Arthur Levy who had been installed as the president of Petrobras a week earlier on March 31, the eve of the coup. Levy witnessed the arrest of the former Petrobras president, Alves, on the premises. See Arthur Levy, Depoimento (1987), 308–13, CPDOC/FGV.

30. Artur Levy Archive, 1964.01.30, 116, CPDOC/FGV.

31. Artur Levy Archive, 1964.01.30, 75, CPDOC/FGV. On the consolidated labor legislation, see Skidmore, *Politics of Military Rule*, 33–34.

32. Artur Levy Archive, 1964.01.30, 98, CPDOC/FGV.

33. Resolução no. 32/64, Ademar de Queiroz, President of Petrobras, Rio de Janeiro, September 28, 1964.

34. Artur Levy Archive, 1964.01.30, 94, 117, CPDOC/FGV.

35. Artur Levy Archive, 1964.01.30, 94, 117, CPDOC/FGV.

36. Gaspari, *A ditadura derrotada*, 199.

37. Artur Levy Archive, 1964.01.30, 94, 119, CPDOC/FGV.

38. Zerbine, *Anistia; Maria Quitéria: Boletim do Movimento Feminino pela Anistia* 1, no. 2 (June 1977).

39. Fernando Gabeira—who had participated in the 1969 kidnapping of the US ambassador to Brazil, then was captured, tortured, imprisoned, and finally expelled from Brazil—mentions the committees that formed throughout Europe. See Gabeira, *Carta Sobre a Anistia*, 12.

40. An internal Women's Movement for Amnesty squabble, coupled by a pressing need for coordinated action, reportedly resulted in the creation of the Brazilian Committee for Amnesty. See Benjamin, with Autran, *Ofício de mãe*, 70. On the committee's conferences and the actions of professional associations, see Fundo Comitê Brasileiro pela Anistia, 50, 66, 67, Edgard Leuenroth Archive, Campinas, São Paulo.

41. Carla Simone Rodeghero argues that two trajectories formed during the period. One associated amnesty with national reconciliation and the "pacification of the Brazilian family"; the other sought the "radical dismantling of the dictatorship." See Rodeghero, "A anistia entre a memória e o esquecimento," 131.

42. R. Martins, *Liberdade para os brasileiros* (on references to this work, see Comissão Mista Sobre Anistia, *Anistia*, 1:617, 692); J. Ferreira, *Anistia*; R. Moraes, *O poder de graça*.

43. "A repressão perdoada," *Veja*, July 4, 1979, 16–17. See also A. Schneider, "Legislative Efforts."

44. The inclusive dates of the amnesty were extended to August 15, 1979, by amendment to the proposed law.

45. Comissão Mista Sobre Anistia, *Anistia*, 1:23–25.

46. The hunger strike began in Rio de Janeiro, but prisoners in Pernambuco and São Paulo later joined in. See G. Viana, *Fome de liberdade*.

47. "Presos do Rio entram em greve por anistia," *Jornal do Brasil*, July 23, 1979, 4; "Comissão Mista da anistia visitará presos políticos," *Jornal do Brasil*, August 3, 1979, 4.

48. Márcio Alves, *Teotônio, guerreiro da paz*, 176–77.

49. Citing data from a *Veja* article in the June 27, 1979, issue, M. Motta, *Teotônio Vilela*, 168.

50. "Anistia exclui 195 pêssoas mas poderá chegar a mais," *Jornal do Brasil*, July 1, 1979, 3.

51. Letter from the attorney general of military justice, Milton Menezes da Costa Filho, to the secretary general of the Ministry of Justice, Walter Costa Porto, September 12, 1979, Fundo TT, Divisão de Segurança e Informações do Ministério da Justiça, Série movimentos contestatórios, avulsos 106, 1, AN.

52. Rousseff joined the Vanguarda Armada Revolucionária Palmares (Palmares Armed Revolutionary Vanguard, VAR-Palmares) in São Paulo while Genoíno participated in the guerrilla movement in Araguaia that took the struggle against the regime to a rural region. In each case, after their rise to power, their political stars fell dramatically. By 2002, Genoíno was the president of the Workers' Party. Ten years later, he was among the highest profile figures to be convicted in the *mensalão* (the "big monthly payment" scandal). Rousseff was removed from office by impeachment in 2016. Prior to her election she had served on the board of Petrobras and approved purchases that were later a target

in the *lavo jato* ("car wash") investigations, which focused primarily on corruption in Petrobras and the Odebrecht construction conglomerate. See Serbin, *From Revolution to Power*, 253, 290–91, 302–3.

53. Oliveira, *Atos Institucionais*.

54. Comissão Mista Sobre Anistia, *Anistia*, 1:24.

55. Associação de Defesa dos Direitos e Pró-Anistia dos Atingidos por Atos Institucionais (Association for the Defense of Rights and for Amnesty for those Punished by Institutional Acts, AMPLA), "Declaração Sobre a Anistia," Ernani do Amaral Peixoto Archive, Aplicação da Lei da Anistia, 79.07.13, CPDOC/FGV.

56. The bill proposed by Linhares is discussed in a letter from Jose Moreira dos Santos to Ernani do Amaral Peixoto, July 23, 1979, Ernani do Amaral Peixoto Archive, 79.07.13, CPDOC/FGV.

57. Law no. 6,683, August 28, 1979. A substitute version of the proposed amnesty, which would have broadened its application, was defeated by just five votes. "Anistia do Governo passa por 5 votos," *Jornal do Brasil*, August 23, 1979, 1. See also "A página virada," *Veja*, August 29, 1979.

58. See reports of the Ministério das Minas e Energia, *Diário Oficial*, June 14, 25, July 4, 1980.

59. Report of the Ministério do Trabalho, *Diário Oficial*, December 28, 1981, 24915.

60. "MT anistia 260 e reintegra 30," *Jornal do Brazil*, April 26, 1980, 12.

61. "Documentos sobre reversão," dossiê reintegração polícia federal, Fundo TT, Divisão de Segurança e Informações do Ministério da Justiça, série pessoal, avulsos 3, AN.

62. "Anistia tem um beneficiado na Caixa Econômica, 17 na Marinha e 17 na Agricultura," *Jornal do Brasil*, March 29, 1980, 17.

63. "Marinha anistia 21 oficiais, 50 praças e 25 servidores," *Jornal do Brasil*, March 12, 1980, 17.

64. Mezarobba, *Um acerto de contas com o futuro*, 54; "Aeronáutica anistia 78 militares," *Jornal do Brasil*, February 26, 1980, 4; "Marinha anistia 21 oficiais, 50 praças e 25 servidores," *Jornal do Brasil*, March 12, 1980, 17; N. Schneider, "Forgotten Voices," 314.

65. N. Schneider, "Forgotten Voices," 335.

66. Many members of the association had also been involved in the "Sergeants' Revolt," which took place in Brasília and São Paulo in September 1963 following the rejection by the Federal Supreme Court of the candidacy of a military sergeant. See F. Rodrigues, *Vozes do mar*, 97. For a personal account of this event, see Batista, *Cantata de um anistiado*.

67. Capitani, *A Rebelião dos Marinheiros*, 51, 70; F. Rodrigues, *Vozes do mar*, 108–9; Chirio, *Politics in Uniform*, 44. See also F. Machado, "As Forças Armadas," 117.

68. Archdiocese of São Paulo, *Brasil nunca mais*, 118–20; Mitchell, "FH anistia," 4. On the significance of the events, see also Gandra, Castro, and Silva, "No rumo da memória."

69. Capitani, *A Rebelião dos Marinheiros*, 72.

70. "Velhos militares aguardam reintegração," *Jornal do Brasil*, May 26, 1985, 4. On Petrobras, see Mezarobba, *Um acerto de contas*, 54.

71. Greenhalgh, *I Seminário do Grupo Tortura Nunca Mais*, 113.

72. "Dossiê dos marinheiros, cabos e soldados da aeronáutica punidos pelo ato institucional no. 1/64 [AI-1] e ate o momento não foram anistiados," Fundo Mário Lago, Série atividades politicas, textual 4, AN; Mezarobba, *Um acerto de contas*, 54.

73. Letter to the President of the Republic from CONAPE/Bahia, June 1, 1983, Ernani do Amaral Peixoto Archive, 79.07.13, CPDOC/FGV.

74. The organization formalized itself as the Associação Nacional dos Anistiados da Petrobras (National Association of the Amnestied of Petrobras, CONAPE). See "Nossa História," Associação Nacional dos Anistiados da Petrobrás, http://conape.org.br/nossa-historia.

75. F. Machado, "As Forças Armadas," 120–24. Additional organizations included the Associação dos Militares Incompletamente Não Anistiados (Association of Incompletely Non-Amnestied Military Members), Unidade de Mobilização Nacional pela Anistia (Unit of National Mobilization for Amnesty), and the Movimento Democrático pela Anistia e Cidadania (Democratic Movement for Amnesty and Citizenship). See P. da Cunha, "Militares e anistia," 32.

76. "Governador de Sergipe está preso na Bahia," *A Tarde* (Bahia), April 4, 1964, courtesy of Mário Lima.

77. "Notificação," *A Tarde* (Bahia), August 27, 1964. See also "Petrobrás divulga nomes: demissões," *Jornal da Bahia*, September 11, 1964, courtesy of Mário Lima.

78. "Geisel: não há tortura dos presos políticos," *A Tarde* (Bahia), September 17, 1964, 1, courtesy of Mário Lima.

79. "Relação dos Cassados em Virtude do Ato Institucional no. 1," *Diário Oficial*, November 15, 1965; "Liberdade de Mário depende do Auditor," *Jornal da Bahia*, October 5, 1971, 6; "Subversão na Petrobrás está agora na Justiça do Exército," *A Tarde* (Bahia), September 1, 1970; "Mário Lima—1964–1970, Prisões," courtesy of Mário Lima.

80. "Ex-líder sindical quer reintegração de antigos empregados da Petrobrás," *A Tarde* (Bahia), October 2, 1980; "Ex-líderes da Petrobrás querem a reintegração," *Correio Brasiliense*, October 14, 1980, 7; "Abi-Ackel estuda reintegração de 289 a Petrobrás," *O Globo*, February 27, 1981, 7, courtesy of Mário Lima.

81. "Ex-líder sindical quer reintegração de antigos empregados da Petrobrás," *A Tarde* (Bahia), October 2, 1980; "Ex-líderes da Petrobrás querem a re-

integração," *Correio Brasiliense*, October 14, 1980, 7. See also "Aplicação de Penalidades em Empregados," Informativo Petrobrás, Edição Especial, courtesy of Mário Lima.

82. "Mário Lima quer volta a Petrobras," *A Tarde* (Bahia), April 30, 1982, courtesy of Mário Lima.

83. Sebastião Nery, "Lula e Mário, duas histórias de operários," *Tribuna da Imprensa*, October 4, 2002, courtesy of Mário Lima. See also Cano and Ferreira, "Reparations Program," 106.

84. Mezarobba, *Um acerto de contas*, 54.

85. Letter to President Figueiredo, July 24, 1984, Ernani do Amaral Peixoto Archive, 79.07.13, CPDOC/FGV. See also "Carta ao Congresso Sobre a Rejeição do Veto ao Projeto 'Célio Borja,'" Ernani do Amaral Peixoto Archive, 79.07.13, CPDOC/FGV.

86. Santayana, *Conciliação e transição*.

87. "Anistia: Um Fato Histórico," letter from Jorge Vianna to Mário Lima, March 31, 2006, courtesy of Mário Lima.

88. Constitutional Amendment no. 26, November 27, 1985.

89. Ato das Disposições Constitucionais Transitórias (ADCT), article 8, Constitution of the Federal Republic of Brazil, October 5, 1988; Cano and Ferreira, "Reparations Program," 105.

90. Decree no. 611, July 21, 1992, Seção VIII, "Da Aposentadoria Excepcional de Anistiado," and Decree no. 1,500, May 24, 1995. See brief discussion of the laws in D. Gonçalves, *O preço do passado*, 57–58.

91. The commission was first established under a provisional measure and then instituted through Law no. 10,559, November 13, 2002.

92. P. da Cunha, "Militares e anistia," 32; "Retornar não quer dizer ficar na empresa," *Informativo CONAPE*, no. 2 (June–July 1985).

93. *Jornal Petrobras* 4, no. 70 (January–February 1986), 4; *Jornal Petrobras* 7, no. 71 (March 1986), 2.

94. Processos no. 2002.01.09503, 3; no. 2002.01.10644, 3; no. 2002.01.11927, 3, Arquivo da Comissão de Anistia (Archive of the Amnesty Commission; hereafter cited as ACA).

95. *Diário Oficial*, July 18, 1987.

96. *Jornal Petrobras* 6, no. 68 (November 1985), 3.

97. Evandro Éboli, "Uma conta do passado ainda por pagar," *O Globo*, August 8, 2004, 8. Processos no. 2002.01.09503, 3, 220–22, 224, 227; no. 2002.01.10644, 272–73; no. 2002.01.11927, 238, 244, ACA; processo no. 2003.01.14903, courtesy of Mário Lima.

98. Evandro Éboli, "Anistia: ex-servidores da Petrobras têm 70 das cem maiores indenizações," *O Globo*, February 9, 2015, https://oglobo.globo.com/brasil/anistia-ex-servidores-da-Petrobras-tem-70-das-cem-maiores-indeni zacoes-15281945.

99. CONAPE (Associação Nacional dos Anistiados da Petrobras), accessed January 9, 2021, http://conape.org.br.

100. A number of rulings from the Amnesty Commission distinguish between prior settlements reached and the new calculus applied under a "juridical framework" of reparations that was established by Law 10,559, November 13, 2002.

101. Evandro Éboli, "Uma conta do passado ainda por pagar," *O Globo*, August 8, 2004, 8.

102. Evandro Éboli, "Anistia: ex-servidores da Petrobras têm 70 das cem maiores indenizações," *O Globo*, February 9, 2015. The "car wash" investigation is the largest corruption probe in Brazilian history. It has exposed billions of dollars illicitly channeled from Petrobras projects to Petrobras officials, politicians, and contract directors. See Serbin, *From Revolution to Power*, 303.

Chapter 7: Two Long Shadows

1. "Médici pune 43 agentes da Polícia Federal pelo AI-5," *Jornal do Brasil*, August 3, 1973, 18.

2. Ministério da Justiça, Comissão Geral de Investigações Sub-Comissão de São Paulo, "Processo no. MJ 53.162/73, enriquecimento ilícito," Fundo 1M, Comissão Geral de Investigações, document 816.12, 1–27, AN.

3. A total of 78,667 cases had been received as of June 2020. See Ministério da Mulher, da Família e dos Direitos Humanos, "Transparência," accessed July 29, 2020, https://www.gov.br/mdh/pt-br/navegue-por-temas/comissao-de-anistia-1/transparencia.

4. "Comissão de Anistia: requerimentos arquivados, Segundo ano de publicação da portaria," accessed January 3, 2020, mdh.gov.br/navegue-por-temas/comissao-de-anistia-1/numerosnovember2019.pdf.

5. Nina Schneider discusses the tendency to homogenize military members and to associate all of them as oppressors, ignoring that many oppressed by the regime were military members themselves. See N. Schneider, "Forgotten Voices," 315. See also F. Machado, "As Forças Armadas."

6. The federal police department was established in 1940 to be a judicial force with national reach; chiefs during the dictatorship were all military officers, and most of them were generals. See CNV, *Relatório*, 1:113.

7. OBAN stands for Operação Bandeirantes (Operation Bandeirantes).

8. Unless otherwise noted, references to petitions to or rulings from the Amnesty Commission concerning former federal police agents are derived from and/or were informed by the following cases: processo nos. 2001.01.00055, 00130, 02466, 2002.01.07957, 2003.01.15645, 18316, 18647, 2008.01.61219, all in ACA.

9. Chirio, *Politics in Uniform*, 60–61, 83.

10. Chirio, *Politics in Uniform*, 80.

11. Chirio, *Politics in Uniform*, 79–85.

12. Thomas Skidmore notes that the regime rejected a one-party formula for legitimizing authoritarian rule as had been installed in Mexico. See Skidmore, *Politics of Military Rule*, 48.

13. In the beginning, given the artificial nature of their formation, the two parties were largely indistinguishable and basically functioned only to sanction the regime's initiatives. Critics distinguished only between the "yes" party (the MDB) and the "yes, Sir" party (the ARENA). Motta, *Partido e sociedade*, 46.

14. Gaspari, *A ditadura envergonhada*, 345. Gaspari himself had been an early target of the regime when, as a student, he was expelled from his university soon after the 1964 coup.

15. Chirio, *Politics in Uniform*, 130–31; Skidmore, *Politics of Military Rule*, 79–81. The final vote tally was 216 to 141, with fifteen abstentions.

16. Skidmore, *Politics of Military Rule*, 81.

17. Motta, *Partido e sociedade*, 134.

18. Daniel Aarão Reis and Denise Rollemberg, "O Ato Institucional no. 5," *Memorias Reveladas*, accessed July 29, 2020, http://www.memoriasreve ladas.arquivonacional.gov.br/campanha/edicao-do-ai-5 (no longer available). See also Maria Celina D'Araujo, "O AI-5," CPDOC/FGV, http://cpdoc.fgv .br/producao/dossies/FatosImagens/AI5.

19. Joffily, *No centro da engrenagem*, 27.

20. Langland, *Speaking of Flowers*, 215–16.

21. Langland, *Speaking of Flowers*, 153; Gaspari, *A ditadura envergonhada*, photographs (unnumbered pages).

22. N. Schneider, *Brazilian Propaganda*, 19, 109.

23. OBAN used personnel from the navy, army, air force, federal police, civil police, and civil guard, as well as the DOPS and the Serviço Nacional de Informações (National Intelligence Service). See Godoy, *A casa da vovó*, 133.

24. Leigh Payne notes that "whether business contributions to OBAN were voluntary remains in dispute." See Payne, "Corporate Complicity," 167–68. See also CNV, *Relatório*, 1:320.

25. Chirio, *Politics in Uniform*, 139.

26. CNV, *Relatório*, 1:138, 322–23.

27. "Brazil: Government by Torture," *Look Magazine* 34, no. 14, July 14, 1970. On the dissemination of news about torture in Brazil, see Green, *We Cannot Remain Silent*, 148–61.

28. Amnesty International, *Report on Allegations of Torture*, 61–63, 36.

29. Amnesty International, *Report on Allegations of Torture*, 36.

30. The majority of the original staff hailed from the military police of the state of São Paulo but also included members of the civil police, the army, the air force, and the federal police. The agents who worked at the Tutóia Street

address called it "grandma's house," because "that is where things were good." Godoy, *A casa da vovó*, 19. See also CNV, *Relatório*, 1:146, 319, 755.

31. Godoy, *A casa da vovó*, 33–34. In an earlier collaborative work, Martha Huggins, Mika Haritos-Fatouros, and Philip Zimbardo aimed to understand the "causes and support for police violence." They found that "violence workers" had been "funneled" into it, and that these workers then rationalized what they did, and were, in significant ways, deeply damaged by it. See Huggins, Haritos-Fatouros, and Zimbardo, *Violence Workers*. See also Chirio, *Politics in Uniform*, 122–24.

32. CNV, *Relatório*, 1:544. Although the use of torture was widespread, some in the military and police opposed it, as they did the expanding autonomy of the security apparatus. See Stepan, *Rethinking Military Politics*, 31; Weschler, *Miracle*, 66–67.

33. Tiago Dantas, "Ato no prédio do Doi-Codi, em SP, pede fim da anistia a torturadores," *O Globo*, March 31, 2014.

34. At the beginning the force totaled 112, including 18 from the army, 72 from the military police, 20 from civil police, and one each from the air force and the federal police. In his "biography" of some of the individuals and the institutions linked to "grandma's house," Marcelo Godoy identified five federal police agents who, over time, had been part of the DOI. See Godoy, *A Casa da Vovó*, 133, 557–58. On the jurisdiction of military police, see Huggins, Haritos-Fatouros, and Zimbardo, *Violence Workers*, 1–2.

35. Grabois, *Mauricio Grabois*, 28.

36. J. Teles, "Dói gostar dos outros," 265; E. Teles, "Quem é essa pessoa que tem a voz da minha mãe?" 257–59. Their parents were ultimately charged with crimes and imprisoned at the Carandiru prison in São Paulo until their release in October 1973. Their father was imprisoned again in 1975. After the passage of the amnesty law in 1979, both parents were included on the list prepared of former prisoners who were beneficiaries. See Superior Tribunal Militar, "Relação de Anistiados," Fundo TT, Divisão de Segurança e Informações do Ministério da Justiça, Série movimentos contestatórios, avulsos 106, 44–79, AN.

37. J. Teles, "Dói gostar dos outros," 261–66.

38. E. Teles, "Quem é essa pessoa."

39. N. Schneider, *Brazilian Propaganda*, 3, 182.

40. N. Schneider, "Breaking the 'Silence,'" 201.

41. Unless otherwise noted, biographical details about Bandeira are derived from "Antonio Bandeira," *DHBB*, CPDOC/FGV, http://www.fgv.br/cpdoc/acervo/dicionarios/verbete-biografico/bandeira-antonio.

42. CNV, *Relatório*, 1:857, 878; Chirio, *Politics in Uniform*, 186.

43. Ministério da Justiça, Comissão Geral de Investigações Sub-Comissão de São Paulo, "Processo no. MJ 53.162/73, enriquecimento ilícito," Fundo 1M, Comissão Geral de Investigações, document 816.12, 1–27, AN.

44. Ministério da Justiça, Departamento de Polícia Federal, "Funcionários do DPF Atingidos pelo AI-5," July 30, 1973, Fundo V8, Serviço Nacional de Informações, Série agência central, 73060402, AN.

45. On the investigations and purges, see Presidência da República, Gabinete Militar, "Aposentadoria e Demissão do Serviço Público com base no AI/5 e AC/39," August 3, 1972, Fundo N8, Conselho de Segurança Nacional, Série processos, Subsérie cassações 1168, 3–22, AN; Letter to the President of the Republic from the Minister of Justice, February 23, 1972, Fundo N8, Conselho de Segurança Nacional, Série processos, Subsérie cassações 623, 38–40, AN.

46. Ministério da Justiça, Departamento de Polícia Federal, "Funcionários do DPF Atingidos pelo AI-5," July 30, 1973, Fundo V8, Serviço Nacional de Informações, Série agência central, 73060402, AN.

47. "Funcionários do Departamento de Polícia Federal Demitidos ou Aposentados com base no AI-5," Fundo H8, Delegacia de Polícia Federal em Dourados, Série pessoas físicas, dossiê 343, 1–13, AN.

48. Processo MJ 53.162/73, Fundo N8, Conselho de Segurança Nacional, Série processos, Subsérie cassações 1893, AN.

49. "Presidente demite 21 policiais," *Jornal do Brasil*, August 3, 1973, 1; see also the request by the Ministry of Justice for these dismissals and forced retirements as well as the formal declarations by the president, Fundo N8, Conselho de Segurança Nacional, Série processos, Subsérie cassações 6, 5–17, AN.

50. "Médici pune 43 agentes da Polícia Federal pelo AI-5," *Jornal do Brasil*, August 3, 1973, 18.

51. "Brio Policial," *Jornal do Brasil*, August 3, 1973, 6.

52. In his filings to the Amnesty Commission, the agent included a copy of a letter from Fleury to the president of the investigative commission. See also Ministério da Justiça, Departamento de Polícia Federal, "Relatório parcial da investigação sumária instituída pela Portaria n. 0106 de 26 de Janeiro de 1977," Fundo TT, Divisão de Segurança e Informações do Ministério da Justiça, Série irregularidades politico-administrativas, processo no. 644, 2–13, AN; Serviço Nacional de Informações, "Envolvimento de funcionários do DPF/SP em contrabando," February 18, March 17, 1977, Fundo V8, Serviço Nacional de Informações, Série agência São Paulo, 80005322, 1–2, 8, AN.

53. Divisão de Segurança e Informações, Ministério da Justiça, "Anistia no âmbito do Ministério da Justiça—Decreto no. 84.143 de 31 Out 79," July 17, 1980, Fundo V8, Serviço Nacional de Informações, Série agência central, 80011286, 2–16, AN. See also "Documentos sobre Reversão," Fundo TT, Divisão de Segurança e Informações do Ministério da Justiça, Série pessoal, avulsos 3, AN.

54. "Relação Nominal," Fundo TT, Divisão de Segurança e Informações do Ministério da Justiça, Série pessoal, avulsos 3, 90–99, AN.

55. Constitutional Amendment no. 26, November 27, 1985.

56. Ministério da Justiça, Departamento de Polícia Federal, "Reversão ao serviço ativo dos servidores do Departamento de Polícia Federal atingidos pelo Ato Institucional n. 5," September 1, 1986, in processo no. 2001.01.00130, 2:11, ACA.

57. Ministério da Justiça, Departamento de Polícia Federal, "Reversão ao serviço ativo dos servidores do Departamento de Polícia Federal atingidos pelo Ato Institucional n. 5," September 1, 1986, in processo no. 2001.01.00130, 2:11–20, ACA.

58. *Diário Oficial*, Section 2, September 18, 1986, 5257.

59. Abrão, Bellato, Alvarenga, and Torelly, "Justiça de Transição," 12.

60. Mezarobba, "O processo de acerto de contas," 112–13.

61. J. Teles, *Mortos e desaparecidos políticos*, 168–69.

62. Law no. 9,140, December 4, 1995.

63. Mezarobba, "O processo de acerto de contas," 112.

64. N. Schneider, "Waiting for a Meaningful State Apology."

65. Abrão, Bellato, Alvarenga, and Torelly, "Justiça de Transição," 16.

66. Abrão and Torelly, "Resistance to Change," 155–56.

67. Mezarobba, "O processo de acerto de contas," 116–17.

68. Evandro Éboli, "Uma conta do passado ainda por pagar," *O Globo*, August 8, 2004, 8.

69. Evandro Éboli, "Não existe anistia para quem torturou," *O Globo*, February 25, 2007, 15.

70. Evandro Éboli, "Uma conta do passado ainda por pagar," *O Globo*, August 8, 2004, 8; Paulino, *O julgamento*, 1:59.

71. Processo no. 2001.01.00019, in Paulino, *O julgamento*, 1:273–77.

72. Processo no. 2003.01.36041, in Comissão de Anistia, *Livro dos votos da Comissão de Anistia*, 133–37.

73. Processo no. 2003.01.36041, in Comissão de Anistia, *Livro dos votos da Comissão de Anistia*, 511–14.

74. Processo no. 2001.01.00029, in Paulino, *O julgamento*, 1:163–64, 184–85.

75. Processo no. 2001.01.00037, in Paulino, *O julgamento*, 1:196–98.

76. The commission rounded up the time frame to eight years. Processo no. 2007.01.57675, in Comissão de Anistia, *Livro dos votos da Comissão de Anistia*, 295–98.

77. Processo no. 2001.02.01528, in Comissão de Anistia, *Livro dos votos da Comissão de Anistia*, 100–102.

78. Evandro Éboli, "Uma conta do passado ainda por pagar," *O Globo*, August 8, 2004, 8.

79. Paulino, *O julgamento*, 2:133–43, especially 135, 138–39.

80. Paulino, *O julgamento*, 2:133.

81. Processo no. 2000.01.00144, in Paulino, *O julgamento*, 2:154–59.

82. Evandro Éboli, "Uma conta do passado ainda por pagar," *O Globo*, August 8, 2004, 8.

83. Tiago Angelo, "Anulação de anistia a militares em por base decisão proferida pelo STF em 2019," June 9, 2020, https://www.conjur.com.br/2020-jun-09/anulacao-anistia-militares-baseada-decisao-stf-2019; and "OAB contesta anulação de anistias políticas pelo Ministério da Mulher e dos Direitos Humanos," December 20, 2020, https://www.rotajuridica.com.br/oab-contesta-anulacao-de-anistias-politicas-pelo-ministerio-da-mulher-e-dos-direitos-humanos.

84. Processo no. 2006.01.55584, in Comissão de Anistia, *Livro dos votos da Comissão de Anistia*, 206–9.

85. Maiá Menezes, "Militares vão a Justiça contra promoção de Lamarca," *O Globo*, September 15, 2007, 13.

86. "Justiça cancela indenização à família de Carlos Lamarca," *Estadão*, May 12, 2015, https://noticias.uol.com.br/ultimas-noticias/agencia-estado/2015/05/12/justica-cancela-indenizacao-a-familia-de-carlos-lamarca.htm. See also Matheus Leitão, "Presidente da Comissão de Anistia entrou com ação que suspendeu indenização à família de Lamarca," *O Globo*, April 10, 2019, https://g1.globo.com/politica/blog/matheus-leitao/post/2019/04/10/presidente-da-comissao-de-anistia-entrou-com-acao-para-suspender-indenizacao-a-familia-de-lamarca.ghtml.

87. "Comissão de Anistia divulga Nota Oficial sobre Carlos Lamarca," Ministério da Justiça e Segurança Pública, May 13, 2015, https://www.novo.justica.gov.br/news/comissao-de-anistia-divulga-nota-oficial-sobre-carlos-lamarca.

88. For at least one case, the commission denied the petitioner in a 2007 ruling finding that "the descriptions of the facts . . . do not show exclusively political motivation" for the actions taken against him. Five years later, after appeals, the commission reversed that finding, noting that AI-5 was the only basis for his firing, further noting that his retirement pension had been granted under the 1979 amnesty law. The commission also extended an official apology but denied economic reparations.

89. Abrão and Torelly, "Resistance to Change," 154–55.

90. Some of the individuals with rulings from 2008 to 2010, were declared amnestied, granted reparations, and extended an apology. Others were declared amnestied and extended an apology but were denied reparations beyond settlements previously reached. At least one was only declared amnestied.

91. Abrão and Torelly, "Mutações do conceito de anistia," 368.

92. Abrão, Bellato, Alvarenga, and Torelly, "Justiça de Transição," 17.

93. Abrão, "Os votos da Comissão de Anistia."

94. Ministério da Justiça, *Ações educativas da Comissão de Anistia*, 15–16.

95. Comissão de Anistia, *Caravanas da anistia*, 14–15.

96. Pistori and Da Silva Filho, "Memorial da Anistia Política," 114.

97. Pistori and Da Silva Filho, "Memorial da Anistia Política," 125.

98. Abrão and Torelly, "Resistance to Change," 152.

99. Pistori and Da Silva Filho, "Memorial da Anistia Política," 114.

CHAPTER 8: CONNECTED TO AMNESTY

1. Comissão de Legislação e Normas, Secretaria de Estado de Educação e Cultura, Parecer no. 609/81, in Processo no. 2004.01.39840, 18–19, ACA.

2. Olímpio, "Não tem luto," 293.

3. Grabois, *Maurício Grabois*, 88; Grabois, "Nome falso," 267.

4. Olímpio, "Não tem luto," 296; "Saiba quem é Luiz Eduardo Greenhalgh," *Folha de São Paulo*, February 15, 2005, http://www1.folha.uol.com.br/folha/brasil/ult96u67202. Lula had been arrested multiple times during the general strikes in São Paulo. Twenty-five years later, he upended entrenched elite politics with his election as president. Greenhalgh, a longtime supporter of Lula, would later himself pursue a political career.

5. Lamia Oualalou, "Parentes desaparecidos nunca mais: a luta de Victória Grabois," *Vermelho*, October 17, 2009, https://vermelho.org.br/2009/10/17/parentes-desaparecidos-nunca-mais-a-luta-de-victoria-grabois.

6. Processo no. 2004.01.39840, 103, ACA; Dos Santos, "Quem dará o golpe."

7. Grabois, "Uma trajetória," 181; Grabois, *Maurício Grabois*, 25, 46.

8. Skidmore, *Politics of Military Rule*, 15, 24; Alves, *Estado e oposição*, 143.

9. CNV, *Relatório*, 1:98; Skidmore, *Politics of Military Rule*, 203.

10. Skidmore, *Politics of Military Rule*, 85; Chirio, *Politics in Uniform*, 189. The targeting of the PCB occurred through an operation known as "Operação Radar." CNV, *Relatório*, 1:158, 642.

11. CNV, *Relatório*, 1:681; Alves, *Estado e oposição*, 143.

12. Skidmore, *Politics of Military Rule*, 85–87, 121–122; Chirio, *Politics in Uniform*, 178; Alves, *Estado e oposição*, 143.

13. Freire, *Pedagogy of the Oppressed*.

14. Processo no. 2004.01.39840, 183, ACA. See also Grabois, "Memória, esquecimento e verdade," 379–80.

15. Grabois, "Nome falso," 265. On the events at the headquarters of the National Student Union and the law school, see also Langland, *Speaking of Flowers*, 88–90.

16. Grabois, "Memória, esquecimento e verdade," 379; "UFRJ reintegra 19 alunos expulsos durante ditadura," in Processo no. 2004.01.39840, 116, ACA.

17. Those expelled on July 2, 1964, included Yeda Salles, Sergio Salomé, Rachel Teixeira, Amaury Cano, Wilson Barbosa, Adyr Moisés Luis, Falvio Silva, Regina do Prado, Victória Grabois, and Elio Gaspari. See Processo no. 2004.01.39840, 98, ACA.

18. N. Schneider, *Brazilian Propaganda*, 68.

19. Márcia Telles, "Vítimas da intolerância política," *Jornal do Brasil*, in Processo no. 2004.01.39840, 117, ACA.

20. Processo no. 2004.01.39840, 98, 100, ACA.

21. Processo no. 2004.01.39840, 101, ACA.

22. "UFRJ reintegra 19 alunos que foram expulsos em 64" in Processo no. 2004.01.39840, 113, ACA.

23. Márcia Telles, "Vítimas da intolerância política," *Jornal do Brasil*, in Processo no. 2004.01.39840, 117, ACA.

24. Grabois, "Uma trajetória," 180.

25. Grabois, "Nome falso," 266. Another woman who assumed a false name during the dictatorship described the mental energy necessary to respond to her assumed name. "When someone called out 'Alice,' I had to think quickly—it wasn't always a reflex—and this kind of thing makes us waste a lot of energy." See Ferreira, "Oral History," 25.

26. Grabois, "Nome falso," 266; Wilson Tosta, "Dada como morta, anistiada passou 16 anos na clandestinidade," *O Estado de S. Paulo*, August 22, 2009; Grabois, "Nome falso," 267.

27. Grabois, *Maurício Grabois*, 87–88; see also biography of Gilberto Olímpio Maria in Grupo Tortura Nunca Mais, Dossiê Desaparecidos Brasil, https://www.torturanuncamais-rj.org.br/dossie-mortos-desaparecidos/brasil. Several party members that eventually became guerrilla fighters in Araguaia received training in Beijing and Nanjing, beginning in 1964. See CNV, *Relatório*, 1:682.

28. Skidmore, *Politics of Military Rule*, 85; *Gomes Lund et al.*, Report, §21; see also biography of André Grabois in Grupo Tortura Nunca Mais, Dossiê Desaparecidos Brasil, https://www.torturanuncamais-rj.org.br/dossie-mortos-desaparecidos/brasil.

29. Dassin, "Testimonial Literature," 179; Alves, *Estado e oposição*, 142–43.

30. CNV, *Relatório*, 1:679–82; *Gomes Lund et al.*, Memorial, 28–29; Nossa, *Mata!*, 132.

31. *Gomes Lund et al.*, Memorial, 28.

32. *Gomes Lund et al.*, Memorial, 38–43.

33. Nossa, *Mata!*, 127.

34. CNV, *Relatório*, 1:685; Processo no. 2004.01.39840, ACA; Lamia Oualalou, "Parentes desaparecidos nunca mais: a luta de Victória Grabois," *Vermelho*, October 17, 2009.

35. *Gomes Lund et al.*, Memorial, 38–43; "Latin Guerrillas Fail to Organize Uprising: Survey of Terrorist Movements Reveals Their Status as Fragmented Kaleidoscope," *Los Angeles Times*, December 14, 1972.

36. Processo no. 2004.01.39840, 70, ACA; Grabois, *Maurício Grabois*, 33.

37. Rinaldo Gama, "O fim da guerra no fim do mundo" *Veja*, Edição 1309, October 13, 1993, 18–19; Nossa, *Mata!*, 183. See also CNV, *Relatório*, 1:710; *Gomes Lund et al.*, Memorial, 43.

38. Of the total, fifteen were under the age of twenty-five; thirty-eight were between twenty-five and thirty; and just nine were older than thirty-five. *Gomes Lund et al.*, Memorial, 29–30.

39. *Gomes Lund et al.*, Memorial, 4, 22, 31–37.

40. Cabral, *Xambioá: Guerrilha no Araguaia*; see discussion of the book in Payne, *Unsettling Accounts*, 206. On the publication of the novel, see also Lesser, *Discontented Diaspora*, 110.

41. Payne, *Unsettling Accounts*, 214, 223.

42. Payne, *Unsettling Accounts*, 205.

43. The October 1993 special edition of the newsweekly *Veja* ran with the cover title, "Eu vi os corpos queimados," which was a quote from Gama's exclusive interview with Cabral. See Rinaldo Gama, "O fim da guerra no fim do mundo," *Veja*, Edição 1309, October 13, 1993, 16, 19, 24; Sebastião Curió Rodrigues de Moura, Brasília, letter, *Veja* 1310, October 20, 1993, 14. Vargas Llosa's book, *The War of the End of the World*, was first published in 1981.

44. Nossa, *Mata!*, 327, 350, 387.

45. CNV, *Relatório*, 1:718.

46. CNV, *Relatório*, 1:712.

47. Processo no. 2004.01.39840, 209, ACA. See also Olímpio "Não tem luto."

48. Chirio, *Politics in Uniform*, 193.

49. Processo no. 2004.01.39840, 1, 27, 44, ACA.

50. First Vara Federal, Processo no. 225/1981, June 1980, in Processo no. 2004.01.39840, 27, ACA.

51. Processo no. 2004.01.39840, 35, 38, 36, ACA.

52. Nossa, *Mata!*, 113.

53. Cano and Ferreira, "Reparations Program," 106.

54. Weschler, *Miracle*, 16, 71; Archdiocese of São Paulo, *Brasil nunca mais*, 291–93.

55. *I Seminário do Grupo Tortura Nunca Mais*, 17–20; Comissão de Familiares dos Mortos e Desaparecidos Políticos, "Mortos e desaparecidos políticos."

56. Salgado and Grabois, "O Grupo Tortura Nunca Mais/RJ," 61–63. See also Cano and Ferreira, "Reparations Program," 107.

57. Processo no. 2004.01.39840, 148, ACA.

58. Processo no. 2008.01.60684, 66, 76, ACA.

59. *Gomes Lund et al.*, Memorial, 7–10.

60. Payne, *Unsettling Accounts*, 211–12; Cano and Ferreira, "Reparations Program," 109.

61. *Gomes Lund et al.*, Demanda, §133. On reference to amnesty law, see article 6, Law no. 6,683, August 28, 1979.

62. Comissão Mista sobre Anistia, *Anistia*, 2:533–35.

63. Cano and Ferreira, "Reparations Program," 106.

64. On the various amendments, see A. Schneider, "Legislative Efforts." On Fleury's death and the amnesty debate, see Skidmore, *Politics of Military Rule*, 218.

65. Comissão Mista, *Anistia*, 2:451.

66. Comissão Mista, *Anistia*, 2:433.

67. Fico, "A negociação parlamentar," 324–27; A. Schneider, "Legislative Efforts," 26–29.

68. Comissão Mista, *Anistia*, 1: 112, 67, 150, 134.

69. Cano and Ferreira, "Reparations Program," 108–9; *Gomes Lund et al.*, Report, §§23–24, 42–47.

70. *Gomes Lund et al.*, Report, §57. On the response of the petitioners to the Law of the Disappeared, see *Gomes Lund et al.*, Report, §25.

71. *Gomes Lund et al.*, Memorial, 6.

72. Mechi and Justamand, "Arqueologia," 115–16. The remains of Lourival Moura Paulino were located in the cemetery of Marabá in 2008. *Gomes Lund et al.*, Judgment, §95.

73. *Gomes Lund et al.*, Report, §§33–34.

74. *Gomes Lund et al.*, Report, §25; Franco, "Notion of Ramifications," 136.

75. Relatório de Mérito No. 91/08, as described in *Gomes Lund et al.*, Memorial, 12.

76. *Gomes Lund et al.*, Report, §57.

77. *Gomes Lund et al.*, Memorial, 1.

78. Binder, "Prohibition of Amnesties," 1209, 1210.

79. On the norms of international law, see discussion of *jus cogen* in Veçoso, "Whose Exceptionalism?" 189.

80. *Gomes Lund et al.*, Judgment, 114.

81. N. Schneider, "Impunity in Post-authoritarian Brazil," 43, 49–50.

82. Veçoso, "Whose Exceptionalism?," 200–201.

83. ADPF 153, Ordem dos Advogados do Brasil (2008), 9.

84. ADPF 153, Acordão, Suprema Tribunal Federal (2010), §§9, 21, 29, 29; for discussion of the matter of "connected crimes," see §§26, 28, 38.

85. Simon Romero, "An Uneasy Search for Truth as Ghosts from Military Rule Start to Stir," *New York Times*, December 20, 2011.

86. V. Grabois, *Mauricio Grabois*, 146; Kucinski, *K*, 78.

87. Skaar, Collins, and García-Godos, "Uneven Road," 288.

88. The Caravan of Death case was preceded by a decision in the Poblete-Córdoba case in September 1998 that likewise accepted the disappearance-as-kidnapping argument. See Skaar, *Judicial Independence*, 103.

89. Roht-Arriaza, *Pinochet Effect*, 74–79.

90. Reinaldo Azevedo, "Justiça Federal em Marabá rejeita denúncia contra o major Curió," *Veja*, March 16, 2012, https://veja.abril.com.br/blog/reinaldo/

juiz-federal-recusa-denuncia-contra-major-curio-e-critica-ministerio-publi-
co-por-tentar-driblar-lei-da-anistia.

91. See Justiça Federal, Seção Judiciária do Pará, "Militares são processados
por crimes durante Guerrilha do Araguaia," August 30, 2012, https://portal
.trf1.jus.br/sjpa/comunicacao-social/imprensa/noticias/militares-sao-pro
cessados-por-crimes-durante-guerrilha-do-araguaia.htm; Juliana Bigatão Puig
and Laura M. Donadelli, "Entre máscaras e armas, Brasil de Bolsonaro
escolhe seus heróis: Notórios torturadores são chamados pelo governo de
'heróis,' enquanto mortes pela pandemia não são lamentadas," *Brasil de Fato*
(São Paulo), June 3, 2020, https://www.brasildefato.com.br/2020/06/03/artigo
-entre-mascaras-e-armas-brasil-de-bolsonaro-escolhe-seus-herois.

92. The assessments included, among others, "the amnesty dimension of accountability," "the trial dimension of accountability," and the "overall accountability trends." See Skaar, Collins, and García-Godos, "Uneven Road," 278,
280, 282–83, 286, 288, 292.

93. Fátima Peña, "Juez ordena reapertura del caso El Mozote y abre proceso
contra el Alto Mando de 1981," *El Faro*, September 30, 2016, https://elfaro.net/
es/201609/el_salvador/19339/Juez-ordena-reapertura-del-caso-El-Mozote-y
-abre-proceso-contra-el-Alto-Mando-de-1981.htm.

94. Skaar, Collins, and García-Godos, "Uneven Road," 281, 288.

95. The authors called this the "acknowledgement function." See Skaar,
Collins, and García-Godos, "Uneven Road," 285, 290.

Epilogue: The *Política* of Amnesty in Brazil

1. "Em carta a Damares, ex-presa política denuncia destruição deliberada
da Comissão de Anistia pelo governo Bolsonaro e deixa órgão," *Vio Mundo*,
May 28, 2019, https://www.viomundo.com.br/denuncias/em-carta-a-damares
-ex-presa-politica-denuncia-destruicao-deliberada-da-comissao-de-anistia
-pelo-governo-bolsonaro-e-deixa-orgao-leia-integra.html.

2. Serbin, *From Revolution to Power*, 328.

3. "Em carta a Damares, ex-presa política denuncia destruição deliberada
da Comissão de Anistia pelo governo Bolsonaro e deixa órgão," *Vio Mundo*,
May 28, 2019, https://www.viomundo.com.br/denuncias/em-carta-a-damares
-ex-presa-politica-denuncia-destruicao-deliberada-da-comissao-de-anistia-pe
lo-governo-bolsonaro-e-deixa-orgao-leia-integra.html.

4. Luiz Felipe Barbiéri, "Damares amplia número de integrantes e determina auditoria em atos da Comissão de Anistia," *O Globo*, March 27, 2019, https://
g1.globo.com/politica/noticia/2019/03/27/damares-amplia-numero-de-inte
grantes-e-determina-auditoria-em-atos-da-comissao-de-anistia.ghtml.

5. Matheus Leitão, "Nomeados por Damares para Comissão de Anistia têm
postura 'incompatível' com órgão, diz MPF," *O Globo*, May 7, 2019, https://g1
.globo.com/politica/blog/matheus-leitao/post/2019/05/07/nomeados-por-dam

ares-para-comissao-de-anistia-tem-postura-incompativel-com-orgao-diz-mpf
.ghtml. See also "Novo chefe da Comissão da Anistia travou indenização a cam-
poneses do Araguaia," *Folha de São Paulo*, March 27, 2019, https://www1.folha
.uol.com.br/poder/2019/03/novo-chefe-da-comissao-da-anistia-travou-indeniz
acao-a-camponeses-do-araguaia.shtml; João Henrique Nascimento de Freitas,
"A #ComissãodeAnistia negou todos o requerimentos da temática Guerrilha do
Araguaia," https://twitter.com/JHNdeF/status/1229943315090546689. Freitas
had also been behind the lawsuit that resulted in the annulment of the amnesty
granted posthumously to Carlos Lamarca. See Talita Marchão, "Sob Bolsonaro,
Comissão de Anistia muda critérios e vítima vira terrorista," *UOL*, August 10,
2019, https://noticias.uol.com.br/politica/ultimas-noticias/2019/08/10/anistian
do-terrorista-e-decisao-com-base-em-infancia-militar-as-decisoes.htm.

6. "Memorial da Anistia, que já custou R\$ 28 mil, será cancelado, diz
Damares," *Veja*, August 13, 2019, https://veja.abril.com.br/politica/memorial
-da-anistia-que-ja-custou-r-28-mi-sera-cancelado-diz-damares.

7. Talita Marchão, "Sob Bolsonaro, Comissão de Anistia muda critérios e vítima vira terrorista," *UOL*, August 10, 2019, https://noticias.uol.com.br/politica/
ultimas-noticias/2019/08/10/anistiando-terrorista-e-decisao-com-base-em-in
fancia-militar-as-decisoes.htm.

8. Ricardo Della Coletta, "Orientação na Comissão de Anistia é negar pedi-
dos em massa, diz Conselheiro do órgão," *Folha de São Paulo*, September 12, 2019,
https://www1.folha.uol.com.br/poder/2019/09/orientacao-na-comissao-de
-anistia-e-negar-pedidos-em-massa-diz-conselheiro-do-orgao.shtml.

9. In DaMatta's words, the core of the Brazilian dilemma is that "univer-
salizing laws that are supposed to correct inequalities end up helping to legit-
imatize and perpetuate them." Further, for Brazil, the "double code" resulted
in the "paradoxical institutionalization of ambiguity." See DaMatta, *Carnivals,
Rogues, and Heroes*, 187–88, 196.

10. As of February 2020, the Amnesty Commission reported that it had
received 78,589 petitions, of which 38,966 have been approved and 25,307
have been denied. See Comissão de Anistia, "Comissão de Anistia Feb. 2020,"
https://www.gov.br/mdh/pt-br/navegue-por-temas/comissao-de-anistia-1/
CAnumerossitiofev2020.pdf; Comissão de Anistia, "Requerimentos de Anistia deferidos (actualização 02/2020)," https://www.gov.br/mdh/pt-br/navegue
-por-temas/comissao-de-anistia-1/CAnumerosfev2020DEFERIDOS.pdf.

BIBLIOGRAPHY

ARCHIVES

Arquivo da Comissão de Anistia (Archive of the Amnesty Commission), Brasília (ACA)

Arquivo Edgard Leuenroth (Edgard Leuenroth Archive), Campinas, São Paulo

Arquivo Nacional (National Archive), Rio de Janeiro and Brasília (AN)

Arquivo Público do Estado do Rio de Janeiro (Public Archive of Rio de Janeiro State), Rio de Janeiro (APERJ)

Centro de Pesquisa e Documentação de História Contemporânea do Brasil, Fundação Getúlio Vargas (Center for the Research and Documentation of Contemporary Brazilian History, Getúlio Vargas Foundation), Rio de Janeiro (CPDOC/FGV)

Fundação Casa Rui Barbosa (Rui Barbosa House Foundation), Rio de Janeiro

PERIODICALS

Brasil de Fato (São Paulo)

Careta

Chicago Tribune

Correio Brasiliense

Correio da Manhã (Rio de Janeiro)

Diario da Noite (Rio de Janeiro)

Diário de Notícias (Rio de Janeiro)

Diário Oficial

O Direito: Revista Mensal de Legislação, Doutrina e Jurisprudencia

Estadão

O Estado de S. Paulo

El Faro

Folha da Tarde

Folha de São Paulo

Gazeta de Notícias

O Globo

The Guardian

Informativo CONAPE

Informativo Petrobrás

O Jornal (Rio de Janeiro)

Jornal da Bahia

Jornal do Brasil (Rio de Janeiro)

Jornal GGN

Jornal Petrobras

London Times

Los Angeles Times

O Malho

New York Times

Philadelphia Inquirer

Revista Anistia Política e Justiça Transição

Revista de Direito Administrativo

A Tarde (Bahia)

Times of Israel

Tribuna de Imprensa (Bahia)

UOL

Veja

Vermelho

Washington Post

GENERAL WORKS

Abrão, Paulo. "Os votos da Comissão de Anistia." In Comissão de Anistia, Ministério da Justiça, *Livro dos votos da Comissão de Anistia: verdade e reparação aos perseguidos políticos no Brasil*, edited by Maria José H. Coelho and Vera Rotta. Brasília and Florianópolis: Comunicação, Estudos e Consultoria, 2013.

Abrão, Paulo, Sueli Aparecida Bellato, Roberta Vieira Alvarenga, and Marcelo D. Torelly. "Justiça de Transição no Brasil: o papel da Comissão de Anistia do Ministério da Justiça." *Revista Anistia Política e Justiça Transição*, no. 1 (January–June 2009): 12–21.

Abrão, Paulo, and Marcelo D. Torelly. "Mutações do conceito de anistia na justiça de transição brasileiro: a terceira fase de luta pela anistia." *Revista de Direito Brasileira* 3 (2012): 357–79.

Abrão, Paulo, and Marcelo D. Torelly. "Resistance to Change: Brazil's Persistent Amnesty and Its Alternatives for Truth and Justice." In *Amnesty in the Age of*

Human Rights Accountability: Comparative and International Perspectives, edited by Francesca Lessa and Leigh A. Payne, 152–81. New York: Cambridge University Press, 2012.

Alveal Contreras, Edelmira del Carmen. *Os desbravadores: a Petrobrás e a construção do Brasil industrial.* Rio de Janeiro: Relume Dumará, 1994.

Alves, Márcio Moreira. *Teotônio, guerreiro da paz.* Petrópolis: Vozes, 1983.

Alves, Maria Helena Moreira. *Estado e oposição no Brasil, 1964–1984.* Petrópolis: Vozes, 1984.

Amado, Jorge. *Vida de Luis Carlos Prestes: o cavaleiro da esperança.* Rio de Janeiro: Record, 2002.

Amnesty International. *Report on Allegations of Torture in Brazil.* London: Amnesty International Publications, March 1976.

Annães do Senado Federal, segunda sessão da primeira legislatura, sessões de 28 de abril a 15 de junho de 1892. Vol. 1. Rio de Janeiro: Imprensa Nacional, 1892.

Archdiocese of São Paulo. *Brasil nunca mais: um relato para a história.* 20th ed. Petrópolis: Vozes, 1987.

Arguição de descumprimento de preceito fundamental (ADPF) 153. Acórdão, Supremo Tribunal Federal, 2010.

Arguição de descumprimento de preceito fundamental (ADPF) 153. Ordem dos Advogados do Brasil, Conselho Federal, 2008.

Atencio, Rebecca J. *Memory's Turn: Reckoning with Dictatorship in Brazil.* Madison: University of Wisconsin Press, 2014.

Atencio, Rebecca J. "Toward a Culture of Memory in Brazil: Reading Bernardo Kucinski's *K.* as Testimony and Literature." *Luso-Brazilian Review* 53, no. 2 (2016): 117–33.

Azevedo, Rafael Sânzio de. *Adolfo Caminha: vida e obra.* 2nd ed. Fortaleza: Universidade Federal do Ceará, UFC Edições, 1999.

Barbosa, Rui. "Acórdão do Supremo Tribunal em 27-IV-1892." In *Trabalhos jurídicos, 1892.* Vol. 19, bk. 3 of *Obras completas de Rui Barbosa*, 355–61. Rio de Janeiro: Ministério de Educação e Cultura, 1956.

Barbosa, Rui. "Anexos." In *Trabalhos jurídicos, 1895.* Vol. 22, bk. 1 of *Obras completas de Rui Barbosa*, 319–37. Rio de Janeiro: Ministério de Educação e Cultura, 1952.

Barbosa, Rui. "Anistia aos marinheiros rebeldes (sessão do Senado Federal em 24 de novembro de 1910)." In *Discursos parlamentares, 1910.* Vol. 37, bk. 3 of *Obras completas de Rui Barbosa*, 169–84. Rio de Janeiro: Ministério da Educação e Cultura, Fundação Casa de Rui Barbosa, 1971.

Barbosa, Rui. "Anistia inversa: caso de teratologia juridica." In *Trabalhos jurídicos, 1897.* Vol. 24, bk. 3 of *Obras completas de Rui Barbosa*, 1–196. Rio de Janeiro: Ministério da Educação e Cultura, 1955.

Barbosa, Rui. "Anistia para os marinheiros (sessão do Senado Federal em 24 de novembro de 1910)." In *Discursos parlamentares, 1910.* Vol. 37, bk. 3 of *Obras completas de Rui Barbosa*, 155–68. Rio de Janeiro: Ministério da Educação e Cultura, Fundação Casa de Rui Barbosa, 1971.

Barbosa, Rui. "Estado de Sítio." In *Trabalhos jurídicos, 1892*. Vol. 19, bk. 3 of *Obras completas de Rui Barbosa*, 1–343. Rio de Janeiro: Ministério de Educação e Cultura, 1956.

Barbosa, Rui. *Martial Law: Its Constitution, Limits and Effects, Application made to the Federal Supreme Court for Habeas-Corpus on behalf of the Persons arrested in virtue of Decrees of April 10 and 12, 1892*. Rio de Janeiro: Typ. Aldina de A.J. Lamoureux, 1892.

Barbosa, Rui. "Os atos inconstitucionais do congress e do executivo perante a justiça federal." In *Trabalhos jurídicos, 1893*. Vol. 20, bk. 5 of *Obras completas de Rui Barbosa*, 1–233. Rio de Janeiro: Ministério da Educação e Cultura, 1958.

Barbosa, Rui. "O caso Wandenkolk—Parecer n. 203." In *Discursos parlamentares, 1893*. Vol. 20, bk. 1 of *Obras completas de Rui Barbosa*, 287–92. Rio de Janeiro: Ministério da Educação e Cultura, 1948.

Barbosa, Rui. "Os castigos corporais na marinha (sessão do Senado Federal em 24 de November de 1910)." In *Discursos parlamentares, 1910*. Vol. 37, bk. 3 of *Obras completas de Rui Barbosa*, 185–210. Rio de Janeiro: Ministério da Educação e Cultura, Fundação Casa de Rui Barbosa, 1971.

Barkan, Elazar. *The Guilt of Nations: Restitution and Negotiating Historical Injustices*. New York: W. W. Norton, 2000.

Batista, Estanislau Fragoso. *Cantata de um anistiado . . . para depois*. São Paulo: Edições Loyola, undated.

Beattie, Peter. "Adolfo Ferreira Caminha: Navy Officer, Ardent Republican, and Naturalist Novelist." In *The Human Tradition in Modern Brazil*, edited by Peter M. Beattie, 89–106. Wilmington, DE: Scholarly Resources, 2004.

Beattie, Peter. "Conflicting Penile Codes: Modern Masculinity and Sodomy in the Brazilian Military." In *Sex and Sexuality in Latin America*, edited by Daniel Balderston and Donna J. Guy, 65–85. New York: New York University Press, 1997.

Beattie, Peter. "Conscription versus Penal Servitude: Army Reform's Influence on the Brazilian State's Management of Social Control, 1870–1930." *Journal of Social History* (Summer 1999): 847–78.

Beattie, Peter. "The House, the Street, and the Barracks: Reform and Honorable Masculine Social Space in Brazil, 1864–1945." *Hispanic American Historical Review* 76, no. 3 (August 1996): 439–73.

Beattie, Peter M. *The Tribute of Blood: Army, Honor, Race, and Nation in Brazil, 1864–1945*. Durham: Duke University Press, 2001.

Benjamin, Iramaya, with Margarida Autran. *Ofício de mãe: a saga de uma mulher*. Rio de Janeiro: Editora Marco Zero, 1982.

Berger, Peter. "On the Obsolescence of the Concept of Honor." In *Revisions: Changing Perspectives in Moral Philosophy*, edited by Stanley Hauerwas and

Alasdair MacIntyre, 172–81. Notre Dame, IN: University of Notre Dame Press, 1983.

Bethell, Leslie. "Brazil." In *Latin America between the Second World War and the Cold War, 1944–1948*, edited by Leslie Bethell and Ian Roxborough, 33–65. New York: Cambridge University Press, 1992.

Bethell, Leslie. *Brazil: Essays on History and Politics*. London: School of Advanced Study, Institute of Latin American Studies, University of London, 2018.

Binder, Christina. "The Prohibition of Amnesties by the Inter-American Court of Human Rights." *German Law Journal* 12, no. 5 (2001): 1203–29.

Bois-Pedaín, Antje du. "Accountability through Conditional Amnesty: The Case of South Africa." In *Amnesty in the Age of Human Rights Accountability: Comparative and International Perspectives*, edited by Francesca Lessa and Leigh A. Payne, 238–62. New York: Cambridge University Press, 2012.

Borges, Dain. "Intellectuals and the Forgetting of Slavery in Brazil." *Annals of Scholarship* 11, nos. 1–2 (1996): 37–60.

Borges, Dain. "'Puffy, Ugly, Slothful and Inert': Degeneration in Brazilian Social Thought, 1880–1940." *Journal of Latin American Studies* 24, no. 2 (May 1993): 235–56.

Borges, Dain. "The Relevance of Machado de Assis." In *Imagining Brazil*, edited by Jessé Souza and Valter Sinder, 235–49. Lanham, MD: Lexington Books, 2005.

Borges, Dain. "Salvador's 1890s: Paternalism and Its Discontents." *Luso-Brazilian Review* 30, no. 2 (Winter 1993): 47–57.

"Brazil: Government by Torture." *Look Magazine* 34 (July 1970): 70–71.

Cabral, Pedro Corrêa. *Xambioá: Guerrilha no Araguaia*. Rio de Janeiro: Editora Record, 1993.

Câmara dos Deputados. *Anistia: Legislação brasileira, 1822–1979*. Brasília: Câmara dos Deputados, 1980.

Câmara dos Deputados. "Sessão em 14 de agosto de 1896." *Annães de Camara*, no. 50A, 1896.

Caminha, Adolfo. *The Black Man and the Cabin Boy*. Translated by E. A. Lacey. San Francisco: Gay Sunshine Press, 1982.

Cano, Ignacio, and Patrícia Salvão Ferreira. "The Reparations Program in Brazil." In *The Handbook of Reparations*, edited by Pablo De Greiff, 102–53. New York: Oxford University Press, 2008.

Capitani, Avelino Biden. *A Rebelião dos marinheiros*. Porto Alegre: Artes e Ofícios, 1997.

Carvalho, Getúlio Pereira. "Petrobrás: A Case Study of Nationalism and Institution Building in Brazil." PhD dissertation. University of Connecticut, Storrs, 1976.

Carvalho, José Carlos de. *O livro da minha vida: na guerra, na paz e nas revoluções, 1847–1910*. Rio de Janeiro: Typ. do *Jornal do Commercio*, de Rodrigues, 1912.

Carvalho, José Murilo de. *Os bestializados: o Rio de Janeiro e a República que não foi*. São Paulo: Companhia das Letras, 1987.

Carvalho, José Murilo de. "Brazil, 1870–1914: The Force of Tradition." *Journal of Latin American Studies* 24 (1992): 154–55. Quincentenary supplement, "The Colonial and Post-colonial Experience, Five Centuries of Spanish and Portuguese America."

Carvalho, José Murilo de. *Cidadania no Brasil: o longo caminho*. Rio de Janeiro: Civilização Brasileira, 2007.

Carvalho, José Murilo de. *Pontos e bordados: escritos de história e política*. Belo Horizonte: Editora Universidade Federal Minas Gerias, 1999.

Caulfield, Sueann. *In Defense of Honor: Sexual Morality, Modernity, and Nation in Early-Twentieth-Century Brazil*. Durham: Duke University Press, 2000.

Chasteen, John Charles. "Background to Civil War: The Process of Land Tenure in Brazil's Southern Borderland, 1801–1893." *Hispanic American Historical Review* 71, no. 4 (November 1991): 737–60.

Chasteen, John Charles. "Fighting Words: The Discourse of Insurgency in Latin American History." *Latin American Research Review* 28, no. 3 (1993): 83–111.

Chirio, Maud. *Politics in Uniform: Military Officers and Dictatorship in Brazil, 1960–80*. Pittsburgh, PA: University of Pittsburgh Press, 2018.

Comisión Nacional de Verdad y Reconciliación, Chile. *Informe*. February 1991.

Comisión Nacional sobre la Desaparición de Personas, Argentina. *Nunca Más: The Report of the Argentine National Commission on the Disappeared*. New York: Farrar, Straus and Giroux, 1986.

Comissão de Anistia, Ministério da Justiça. *Caravanas da anistia: o Brasil pede perdão*. Edited by Maria José H. Coelho and Vera Rotta. Brasília and Florianópolis: Comunicação, Estudos e Consultoria, 2012.

Comissão de Anistia, Ministério da Justiça. *Livro dos votos da Comissão de Anistia: verdade e reparação aos perseguidos políticos no Brasil*. Edited by Maria José H. Coelho and Vera Rotta. Brasília and Florianópolis: Comunicação, Estudos e Consultoria, 2013.

Comissão de Familiares de Mortos e Desaparecidos Políticos. *Dossiê dos mortos e desaparecidos políticas a partir de 1964*. Recife: Companhia Editora de Pernambuco, 1995.

Comissão de Familiares dos Mortos e Desaparecidos Políticos. "Mortos e desaparecidos políticos: um resgate da memória brasileira." In *Mortos e desaparecidos políticos: reparação ou impunidade?*, 154–55. São Paulo: Humanitas, 2000.

Comissão Mista sobre Anistia. *Anistia*, Vols. 1 and 2. Edited by Teotônio Vilela. Brasília: Centro Gráfico do Senado Federal, 1982.

Comissão Nacional da Verdade. *Relatório*. 3 vols. December 2014.

Comissão Revisora. *Pareceres*. Rio de Janeiro: Imprensa Nacional, 1938.

Congresso Nacional. "Suppresão de restricções a amnistia decretada em 1895." *Annaes do Senado*. Rio de Janeiro: Imprensa Nacional, undated.

Costa, Emilia Viotti da. *The Brazilian Empire: Myths and Histories*. Revised ed. Chapel Hill: University of North Carolina Press, 2000.

Costa, João Cruz. *Contribuição à história das idéias no Brasil*. 2nd ed. Rio de Janeiro: Civilização Brasileira, 1967.

Cunha, H. Pereira da. *A revolta na esquadra brasileira em novembro e dezembro de 1910*. Rio de Janeiro: Imprensa Naval, 1953.

Cunha, Paulo Ribeiro da. "Militares e anistia no Brasil: um dueto desarmônico." In *O que resta da ditadura: a exceção brasileira*, edited by Edson Teles and Vladimir Safatle, 15–40. São Paulo: Boitempo, 2010.

Da Cunha, Euclides. *Rebellion in the Backlands*. Translated by Samuel Putnam. Chicago: University of Chicago Press, 2010.

Da França, Geminiano. "Instituto jurídico da graça: amnistia." *Revista Forense* 61 (1933): 247–52, 366–74.

DaMatta, Roberto. *Carnivals, Rogues, and Heroes: An Interpretation of the Brazilian Dilemma*. Translated by John Drury. Notre Dame, IN: University of Notre Dame Press, 1991.

Dassin, Joan. "Testimonial Literature and the Armed Struggle in Brazil." In *Fear at the Edge: State Terror and Resistance in Latin America*, edited by Juan E. Corradi, Patricia Weiss Fagen, and Manuel Antonio Garretón, 161–83. Berkeley: University of California Press, 1992.

Debrun, Michel. *A "conciliação" e outras estratégias*. São Paulo: Brasiliense, 1983.

Della Cava, Ralph. "Brazilian Messianism and National Institutions: A Reappraisal of Canudos and Joaseiro." *Hispanic American Historical Review* 48, no. 3 (August 1968): 402–20.

Dewey, Donald O. *Marshall versus Jefferson: The Political Background of* Marbury v. Madison. New York: Knopf, 1970.

Dos Santos, Wanderley Guilherme. "Quem dará o golpe no Brasil." *Cadernos do Povo Brasileiro* 5 (1962): 1–52.

Duarte, Eduardo de Assis. "Jorge Amado: Exile and Literature." *Comparative Political Studies* 49, no. 3 (2012): 382–94.

Duff, Ernesto A. "Luis Carlos Prestes and the Revolution of 1924." *Luso-Brazilian Review* 4, no. 1 (Spring 1967): 3–16.

Dulles, John W. F. *Anarchists and Communists in Brazil, 1900–1935*. Austin: University of Texas Press, 1973.

Dulles, John W. F. *Sobral Pinto, "The Conscience of Brazil": Leading the Attack against Vargas, 1930–1945*. Austin: University of Texas Press, 2002.

Eloysa, Branca, ed. *I Seminário do Grupo Tortura Nunca Mais: depoimentos e debates*. Petrópolis: Vozes, 1987.

Ensalaco, Mark. *Chile Under Pinochet: Recovering the Truth*. Philadelphia: University of Pennsylvania Press, 2000.

Fausto, Boris. *A Concise History of Brazil*. Translated by Arthur Brakel. New York: Cambridge University Press, 1999.

Ferreira, Elizabeth F. Xavier. "Oral History and the Social Identity of Brazilian Women under Military Rule." *Oral History Review* 24, no. 2 (Winter 1997): 1–33.

Ferreira, José Ignacio. *Anistia, caminho e solução: ensaio sobre hipóteses de desconstituição dos atos punitivos da revolução de 1964 no Brasil*. Vitória, Espírito Santo, Brazil: JANC Editora e Publicidade, 1979.

Fico, Carlos. "A negociação parlamentar da anistia de 1979 e o chamado 'perdão aos torturadores.'" *Revista Anistia: Política e Justiça de Transição* 4 (2011): 318–33.

Figueiredo, Euclides. *Contribuição para a história da Revolução Constitucional de 1932*. 2nd ed. São Paulo: Livraria Martins Editora, 1977.

Fijalkowski, Agata. "Amnesty." In *An Introduction to Transitional Justice*, edited by Olivera Simic, 113–36. New York: Routledge, 2017.

Franco, Shirley Carvalhêdo. "The Notion of Ramification of Archival Documents: The Example of the *Fonds* Related to the Brazilian Political Movement Araguaia Guerrilla." *American Archivist* 78, no. 1 (Spring–Summer 2015): 133–53.

Freire, Paulo. *Pedagogy of the Oppressed*. 50th anniversary edition. Translated by Myra Berman Ramos. New York: Bloomsbury Academic, 2018.

French, John D. "The Populist Gamble of Getúlio Vargas in 1945: Political and Ideological Transitions in Brazil." In *Latin America in the 1940s: War and Postwar Transitions*, edited by David Rock, 141–65. Berkeley: University of California Press, 1994.

Freyre, Gilberto. *The Masters and the Slaves*. Translated by Samuel Putnam. New York: Alfred A. Knopf, 1956.

Freyre, Gilberto. *Order and Progress: Brazil from Monarchy to Republic*. Edited and translated by Rod W. Horton. New York: Alfred A. Knopf, 1970.

Gabeira, Fernando. *Carta sobre a anistia: a entrevista do Pasquim, conversaçao sobre 1968*. Rio de Janeiro: Codecri, 1979.

Gallotti, Luis. "Alcance e efeitos da anistia." *Arquivos do Ministério da Justiça e Negócios Interiores* 3, no. 14 (August 1945): 1–6.

Galvão, João Carlos Jr. *Rui Barbosa e a doutrina brasileira do habeas corpus*. Rio de Janeiro: Fundação Casa de Rui Barbosa, 2005.

Galvão, Laila Maia. "História constitucional brasileira na primeira república: un estudo da intervenção federal no Estado o Rio de Janeiro em 1923." Master's thesis. Universidade Federal de Santa Catarina, Florianópolis, 2013.

Gandra, Edgar Ávila, Robert Wagner Porto da Silva Castro, and Thiago Cedrez Silva. "No rumo da memória: radicalização do movimento dos marinheiros em 1964." *Cadernos de História, Belo Horizonte* 15, no. 23 (2014): 130–52.

Gaspari, Elio. *A ditadura derrotada: o sacerdote e o feiticeiro*. São Paulo: Companhia das Letras, 2003.

Gaspari, Elio. *A ditadura envergonhada*, São Paulo: Editora Schwarcz, 2002.

Godoy, Marcelo. *A casa da vovó: biografia do DOI-Codi, 1969–1991*. São Paulo: Alameda, 2014.

Gomes Lund et al. ("Guerrilha de Araguaia"). Inter-American Commission of Human Rights. Report no. 33/01, Case 11.552. March 6, 2001.

Gomes Lund et al. ("Guerrilha de Araguaia") v. Brasil. Inter-American Commission of Human Rights. Demanda ante la Corte Interamericana de Derechos Humanos, Case 11.552. March 26, 2009.

Gomes Lund et al. ("Guerrilha de Araguaia") v. Brasil. Inter-American Court of Human Rights. Judgment of November 24, 2010.

Gomes Lund et al. ("Guerrilha de Araguaia") v. Brasil. Inter-American Court of Human Rights. Memorial de Requerimentos, Argumentos e Provas. July 18, 2009.

Gonçalves, Danyelle Nilin. *O preço do passado: anistia e reparação de perseguidos políticos no Brasil*. São Paulo: Editora Expressão Popular, 2009.

Gonçalves, William Couto. "Judiciabilidade dos atos políticos ou de governo do Brasil no contexto dos direitos e garantias fundamentais do cidadão em homenagem aos vinte anos da constituição cidadão." *Revista de Direitos e Garantias Fundamentais*, no. 4 (July–December 2008): 169–212.

Grabois, Victória Lavínia. *Maurício Grabois: Meu Pai*. Rio de Janeiro: Hexis, 2012.

Grabois, Victória Lavínia. "Memória, esquecimento e verdade." In *68 a geração que queria mudar o mundo: relatos*, edited by Eliete Ferrer, 379–82. Brasília: Ministério da Justiça, Comissão de Anistia, 2011.

Grabois, Victória Lavínia. "Nome falso: um adjetivo." In *68 a geração que queria mudar o mundo: relatos*, edited by Eliete Ferrer, 265–67. Brasília: Ministério da Justiça, Comissão de Anistia, 2011.

Grabois, Victória Lavínia. "Uma trajetória." In *Nossa paixão era inventar um novo tempo*, edited by Daniel Souza and Gilmar Chaves, 180–86. Rio de Janeiro: Editora Rosa dos Tempos, 1999.

Grabois, Victória Lavínia. "A vida na clandestinidade de meu filho." In *Infância roubada: crianças atingidas pela ditadura militar no Brasil*, edited by Tatiana Merlino, 299. São Paulo: ALESP, 2014.

Graham, Lawrence S. *Civil Service Reform in Brazil: Principles versus Practice*. Austin: University of Texas Press, 1968.

Graham, Richard. *Patronage and Politics in Nineteenth-Century Brazil*. Stanford, CA: Stanford University Press, 1990.

Granato, Fernando. *O negro da chibata*. Rio de Janeiro: Editora Objetiva, 2000.

Green, James N. *We Cannot Remain Silent: Opposition to the Brazilian Military Dictatorship in the United States*. Durham: Duke University Press, 2010.

Greenhalgh, Luiz Eduardo. "Dr. Luiz Eduardo Greenhalgh, 3a mesa—30/10/85—Um regime que destrói." In *I Seminário do Grupo Tortura Nunca Mais: depoimentos e debates*, edited by Branca Eloysa, 109–20. Petrópolis: Vozes, 1987.

Haskins, George L., and Herbert A. Johnson. *The Foundations of Power: John Marshall, 1801–1815*. New York: Macmillan, 1981.

Hayes, Robert A. *The Armed Nation: The Brazilian Corporate Mystique*. Tempe: Arizona State University Press, 1989.

Hayner, Priscilla. *Unspeakable Truths: Transitional Justice and the Challenge of Truth Commissions*. 2nd ed. New York: Routledge, 2011.

Hilton, Stanley E. *Brazil and the Soviet Challenge, 1917–1947*. Austin: University of Texas Press, 1991.

Holanda, Sérgio Buarque de. *Raízes do Brasil*. 20th ed. Rio de Janeiro: J. Olympio Editora, 1988.

Huggins, Martha K., Mika Haritos-Fatouros, and Philip G. Zimbardo. *Violence Workers: Police Torturers and Murderers Reconstruct Brazilian Atrocities*. Berkeley: University of California Press, 2002.

Huntington, Samuel P. *The Third Wave: Democratization in the Late Twentieth Century*. Norman: University of Oklahoma Press, 1991.

Jesus, Christianne Theodoro de. "O diário do almirante." *Revista de História*, November 3, 2011.

Joffily, Mariana. *No centro da engrenagem: os interrogatorios na operação bandeirante e no DOI de São Paulo, 1969–1975*. São Paulo: EDUSP, 2013.

Juizo Seccional do Districto Federal. "Acçao summaria especial, Jul. 26, 1896." *O Direito: Revista Mensal de Legislação, Doutrina e Jurisprudencia* 71 (September–December 1896): 101–4.

Klinger, Bertholdo, Euclydes Figueiredo, Othelo Franco, José Lôbo, and Argemiro de Assis Brasil. *Nós e a dictadura: a jornada revolucionaria de 1932*. N.p., 1933.

Kucinski, Bernardo. *K.* Translated by Sue Branford. N.p.: Practical Action Publishing, 2015.

Lacombe, Américo Jacobina. *A sombra de Rui Barbosa*. Brasiliana, Vol. 365. São Paulo: Ministério da Educação e Cultura, Companhia Editora Nacional, 1978.

Lago, Laone. *Rui Barbosa e o habeas corpus: o "nascimento" de uma doutrina*. Rio de Janeiro: Fundação Casa de Rui Barbosa, 2005.

Langland, Victoria. *Speaking of Flowers: Student Movements and the Making and Remembering of 1968 in Military Brazil*. Durham: Duke University Press, 2013.

Leão, Joaquim Marques Baptista de. *Relatório apresentado ao Presidente da República dos Estados do Brasil*. May 1911.

Lemos, Renato. "Anistia e crise política no Brasil pós-1964." *Topoi: Revista de História* 5 (September 2002): 287–313.

Lessa, Francesca, and Leigh A. Payne, eds. *Amnesty in the Age of Human Rights Accountability: Comparative and International Perspectives.* New York: Cambridge University Press, 2012.

Lesser, Jeffrey. *A Discontented Diaspora: Japanese Brazilians and the Meanings of Ethnic Militancy, 1960–1980.* Durham: Duke University Press, 2007.

Levi, Primo. *Survival in Auschwitz: The Nazi Assault on Humanity.* Translated by Stuart Woolf. New York: Touchstone, 1996.

Levine, Robert M. *Father of the Poor: Vargas and His Era.* New York: Cambridge University Press, 1998.

Levine, Robert M. "'Mud-Hut Jerusalem': Canudos Revisited." *Hispanic American Historical Review* 68, no. 3 (August 1988): 525–72.

Levine, Robert M. *Vale of Tears: Revisiting the Canudos Massacre in Northeastern Brazil, 1893–1897.* Berkeley: University of California Press, 1995.

Lima Barreto, Afonso Henriques de. *Triste Fim de Policarpo Quaresma.* 9th ed. São Paulo: Editôra Brasiliense, 1971.

Lins, Ivan. *História do positivismo no Brasil.* Brasiliana, vol. 322. São Paulo: Campanhia Editôra Nacional, 1964.

Linz, Juan J., and Alfred Stepan. *Problems of Democratic Transition and Consolidation: Southern Europe, South America, and Post-communist Europe.* Baltimore: Johns Hopkins University Press, 1996.

Lourdes, Maria de, and Monaco Janotti. "The Monarchist Response to the Beginnings of the Brazilian Republic." *The Americas* 48, no. 2 (October 1991): 223–43.

Love, Joseph L. *The Revolt of the Whip.* Stanford, CA: Stanford University Press, 2012.

Love, Joseph L. *Rio Grande do Sul and Brazilian Regionalism, 1882–1930.* Stanford, CA: Stanford University Press, 1971.

Machado, Flávia Burlamaqui. "As Forças Armadas, a anistia de 1979 e os militares cassados." *Militares e Políticos*, no. 6 (January–June 2010): 114–40.

Machado de Assis, Joaquim Maria. "The Rod of Justice." In *The Psychiatrist and Other Stories*, translated by William L. Grossman and Helen Caldwell. Berkeley: University of California Press, 1963.

Madden, Lori. "The Canudos War in History." *Luso-Brazilian Review* 30, no. 2 (Winter 1993): 5–22. Special issue, "The World Out of Which Canudos Came."

Maier, Charles S. "Overcoming the Past? Narrative and Negotiation, Remembering, and Reparations: Issues at the Interface of History and the Law." In *Politics and the Past: On Repairing Historical Injustices*, edited by John Torey, 295–304. New York: Rowman and Littlefield, 2003.

Malamud-Goti, Jaime. *Game without End: State Terror and the Politics of Justice.* Norman: University of Oklahoma Press, 1996.

Martins, Hélio Leôncio. *A Revolta da Armada.* Rio de Janeiro: Biblioteca do Exército Editora, 1997.

Martins, Roberto Ribeiro. *Liberdade para os brasileiros: Anistia ontem e hoje.* Rio de Janeiro: Editora Civilização Brasileira, 1978.

Maximiliano, Carlos. *Comentários à Constituição brasileira.* 5th ed. Vol. 1. Rio de Janeiro: Livraria Freitas Bastos, 1954.

McCann, Bryan. "Carlos Lacerda: The Rise and Fall of a Middle-Class Populist in 1950s Brazil." *Hispanic American Historical Review* 83, no. 4 (2003): 661–96.

McCann, Frank. "The Brazilian General Staff and Brazil's Military Situation, 1900–1945." *Journal of Interamerican Studies and World Affairs* 25, no. 3 (August 1983): 299–324.

McCann, Frank. "The Formative Period of Twentieth-Century Brazilian Army Thought, 1900–1922." *Hispanic American Historical Review* 64, no. 4 (November 1984): 737–65.

Meade, Teresa A. *"Civilizing" Rio: Reform and Resistance in a Brazilian City, 1889–1930.* University Park: Pennsylvania State University Press, 1997.

Mechi, Patricia Sposito, and Michel Justamand. "Arqueologia em contextos de repressão e resistência: a Guerrilha do Araguaia." *Revista de Arqueologia Pública* 10 (December 2014), 108–20.

Mello, Maria Tereza Chaves de. *A República consentida: cultura democrática e científica do final do Império.* Rio de Janeiro: Editora FGV, 2007.

Melo, Ana Amélia M.C. de. "Jorge Amado: a militância das letras." *Latin American Research Review* 51, no. 1 (2016): 181–97.

Mezarobba, Glenda. *Um acerto de contas com o futuro: a anistia e suas consequências, um estudo do caso brasileiro.* São Paulo: Associação Editorial Humanitas, 2006.

Mezarobba, Glenda. "Between Reparations, Half Truths and Impunity: The Difficult Break with the Legacy of the Dictatorship in Brazil." *Sur, International Journal on Human Rights* 7, no. 13 (December 2010): 7–24.

Mezarobba, Glenda. "O processo de acerto de contas e a lógica do arbítrio." In *O que resta da ditadura,* edited by Edson Teles and Vladimir Safatle, 109–19. São Paulo: Boitempo, 2010.

Mezarobba, Glenda. "The Torturous Path to Truth and Justice." In *Transitional Justice in Latin America: The Uneven Road from Impunity toward Accountability,* edited by Elin Skaar, Jemima García-Godos, and Cath Collins, 103–25. New York: Routledge, 2016.

Mignone, Emilio Fermin, Cynthia L. Estlund, and Samuel Issacharoff. "Dictatorship on Trial." *Yale Journal of International Law* 10 (1984): 118–50.

Ministério da Agricultura, Industria e Commercio, Diretória Geral de Estatísticas. *Annuario Estatístico do Brazil, 1908–1912.* Vol. 1, *Território e População.* Rio de Janeiro: Typographia da Estatística, 1916.

Ministério da Justiça. *Ações educativas da Comissão de Anistia: relatório de gestão 2007–2010.* Brasília: Ministério da Justiça, 2010.

Mitchell, José. "FH anistia 700 marinheiros cassados em 1964, medida beneficia o úiltimo grande grupo de militares acusados de subversão politica depois do golpe militar." *Informativo do MODAC* 1, no. 5 (August–September 2002): 4.

Moraes, Railda Saraiva de. *O poder de graça.* Rio de Janeiro: Forense 75, 1979.

Moraes Filho, Alexander José de Mello. *Um estadista da república: Dr. J.J. Seabra.* Rio de Janeiro: Laemmert, 1903.

Morel, Edmar. *A revolta da chibata.* 6th ed. Rio de Janeiro: Paz e Terra, 2016.

Morgan, Zachary R. *Legacy of the Lash: Race and Corporal Punishment in the Brazilian Navy and the Atlantic World.* Bloomington: Indiana University Press, 2014.

Motta, Marly Silva da. *Teotônio Vilela.* Brasília: Senado Federal, 1996.

Motta, Rodrigo Patto Sá. "A 'Intentona Comunista' ou a construção de uma legenda negra." *Tempo* 13 (July 2002), 189–207.

Motta, Rodrigo Patto Sá. *Partido e sociedade: A trajetória do MDB.* Ouro Preto: Editora Universidade Federal de Ouro Preto, 1997.

Moura, Gerso. *A campanha do petróleo.* São Paulo: Brasiliense, 1986.

Nascimento, Álvaro Pereira do. *Cidadania, cor e disciplina na revolta dos marinheiros de 1910.* Rio de Janeiro: MAUAD Editora Ltda, 2008.

Nascimento, Álvaro Pereira do. *A ressaca da marujada: recrutamento e disciplina na Armada Imperial.* Rio de Janeiro: Arquivo Nacional, 2001.

Needell, Jeffrey D. "The Revolta Contra Vacina of 1904: The Revolt against 'Modernization' in Belle-Époque Rio de Janeiro." *Hispanic American Historical Review* 67, no. 2 (May 1987): 233–69.

Needell, Jeffrey D. *A Tropical Belle Époque: Elite Culture and Society in Turn-of-the-Century Rio de Janeiro.* New York: Cambridge University Press, 1987.

Nino, Carlos Santiago. "The Human Rights Policy of the Argentine Constitutional Government: A Reply." *Yale Journal of International Law* 11 (1985): 217–30.

Nogueira, Rubem. *O advogado Rui Barbosa.* 2nd ed. Salvador: Edições GRD, 1967.

Nossa, Leonencio. *Mata! o Major Curió e as guerrilhas no Araguaia.* São Paulo: Campanhia das Letras, 2012.

Official da Armada. *Política versus Marinha.* Rio de Janeiro: Livraria H. Garnier, undated.

Olímpio, Igor Grabois. "Não tem luto. São vazios." In *Infância Roubada: Crianças atingidas pela Ditadura Militar no Brasil,* edited by Tatiana Merlino, 292–98. São Paulo: ALESP, 2014.

Oliveira, Celso Lemos de. "The Early Jorge Amado." In *Jorge Amado: New Critical Essays*, edited by Keith H. Brower, Earl E. Fitz, and Enrique Martínez-Vidal, 159–72. New York: Routledge, 2001.

Oliveira, Paulo Affonso Martins de. *Atos Institucionais: Sanções Políticas*. Brasília: Centro de Documentação e Informação, Coordenação de Publicações, Câmara dos Deputados, 2000.

Paulino, José Alves. *O julgamento dos anistiados políticos: o plenário*. 2 vols. Brasília: Projeto Editoria, 2003, 2004.

Payne, Leigh A. "Corporate Complicity in the Brazilian Dictatorship." In *The Brazilian Truth Commission: Local, National and Global Perspectives*, edited by Nina Schneider, 157–81. New York: Berghahn, 2019.

Payne, Leigh A. *Unsettling Accounts: Neither Truth nor Reconciliation in Confessions of State Violence*. Durham: Duke University Press, 2008.

Pistori, Edson Claudio, and José Carlos Moreira da Silva Filho. "Memorial da Anistia Política do Brasil." *Revista Anistia Política e Justiça Transição*, no. 1 (January–June 2009): 113–33.

Pontes de Miranda, Francisco Calvacanti. *Comentários à Constituição de 1946*. 3rd ed. Vol. 1. Rio de Janeiro: Editor Borsoi, 1960.

Prates, Mariana, Sara Loup, and Rebeca Gois. "Cemitério São João Batista e suas histórias fantásticas." *Livro-Reportagem* 7 (April–June 2018). https://livro-reportagem.com.br/cemiterio-sao-joao-batista-e-suas-historias-fantasticas/. Last accessed January 8, 2021.

Queiroz, Suely Robles Reis de. "Reflections on Brazilian Jacobinism of the First Decade of the Republic (1893–1897)." *The Americas* 48, no. 2 (October 1991): 181–205.

Randall, Laura. *The Political Economy of Brazilian Oil*. Westport, CN: Praeger, 1993.

Ribeiro, Atanagildo Barata. *Sonho no cárcere: dramas da revolução de 1893 no Brazil: poema pelo primeira tenente reformado do Armada Imperial, o engenheiro constructor naval*. Rio de Janeiro: Casa Mont'Alverne, 1895.

Ricoeur, Paul. *Memory, History, Forgetting*. Translated by Kathleen Blamey and David Pellauer. Chicago: University of Chicago Press, 2004.

Rodeghero, Carla Simone. "A anistia entre a memória e o esquecimento." *História Unisinos* 13, no. 2 (May–August 2009): 131–39.

Rodeghero, Carla Simone, Gabriel Dienstmann, and Tatiana Trinidade. *Anistia ampla, geral, e irrestrita: história de uma luta inconclusa*. Santa Cruz do Sul: Edunisc, 2011.

Rodrigues, Flávio Luís. *Vozes do mar: o movimento dos marinheiros e o golpe de 64*. São Paulo: Editora Cortez, 2004.

Rodrigues, José Honório. *Conciliação e reforma no Brasil: um desafio histórico-político*. Rio de Janeiro: Editora Civilização Brasileira, 1965.

Rodrigues, Lêda Boechat. *História do Supremo Tribunal Federal*. Vol. 1, bk 1, 1891–1898, Defesa das Liberdades Civis. Rio de Janeiro: Editora Civilização Brasileira, 1965.

Roht-Arriaza, Naomi. "The New Landscape of Transitional Justice." In *Transitional Justice in the Twenty-First Century: Beyond Truth versus Justice*, edited by Naomi Roht-Arriaza and Javier Mariezcurrena, 1–16. New York: Cambridge University Press, 2006.

Roht-Arriaza, Naomi. *The Pinochet Effect: Transnational Justice in the Age of Human Rights*. Philadelphia: University of Pennsylvania Press, 2005.

Roht-Arriaza, Naomi. "Reparations in the Aftermath of Repression and Mass Violence." In *My Neighbor, My Enemy: Justice in the Aftermath of Mass Atrocity*, edited by Eric Stover and Harvey M. Weinstein, 121–40. New York: Cambridge University Press, 2004.

Roland, Maria Inês. *A revolta da chibata: Rio de Janeiro, 1910*. São Paulo: Editôra Saraiva, 2000.

Romero, José Luis. *Latinoamérica: Las ciudades y las ideas*. Mexico: Siglo XXI, 1976.

Salgado, Lívia de Barros, and Victória Grabois. "O Grupo Tortura Nunca Mais/RJ: um olhar etnográfico." *História Oral* 20, no. 2 (July–December 2017): 59–79.

Santayana, Mauro. *Conciliação e transição: as armas de Tancredo*. Rio de Janeiro: Paz e Terra, 1985.

Santos, J. M. de Carvalho. *Repertorio enciclopédico do direito brasileiro*. Vol. 3. Rio de Janeiro: Editor Borsoi, undated.

Scaletsky, Eduardo Carnos. *O patrão e o petroleiro: um passeio pela história do trabalho na Petrobras*. Rio de Janeiro: Relume Dumará, 2003.

Schneider, Ann M. "Legislative Efforts against Impunity in the 1979 Amnesty Debate in Brazil." *Bulletin of Latin American Research* 37, no. 1 (January 2018): 18–32.

Schneider, Ann M. "Truth Commissions and Their Archives in El Salvador, Peru and Brazil." In *The Brazilian Truth Commission: Local, National and Global Perspectives*, edited by Nina Schneider, 265–85. New York: Berghahn Books, 2019.

Schneider, Ann M. "The Unsettling and Unsettled Monument against Torture in Rio de Janeiro, Brazil." *Peace & Change* 37, no. 4 (October 2012): 489–515.

Schneider, Nina. *Brazilian Propaganda: Legitimizing an Authoritarian Regime*. Gainesville: University Press of Florida, 2014.

Schneider, Nina. "Breaking the 'Silence' of the Military Regime: New Politics of Memory in Brazil." *Bulletin of Latin American Research* 30, no. 2 (2011): 198–212.

Schneider, Nina. "The Forgotten Voices of the Militares Cassados: Reconceptualising 'Perpetrators' and 'Victims' in Post-1985 Brazil." *Brasiliana, Journal for Brazilian Studies* 2 (2003): 313–44.

Schneider, Nina. "Impunity in Post-authoritarian Brazil: The Supreme Court's Recent Verdict on the Amnesty Law." *European Review of Latin American and Caribbean Studies* 90 (April 2011): 39–54.

Schneider, Nina. "Waiting for a Meaningful State Apology: Has Post-authoritarian Brazil Apologized for State Repression?" *Journal of Human Rights* 13, no. 1 (2014): 69–84.

Schwarcz, Lilia Moritz. *The Emperor's Beard: Dom Pedro II and the Tropical Monarchy of Brazil.* Translated by John Gledson. New York: Farrar, Straus and Giroux, 2004.

Schwarcz, Lilia Moritz. *Lima Barreto: triste visionário.* São Paulo: Companhia das Letras, 2017.

Serbin, Kenneth P. "The Ghosts of Brazil's Military Dictatorship: How a Politics of Forgetting Led to Bolsonaro's Rise." *Foreign Affairs,* January 1, 2019.

Serbin, Kenneth P. *From Revolution to Power in Brazil: How Radical Leftists Embraced Capitalism and Struggled with Leadership.* Notre Dame, IN: University of Notre Dame Press, 2019.

Siegel, Gilbert B. "The Strategy of Public Administration Reform: The Case of Brazil." *Public Administration Review* 26, no. 1 (March 1966): 45–55.

Sikkink, Kathryn. *The Justice Cascade: How Human Rights Prosecutions Are Changing World Politics.* New York: W. W. Norton, 2011.

Silva, Marcos A. da. *Caricata República: Zé Povo e o Brasil.* São Paulo: Editora Marco Zero, 1990.

Simmons, Charles Willis. "Deodoro da Fonseca, Fate's Dictator." *Journal of Inter-American Studies* 5, no. 1 (January 1963): 45–52.

Skaar, Elin. *Judicial Independence and Human Rights in Latin America: Violations, Politics, and Prosecutions.* New York: Palgrave Macmillan, 2011.

Skaar, Elin, Cath Collins, and Jemima García-Godos. "The Uneven Road towards Accountability in Latin America." In *Transitional Justice in Latin America: The Uneven Road from Impunity towards Accountability,* edited by Elin Skaar, Jemima García-Godos, and Cath Collins, 275–309. New York: Routledge, 2016.

Skidmore, Thomas E. "Failure in Brazil: From Popular Front to Armed Revolt." *Journal of Contemporary History* 5, no. 3 (1970), 137–57.

Skidmore, Thomas E. *Politics in Brazil, 1930–1964: An Experiment in Democracy.* New York: Oxford University Press, 1967.

Skidmore, Thomas E. *The Politics of Military Rule in Brazil, 1964–1985.* New York: Oxford University Press, 1988.

Smith, Peter Seaborn. "Petrobras: The Politicizing of a State Company, 1953–1964." *Business History Review* 46, no. 2 (Summer 1972): 182–201.

Stepan, Alfred. *Rethinking Military Politics: Brazil and the Southern Cone*. Princeton, NJ: Princeton University Press, 1988.

Teitel, Ruti G. *Transitional Justice*. New York: Oxford University Press, 2000.

Teitel, Ruti G. "Transitional Justice Genealogy." *Harvard Human Rights Journal* 16 (2003): 69–94.

Teles, Edson. "Entre justiça e violência: estado de exceção nas democracias do Brasil e da África do Sul." In *O que resta da ditadura: a exceção brasileira*, edited by Edson Teles and Vladimir Safatle, 299–318. São Paulo: Boitempo, 2010.

Teles, Edson. "Quem é essa pessoa que tem a voz da minha mãe?" In *Infância roubada: crianças atingidas pela ditadura militar no Brasil*, edited by Tatiana Merlino, 257–59. São Paulo: ALESP, 2014.

Teles, Janaína. "Dói gostar dos outros." In *Infância roubada: crianças atingidas pela ditadura militar no Brasil*, edited by Tatiana Merlino, 260–66. São Paulo: ALESP, 2014.

Teles, Janaína, ed. *Mortos e desparecidos políticos: reparação ou impunidade*. São Paulo: Humanitas, 2000.

Topik, Steven C. "Brazil's Bourgeois Revolution?" *The Americas* 48, no. 2 (October 1991): 245–71.

Vargas Llosa, Mario. *The War of the End of the World*. Translated by Helen R. Lane. New York: Farrar, Straus and Giroux, 1984.

Veçoso, Fabia Fernandes Carvalho. "Whose Exceptionalism? Debating the Inter-American View on Amnesty in the Brazilian Case." In *Anti-impunity and the Human Rights Agenda*, edited by Karen Engle, Zinaida Miller, and D. M. Davis, 185–215. New York: Cambridge University Press, 2016.

Viana, Arízio de. *D.A.S.P.: instituição a serviço do Brasil*. Rio de Janeiro: Imprensa Nacional 1953.

Viana, Gilney. *Fome de liberdade: a luta dos presos políticos pela anistia*. Victória, Espírito Santo, Brazil: Fundação Ceciliano Abel de Almeida, 1992.

Wasserman, Renata R. Mautner. "Lima Barreto, the Text and the Margin: On 'Policarpo Quaresma.'" *Modern Language Studies* 22, no. 3 (Summer 1992): 53–69.

Weschler, Lawrence. *A Miracle, a Universe: Settling Accounts with Torturers*. Chicago: University of Chicago Press, 1998.

Whitehead, Laurence. *Democratization: Theory and Experience*. Oxford: Oxford University Press, 2002.

Williams, Raymond Leslie, and Mario Vargas Llosa. "The Boom Twenty Years Later: An Interview with Mario Vargas Llosa." *Latin American Literary* 15, no. 29 (January–June 1987): 201–6.

Wilson, Richard. *The Politics of Truth and Reconciliation in South Africa*. Cambridge: Cambridge University Press, 2001.

Zerbine, Therezinha Godoy. *Anistia: semente da liberdade*. São Paulo: Escolas Profissionais Salesianas, 1979.

INDEX

abolition in Brazil, 23, 32, 47, 48, 65; movement for, 35; process of, 28, 34
abolitionists, in US, 37
abolitionist thought, 70
Abrão, Paulo, 15, 176, 186, 187, 188, 223n25
accommodation, in politics, 12. *See also* conciliation
accountability for human rights violations, 188, 213, 223n22; absence of, 181, 213, 218; amnesty as obstacle to, 135, 190; individual criminal, 134, 212, 218
acknowledgment of human rights abuses, 6, 15, 138, 204
AI-1 (*Ato Institucional no. 1*, First Institutional Act), 147, 149, 155, 242n22
AI-2 (*Ato Institucional no. 2*, Second Institutional Act), 169–70
AI-5 (*Ato Institucional no. 5*, Fifth Institutional Act), 171; adjudication of amnesty and, 179, 180, Amnesty Commission and, 165, 186; enactment of, 169, 170, 171; purges by, 176, 177, 178; repression under, 171, 172, 173

Almeida, Criméia Alice Schimdt de, 174, 199
Almeida Barreto, José de, 24, 26, 28, 31; exile of, 27, 33; habeas petition for, 34; civil suit for restitution of, 28, 38–39, 40, 42, 46, 56
Almonacid v. Chile, 209
ALN (*Ação Libertadora Nacional*, National Liberation Action), 136, 193
ANL (*Aliança Libertadora Nacional*, National Liberation Alliance), 88, 104
Alves, Damares, 214, 215, 216
Alves, Francisco de Paula Rodrigues, 66, 67, 68
Alves, Márcio Moreira, 170–71
Alves, Osvino Ferreira, 146, 147, 158
Amado, Jorge, 84, 87–88, 93, 105, 116, 197
Amazon, exile to, 19, 23, 24, 27, 63. *See also* Cucuhy; Tabatinga
American Civil War, 52, 59, 128
amnestied (*anistiados*), 10, 13, 14, 59, 112; by the Amnesty Commission, 168, 187, 215, 219
amnesty, committees on, 117–18, 152–53, 159, 191, 202

amnesty, defined as: conciliation, 12, 15, 24, 122, 128, 138, 154, 164; forgetting, 40, 41, 60, 120, 128–129, 188; impunity, 5, 135, 188, 208–9; institution, 24, 60, 85, 166, 187, 188, 219; interrupting violence, 11, 13; memory, 13, 187–88, 215, 218; pacifying, 52, 59, 89, 101, 122, 128–29, 243n41; pact of honor, 86; penalty, 25, 45, 55; political tool, 12, 24, 46, 60, 83, 87; recourse, 24, 45, 79, 217; reparations, 4, 6, 15, 60, 138, 165, 218; restitution, 3, 5, 6, 13, 39, 46, 109, 218; settlement, 10, 13, 14, 15, 58, 219; state weakness, 96; trap, 86; vindication, 87, 111, 117, 135, 143

amnesty, history/evolution of (Brazil), 10–11, 13, 30–31, 59, 153, 223n25

amnesty, professional associations of, 117, 153, 156, 158, 160

amnesty (1895), 21, 45, 117; debates about, 52–54; Federal Supreme Court ruling on, 56; reflections on, 83, 85. *See also* Anistia Inversa

amnesty (1910), 22, 62, 63–64, 78; aftermath of, 77–78, 79–80; critiques of, 76–77; demands for, 62, 68

amnesty (1930), 80, 93, 97–100

amnesty (1934), 60, 94, 102, 113, 120

amnesty (1945), 90, 115, 118–19; civil society campaign for, 10–11, 115–18; constituent assembly and, 120–21

amnesty (1961), 127

amnesty (1979), 3, 6, 162, 203, 218; civil society campaign for, 11, 152–53; congressional debates over, 153–56, 206–7; evolution of, 138, 181; Federal Supreme Court rulings, 135, 190, 210–11; Inter-American Court of Human Rights ruling, 191, 209–10

amnesty (1985 constitutional amendment), 137–38, 142–43, 162–63, 168, 179

amnesty commission (1935). *See* Review Commission

amnesty commission(s) (1945), 110, 111–12, 119, 122–28, 162

amnesty commission(s) (1979), 142, 154, 156–60, 167–68, 178–80

Amnesty Commission (*Comissão de Anistia*, 2001), 6, 14–15, 138, 164, 213; Paulo Abrão and, 185–87; administration of Bolsonaro and, 15, 214–16; cases from, 165, 183–86, 204; comprehensive data about, 168, 184, 186, 215, 219, 258n10; critiques of, 181–82, evolution of, 186–88, 216; institution of, 3–4, 181, 221n2; leaders of, 13, 182; structure of, 166, 180–81

amnesty-ing (*anistiando*), 13, 129, 214, 219

Amnesty International, 172–73

Anistia Inversa, 45; arguments of, 27–28, 40, 42, 46, 54–55; legacy of, 58, 59–60, 83; references to, 121, 128, 216–17; ruling on, 55–56

apology, official: by Amnesty Commission, 6, 186, 215; for disappearances, 138; by Institute of Chemistry, University of São Paulo, 139

Araguaia, 189, 198; Amnesty Commission and, 215; Canudos and, 201; decimation of guerrillas at, 190, 202; denial of killings at, 190; disappeared of 174, 190, 191, 202, 204; efforts for justice for, 191, 205, 207, 213; fact-finding missions to, 191, 205, 207, 208; guerrilla movement of, 140, 174, 190, 197–98, 199, 200, 203; Inter-American Court of

Human Rights and, 191, 209, 210; military campaigns against, 174, 189, 198–99, 201; novel about, 200; Truth Commission investigation of, 201

Aranha, Oswaldo, 115

ARENA (*Aliança Renovador Nacional*, National Renewal Alliance), 170–71, 248n13

Argentina: amnesty in, 135, 209; dirty war in, 4; economy of, 144; exile to, 20, 84, 88, 113; transitional justice in, 133–35, 209. *See also* Perón, Juan

Argentine Forensic Anthropology Team (*Equipo Argentino de Antropología Forense*), 208

Arruda, Firmiano Pacheco de, 176

Atencio, Rebecca, 133, 223n22

atrocity testimony, genre of, 133

authoritarianism, in Brazilian politics, 12; during the First Republic, 23, 32, 35, 59; regimes of, 190; response to legacy of, 129, 185; resistance against, 215; return to, 122; under Getúlio Vargas, 113, 119, 143; transition from, 111

Bahia (cruiser), 62, 63

Bahia (state), 40, 87, 193,162, 185; Canudos, 46, 48; Petrobras and, 160, 161

Bandeira, Antônio, 174, 175, 177

Barbosa, Rui, person of, 20, 23, 31, 32, 44, 68. *See also* Almeida Barreto, José de; amnesty (1895); amnesty (1910); *Anistia Inversa*; habeas corpus, Revolt of the Lash

barracks revolt (1935). *See* Intentona Comunista

Barrios Altos v. Peru, 209

Beattie, Peter, 75

Belle Époque, 49, 67, 229n18

Belo Horizonte, amnesty monument project in, 187, 215

Benário, Olga, 114–15

benevolence: amnesty as, 83, 84; pardon as, 12, 117, 128

Berger, Harry, 114

Berger, Peter, 73

Bernandes, Artur, 95–96

Bethell, Leslie, 104

Blackstone, William, 36

Bocaiúva, Quintino, 52–53

Bolivia, exile to, 84, 93

Bolsonaro, Jair, 15, 214

Bom Crioulo (Caminha), 72–72, 230n41

Borja, Célio, 162

Borges, Dain, 46, 66, 73, 222n18

Brasil nunca mais (Brazil never again), 137, 191, 203

Brazilian Bar Association (*Ordem dos Advogados do Brasil*), 117, 153, 191, 205, 207; case challenging 1979 amnesty, 210–11

Brazilian Committee for Amnesty, 153, 159, 242n39

Brazilian Workers Party (*Partido Trabalhista Brasileiro*), 144, 146

Brizola, Leonel, 144

Buarque de Holanda, Sérgio, 222n17

bureaucracy, 86, 95, 111; of amnesty, 80, 88, 89–90, 94–95, 109, 112; of amnesty (1945), 111–12, 125, 126, 128, 129; of Amnesty Commission, 5

Cabral, Pedro Corrêa, 200–201

Caminha, Adolfo, 72, 73. *See also* Bom Crioulo

Campos, Aureliano, 55–56

Campos Sales, Manuel Ferraz de, 53, 229n18

Camus, Albert, 87

Cândido, João, 21–23, 158, 231n75; as
    able seaman, 76; as emblematic of
    Brazilian sailors, 71; imprisonment
    of, 78; posthumous amnesty for, 80;
    in the press, 77. *See also* Revolt of
    the Lash
Cantuta v. Peru, La, 209
Canudos, 46, 48–49, 51, 66, 101, 201
Caravans of Amnesty, 187
Cardoso, Fernando Henrique, 3
Carone, Nysia Coimbra Flores, 183
Carvalho, José Carlos de, 68, 75–76
Carvalho, José Murilo de, 35, 67
"car wash" (*lavo jato*) investigation,
    165, 243n52, 247n102
Cascardo, Herculino, 91–92, 93, 95;
    and ALN, 104; and Getúlio Vargas,
    96, 98–99
Castelo Branco, Humberto de
    Alencar, 147, 169
Castilhistas, 50
Castilhos, Júlio de, 50
Castro, Fidel, 146, 197
"cavalier of hope," moniker of Luis
    Carlos Prestes, 93, 115; biography
    of Luis Carlos Prestes, 84
Central Station, rally (1964), 147, 152
Cervantes, Miguel de, 47
Chamber of Deputies (lower house of
    Brazilian Congress), 30; bills intro-
    duced to, 53, 107, 127; committees
    of, 57, 162; commissions in, 207;
    debates of, 57, 76; members of, 27,
    34, 41, 75, 127, 162; purges from,
    147, 152, 183; publications of, 155
Chaves, Aureliano, 164
Chile: amnesty in, 135, 209; chal-
    lenges to amnesty in, 5, 212;
    indemnity payments to victims, 4;
    truth commission of, 133, 135. *See
    also* Pinochet, Augusto; *Almonacid
    v. Chile*

China, 146, 197, 200
Chirio, Maud, 105, 169, 172
Civil Police, 173, 248n23, 248n30,
    249n34
Cohen Plan, 106
Coimbra, Roberto, 148–49
Cold War: dictatorships in Latin
    America, 4, 133–34, 169; repression
    of PCB/communists in Brazil, 88,
    90, 112
Colombia, 201
colonialism, Portuguese, 10, 28,
    29–30, 85, 222n17
Comintern (Communist Internation-
    al), 104, 114
Commission for the Repression of
    Communism (*Comissão de Repressão
    do Comunismo*), 105
communism (in Brazil), 85, 105, 117,
    113–24, 146, 170; repression of,
    112, 113–14; Luis Carlos Prestes
    and, 84, 104. *See also* Intentona
    Comunista; Cohen Plan; PCB;
    PCdoB
Comte, Aguste, 29. *See also* positivism
CONAPE (*Associação Nacional dos
    Anistiados da Petrobras*, National
    Association of the Amnestied of
    Petrobras), 160, 161, 164–65
Conciliation, political, 90, 138; as
    defining characteristic of Brazil, 12,
    15, 30, 153, 222n19, 223n22
Congress (Brazilian): amnesty laws
    enacted by, 52, 62, 76, 127, 156,
    162–63; authoritarianism and, 105;
    bills considered by, 96, 143; closing
    or suspension of, 19, 147, 171;
    criticism of, 77–78; debates in, 52,
    76, 206; purges from, 171; speeches
    in, 153, 162
connected crimes: amnesty (1945)
    and, 118–19; amnesty (1979) and,

140, 142, 153–54, 190, 206–7;
interpretation by Federal Supreme
Court (2010), 210; Victoria Grabois
and, 190, 196, 203
Conselheiro, Antônio, 48. *See also*
Canudos
consolidation, political, 12, 48, 112,
134, 217
Constant, Benjamin, 28–29, 225n10
constituent assembly (1890–1891), 30
constituent assembly (1946), 111–12,
119–20
constitution (1824), 30–31, 73
constitution (1891), 20, 30, 73, 130;
violation of, 38–39, 42, 55
constitution (1934), 60, 94, 103;
amendment to, 110, 124
constitution (1937), 105, 126
constitution (1946), 88, 112, 120, 128
constitution (1967), 170
constitution (1988), 138, 163, 165,
182, 210–11
Constitutional Transitional Provisions
Act (*Ato das Disposições Constituicio-
nais Transitórias*), 103, 107, 163
Constitutionalist Revolution (1932),
94, 113; amnesty and, 101–2
Copacabana, beach, 91
Copacabana Fort, 91, 92, 94, 119
Costa e Silva, Artur da, 169–71
Cucuhy, 27, 33
Curió Rodrigues de Moura, Sebastião
(Major Curió), 201, 212
crimes against humanity, 209
Cruz, Oswaldo, 67
Cuba, 197; travel to/training in, 147,
148, 200

Da Cunha, Euclides, 46, 48–49, 100.
See also Canudos
Da França, Geminiano, 83–84,
85–86, 87, 89, 108

DaMatta, Roberto, 66, 67, 71, 217,
258n9
DASP (*Departamento Administrativo
do Serviço Público*, Administrative
Department of Public Service), 122,
124
Dassin, Joan, 197
Debrun, Michel, 12
degeneration, doctrine of racial, 50,
65, 66, 72, 85. *See also* race/racism
"democratic experiment," 119, 128
democratization: Amnesty Commission and, 187; from dictatorship
(1964–1985), 152, 161–62; from
Estado Novo, 111, 116, 118, 143;
and past atrocities, 134
Deodoro. *See* Fonseca, Deodoro da
Deodoro (cruiser), 62
dependency theory, 222n20
desprotegidos (unprotected ones), 65,
70. *See also* patronage
determinism, geographic, 49. *See also*
Rebellion in the Backlands
Diário Oficial, 27, 160, 175, 180
Dias, Walter, 175, 176
Dies Committee (US), 124
dignity, principle of, 64, 73, 79, 217
Diretas já (Direct elections now)
movement, 162
disappearance, forced, 134; Araguaia
and, 191, 209; in brazil, 4–5,
136–37, 140, 204; impunity for in
Brazil, 135, 173, 181, 210, 212; as
on-going crime of kidnapping, 5,
212, 213
DOI-CODI (*Destacamento de Operações de Informação, Centro de Operações de Defesa Interna*, Detachment
of Information Operations, Center
of Operations of Internal Defense),
136, 169, 172, 173, 174–75, 180
Dom Pedro II, 28, 32, 71

Don Quixote, 47

DOPS (*Departamento de Ordem Político e Social*, Department of Political and Social Order), 136, 169, 172–73, 180, 183, 192; investigations at Petrobras, 141, 148, 149, 151–52. *See also* Fleury, Sergio

Dos Santos, Wanderley Guilherme, 192

Duarte, Nélson, 177

Duque de Caxias, 141, 148, 158. *See also* Reduc

Dutra, Eurico Gaspar, 117; election of, 119, 120; review of amnesty petitions by, 124, 126, 127, 128

economy, Brazilian, 86, 95, 100–101, 119, 143–44, 146

Elbrick, Charles, 136

El Salvador, 135, 208, 213

El Mozote massacre, 208, 213

England, 22, 69

entitlements, 6, 25, 54, 79, 94, 166

Estado Novo, 84, 105–6, 114, 115, 234n51; Jorge Amado and, 88; dismantling of, 111, 119. *See also* Vargas, Getúlio

eugenics, 46, 65. *See also* race/racism

Ewert, Arthur, 114–15

FARC (Colombia), 201

Farias, Bergson Gurjão, 200, 208

fascism, 88, 105, 111, 114, 117, 126; Estado Novo and, 77, 234n51; integralism and, 112

Federalist Revolution, 50. *See also* Rio Grande do Sul Civil War

Federal Police, 247n6; amnesty commission for, 178–80; internal investigation by, 175–77; involvement in repression, 171–72, 174; purges in, 177

Federal Supreme Court (*Supremo Tribunal Federal*), 26; 1934 amnesty case (1947), 60; 1979 amnesty case (2010), 135, 190, 191, 210–11; Almeida Barreto case (1895), 40, 42; *Anistia Inversa* case (1897), 45, 56, 58, 83–84, 216; habeas petition (1892), 20, 27, 33, 34–38; and Geminiano da França, 83, 85; security measures filed to, 107, 159

Fernandes, Elza, 236n18

Ferreira, Joaquim Câmara, 136

Ferreira, José Ignacio, 153

fiction, as form of reckoning, 133, 200

Figueiredo, Euclides, 102, 112; at constituent assembly (1946), 120, 162

Figueiredo, João, 130, 152, 160, 162

First Republic (1889–1930), 10, 29, 30, 46, 65, 70; establishment of, 20, 28–29, 45

Flaubert, Gustave, 47–48

Fleury, Sergio: Amnesty International and, 173; death of, 206; federal police agents and, 177; as head of DOPS, 136, 172, 173; team of, 174; torture by/under, 136, 172, 183. *See also* DOPS

Flores da Cunha, José Antônio, 101, 121

Florianistas, 31

Floriano. *See* Peixoto, Floriano

Florianopolis, 51

foco, 196; Araguaia and, 198; theory of, 197

Fonseca, Deodoro da, 26, 28–29, 31–32, 51

Fonseca, Hermes Rodrigues da, 68, 69, 77

Franco, Francisco, 115

fraud, ideological, 190

Freire, Alpírio Raimundo Viana, 183–84

Freire, Paulo, 193
Freitas, João Henrique Nascimento de, 215, 257n5
Freitas, Jorge, 189
Freitas, Teresa de Rosa, 189, 195
French Revolution: allusion to, 49; figures of, 29, 31; satire of, 47
Freyre, Gilberto, 29–30, 64, 65, 222n17

Gabeira, Fernando, 242n39
Gallotti, Luis, 100, 234n55
Gama, Rinaldo, 201
Gaspari, Elio, 170, 194
Geisel, Ernesto, 152, 160
Genoíno, José, 155, 203, 243n52
Globo, O, 165
Godoy, Marcelo, 173
Gomes, Eduardo, 92, 119
Goulart, João: coup against, 141, 147, 158, 194; as president, 146–47, 169; Getúlio Vargas and, 144
Grabois, André, 197, 199, 212
Grabois, Igor. See Olímpio, Igor Grabois
Grabois, Mauricio, 120, 191, 192, 193, 203, 212
Grabois, Victória: "connected crimes," 190, 196; on day of the coup, 192, 193–94; exit from clandestine life, 189, 191–92, 202–3; entrance to clandestine life, 192, 195–96; expulsion from university, 194–95; fact-finding mission to Araguaia, 205; family members in guerrilla movement, 197, 198; Grupo Tortura Nunca Mais, 204, 205; at Inter-American Court of Human Rights, 191, 205; motherhood and, 191, 197; in New York Times article, 210–11; PCdoB, 193; as "Teresa", 199, 202; university study by, 192, 202

grace, in politics, 83, 85, 153
"grandma's house," 173, 248n30. See also OBAN
Great Depression, 90, 128
Greenhalgh, Luiz Eduardo, 159, 191, 196, 202, 205, 253n4
Grupo Tortura Nunca Mais, 3, 4–5, 204, 205
Guanabara Bay (Rio de Janeiro), 85, 91; navy revolt in (1893), 21, 50; navy revolt in (1910), 22
Guerrilha de Araguaia v. Brazil (Inter-American Court decision, 2010), 209–10
Guerrilla Movement of Araguaia (Guerrilha do Araguaia), 140, 190. See also Araguaia
Guerrilla training, 197, 254n27
Guevara, Che, 146
Guilt of Nations, The (Barkan), 4
Guiratinga (Mato Grosso), 196–97. See also foco

habeas corpus: under Floriano Peixoto, 20, 27, 30, 33–38; during military dictatorship, 171
Heck, Conrado, 98, 169
Heck, Sílvio de Azevedo, 169
Higino, José, 56
Hitler, Adolf, 84
honor, 13, 64–65, 67, 69–71, 73, 75
"House of Death" (Casa da Morte), 136, 155
human rights, 140, 154, 218; advocacy for, 3, 5, 59, 155, 187; defense of, 139; Inter-American system of, 191, 209; government ministries of, 15, 182, 214; redress for violations of, 133, 134, 135, 211; violations of, 135, 153, 154, 175
hunger strike, for amnesty, 154–55, 206
Huntington, Samuel, 134

Ibiúna (São Paulo), 171, 200. *See also* National Student Union

immigration, 66, 86; laws, 113

impressment, in the navy, 70–71

impunity, 218; amnesty as, 5, 6, 135, 188, 207, 210; and Araguaia case, 208, 209

indemnity, 4, 44, 98–99; amnesty as, 60, 138; prohibited in amnesty laws, 118–19; and the Amnesty Commission, 164–65, 180–83, 185–87, 215; and Law of the Disappeared, 208

independence of Brazil, 31, 152; commemoration of, 170

industrialization, Brazil, 32, 64, 143

Ilha das Cobras, 21, 77–78

Ilha Grande, 118

Institute of Philosophy and Social Sciences, Federal University of Rio de Janeiro, 192

integralism, 112, 114, 126

integralistas, 113, 114; and amnesty commissions, 122, 125, 126, 127; revolt of (1938), 114, 115, 123, 175

Intentona Comunista (barracks revolt of 1935), 84, 104–5, 121, 182, 193; crackdown following, 110, 111, 114–15, 193, 218; preparation for, 88, 104; Luis Carlos Prestes and, 123, 182

Inter-American Commission on Human Rights, 191, 204, 207, 208–9

Inter-American Court of Human Rights, 140, 191, 205, 209–10, 213

Jacobins, 31, 32, 51, 68

Joffily, Mariana, 171

Jornal do Brasil, 106, 107, 177, 192, 195

Jubiabá (Amado), 87–88

Júpiter (packet boat), 18

K (Kucinski), 133, 136–37, 212

Kubitschek, Juscelino, 127, 169

Kucinski, Ana, 135–39, 155, 193–94

Kucinski, Bernardo, 133, 136–37, 206, 212

labor: leaders, 139, 141, 142, 147, 150, 160; laws or regulations, 139, 149, 150, 152, 156; rights, 143; strikes, 121

Lacerda, Carlos, 144, 146

Lamarca, Carlos, 184–85, 257n5

Langland, Victoria, 172

Lapa (São Paulo), 202

Lavenère, Marcello, 182

Law of the Disappeared (*Lei dos Desaparecidos*, 1995), 138, 163, 181, 204, 213

Leão, Joaquim Marques Baptista de, 73, 75, 76

Levi, Primo, 133

Liberal Alliance (*Aliança Liberal*), 95, 96, 112–13

liberalization, in Brazilian politics, 59, 110–12, 119, 135, 216. *See also* democratization

Life of Luís Carlos Prestes, The (Amado), 84, 88

Lima, Fausto Thomaz de, 183

Lima, Mário, 160–61, 162, 164. *See also* CONAPE

Lima, Pedro Ivo Moézia de, 211

Lima Barreto, Afonso Henriques, 46, 47, 48, 51, 66

Linhares, Marcelo, 156

Long March, 84, 86, 182. *See also* Prestes Column

Look Magazine, 172

López, Francisco Solano, 20

Los Angeles Times, 199

Luis, Washington, 96, 100

Lula da Silva, Luiz Inácio, 80, 191

Machado de Assis, Joaquim Maria, 75

Maciel, Antônio Vicente Mendes, 48. *See also* Canudos

Malvinas/Falkland Wars, 134. *See also* Argentina

"Manifesto of the Thirteen Generals" (1892), 19, 26, 32–33

Marabá, 198–99

Marbury v. Madison, 37, 39

Marighella, Carlos, 136, 193

Mariscot, Mariel, 177

Marks of Memory (*Marcas de Memória*), 187

martial law, 20, 34, 35, 38, 41, 171

Martins, Roberto Ribeiro, 153

Mata! (Nossa), 201

Maximiliano, Carlos, 128–29

McCann, Bryan, 144

MDB (*Movimento Democrático Brasileiro*, Brazilian Democratic Movement), 170, 171, 248n13

Médici, Emílio Garrastazu, 4, 167, 172, 175, 198

Melo, Custódio José de, 51, 60, 103

memory, politics of, 13, 15, 187–88, 215, 218

Mendes da Silva, Adalberto, 148

Menezes, Marcelino Rodrigues, 62

mensalão ("big monthly payment"), scandal 243n52

mercy, compared to amnesty, 12, 128–29

Metalworkers Union Rally, 158, 184

Mezarobba, Glenda, 181

Military Police, 163, 174, 248n30, 249n34; amnesty commission for, 122

Minas Geraes (dreadnaught), 62, 63, 69

Minas Gerais (state), 95, 127, 187

Ministry of Defense, 208

Ministry of Education and Culture, 193, 204

Ministry of Justice: Amnesty Commission and, 3, 15; readmission to under amnesty (1979), 167, 178–80

Ministry of Mines and Energy, 161, 164

Ministry of Women, Family and Human Rights, 214

Miranda, Nilmário de, 182–83

"moderating power", 30–32, 38, 225n19

modernization, 29, 64, 79

monarchy, Brazilian, 20, 28, 34, 42

Monnerat, Elza de Lima, 203

Monteiro, Góis, 113

monument to amnesty, 187

Moraes, Railda Saraiva de, 153

Morais, Prudente de: amnesty (1985), 24, 39, 42–43, 52, 53; assassination attempt against, 51; election of, 21, 39, 44–45, 95

Morel, Edmar, 62

Müller, Filinto, 113

Nabuco, Joaquim, 69

nation as body, metaphor of, 65, 70

National Literacy Program (*Programa Nacional de Alfabetização*), 193, 204

National Security Council (*Conselho de Segurança Nacional*), 150, 171

National Security Tribunal (*Tribunal de Segurança Nacional*), 105, 115, 118–19, 236n17

National Student Union (*União Nacional dos Estudantes*), 171, 194, 200. *See also* Ibiúna

navy, Brazilian: amnesty (1930), 97–99; amnesty (1979), 157, 158–59; history of, 64, 70–72, 74–75; revolt of (1893), 21, 44, 46–47, 50–51, 83; revolt of (1910), 22–23, 61–65, 68,

75–78, 80; purges from, 23, 69; and technology, 22, 65

Nazi/Nazism, 4, 114–15, 119, 126, 133, 192

Needell, Jeffrey, 67

Neves, João Batista das, 62

Neves, Tancredo, 162

New York Times, 61, 77, 211

Nogueira, Rubem, 40–41, 226n59

Nossa, Leonencio, 201

OBAN (*Operação Bandeirantes*, Operation Bandeirantes), 169, 173, 174; formation of, 172; targets of, 174, 180, 184, 199

Olímpio, Igor Grabois, 191, 197, 202, 203; as Jorge, 189, 199

Olímpio Maria, Gilberto, 189, 212; in China, 197; death certificate for, 204; in Guiratinga, 197; marriage to Victória Grabois, 195

"O petróleo é nosso" (the petroleum is ours!), campaign, 143, 158

Organization of American States, the, 191

Pará (state), 33, 174, 189, 198, 212. *See also* Araguaia

Paraguayan War (1865–1870), 20, 50, 71

patronage, 31, 65, 68, 70, 89, 95, 222n18

Paulino, José Alves, 13

Paulino, Lourival Moura, 200

PCB (*Partido Comunista Brasileiro*, Brazilian Communist Party), 86; ALN and, 88, 104; amnesty and, 115, 127; defections from, 136, 174, 192, 193; under the dictatorship (1964–1985), 192–93, 253n10; Mauricio Grabois and, 192, 195; legality of, 88, 120–21, 192; Luis

Carlos Prestes and, 119, 123, 127, 147, 192; renewed criminalization of, 122, 125, 195

PCdoB (*Partido Comunista do Brasil*, Communist Party of Brazil), 174, 193; at Araguaia, 197–99, 208; in São Paulo, 202, 203. *See also* Araguaia

Peixoto, Floriano, 19–21, 26–28, 31–34, 38–39, 44, 50–51. *See also* Sad End of Policarpo Quaresma, The

Peron, Juan, 88, 144

Pertence, José Paulo, 207

Petit, Maria Lucia, 200, 208

Petrobras: amnesty commission for, 156–57; Amnesty Commission and, 164–65; history of, 143–47; purges from, 147–52, 157; reintegration to, 160–64

petroleiros, 139, 142–43. *See also* Reduc

Pinochet, Augusto, 4, 135. *See also* Chile

political crimes, 10, 11; amnesty of (1934), 60, 103; amnesty of (1945), 118; amnesty of (1961), 127; amnesty of (1979), 154, 155; prosecuted by National Security Tribunal, 126; interpretation by Federal Supreme Court (2010), 210

political policing, 105–6, 122, 150

political prisoners: amnesty (1945) and, 111, 112, 115–19, 120, 218; hunger strike of, 154–55; kidnapping of Charles Elbrick and, 136; torture of, 168, 169, 171, 173–75, 207

Pontes de Miranda, Francisco Cavalcante, 128–29

Popular Revolutionary Vanguard (*Vanguarda Popular Revolucionária*), 185

Porto Alegre, 195, 196; archbishop of, 101

positivism, 29, 225n10

Potemkin, 69

Prestes, Júlio, 96, 100

Prestes, Luis Carlos: amnesty (1945), 88, 97, 112, 117, 122–23; amnesty campaigns and, 115, 116, 120, 127; Amnesty Commission ruling on, 182–83; and Olga Benário, 114–15; biography of, 84, 88, 89; constituent assembly (1946) and, 112, 121; dictatorship (1964–1985) and, 147, 160, 192; imprisonment of, 236n18; revolt in Rio Grande do Sul (1924), 91–92; Getúlio Vargas and, 96, 113, 118, 119. *See also* Intentona Comunista, PCB, Prestes Column

Prestes, Luis Carlos Ribeiro, 183

Prestes Column, 86, 92, 93, 94, 97. *See also* Long March

Prudente. *See* Morais, Prudente de

Quadros, Jânio, 146

Queiroz, Ademar de, 148, 149, 150, 152

Quitéria, Maria, 152

race/racism, 21, 35, 46–47, 49–50, 65–66, 72–74

Ramos, Graciliano, 197

Rebellion in the Backlands (Da Cunha), 46, 48, 49, 100. *See also* Canudos

Rebellion of the Sailors (1964), 158

reconciliation, national, 122, 125, 129, 138, 153, 216; of Brazilian "family", 116; South Africa and, 6

Reduc (Refinery of Duque de Caxias), 141–42, 145; DOPS surveillance at, 141, 148; following the coup (1964) at, 147, 148–49; purges at, 142, 152;

readmission of employees to, 164; visit by sailors to, 158

reparations, 223n24; Brazilian paradigm of, 4, 138, 163, 165–66, 181–82, 186. *See also* transitional justice

restitution, 223n24; Brazilian history of, 60; material, 129; moral 129. *See also* amnesty, defined as

República (cruiser), 21

Retumba, João da Silva, 34, 50, 57

Review Commission (*Comissão Revisora*, 1935), 90, 94, 103–4; sessions of, 106–8

Revolt of the Lash (*Revolta da Chibata*, 1910), 62, 68; Gilberto Freyre on, 64–65; responses to, 75–78. *See also* Cândido, João; navy

Ribeiro de Carvalho, Thomas, 126, 127–28

Ricoeur, Paul, 11

rights, balancing of, 87

Rio de Janeiro (city), 19, 49, 65–66, 117

Rio de Janeiro (state), 95

Rio Grande do Sul (ship), 77

Rio Grande do Sul (state), 95, 156; politicians from, 144, 146; Luis Carlos Prestes and, 91, 92, 93, 97; Getúlio Vargas and, 97, 101

Rio Grande do Sul Civil War (1893), 20–21, 50–51, 67, 101; amnesty for, 28, 39, 52; pardon for 52; peace accords for, 44

Rivera, Diego, 88

Rocha, Alceu Andrade, 162

Rodeghero, Carla Simone, 229n41

Rodrigues, José Soares, 170

Romeu, Ines Etienne, 141

Rondon, Cândido, 79

Rousseff, Dilma, 155, 211, 214, 243n52

Russia, 69, 123, 192

Sad End of Policarpo Quaresma, The
(Lima Barreto), 46–48, 51, 66
Saldanha da Gama, Luís Felipe de, 51
Salgado, Plinio, 114, 127
Santa Catarina, 21
São Paulo (city), 49; PCdoB in, 202;
rebellion in (1924), 92
São Paulo (dreadnaught), 62, 69, 91–92
São Paulo (state): amnesty conference in, 153; archbishop of, 203;
"Constitutionalist Revolution" in
(1932), 94, 97; DOI-CODI in, 136;
DOPS in, 136, 172, 183, 206, 215;
elites from, 39, 94, 100; federal
court in, 189, 190; federal police
from, 139, 167, 175–76, 177; OBAN
in, 172, 199; planter class of, 39;
politicians of/from, 32, 53, 183;
presidents from, 21, 67, 96; purges
of civil servants in, 159; rebels from,
101, 113; repression in, 133, 173–75;
republicans from, 67; review
commission for, 107
Santos, Max da Costa, 152
Sarney, José, 162
Schneider, Nina, 247n5
Schwarcz, Lilia Moritz, 28
Seabra, José Joaquim, 27, 34, 35, 42
Senate (Brazilian Congress), 30; bills
introduced to, 53; committees of,
154, 162; members of, 19, 20, 21,
52; speeches in, 33, 73; votes in,
53, 76
Sergeants' Revolt (1963), 244n66
sertão, 48, 49
Sertões, Os (Da Cunha), 46, 49. *See also*
Rebellion in the Backlands
Sesame Street, 174
shame, 79. *See also* honor
siege, state of, 32, 38, 42, 78, 105
Sipahi, Rita, 214–16
Siqueira Campos, Antônio de, 92

Siqueiros, David, 88
Skidmore, Thomas, 144, 193, 237n46
slavery, in Brazil, 28, 34–35, 47, 70,
86, 226n35
South Africa, 5–6
Souta, Edson Luis de Lima, 171, 174
Soviet Union: travel to, 147–48; exile
to, 183
Spanish Civil War, 115
Special Commission of Amnesty,
(*Comissão Especial de Anistia*, 1995),
163
Special Commission on Political
Death and Disappearances
(*Comissão Especial sobre Mortos e
Desparecidos Políticos*), 138, 181–82,
204, 213
Stalin, Joseph, 88
Story, Joseph, 36–37
Supreme Military Council (*Conselho
Supremo Militar*), 26, 31
Switzerland, 4

Tabatinga, 19, 20, 23, 27
Tancredo. *See* Neves, Tancredo
Teitel, Ruti, 134
Teixeira, Raquel, 195
Teles, family, 174–75, 199
Temer, Michel, 215
tenentes, 80, 92, 95–96, 99, 113, 218
tenetismo, 92
Tiradentes, 22
Torelly, Marcelo, 15, 188
torture, in Brazil, 61, 114, 136–37,
155, 193, 202; AI-5 and, 168–69,
171–75; Amnesty Commission and,
180, 181–82, 183, 216; amnesty
debate about, 206–7; Araguaia and,
190, 198, 199, 208, 215; impunity
for, 135, 153, 181, 191, 204, 210;
survivors of, 3, 4
transitional justice, 112, 115, 130,

134–35, 165, 223n25; processes in
Brazil, 15, 137–38, 181, 186–88,
213, 218–19
trials, human rights, 5–6, 134–35;
lack of in Brazil, 181, 188, 213
Tribuna de Imprensa, 144
truth commission(s), 133–36, 173,
190, 201, 211, 213; absence of in
Brazil, 188, 181, 203
Truth and Reconciliation Commission, South Africa, 5–6
Tutóia Street, 173, 174, 248n30. *See
also* "grandma's house"
Tutu, Desmond, 6, 222n12

UDN (*União Democrática Nacional,*
National Democratic Union), 144,
146, 170
Union of Non-Amnestied Military
Members (*União dos Militares
Não-Anistiados*), 159
United Front, 101
University of Brasília, 171
University of Brazil, 192
University of Moema, 202
University of São Paulo, 136
Ustra, Carlos Alberto Brilhante, 175,
214

vaccine, revolt against (1904), 51,
67–68
Vargas, Getúlio: 1930 revolution,
24, 80, 93, 100; amnesty and,
80, 89, 217–18; amnesty (1930),
93–94, 97; amnesty (1934), 101–2;
amnesty (1945), 111–12, 115–17,
118; "Constitutionalist Revolution"

against (1932), 94, 113; era of, 10,
89, 93, 94, 96–97, 150; and Estado
Novo, 84, 88, 90, 105–6, 111; and
Figueiredo, Euclides, 112–13;
integralistas, 112, 114; Intentona
Comunista (or barracks revolt), 84,
105; and Petrobras, 143–44; and
Luis Carlos Prestes, 112–13, 118,
119; Review Commission, 103, 104,
106–7, 108; tenentes and, 80, 96,
98, 99, 113, 218; suicide of, 144–45
Vargas Llosa, Mario, 49, 201
Viana, Eremildo Luiz, 194
Vianna, Jorge, 162
Vilela, Teotônio, 154, 206

Wandenkolk, Eduardo, 19–21, 23, 27,
28, 31; and habeas corpus (1893),
34, 35
war, state of, 103, 105, 108
Washington Post, 52, 77
Women's Movement for Amnesty
(*Movimiento Feminino pela Anistia*),
152
Workers' Party (*Partido dos Trabalhadores*), 155
World War I (First World War),
context of, 83, 84
World War II (Second World War):
Brazilian forces in, 111, 123; context of, 84, 90, 218; and individual
accountability for violations of, 134

Xambioá, 198, 208. *See also* Araguaia
Xambioá (Cabral), 200

Zerbine, Terezinha Godoy, 152